Culture and Customs
of Mexico

1 MÉXICO
2 MORELOS
3 PUEBLA
4 TLAXCALA
5 HIDALGO
6 QUERÉTARO
7 GUANAJUATO
8 AGUASCALIENTES
9 MEXICO
10 MORELOS
⊗ FEDERAL DISTRICT

Culture and Customs of Mexico

❦

Peter Standish and Steven M. Bell

Culture and Customs of Latin America
and the Caribbean
Peter Standish, Series Editor

GREENWOOD PRESS
Westport, Connecticut • London

Library of Congress Cataloging-in-Publication Data

Standish, Peter.
 Culture and customs of Mexico / Peter Standish and Steven M. Bell.
  p. cm. — (Culture and customs of Latin America and the Caribbean, ISSN 1521–8856)
 Includes bibliographical references and index.
 ISBN 0–313–30412–2 (alk. paper)
  1. Mexico—Civilization—20th century. 2. Mexico—Social life and customs—20th century.
 I. Bell, Steven M. II. Title. III. Series.
F1234.S73 2004
972—dc21   2003052844

British Library Cataloguing in Publication Data is available.

Library of Congress Catalog Card Number: 2003052844
ISBN: 0–313–30412–2
ISSN: 1521–8856

First published in 2004

Greenwood Press, 88 Post Road West, Westport, CT 06881
An imprint of Greenwood Publishing Group, Inc.
www.greenwood.com

Printed in the United States of America

Contents

Series Foreword

Culture is a problematic word. In everyday language we tend to use it in at least two senses. On the one hand, we speak of cultured people and places full of culture—uses that imply a knowledge or presence of certain forms of behavior or of artistic expression that are socially prestigious. In this sense, large cities and prosperous people tend to be seen as the most cultured. On the other hand, there is an interpretation of culture that is broader and more anthropological; culture in this broader sense refers to whatever traditions, beliefs, customs, and creative activities characterize a given community—in short, it refers to what makes that community different from others. In this second sense, everyone has culture; indeed, it is impossible to be without culture.

The problems associated with the idea of culture have been exacerbated in recent years by two trends: less respectful use of language and a greater blurring of cultural differences. Nowadays, culture often means little more than behavior, attitude, or atmosphere. We hear about the culture of the boardroom, of the football team, of the marketplace; there are books with titles like *The Culture of War* by Richard Gabriel (1990) or *The Culture of Narcissism* by Christopher Lasch (1979). In fact, as Christopher Clausen points out in an article published in the *American Scholar* (Summer 1996), we have got ourselves into trouble by using the term so sloppily.

People who study culture generally assume that culture (in the anthropological sense) is learned, not genetically determined. Another general assumption made in these days of multiculturalism has been that cultural differences should be respected rather than put under pressure to change. But these assumptions, too, have sometimes proved to be problematic. Multicultural-ism is a fine ideal, but in practice it is not always easy to reconcile with the beliefs of the very people who advocate it— for example, is female circumci-sion an issue of human rights or just a different cultural practice?

The blurring of cultural differences is a process that began with the steamship, increased with radio, and is now racing ahead with the Internet. We are becoming globally homogenized. Since the English-speaking world (and the United States in particular) is the dominant force behind this pro-cess of homogenization, it behooves us to make efforts to understand the sen-sibilities of members of other cultures.

This series of books, a contribution toward that greater understanding, deals with the neighbors of the United States, with people who have just as much right to call themselves Americans. What are the historical, institu-tional, religious, and artistic features that make up the modern culture of such peoples as the Haitians, the Chileans, the Jamaicans, and the Guatemalans? How are their habits and assumptions different from our own? What can we learn from them? As we familiarize ourselves with the ways of other countries, we come to see our own from a new perspective.

Each volume in the series focuses on a single country. With slight variations to accommodate national differences, each begins by outlining the historical, political, ethnic, geographical, and linguistic context, as well as the religious and social customs, and then proceeds to a discussion of a variety of artistic activi-ties, including the media, cinema, literature, and the visual and performing arts. The authors are all intimately acquainted with the countries concerned; some were born or brought up in them, and each has a professional commitment to enhancing the understanding of the culture in question.

We are inclined to suppose that our ways of thinking and behaving are nor-mal. And so they are...for us. We all need to realize that ours is only one cul-ture among many, and that it is hard to establish by any rational criteria that ours as a whole is any better (or worse) than any other. As individual mem-bers of our immediate community, we know that we must learn to respect our differences from one another. Respect for differences between cultures is no less vital. This is particularly true of the United States, a nation of immi-grants, but one that sometimes seems to be bent on destroying variety at home and, worse still, on having others follow suit. By learning about other people's cultures, we come to understand and respect them; we earn their respect for us; and, not least, we see ourselves in a new light.

Peter Standish
East Carolina University

Acknowledgments

THANKS ARE DUE TO Mattie Rasberry, who read and commented on the manuscript from the point of view of a typical reader. Steven Bell would like to thank the Fulbright College of the University of Arkansas for granting him a research assignment.

Introduction: Mexico and Culture

MEXICO FOR MANY FOREIGNERS is an exotic, strange place. It is a land of fine beaches and of Latin rhythms, the home of the legendary Pancho Villa, of romantic and revolutionary ballads, of moustaches, huge sombreros, tortillas, and tamales. It is a land of Indians and ancient ruins swallowed up by jungles or huddled in the shadows of smoldering volcanoes. We may think of it as a land to which we can escape into exotic adventure, safely to return to the reassuring familiarity of our own world. At least, that is an idea of Mexico that tourist campaigns like to promote. Yet, in the process, a myth is being foisted upon us and reality is being distorted by the use of selective and exaggerated images. The aim of this book is to explore and question such visions of Mexico, to look beyond them.

Mexico takes its name from the Mexica tribes (commonly known as Aztecs) that once dominated the central plateau where today's Mexico City is located. When the Spaniards conquered the land in the early sixteenth century, the official name they gave to it, and much other land besides, was New Spain. However, for the three hundred–odd years of colonial rule, Mexico was the de facto name and, once independence from Spain was won, that name became official. It is now a land of some 90 million people, a large, complex, dynamic, and distinctive country. Mexico's contact with its northern neighbor has increased to the point where it impinges on everyday life in virtually every corner of the United States.

One might imagine that Mexico's position, both its geographical position and its position in the U.S. psyche, has brought it certain advantages, allowing it to enjoy more attention or more substantial foreign aid than other Latin American countries; but nearness to the United States has in fact been double edged. For example, Mexico lost nearly half of its territory to the United States in the Mexican-American War of 1846–47, territory that included present-day California, Nevada, Colorado, Utah, Arizona, and New Mexico.

The fact that Mexico shares the North American continent with the United States and Canada was brought home to many people by the establishment of the North American Free Trade Agreement (NAFTA). Perhaps NAFTA will encourage a greater respect for Mexico, a deeper appreciation of its distinctiveness among the Latin American nations and of the degree to which the cultural identities of Mexico and the United States are linked. Certainly the United States now admits more readily that it is undergoing rapid Latinization, something that is apparent in the continuing influx of immigrants and in the popularity of Hispanic foods, music, film stars, and so on. Immigration's effect by 2025, it is thought, will be to make the United States the country with the largest number of Spanish speakers in the world. However, bubbles are inclined to burst and, though we may hope that we are entering an era of greater respect and mutual understanding, lurking in the background is the penchant for an imperialist U.S. mind-set not unlike the one that reigned among the Spaniards in 1492.

As our world becomes ever more obviously interconnected, interdependent and, on the face of it, homogeneous, it is particularly appropriate for us to try to improve our understanding of the sensibilities of members of other cultures. But if we are to achieve anything approaching an understanding of others, we must move beyond the comforting but naive notion that we are disinterested observers of their culture. In this particular instance, we need briefly to explore our concepts of "culture" and "Mexico" and the nature of their historical interaction. We must try to get beyond simple, romantic notions of a monolithic Mexican culture as portrayed in popular stereotypes and political rhetoric. We might then come closer to understanding that we are dealing with a dynamic and multifaceted process.

Culture is an extremely complicated concept, and we could hardly find a richer and more controversial terrain than Mexico's in which to explore it. Culture at once unites and divides us; it is the means by which we identify ourselves with and distinguish ourselves from others. Culture embraces both the very mundane question of how we live from day to day and the philosophical one of who we are. Culture is, on the one hand, something lived in, something that is usually unconscious, but it is also something that is consciously constructed in the many forms of artistic activity and symbolic representation that are produced. Traditional anthropology has taken as its primary subject the former aspect of culture—that is to say, the everyday material practices, most typically those of non-European or "primitive" peoples. In contrast, in the cultural studies of today the trend has been increasingly to emphasize the latter understanding of culture—culture as a discursive construct, as something deliberately expressed, not just through the fine arts but through popular forms too. This is not to deny the material realities of culture in the anthropological sense; and it certainly is not meant to suggest that to view culture as a discursive construct makes it any less real. The truth is that at root these two apparently disparate ways of looking at culture are closely related—the very notion of culture as a preexisting or non-verbalized reality has been made up.

In principle, all groups, all individuals, possess culture equally. All countries establish identity and difference, internally and externally, by distinctions of class and gender, language and ethnicity, and so forth. But no country's culture exists in a vacuum. Nor does one generally undertake to examine a culture in the abstract but, rather, responds to particular historical circumstances, and compares it to the culture of others. To cite the classic illustration, the Indians of Latin America never thought of themselves as Indians until the Europeans showed up, revealing that their own ways were different. It was the Europeans who first used the term Indians (though the Indians did quickly come to adopt it and to use it to their advantage in their struggle for cultural and physical survival). Something similar holds true today for the relationship between Mexico and the United States; each is a means by which the other defines itself.

Consider that moment when the Spanish conquistador Hernán Cortés and his troops first managed to traverse the twin volcanoes on the ridge of Anahuac, Mexico's central valley, and glimpse the grandeur of the Aztec capital, Tenochtitlán. The world, or more accurately the European and Indian understanding of it, was forever changed. In a cultural sense, each discovered the other, and each could only struggle to make sense of the other's existence in terms of their own limited worldviews. Thus, the Indians saw Cortés as the returning legendary white, bearded god, Quetzalcóatl. Thus, the Spaniards saw in the Indians—beyond the basic error encapsulated in the name Indian itself—the lost tribes of Atlantis, or the Amazons of Greek mythology, while they saw themselves as crusaders in shining armor from the medieval chivalric tradition.

Mexico itself has almost been obsessed with defining its national character and, because of some of the historical particulars—the need internally to overcome diversity, the need to confront external challenges—the inclination to over-determine and exceptionalize has been noticeably evident in Mexico's own efforts to explain itself. For that very reason, we must try to recognize the historical conditions that have determined the distinctive flavor of Mexican culture. In other words, we must ask what are the factors that have made Mexico such a rich terrain in which to explore the operations of culture, the factors that have made Mexicans so conscious of their culture and made matters related to it so politically charged.

Mexico is Indian and Spanish, ancient and modern. It has constructed an impressive culture while managing to weather a number of historical watersheds. It has fused the most disparate of traditions into something new. Mexico is developed and developing, caught between the Old World and the New World; it is the place par excellence of mestizos born of the mixture of Europeans and indigenous Americans. It is a country that has preserved a great deal, yet at the same time has been at pains to modernize.

Not only was Mexico the site of the most important of all the Spanish viceregal capitals during the Latin American colonial period, but also prior to that it was the site of two of the three major Latin American indigenous civilizations, the Maya and the Aztec. The Aztecs, in particular, had imposed their rule upon other pre-Hispanic peoples. Later, external pressures upon Mexico, together with internal diversity, conspired to produce a strong sense of national pride. The Mexico of today is still beset by tremendous external and internal pressures. One could easily argue that Mexico is at once more diverse and more unified than the United States. Mexico, like the United States, is "Western" in its dominant culture and institutions, and it is also a modern nation in the sense that its autonomy dates from about the same time as that of the United States. Yet such characteristics account for only one dimension of Mexico's national culture.

It is the synthesis of the Spanish and the Indian that makes Mexico so distinctive; that synthesis is observable in all aspects of society, and is still being realized. In effect, basic questions of the national collective identity have yet to be resolved, some of them of an ethical nature. For example, were the Indians, with their human sacrifices and pagan rituals, barbarians whom the Christians redeemed, or were the Spaniards the true barbarians, because of their arrogance and the destruction they inflicted upon the indigenous peoples? In 1992, at the time of the Quincentennial of Christopher Columbus's first voyage, there was much debate about whether one should talk of the New World and whether the arrival of the Spaniards marked a discovery or an encounter. An NPR radio essay by Richard Rodriguez, broadcast in 1992, provides a telling angle on this. Rodriguez, a mestizo (a man of mixed white and Indian parentage) from the southwestern United States, was on the one hand viewed by most of his fellow U.S. citizens as an outcast, as a member of a minority Indian group, and on the other hand viewed by the full-blooded descendants of the original Indians of the region, such as the Pueblo and the Navajo, as a Spaniard, a white European, a descendant of conquerors and oppressors. What was such a person to make of the hullabaloo about whether Columbus's voyage should be a cause for celebration or condemnation? As he saw it, the most significant thing about 1492 was that it marked the birthday of the new mixed race that he represented.

What most divides Mexicans today is not so much ethnic lines or systems of belief but, rather, disparities in such material areas as income and education. The hard realities of day-to-day life for many ordinary Mexicans do not leave much room for soul searching and wondering about national identity; in other words, for all the talk about culture and identity, many of the people concerned have not been parties to the debate. They are often the focus of cultural discourse, however, and they may well be aware of ways in which those who have the authority or ability to define national culture can have a powerful indirect effect on their lives. The "lived-in" culture and the culture as projected feed into and implicate each other: as soon as cultural theories and concepts take shape, they themselves become a part of culture and they influence precisely the things they have attempted to explain. Authoritative or official pronouncements on culture, in particular, can make a powerful impression on the individual psyche; they can work as self-fulfilling prophecies and can impose limits on creativity.[1]

We have raised some questions about our everyday understanding of what culture is, and about what it implies in Mexico. An immense body of literature on Mexico already exists, much of it of considerable quality and interest. There are countless general country surveys, tourist guides, travel accounts and personal impressions, and volumes upon volumes written by historians and anthropologists. Certain Mexican towns and villages have been so studied and revisited by ethnographers and archeologists—one thinks of Tepoztlán in the central highlands, or Chamula in Chiapas—that they seem to have become living museums, cultural laboratories, or meccas, better integrated into networks with international anthropologists and tourists than into their national framework.[2] It could be said that anthropology has created a laboratory or, better yet, a mirror with which to demonstrate its difference and assert its superiority. It is no great surprise that the bulk of the literature on Mexico has come out of Europe and North America; but increasingly it is being supplemented and challenged by work emanating from Mexico itself.

In the literature on Mexico one finds boldly synthetic attempts to distill some kind of national cultural essence, which by definition cannot correspond to the realities and experience of any particular group or individual; at the other extreme, one finds detailed ethnographies of particular locales, in-depth examinations that cannot stand for the whole in all its variety and complexity. Given the difficulties in capturing both the unity and diversity of Mexico, some of the most useful studies have been those that present a series of discrete, individual biographies from many walks of life, with a minimum of synthetic interpretation and analytical depth; examples are Patrick Oster's *The Mexicans: A Personal Portrait of a People* and Judith Adler Hellman's *Mexican Lives*.

Fear has been expressed in many quarters that traditional and culturally distinctive values are on the verge of extinction today, under the onslaught of a new international popular and commercial culture and the homogenizing pressures of globalization. Mexico, so close to the United States and so subject to the imposing shadow it casts, shows that in many ways such fears are justified. Most vestiges of pre-Hispanic rites are fast disappearing, even in the isolated rural regions; the function of the traditional extended family is being eroded and transformed by migration to large urban centers; and a flood of products from the United States has swamped Mexican supermarket and department store shelves. Yet while the causes for concern are very real, just as important, Mexico also shows us, perhaps better than anywhere else, that such fears are easily misplaced and exaggerated; in a great many ways Mexico is still strong and autonomous in its cultural identity. And after all, cultural development has always, everywhere, been a dynamic and multidimensional phenomenon. What is new today is our level of consciousness of the changes, and of the pace at which they are occurring. One positive aspect of the increasing globalization of our time is that it warns us against the dangers of constructing myths about cultural purity.

In this volume we shall be touching on many issues: culture as a force that unites and divides; culture as a tool that builds and challenges unity, community, and identity; culture as a set of material practices, of rites and rituals and corresponding values; culture as a set of symbolic representations, of artifacts that express a certain vision of Mexico. One can only do incomplete justice to Mexican culture in a single volume such as this. We must touch on selected, representative cultural products and processes, and inevitably succumb to some degree of reduction and abstraction. If Mexico's diversity is a hard reality, so too is its degree of unity, based on common practices and a common spirit forged over history.

The first part of this book concentrates on customs, the latter part on cultural products (insofar as they can be separated from one another). That is to say that the first part covers aspects of lived-in culture: the everyday rites, rituals, material practices, and festive traditions, often of religious origin, that provide evidence of common beliefs and values and bind the community together. Later chapters, by contrast, take up culture in the more common and narrow sense, referring to conscious forms of artistic expression. We shall range from the fine arts, to literature and performance, to relatively new media such as television and film. Even in this general survey, however, we are

Mexico, ancient and modern: Oaxaçan dance in Mexico City.
Photo by Carlos Aranda. Courtesy of Imagen Latina.

trying to move away from standard approaches to customs and culture, in certain key emphases and other subtle ways, in the hope of promoting a new, more active understanding. The primary emphasis is modern and contemporary, though not to the exclusion of historical roots. Important though the past is, perhaps this book will go some way toward counterbalancing what seems to be an irresistible tendency to allow the present to be overwhelmed by the weight of the past, a tendency that has led to undervaluing Mexico's dynamism and vitality.

We also hope that this book will help readers appreciate the sophistication of Mexico's cultural products, and that it will help counteract stereotypes. In his classic study excavating the Mexican soul and national character, *The Labyrinth of Solitude,* Octavio Paz affirms that the real measure of a people should not be based on philosophical abstraction and speculation but rather on the creative works produced by those people. By paying attention to examples of products from the full range of cultural production, we should arrive at a respectful appreciation of Mexico's multiplicity and diversity, and at once cast a critical eye on the way in which such works contribute to the discourse that constitutes Mexican culture.

Chapter 1, "Context: History, Land, and Society," explicitly sets out the geographic, demographic, socioeconomic, and ethnic contexts, as well as the historical and political backgrounds. Chapter 2 covers the history and pervasive influence of religion, particularly Catholicism, and chapter 3 deals with secular celebrations and other forms of entertainment, with social relations and the roles of men and women. In line with the general aims of the series, and following recent trends in cultural studies, in the remaining chapters we shall not restrict our attention to refined and sophisticated works of high culture, but shall take into account works of popular culture, from folk art to the mass media. We choose to begin the survey with the mass media (chapter 4) in a further effort to break with the tendency to view Mexico primarily as a museum of primitive folk arts and monumental ruins—something Mexico tends itself to emphasize in its tourist campaigns. Film—very much a modern art—will provide the focus in chapter 5; in this Mexico has been a leader, occupying a position in Latin America and in the Hispanic United States that is in some ways analogous to that of Hollywood in the global arena. The remaining chapters will cover the performing arts (chapter 6), literature (chapter 7), and the visual (or plastic) arts and architecture (chapter 8). In general, these later chapters will be less broadly synthetic and interpretative than the "customs" ones, and will be surveys highlighting major contributions in each area. Overall, the result may have a synchronic flavor, but we have also sought to give the volume an overarching, historical frame of reference.

NOTES

1. Federico Reyes Heroles and Roger Bartra have been two of the fiercest critics of the pernicious effects that derive from the myths about Mexico that have been propagated as part of official culture.

2. Examples of ingenious tactics on the part of the Indians for cultural, material, and spiritual survival abound. Instances include the way the indigenous nobility in the early colonial period quickly converted to Christianity, while secretly preserving the practice of pre-Hispanic beliefs; and the activities of caretakers of pre-Hispanic ruins today, who reflect back at the tourists the images they come to find, even though these images may have no authentic basis.

Chronology

50,000 B.C. ?	First people arrive in America, presumably from Asia.
12,000 B.C.	Approximate date of earliest human remains found in Mexican territory.
9,000 B.C.	Approximate date of first domestication of maize (corn).
1,500 B.C.– A.D. 300	Pre-Classical Period. Early civilizations of note in Meso-America: the Olmecs, with ceremonial sites at La Venta, Tres Zapotes, and San Lorenzo; ancient cultures at Monte Albán, Copilco, and Cuicuilco; and the Maya at Tikal.
A.D. 300–900	Classical Period. Rise of Teotihuacán culture in the central valley. Zapotec development at Monte Albán. Maya civilization at Uxmal, Palenque, and Bonampak.
900–1519	Post-Classical Period. Maya move to Yucatán and establish Chichén Itzá. Toltecs extend influence from Tula throughout central valley before decline. Migration of Nahua tribes from north into central valley and rise of Aztec (Mexica) Empire.
1325	Foundation of Aztec capital of Tenochtitlán, on an island in Lake Texcoco—according to legend, where the Aztecs found an eagle perched on a cactus with a serpent in its beak.
1511	Spanish expedition shipwrecks on the Yucatán coast. Spaniards Jerónimo de Aguilar and Gonzalo Guerrero survive among the Maya.

1519   Landfall of conquistador Hernán Cortés at Yucatán. Encounter with Aguilar in Yucatán and doña Marina/La Malinche in Tabasco; these people served Cortés as translators.

1521   Cortés lays seige to Tenochtitlán; defeats Aztecs.

1522   Cortés named Captain General and Governor of New Spain, as territory is called.

1524   Twelve Franciscan (Catholic) priests arrive to undertake Christian conversion of native population.

1527   Arrival of Mexico's first bishop, Fray Juan de Zumárraga.

1531   Indian Juan Diego believes he sees a vision of the Virgen de Guadalupe at Tepeyac, near Mexico City.

1536   Colegio de Santa Cruz de Tlatelolco founded, for the education and indoctrination of the Indian nobility. Fray Bernardino de Sahagún was a faculty member.

1537   First printing press in Mexico (and the New World).

1542   Las Casas's *Brevísima relación de la destrucción de las Indias.*

1553   Royal and Pontifical University founded (first university in the New World).

circa 1570   Diego de Landa writes *Relación de las cosas de Yucatán.*

1571   Holy Office of the Spanish Inquisition formally established in Mexico.

1572   First Jesuit missionaries arrive.

1577   Bernardino de Sahagún completes Spanish and Náhuatl versions of his four-volume *Historia general de las cosas de Nueva España.* Manuscripts were lost and not discovered for some 200 years.

1597   First permanent outdoor theaters, or *corrales de comedias,* appear in Mexico City.

1648   Birth of Juana Inés de Asbaje (later to become nun Sor Juana Inés de la Cruz, an early writer).

1690   Carlos Sigüenza y Góngora's *Infortunios de Alonso Ramírez.*

1692   Popular riots in Mexico City; government buildings burned.

1712   Indian uprising in Chiapas.

1767   Jesuits expelled from Mexico and other Spanish territories.

1805	First daily newspaper: *Diario de México.*
1810	In the early morning hours of September 16, Father Miguel Hidalgo's Grito de Dolores launches movement for independence from Spain.
1811	José María Morelos takes up leadership of the independence struggle.
1812	Fernández de Lizardi launches his first newspaper.
1816	Fernández de Lizardi's *El Periquillo Sarniento,* commonly considered Latin America's first true novel.
1821	Independence from Spain is consummated as Itúrbide leads victorious troops into Mexico City.
1822	Itúrbide crowned Emperor of newly independent Mexico; rules for 11 months.
1823	Central American Federation of territories declares independence from Mexico.
1824	New constitution establishes federal republic. Itúrbide executed. Guadalupe Victoria elected first president of the Republic.
1830	Antonio López de Santa Anna assumes presidency for the first time; he would assume and abandon the presidency several times between 1830 and 1855.
1833	Valentín Gómez Farías leads efforts to secularize education.
1836	Santa Anna defeated at San Jacinto. Texas declares its independence from Mexico.
1838	Growing interest in Yucatán in the possibility of secession.
1846–47	Mexican-American War. U.S. troops invade Mexico City and Mexican government flees to Querétaro. World's first war photographs taken.
1848	Treaty of Guadalupe Hidalgo signed, in which Mexico cedes more than half of its territory to the United States, including California, Arizona, and New Mexico.
1848–51	Violent caste wars waged in Yucatán.
1854	Liberals, many exiled in New Orleans, proclaim Plan de Ayutla and launch revolt.
1855	Santa Anna abandons Mexico.

1857	Liberal constitution promulgated.
1858–61	Three Years' War between liberals and conservatives, with two different governments claiming legitimacy; Benito Juárez, of Indian heritage, installed as president of liberal government in Veracruz and promulgates Reform Laws.
1862	French troops, allied with the Mexican conservatives, disembark in Veracruz. On May 5, Mexican liberal forces defeat French troops at Puebla.
1864	European royal Maximilian of Hapsburg arrives and is installed at head of Mexico's second empire.
1867	Liberal forces defeat troops loyal to Maximilian, and the restored republic is ushered in. Juárez elected president.
1869	Ignacio Altamirano's literary review *El Renacimiento* begins.
1872	Death of Benito Juárez.
1877–1911	The Porfiriato, a period of stability and infrastructural modernization under the authoritarian leadership of Porfirio Díaz. A hero of the battles to defeat the French, he arranged for his own reelection six times.
1877	National Conservatory of Music established.
1880s	Literary movement known as Modernismo on the rise.
1887	José María Velasco's painting of Oaxaca Cathedral.
1890s	Famous popular engraver José Guadalupe Posada active.
1896	First cinema theater opened.
1910	Mexican revolution, in its political phase, is launched by Francisco I. Madero, seeking the ouster of Díaz and the institution of free elections. Pancho Villa fights in the north; Emiliano Zapata, in the south.
1911	Porfirio Díaz flees into exile; Madero elected president.
1913	Madero assassinated in a coup led by Victoriano Huerta; Villa, Zapata, Carranza, Obregón, and others return to arms.
1913	Manuel M. Ponce publishes *La música y la canción mexicana (Mexican Music and Song)*.
1914	Huerta flees capital and triumphant revolutionary factions march into Mexico City; at the Convención de Aguascalientes the various revolutionary leaders attempt to reconcile their differences but fail.

1915	Revolutionary factions led by northern landholders Carranza, Obregón, and Calles gain ascendancy over more popular revolutionaries Villa and Zapata.
1917	Venustiano Carranza and Constitutional Congress promulgate new Revolutionary constitution. Carranza elected president.
1919	*El automóvil gris,* the outstanding film of the silent era.
1919	Mexican Communist Party founded.
1920	Factions from Sonora led by Obregón and Calles launch rebellion. Carranza flees and is assasinated.
1920–24	Presidency of Alvaro Obregón.
1921	First radio broadcasts.
1921–24	José Vasconcelos leads cultural revolution as minister of education.
1924	Carlos Chávez begins to dominate Mexico's art music, Diego Rivera and the muralists its visual art.
1924–28	Presidency of Plutarco Elías Calles.
1924	Azuela's *Los de abajo,* previously serialized, is published as a book, launching the popularity of the novel of the revolution.
1925	José Vasconcelos publishes *La raza cósmica.*
1926–29	Cristero Rebellion.
1928	Mexican Symphony Orchestra founded.
1928	Obregón is reelected president but is assasinated before taking office.
1929	Calles forms the Partido Revolucionario de la Nación (PRN) and establishes the populist machine politics of the government party.
1930	Radio station XEW begins broadcasting. Russian film director Sergei Eisenstein arrives in Mexico.
1930–50	Golden Age of radio and cinema.
1930s	Migration towards metropolitan area of Mexico City (DF) increases (and will continue in later decades).
1932	Literary group known as the Contemporáneos forms.

1934–40	Social reformist presidency of Lázaro Cárdenas puts many of the ideals of the Revolution into practice.
1935	Cárdenas establishes official peasants' union, Confederación Nacional Campesina (CNC).
1936	Cárdenas establishes official workers' union, Confederación de Trabajadores de México (CTM).
1937	Rodolfo Usigli's *El gesticulador.*
1938	Cárdenas seizes foreign oil company holdings in Mexico and nationalizes petroleum industry. He changes name of official party to Partido de la Revolución Mexicana (PRM) and restructures it.
1939	Conservative opposition party, Partido de Acción Nacional (PAN) founded.
1940	*Ahí está el detalle,* actor Cantinflas's first hit film.
1940s	Refugees from Franco's Spain arrive, among them film director Luis Buñuel.
1942	United States and Mexico start *bracero* program, allowing U.S. employers to take on Mexican agricultural workers.
1943	*Flor silvestre,* the first major film by Fernández and Figueroa.
1943	Goverment establishes national health, disability, and pension system, the Instituto Mexicano del Seguro Social.
1946	Miguel Alemán, first civilian president in the post-Revolutionary period, elected. Mexico's ruling party adopts the name Institutional Revolutionary Party (Partido Revolucionario Institucional, PRI) .
1947	Yáñez's novel *Al filo del agua* is published.
1948	Ballet Nacional de México established.
1950	Buñuel's film *Los olvidados* appears.
1950	Octavio Paz publishes *El laberinto de la soledad (The Labyrinth of Solitude).* Television transmissions begin in Mexico.
1950s	The brash *ruptura* generation of visual artists, such as José Luis Cuevas and Rufino Tamayo, breaks with the prevailing esthetic of the muralists.
1953	Women win the right to vote and hold elective office.
1954	Juan Rulfo's novel *Pedro Páramo* is published.

1959	Ballet Folklórico founded.
1959	Government-funded television starts.
1959	Miguel León Portilla publishes his *Visión de los vencidos.*
1960s	*La Onda:* the "new wave" in fiction.
1961–62	*Nuevo Cine* published.
1962	Carlos Fuentes's *La muerte de Artemio Cruz* (*The Death of Artemio Cruz*), a key novel of the Boom.
1964–65	Bracero program suspended. Mexico starts border industrialization.
1968	Series of student and worker protests culminates when government forces open fire on demonstrators in the Tlatelolco district of Mexico City on October 2; hundreds die. Event instigates a slowly building crisis of legitimacy for governing party. Mexico becomes the first developing country to host the Olympics.
1970s	Influx of political refugees from Chile and Argentina.
1970	Mexico hosts its first World Cup soccer competition.
1971	Luis Alcoriza debuts his film *Mecánica nacional.*
1971	Elena Poniatowska publishes her documentary collage *La noche de Tlatelolco* (*Massacre in Mexico*).
1975	Changes in the Civil Code, protecting women's rights and birth control.
1976	Government orchestrates breakup of staff of *Excelsior* newspaper. Opposition political weekly *Proceso,* newspaper *Unomásuno,* and Octavio Paz's literary monthly *Vuelta* are launched.
1976	The peso suffers a 50 percent devaluation against the U.S. dollar.
1981	Fall in oil prices triggers economic hardships.
1982	The peso again undergoes drastic devaluations. President José López Portillo nationalizes the banking industry.
1985	Major earthquake in Mexico City rallies populace and new civic groups against government corruption. Angeles Mastretta's *Arráncame la vida* (*Mexican Bolero*) appears.
1987	Cuauhtémoc Cárdenas and Porfirio Muñoz Ledo, leading politicians, publicly renounce their PRI membership.

1988	PRI presidential candidate Carlos Salinas de Gortari defeats candidate Cuauhtémoc Cárdenas. Massive protests against apparent fraud in state and federal elections ensue, especially in Chihuahua and on the U.S. border.
1989–93	The Salinas government undertakes new neo-liberal economic reforms, selling off many state-owned enterprises.
1989	The social democratic opposition party, Partido de la Revolución Democrática (PRD), is founded, with Cuauhtémoc Cárdenas as its leading figure.
1989	Jorge Fons's film *Rojo amanecer,* on the Tlatelolco massacre.
1991	Alfonso Arau's film version of Laura Esquivel's novel *Como agua para chocolate (Like Water for Chocolate).*
1993	Newspaper *Reforma* opens.
1993	Second major commercial television network, TV Azteca, brings competition with Televisa empire.
1993	Tratado de Libre Comercio (TLC) (North American Free Trade Agreement [NAFTA]) established.
1994	Ejército Zapatista de Liberación Nacional (EZLN), under the leadership of Comandante Marcos, launches armed rebellion in Chiapas. Rash of political assassinations besets PRI, including PRI presidential candidate Luis Donaldo Colosio.
1995	President Ernesto Zedillo confronts another economic crisis and announces another 50 percent devaluation of the peso.
1996	Zedillo advances real electoral reform, with the creation of an autonomous Federal Elections Institute.
1999	Major student strike shuts down the National University.
2000	Election of PAN presidential candidate Vicente Fox ends 71-year dominance of the PRI.

1

Context: History, Land, and Society

THIS CHAPTER OFFERS an overview of the historical, physical, and social context. We shall be dealing with issues such as continuity versus change, tradition versus modernity, centralism versus regionalism, and unity versus diversity. A powerful sense of nationalism and a strong political will have favored integration, and to the outside world Mexico may present a unified front, but the fact is that it is still a country that suffers from tensions, hierarchies, and stratifications.

In some respects, Mexico's characteristics set it apart from other Spanish American nations. No other country among them has so actively traced its cultural origins though so dramatic a history to such deep roots; none has so thoroughly fused European and non-European cultural influences; and none has made the Indian element so central a part of its official culture. Quite obviously, these things also set Mexico apart from its principal rival, the United States, with which it contrasts in virtually every respect. It would, of course, be absurd to imagine tracing the major roots of the modern United States back beyond the arrival of the first European settlers. Much the same could be said of most Latin American nations as well; for them, non-European ingredients are generally secondary contributors to their cultural identity. At the opposite extreme from Mexico are Argentina and Uruguay which, much like the United States, are primarily nations of transplanted Europeans. As in Mexico, in Perú the Spaniards set up a major administrative center, a viceroyalty, grafting it onto a strong pre-Hispanic base; but modern Perú is different from Mexico in that it is far more socially stratified along colonial lines. By comparison, Mexico is hybrid, it is in-between; it is a bridge between North and South America, between the ancient and the modern, between the developed and the developing worlds.

Two factors in particular account for much of Mexico's distinctiveness. The first is the strength of the two cultures that contributed to early Mexican history—that is to say, the Indian (i.e. Amerindian) and the Spanish cultures. Mexico became the principal seat and the pride of Spanish colonial power in the Americas (from 1521 to 1810, it was even officially called New Spain), and it had been the site of two of the three most sophisticated and powerful pre-Hispanic Meso-American civilizations. The European and Indian cultures did not encounter one another merely by chance; the Spaniards had heard grand accounts of the Indian civilizations and so the expedition led by Hernán Cortés that set out from Cuba in 1519 was aimed precisely at conquering and subjugating them, at gaining power and wealth, at bringing the Indian people to the Christian (Catholic) God. There is a significant historical irony that results from all this: over the subsequent course of history the dominant Spanish element in Mexico has found itself defending and preserving the very Meso-American civilizations whose pagan idolatries Spain originally sought to extirpate and illuminate with the light of Truth. Somewhat paradoxically, it was in colonial New Spain, in precisely the place where Spanish authority was most keenly felt, that the elite became most anxious to establish a separate national identity. So much was this so that by the time of the War of Independence from Spain, in the nineteenth century, anti-Spanish sentiment and pro-Indian rhetoric had become quite natural and provided a highly effective rallying cry.

The second crucial factor relates to modern times: Mexico's proximity to the United States, and the latter's powerful political, economic, and cultural influence. It is sometimes said that the two countries share the longest continuous border between the developed and developing worlds. Mexico's turn-of-the-century President Porfirio Díaz had his own take on the effect of the relationship: "Poor Mexico, so far from God and so close to the United States." The closeness of the United States, coupled with the admixture of the Indian and the European heritages, has helped generate Mexico's strong sense of self, its pride in its special cultural development, and its independence, its impassioned sense of nationalism. But these same factors have also made Mexico's cultural identity problematic, generating vigorous and continuing debate about quite what the nature of that identity is. It is a liking for self-examination that can be read as a sign both of strength and of insecurity.

These same factors have also made Mexico a source of pride and inspiration for other Spanish American nations, who often admire its largely successful resolution of difficult historical circumstances and its relatively harmonious integration of different cultural elements. Mexico has been seen as the brave champion of Latin America, resisting the onslaught of Anglo-American culture. In view of the degree of political stability that it has enjoyed, at least since its 1910 Revolution, Mexico has also provided a safe haven for people from other Hispanic nations. Republican exiles of the Spanish Civil War, for example, came to Mexico in the 1940s in large numbers, many of them greatly enriching its intellectual and academic climate. Likewise, starting in the 1970s, many refugees came from Pinochet's Chile and from the military dictatorships in Argentina. Others who have been less persecuted have felt at home in Mexico—the well-known Colombian novelist Gabriel García Márquez being an example. Interestingly, however, now that migration and globalization are erasing and redrawing cultural boundaries, there is an opposite tendency among Spanish Americans, a tendency to distance themselves from a Mexico that they now see as too close to the United States. Many wish to emphasize their own national or cultural distinctiveness, to avoid being lumped together with the Mexicans and therefore subjected to the negative stereotyping and prejudice that exist particularly in the United States. As all this suggests, a useful way to keep Mexico in perspective is by comparing it, on the one hand, with other Spanish American nations and, on the other, with the United States.

The Spanish conquest and the ensuing three hundred years of colonial rule established the foundations of modern Mexican culture. Spanish customs and institutions, the Spanish language, and the Catholic religion were built (even literally) upon the ruins of the conquered Indian empires and imposed upon a subjugated population. Yet, significantly, both in the popular imagination and in official rhetoric, it is the Indian, rather than the Spanish, side of Mexico's heritage that predominates. The novelist Carlos Fuentes often remarks upon the irony that the most crucial and fundamental period in Mexico's national development (the Spanish colonial era) is the one most frequently and conveniently forgotten. This idea is borne out symbolically, Fuentes suggests, by the glaring absence of any statues of the Spanish conqueror Hernán Cortés—the father, literally and figuratively, of this *mestizo* nation. In contrast, the statue of the vanquished Aztec leader Cuauhtémoc graces a major intersection in Mexico City. Other Spanish figures—Columbus and the Emperor Carlos V, for example—are displayed prominently in civic statuary, but Cortés is a villain, as reflected in Diego Rivera's grotesque depictions in murals at the National Palace in Mexico City.

Similarly, Cortés's Indian mistress and translator Malinche, the mother of the nation, is viewed as a traitor. In fact, the popular term *malinchismo* has come to refer to selling out to foreign interests, and today it is applied primarily to those Mexicans who see everything that comes from the United States as superior. In many people's eyes, this transfer of meaning eloquently sums up the historical trajectory of Mexico since, in the modern period, the United States has taken over the role of foreign oppressor from Spain, starting with the Mexican War of 1846–47, as a result of which Mexico lost vast expanses of the territory that today make up the American Southwest.

The study of pre-Hispanic culture has tended to be dominated by European and North American scholars. In Mexico itself it has run the gamut from utter and indefensible neglect (especially in the latter part of the colonial period and throughout most of the nineteenth century) to idealization and gross oversimplification. This last is particularly true of twentieth-century post-Revolutionary governments, which have appropriated the pre-Hispanic legacy, making it a key part of the official culture. For example, they funded the murals on public buildings that were painted by such artists as Diego Rivera; and they established institutions such as the Museo Nacional de Antropología. The extent to which things Indian are officially regarded as vital parts of the culture was apparent in a traveling art exhibition that was sponsored by the government and the Televisa television empire in 1990, in anticipation of the celebration of the 500th anniversary of Columbus's discovery of America. It was entitled "Splendors of Thirty Centuries" and was completely dominated by pre-Hispanic artifacts, much to the chagrin of modern artists and a number of critics. Many of the latter thought it contradictory for curators working for a government that was claiming to modernize Mexico to be playing upon foreign fascination with the exotic and the primitive. Furthermore, they saw it as another instance of modern Mexican governments, dominated by white Latin American (*criollo*) and mestizo elites, using a smokescreen to hide the marginalization, the injustice, and lack of real opportunities faced by the Indians of today.

Attitudes toward the Indian heritage can verge on the hypocritical. On the one hand, most Mexicans today have learned to take pride in their pre-Hispanic history and their Indian heritage; that is particularly noticeable when they are defending their country's status and identity vis-à-vis others. But, for everyday purposes, things Indian are commonly considered inferior, second-class. Quite understandably, but a little paradoxically, it is often the most modern and especially the most educated Mexicans who espouse the idea of the centrality of Mexico's Indian heritage (a fact that suggests that nationalistic rhetoric and education in the post-Revolutionary period have had the desired effect). The less educated and less empowered—those who ironically tend to be more Indian—are inclined to try to distance themselves from things Indian, probably because they know from personal experience the kind of stigma associated with being thought Indian.

The fact is that pre-Hispanic culture has been irrevocably modified by 500 years of contact with others, first under Spanish colonial and then under Mexican rule, and what we now know of that culture has been filtered through intermediaries, including the local community leaders. As one slightly bizarre illustration of how culture can be so modified, take the case of the contemporary Western anthropologists who, having broken the Mayan code so as to be able finally to read the pre-conquest hieroglyphics, are now attempting to teach descendants of the Mayas to decipher the writings of their ancestors. All of this does not mean, by any stretch of the imagination, that the pre-Hispanic period lacks real influence on the Mexico of today; on the contrary, that influence is present in a thousand conscious and unconscious ways, sometimes so transformed that it is not immediately evident. Indeed, pre-Hispanic influence has considerable explanatory power, as we shall see throughout this volume. The point is simply that that influence is a modified, mediated one, not a direct one.

National and international migration is forever altering the Mexican cultural landscape. Further changes are brought about by increasing telecommunications. Like other developing countries, Mexico is being "electronified" without being fully industrialized, globalized without having fully modernized. The Mayan descendants in the Lacandon jungle of the southern state of Chiapas, traditionally considered one of the most isolated, insular, and least integrated regions of Mexico, are now linked to the World Wide Web through the computer screens of their Zapatista rebel leaders. Commercial television, national and international programming, advertisements for Coca-Cola, Corona, U.S. cleaning and hygiene products, and European and Japanese automobiles have long since pervaded the more remote rural areas. Peasants who since the 1930s and 1940s have flocked to the inner-city neighborhoods and the shantytowns fringing Mexico City are increasingly moving directly—without an elementary education but often with an advanced degree in the school of hard knocks—from the Mexican countryside and provinces, not only into the maquiladoras of the border, not only into large cities like Los Angeles and Chicago, but also into jobs in the poultry-processing plants of northwest Arkansas and the tobacco fields of eastern North Carolina. It is as if they were leaping directly from traditional folk culture right into globalization, bypassing modern Mexico and any attempt at becoming integrated into its mainstream.

Such processes understandably provoke fears that Mexico's distinctive traditions are in danger of extinction. One observer has remarked on how difficult it is today to see regional and national traditions in operation, since "many of the redoubts of regional culture have disintegrated and traditions are modified as never before" (Monsiváis, "Notas...," 250). Yet such processes are never simple, nor do they necessarily lead to the more powerful culture causing the disappearance of the weaker one. Even in Mexico—especially in Mexico, so powerfully under the influence of commercial culture from the United States—any simple notion of Americanization hardly does justice to the complexity of the processes. Just as urban and global ways visit themselves on the provinces, provincial ways also affect the ways of the city and the globe. In fact, the development of culture in Mexico that we have been discussing confirms what recent research has recognized—that processes of global integration tend to strengthen and enhance regional differences as much as erase them.

HISTORICAL PERIODS

Mexican history conveniently separates out into four or five periods. The sequence is punctuated by almost cataclysmic events involving military action and social, political, and cultural upheaval. The first period is the pre-Columbian one, the period of the Indian civilizations until the time of the Spanish conquest (1519). The second period is the one of colonial rule that came to an end with the war for independence from Spain (of 1810–21). The third is the republican era that ends with the Mexican Revolution (of 1910–17). Arguably, the ensuing period reaches another watershed in 1968, when there was a massacre of student protesters at Tlatelolco, a square in Mexico City. We can now see how this event marked the beginning of a crisis of legitimacy for the ruling Institutional Revolutionary Party (PRI), one that finally led to the election to the national presidency of a candidate from outside that party, Vicente Fox, in the year 2000. We should take a moment to compare the length of the periods we have just identified: the pre-Hispanic one spans very many centuries (roughly 1500 B.C. to A.D. 1500), while the colonial period lasts three (1521–1810). In contrast, Mexico's modern history includes the one hundred years of the so-called Republican era (from 1810 to 1910), while the period from the Revolution up to the present day covers some ninety years.

At the end of each of Mexico's historical periods, attempts were made in some way to break with the immediate past, to bring about a fundamental redefinition of Mexico, a new beginning, but one often accompanied by a rededication to the nation's origins. Yet the more things have changed in Mexico, the more there has been resistance to change. There was evidence of this in 1994, in the rash of political assassinations that beset the PRI, which had monopolized power ever since the Revolution. These crimes, which have never been fully clarified or solved, were widely understood to have resulted from internal tensions among the PRI elite, between younger (and often U.S.-educated) technocrats who wanted to open the system up and advocated more democracy, and the "dinosaurs" who sought to retain the traditional networks of patronage. Ominously, the assassinations seemed to echo those that had accompanied the consolidation of the post-Revolutionary, one-party political system in the late 1920s, and suggested that little in the way of political modernization and transparency had been achieved in the intervening years.

In *The Critique of the Pyramid*, the sequel to his classic interpretation of Mexican history entitled *The Labyrinth of Solitude*, Octavio Paz, Mexico's Nobel Prize–winning poet and essayist, suggests an interesting thesis. He argues that one can trace a line of direct descent in the Mexican political system connecting the country's modern and post-Revolutionary presidents to the viceroys of New Spain and reaching back beyond the Spanish conquest to the Tatloani, the high priests of the Aztec empire. What connects them all, says Paz, is their absolute authority over a hierarchy, the almost god-like aura with which they are vested. This sort of tradition distinguishes Mexico from the United States and, to a significant degree, from almost every other Spanish American country as well.

PRE-COLUMBIAN TIMES

Pre-Columbian civilizations have understandably captured the imagination of people all over the world. Even so, they remain cloaked in an aura of mystery and otherness and, given our historical distance and our own cultural viewpoint, it is hard to grasp their scope. To a large extent, modern Mexicans share our difficulty. The achievements of the ancient civilizations, whether social, cultural, artistic, intellectual, or technological, in many ways match those of ancient Egypt, classical Greece, and Rome. Long before the arrival of Europeans on American soil, Meso-America (a region that encompasses parts of Central America as well as modern Mexico) had witnessed the rise and fall of a number of civilizations—from the Olmecs to the Mayas, from the Zapotecs to the Mixtecs, and from the Teotihuacanos and the Toltecs to the Aztecs, to name a few. Of the two greatest civilizations, the Maya, centered first in southern Mexico and Guatemala, then in the Yucatán Peninsula, was in decline by the time the Spaniards arrived. The Aztecs, or Mexica, however, were flourishing; Tenochtitlán, the capital they had founded in 1325 on an island in the middle of Lake Texcoco, was larger than any city in Europe at the time, and cleaner. But its fate was to be destroyed and to have modern Mexico City built over its ruins. How, then, did the Spaniards, who were so heavily outnumbered and in unknown territory, manage to do this?

Believing that the gods had to be satisfied by means of human sacrifice, that only by that means could the future be guaranteed, the Aztecs had come

Aerial view of the Alameda Central, former site of an Aztec market, in Mexico City. Photo by Steven Bell.

to dominate other tribes, sending out raiding parties to bring back live captives who would then become their sacrificial victims. It was because of the hostilities with other tribes that it was possible for Cortés to win allies, supplement his meager force of a few hundred Spaniards, and take on the Aztecs. But there were other factors that worked surprisingly in favor of the invaders. To begin with, the Indians were overawed by their first encounter with horses and firearms, neither of which were known prior to the arrival of the Spaniards. More fortuitous, but every bit as helpful to the invaders, was the fact that Indian legend held that a benign god, Quetzalcóatl, who had been banished from the land, would return at that time, and what is more, that he would assume a physical guise that happened to match that of Cortés. Thus the Spaniards were able to enter Tenochtitlán and establish control through Moctezuma, the Aztec emperor, who became virtually a prisoner. His subjects, however, grew restive, and in an attempt to pacify them the Spaniards brought Moctezuma out into public view. Exactly what followed is a matter of some contention. According to the Spanish version, Moctezuma was stoned to death by his own people; according to the Aztec account, he was stabbed in the back by Cortés. The Spaniards, laden with gold, now fought to retreat from Tenochtitlán. Later they would regroup, lay siege to the city until its inhabitants had starved (or died of the smallpox that the Europeans had inadvertently brought with them), and finally raze the city to the ground.

THE COLONIAL PERIOD

In following years this land, which the Spaniards now called New Spain, would be the location of one of the principal viceroyalties, which were the key administrative units by means of which Spain exercised control and extended its power over newly acquired territories. By the end of the seventeenth century, New Spain had laid claim to an area that ran from the present-day border of Panama in the south, far to the north, into much of what is the southeastern and especially the southwestern and western United States of today. Only in the nineteenth century was this area significantly reduced, first with the break-off of the Central American Confederation of nations in the immediate aftermath of independence from Spain, and then with the independence of Texas and the cession of virtually all of the American West and Southwest to the United States, as a consequence of the Mexican-American War of 1846–47. (Not that Mexico is now a small country; even within its present-day borders, it occupies an area three times the size of Texas.)

In Cholula there is a pyramid that the Spaniards crowned with a colonial church, rather as they had inserted a Catholic chapel into the Moorish mosque at Córdoba, back in Spain, as a symbol of their victory over the infidels. More generally, Spanish authority was imposed, from across the ocean, through the appointment of Spanish-born viceroys and archbishops who served as representatives of the crown. Much as Cortés had used alliances with the disgruntled indigenous groups in order to defeat the dominant Aztecs, so Spanish colonial authorities initially exploited the Indian nobility as intermediaries in order to control and indoctrinate the native population at large. To that same end, they also exploited certain parallels between Catholic and pre-Hispanic religious rituals and icons. (Sometimes they came to regret having done so, as in the case of the patron saint of Mexico, the dark-skinned Virgin of Guadalupe, who became a symbol of the struggle for Mexican independence from Spain.) The very distances that seemed to make rigid measures necessary also made for considerable laxity in their application. In practical terms, this was often for the better, for it allowed considerable creativity and flexibility in the melding of Catholic ritual and pre-Hispanic practices and rites, as thousands upon thousands of Indians were converted to Christianity. Sometimes it was for the worse—witness the difficulty the Spanish crown had in implementing new laws, promulgated in 1542, that had been designed to protect the Indians and limit their exploitation by the colonizers. That attempt to change the way in which Indians were being used came about largely due to an account of their lot, *Brevísima relación de la destrucción de las Indias* (1542), that had been written by a friar named Bartolomé de las Casas. It had become customary for the Spanish crown to grant *encomiendas* to settlers in the newly colonized lands; these encomiendas put groups of Indians under the control of settlers, who could then enjoy the fruits of Indian labor. Las Casas's revelation of how the Indians were being mistreated under this system (he had himself had—and renounced—an encomienda) came to the attention not only of the Spanish monarch but also of Spain's enemies, who profited from it, spreading abroad "the black legend" (*leyenda negra*), the tale of Spanish cruelty. Cruelty and destruction there certainly was, but the Spaniards, partly out of necessity, partly by design, did leave many pre-Hispanic structures (social and economic ones, for example) intact; in many cases they simply overlayed them with Spanish ones.

During the three centuries of Spanish colonial rule, the patterns of interaction between Indians and Spaniards were established, and the processes of cultural synthesis and racial blending that gave rise to the famous castes (*castas*) and produced the mestizo were set in motion. Castas was the term used to refer to the masses of people of mixed race who, as far as the pecking order was concerned, came below the true Spaniards (the *peninsulares*) and the people of Spanish parentage who had been born in the New World (the criollos). Most commentators remark on how, very early on in the colonial period, things took on a notably Mexican flavor, as pride in and appreciation for things American emerged.

Another point to bear in mind is the relative lack of Spanish women in the colonies, as a result of which there was a good deal of racial mixing. One of the first things that Cortés did when he arrived in Yucatán, prior to moving on to found the city of Veracruz and thence traveling to the central valley to conquer Tenochtitlán, was to engage the services of Malinche, an Indian woman who became his interpreter. She also became his mistress and bore him a son who, if not actually the first member, at least symbolically became the first of the new mestizo race. As we have seen, nowadays Malinche is associated with the idea of betrayal—after all, she was instrumental in the downfall of her people. Her union with Cortés, however, also heralds what would become a continental preoccupation with status, with the mistaken but powerful idea that there was such a thing as pure Spanish blood (*limpieza de sangre*). The criollos themselves, though often quite prosperous, and despite being of Spanish descent, were sensitive about the superior standing of the true Spaniards. The latter were appointed by and from Spain to all the positions of administrative and legal power; only at the local council level did the criollos have power.

To understand the racial and cultural fusion that took place in Mexico, it is useful to consider the significant differences between the English and Spanish colonizations of America. In the first place, the English and the Spanish encountered very different circumstances. In the north the Indian groups were mostly small and dispersed, with simple systems of social organization; in Meso-America and farther south there were huge, sophisticated empires, with large populations concentrated in major centers. Furthermore, the Spaniards and the English came to America with very different visions and missions. The English colonizers had in many senses been dissidents or free-thinkers in their home societies. They embodied the new, reformist European ideas of individualism and self-determination, of political, economic, and religious freedom; their vision placed man and the individual at the center, and emphasized his ability to harness nature and shape his own destiny. Even though the Spanish conquest occurred at a time when Renaissance Europe was also emphasizing the importance of mankind, the Spaniards came to America as champions of orthodox Catholicism, with its respect for dogmas, hierarchy, and authority. Ideologically, then, the Spanish conquest was largely an extension of the crusade to reclaim Spain for Christianity, to reconquer the territories that had been occupied by the Moors. The Spaniards were there for the greater glory of God and country, and while they also sought wealth and fame, they were intent on their holy mission of redeeming the Indians. In many respects, the trauma of the conquest has not been overcome, and perhaps it never will be. Nevertheless, one must remember the contrast between the fate of the Indians in Mexico and those in the United States; there is some irony in the fact that Britain was quick to spread the "black legend" about Spanish cruelty, yet the Spaniards did acknowledge the Indians' humanity in principle and in law. Despite all the acts of physical and cultural violence, there were also many great and famous acts of humanity.

There are striking similarities between the pre-Hispanic and the Spanish colonial worldviews, similarities that facilitated cultural synthesis during the Spanish colonial period, providing the basis for Mexico's cultural uniqueness. In both worlds, religious ritual was extremely important. In the pre-Hispanic world church and state were one, while in the Spanish colonial period the powers of both were inextricably linked. It could be said that in the pre-Hispanic era power served pomp; for example, it was the role of the Aztec Tatloani, through the performance of ritual and human sacrifice, to appease the gods and thereby maintain the order of the universe. In the Spanish colonial worldview, in contrast, we might say that pomp served power; thus, for example, the Spaniards could use the symbol of the dark-skinned Virgin of Guadalupe to further the mission of acculturation and conversion of the Indians. In both cases there is a sharp contrast with the modern premise that power should serve the people, a premise still rather halfheartedly embraced in Mexico.

INDEPENDENCE AND THE NINETEENTH-CENTURY REPUBLICAN ERA

The decline of Spain's commercial monopolies and the onset of political turmoil in the old country generated mixed reactions in the New World. Some saw the time as ripe for independence; others rallied around Spain, particularly in view of the French Emperor Napoleon's incursion into it. In the main, the criollos of Mexico opposed Napoleon, but wanted equality with the peoples and provinces of Spain, while the peninsulares (the Spaniards living in New Spain, sometimes referred to disparagingly as *gachupines*) also opposed the Frenchman but refused to accept the idea of Mexican sovereignty or equality. While there were tensions between criollos and peninsulares, while there was a desire for independence, there was also a consciousness of the exceptional power and importance that New Spain had enjoyed under colonial rule. Perhaps that is why, when an independence finally did come, it really amounted to a conservative compromise.

The first spark of rebellion came not from Mexico City but from the village of Dolores, Guanajuato. Father Miguel Hidalgo, a gentle man who nonetheless had had brushes with the Church hierarchy in the past, was, like so many advocates of Spanish American independence, inspired by the ideals of the Enlightenment, by the French Revolution, and the political example of U.S. independence. He and some like-minded people were disaffected with the way that liberals in Mexico City had accepted the imposition of a new viceroy, and together they decided to make a public declaration of independence. But things moved more quickly than they intended: news of their intentions leaked out, Hidalgo was faced with imminent arrest, and so, at midnight on September 15, 1810, he tolled the bells of his church and to those who assembled there in response he proclaimed: "Long live religion; long live America; down with bad government!" That cry became known as the Grito de Dolores (strictly speaking, the "cry from Dolores," though coincidentally and rather appropriately it also suggests a "cry of anguish"); this call for independence is still reenacted each September 15 in major Mexican towns. A rabble army then gathered, composed primarily of poor rural folk who were opposed to both the criollo and the Spanish interests in Mexico City. Under the banner of the Virgin of Guadalupe (a figure associated with the underprivileged Indian community), and armed with little more than farm tools, they took the town of Guanajuato, ransacked it, and killed many creole families. After further advances the "army" was routed in a confrontation with regulars near Guadalajara. Hidalgo attempted to escape but was captured, defrocked, and executed. His intentions had been noble—to better the lot of the rural and indigenous poor—but things had got out of hand, his efforts to impose discipline and be constructive had been thwarted, and he died regretting the violence that had been perpetrated.

The torch of revolution was taken up by another priest, José María Morelos, who had time and organization enough to form a government and declare independence in November 1813. Spain sent forces to fight him, and it was eventually Morelos's fate also to be defrocked and executed. The royalists held Mexico until 1820. By that time, Spain itself was undergoing radical change. Anticlericalism there was strong, as was the drive towards popular participation in the political process; in view of this, even those who had fought against such people as Morelos now came to see this reformed Spain as more threatening than an independent Mexico. One of them, an opportunistic creole soldier called Agustín Itúrbide, now found himself in charge of the imperial forces. He negotiated with another of the rebel leaders, an Indian called Vicente Guerrero, and together they hatched a plan for an independent monarchy in Mexico. Initially the idea was to invite the Spanish monarch to move to Mexico, but the upshot was that Itúrbide managed to insinuate himself into the position, and so he was crowned Emperor Agustín I, on July 25, 1822. Guerrero, however, was disillusioned; things had not improved for the masses, and Itúrbide, amid much Napoleonic pomp, was becoming increasingly dictatorial. Another creole officer, Antonio López de Santa Anna, now drew up a new plan together with Guerrero and Guadalupe Victoria, a rebel leader who had adopted that name in homage to the initiative of Father Hidalgo. As a result, in 1823 Victoria became the first president of the Republic of Mexico, though Santa Anna would continue to be a powerful force for years to come, and the creoles would continue to rule the roost.

In 1839, twenty years after father Hidalgo's Grito de Dolores, Spain formally recognized the independence of Mexico and sent its first ambassador to it. As it happened, his wife was a woman of Scottish descent, and she wrote a lively account of their experiences in Mexico; in it she captures not only the round of socializing among the elite and powerful but also something of the chaos and instability of a country in which revolution and pronouncements of change were frequent, but where little real progress was evident. In 1841 she wrote: "There is no people, nor is there any country where there is a more complete distinction of classes than in this self-styled republic. One government is abandoned, and there is none to take its place, one revolution follows another, yet the remedy is not found."[1] In fact, in the fifteen years following independence there had been a half dozen such changes, and Mexico was well-launched into a cycle of *caudillismo*—rule by strongmen, by petty tyrants. Itúrbide had been forced to abdicate, told to leave the country, and then shot. Victoria had survived a four-year term, despite warring factions of federalists (backed by strong regional figures) and centralists (supported by the creole elite in the big city). New elections in 1828 were won by the centralists, but the federalists and Santa Anna installed Guerrero in the presidency, and chaos followed. Guerrero in due course was overthrown, put on trial, and executed. In 1833 Santa Anna himself was elected. Since governing was going to be difficult, Santa Anna retired to a comfortable location and left his deputy to struggle with the situation; this man, Valentín Gómez Farías, attempted to challenge the colonial order and bring about reforms, but was inevitably frustrated by the opposition that came from vested creole interests and the Church. After Gómez Farías withdrew into exile in New Orleans, Santa Anna took the reins once again, now declaring himself a centralist and changing the constitution so that the established interests were protected. He governed virtually as a dictator, and eventually fell out of favor with both conservatives and liberals to the point where he too was forced into exile, in Cuba, in 1844. The country then reverted to its earlier constitution; but when Mexico found itself at war with the United States, Santa Anna was brought back.

By the middle of the century Mexico had ceded not only Texas but what would become California, Arizona, and New Mexico also, though it did receive some financial compensation from the U.S. government. Santa Anna was once again in disgrace (and in exile, this time in Venezuela), and the country was in even greater chaos. Yet once again they asked Santa Anna to return, lacking a better prospect for holding the country together; this time he ruled with greater pomp and circumstance, squandering money until he was eventually ousted in 1855.

There followed what is known as the Era of Reform. Two important laws were passed, aimed at breaking up lands held by the Church and reducing the privileges of church and military personnel; a new constitution, one that would last into the future, was drawn up in 1857. Naturally, such changes represented major attacks on the established order, and they met with fierce opposition from the creoles and the clergy, whose interests were at stake. Many of these people lived in Mexico City, though their lands, their haciendas, were far away, managed by overseers and worked by poor peasants.

In the mid-nineteenth century Mexico City had perhaps 150,000–200,000 inhabitants, which meant that it was less populous than Tenochtitlán had been in the days of the Aztecs; and the character of the population in the nineteenth century was radically different, consisting largely of creoles, people who lived in fashionable style, while on the outskirts of the city there was squalor of a kind that anticipated the slums that fringe many of today's major Latin American cities. Lake Texcoco, in which the Aztecs had built their capital on reclaimed land (the lake was about seven feet deep), was still four miles wide, and the city was still supplied via canals or via its causeways by pack animals or serfs. The Spanish ambassador's wife observed that there was little in common between the luxurious lives of the city's inhabitants and those of the Indians who served them.[2] Unfortunately, the Reform Laws did not have the desired effect of creating a class of small landowners, but instead more lands fell into the hands of the rich, and of foreign speculators.

The proponent of the law designed to reduce the legal privileges of church and military men (who had been entitled to exemption from the normal processes of the law) was himself a lawyer. Benito Juárez went from the most humble beginnings to being one of the most revered of Mexico's heroes. Born in an isolated Indian community and orphaned at an early age, when he was twelve he made his way on foot to Oaxaca, many miles away, where he was taken in as a servant by a family of Italian origin; later, a friend of that family who was a priest adopted him and gave him an education. Juárez took a degree in law, married the daughter of the family to which he had been servant, and rose to prominence, first in Oaxaca, then nationally, as chief justice. In that capacity, according to the 1857 constitution, he was second in line for the presidency, but when the president was forced to resign, an armed force took over, and Juárez, though now president in the eyes of the liberals, had to escape to Panama. He returned to Veracruz, where he set up as alternative president and decreed more reforms separating church and state, encouraging religious tolerance, and providing for a public (secular) education. After much violence and destruction wrought by both sides, the liberals prevailed, and Juárez was formally elected president in 1861.

The country now faced massive debt, especially with European banks. The French were the main creditors, and France was ruled at that time by the ambitious Napoleon III, who saw a chance to enhance his reputation at home by making Mexico into a puppet state. And so French troops were sent to take over the Juárez government. They were routed at Puebla on May 5, 1862, the famous Cinco de mayo that Mexicans celebrate to this day. However, this only provoked a larger-scale French intervention, supported by Mexican conservatives, who convinced the French that Mexicans would welcome a Catholic European monarch. Accordingly, Napoleon offered the throne of Mexico to Maximilian of Hapsburg, an Austrian prince: he would reign over an independent empire but would be backed by French troops. Maximilian and his wife, Carlotta, established a lavish court in Mexico City. They made efforts to Mexicanize, wearing Mexican dress, eating Mexican food. They even adopted Itúrbide's grandson. There seems to be no doubt that they were well-intentioned, that they wished to continue reforming the role of the church and to improve the lot of the Indians, but they were from another tradition and out of their depth. Mexico's economic problems continued; the French decided that the whole business was too costly and, needing their troops back in Europe, they withdrew them. Juárez, meantime, had gone to the very north of the country, to the town we now know as Ciudad Juárez. Desperate to consolidate his position, Maximilian ordered that all supporters of Juárez should be hunted down and shot as rebels. This made people rally behind Juárez. By 1867 Maximilian himself had been captured and shot, and Juárez made an unceremonious return to the capital. He was reelected president for two further four-year terms. He continued to attempt to balance the budget and to democratize and modernize the country, but he died (of natural causes!) before his term was over.

The last part of the nineteenth century and the first decade of the twentieth were dominated by what amounted to a dictatorship, that of Porfirio Díaz. Although he was from a similarly humble background, Díaz, unlike Juárez, rose to prominence in the military ranks, eventually becoming a general. Along the way he also became a rich landowner, making his fortune through sugar. He supported Juárez against Santa Anna, and made many public declarations in favor of reform and democracy, but when Juárez's successor, an ineffectual though well-meaning leader, sought reelection, Díaz effectively staged a coup, declaring himself provisional president, and subsequently arranging for his own election. After his term, he stepped down, and a friend, Manuel González, assumed the presidency; but Díaz's appointees were still in all the important positions of government. When González's government became embroiled in a corruption scandal, Díaz was able to sweep back into power, ostensibly as a reformer. And there he remained, arranging his own reelection, until 1910.

During the fifty years prior to Porfirio, Mexico had had about fifty different rulers, which may explain the attraction of the relative stability that Díaz brought to the country. But that stability was had at the price of strong-arm rule and compromised ideals. He won over the conservative landowners by forgetting all ideas of land redistribution; after all, he himself was one of them. The clergy regained much of the power they had lost in previous years and were happy because, while Díaz talked about reform, he in fact changed nothing. The intellectuals and liberals were bought off with comfortable jobs. And, as ever, the majority, the poorest and weakest people, particularly the Indians, were left out. Recruiting bandits, Díaz established his own militia, called the *rurales,* whose job was to do away with any disorder in the country. If anyone dared to voice dissent, then he could be silenced by bribery or, failing that, could be arrested on some charge and shot "while attempting to escape." When strikes occurred, they were bloodily suppressed, as were Indian protests.

Díaz was a friend of foreign investment. Money flowed into the development of cattle ranching, mines, oilfields, and railways. Uncharted lands, often appropriated from the Indians, were easily acquired by foreign interests; cheap labor was exploited with no controls. The profits left Mexico to benefit shareholders in such places as the United States, Britain, and Germany. And so Mexico made great industrial progress, employment levels were high, but reinvestment in the country's infrastructure was low. By 1910 there had been great material progress for some people, but most of it was at the expense of the masses of poor people. In effect Díaz was acting a little like a viceroy heading a government of neocolonial creoles. Like many dictators and their supporters, these people seem to have believed that they were their country's saviors. Somewhat ironically, while the monarch installed by the French, Maximilian, had sought to show respect for native traditions and popular Mexican customs, the social elite under Díaz cultivated things European, and particularly French, far more than at any previous time.

THE 1910 REVOLUTION AND THE INSTITUTIONAL REVOLUTIONARY PARTY

The independence movement that opened Mexico's nineteenth century and the Revolution that defines the twentieth were disconcertingly similar. Both were more spontaneous and fragmentary than premeditated or unified. The Revolution had no shared ideology or vision. It came about because of various kinds of social, economic, and political dissatisfaction, and it degenerated quickly into chaos and violence. In 1910 Mexico was preparing to celebrate the centenary of Father Hidalgo's cry for independence from Spain, the famous Grito de Dolores. Porfirio, ready to show off to the world the achievements of his regime, engaged in a large-scale propaganda exercise, inviting representatives of foreign countries to a luxurious and very selective view of Mexico. Then Díaz declared his intention, at the age of eighty, to seek another term of office, and this galvanized the opposition into action. Díaz was overthrown in 1911 and succeeded by various leaders whose rule did not last for long. The first of these was Francisco Madero, who was from a prosperous, landowning family. After two ineffectual years he was ousted and killed by his own commander of the forces, Victoriano Huerta. A year later, Huerta was driven out of the country, which then fell victim to warring factions led by regional caudillos; the main ones were Venustiano Carranza, Alvaro Obregón, Emiliano Zapata, and Pancho Villa. Eventually Carranza came to power with the help of Obregón, who then turned against him and took over. As for Villa, he was a volatile man, often brutal and sometimes tender, but basically a bandit who raped, murdered, and pillaged his way around Mexico; nevertheless, he managed to acquire something of a Robin Hood reputation and also became famous for outwitting U.S. troops after he had launched a raid into New Mexico. This in turn led to his image becoming mythicized in ballads as the romantic hero who cocked a snook at the big brother to the north. If Villa's main area of operation was the north of Mexico, Zapata's was the south. But Zapata stands out as a man who was not motivated by personal ambition and profit. Zapata was an Indian, an idealist who saw the struggle as one to improve the lot of landless peasants. Zapata was shot by Carranza's troops; Obregón had Carranza put to death and was probably also behind the death of Villa; Obregón himself was shot in 1928.

Though the worst of the violence was over by 1920, commonly quoted as the end date of the Revolution, things were hardly peaceful for some years thereafter. Carranza had reluctantly accepted the introduction of a new constitution, one that addressed many of the issues that had caused discontent; it provided for land redistribution, the return of private property to public ownership, a secular education system, and rights for workers, such as minimum wage level and the right to strike. But Carranza did little to implement the constitution's provisions. Widespread disillusionment with the Revolution became encapsulated in the common phrase "the Revolution never reached here" ("La Revolución nunca pasó por aquí"). Literally, that may not have been the case, for few areas or levels of society remained unscathed by it, but figuratively the expression means that for a lot of people the Revolution made no difference for the better. However, the powers of the military and of the ecclesiastical hierarchy were tempered, and some leaders in the post-Revolutionary period did bring about improvements for humble people—one thinks of the presidency of Lázaro Cárdenas, for example (1934–40). Furthermore it was only from then on that presidents were no longer routinely subject to assassination attempts and that there was an orderly transition from one president to another, each serving for a maximum term limit of six years.

Cárdenas was a mestizo, and proud of it, and concerned, too, for the common man. He introduced sweeping nationalization of foreign assets, including the petroleum industry, to great public acclaim, but to the displeasure of the United States. He also made radical changes in land tenure at a time when some 70 percent of Mexicans were working in agriculture, and many of them under the old colonial hacienda system. Unfortunately, the new cooperative system of land tenure proved to be less productive than hoped, and depended on large state subsidies, while there was an international boycott of Mexican oil and other economic sanctions imposed by Washington.

It was under President Miguel Alemán (1946–52) that the ruling party adopted the paradoxical name of Institutional Revolutionary Party (Partido Revolucionario Institucional, or PRI, as it is commonly known). The rationale for the name change (previously it had been called the National Revolutionary Party) was that the main goals of the Revolution had been achieved and that a period of stability should ensue. In fact, by astute organization, by avoidance of political dogma, and by a certain amount of patronage, nepotism, and graft, the PRI remained in power continuously until the end of the century, often with substantial electoral margins! In subsequent chapters, we shall be commenting on how post-Revolutionary governments affected cultural production and, in particular, how they promoted an official image of Mexican culture.

TLATELOLCO AND AFTER

In 1968, a year characterized by protests in several parts of the world, a demonstration against government policies occurred in Mexico City, in a square called the Square of the Three Cultures (La Plaza de las Tres Culturas), so named because in that place were to be found examples of buildings from the pre-Columbian, the colonial, and the modern periods. This place is also known by its Aztec name, Tlatelolco. Mexico was about to host the Olympic Games, and the date of the demonstration had been chosen in an attempt to draw international attention to Mexico's internal problems and thus put pressure on the government for change. The demonstration ended in tragedy when armed police fired on protesters caught in the square. For a long time thereafter official Mexico was unwilling to come clean about the incident and its cost in human lives; estimates vary widely, but at least 350 died, with many more injured. The significance of the massacre, however, was really symbolic. Viewed against the international scene, it seemed comparable to recent acts of repression in Prague and Paris, while at home in Mexico it echoed the tradition of authoritarian regimes such as the Porfiriato, and even the colonial Spanish one. So, at least, it seemed to many intellectuals. Writer Octavio Paz, for example, who was his country's ambassador to India at the time, resigned in protest. Furthermore, Tlatelolco served as a reminder of how far Mexico still had to go along the road to true democracy and more equitable distribution of resources, and a reminder of how little progress had been made since the Revolution at the beginning of the century. Clearly, by this time the Partido Revolucionario Institucional was anything but a revolutionary party, and it was not so much institutionalized as ossified and, furthermore, corrupt. And, while a minority of people were very prosperous, vast numbers of Mexicans were still living in poverty. One byproduct of the protest movement in the late 1960s was the emergence of small foci of guerrilla activity in the 1970s, particularly in the southwestern state of Guerrero. (New guerrilla activity in Guerrero also reemerged in the aftermath of the 1994 Zapatista rebellion.)

Ironically, the government minister most closely associated with the massacre, Luis Echeverría, then became president (1970–76) and proved to be quite popular and left-wing. The number of state enterprises rose, and money was borrowed for subsidies to keep prices of basic items low at a time when most countries were undergoing high inflation. Subsequently, under President López Portillo (1976–82), came the oil boom; new reserves were discovered, making Mexico one of the world's most significant producers. (Its oil reserves are more than twice those of the United States.) The country became too dependent on oil, and corruption siphoned off substantial portions of the revenue. (Mexico City's police chief built himself a house so luxurious that that it was later converted into a government museum intended as a reminder of the level of corruption.) After some help from the International Monetary Fund, during the eighties there was a new wave of privatization (in Mexico as elsewhere in the world), a recovery of confidence among foreign investors, and a reduction of foreign debt. However, once again agricultural workers in remote places were left behind. A significant amendment was made to the system of land tenure, from cooperative to small-scale private ownership, in the belief that this would favor increased levels of productivity. A setback came at the beginning of 1994, when there was news of an armed uprising in Chiapas, the southernmost region, inhabited largely by Indians and one of the poorest regions of Mexico. The rebels, remembering their advocate of revolutionary days, adopted the name Zapatistas. Foreign investors' confidence fell once more, and another international aid package was needed before Mexico recovered some degree of economic stability. On the political front, however, there were tensions between the PRI old guard and its younger leaders, and even assassinations. And corruption on a grand scale reared its ugly head again. By the late nineties the PRI monolith was coming apart; the party was about to lose the presidency for the first time in over seventy years.

GEOGRAPHY

Four fifths of Mexico is mountainous or hilly, and much of the country, especially in the north, suffers from a lack of rainfall. There are few navigable rivers. Two mountain ranges run north-south, the Sierra Madre Oriental and the Sierra Madre Occidental. Between them there is an extensive plateau (*meseta*) whose altitude near Mexico City reaches about 7,000 feet. There are a number of relatively fertile valleys along the meseta, but it is also an area subject to seismic and volcanic activity, particularly near Mexico City, where another range runs east-west, with mountains as high as 18,000 feet. The climate is generally dry and mild, with coldish nights, and it is in this area that several of Mexico's main cities are located. Other major cities of the central plateau are Guadalajara, Puebla, and Monterrey. Mexico City itself is now the world's largest and most crowded conurbation, exceeding 20 million people, and with a daily influx of new immigrants from the provinces estimated at 1,000. It is also one of the world's most polluted cities, partly because industrial and vehicular emissions are trapped in the Anahuac Valley, between the mountains. Mexico is now highly industrialized in some areas such as this, but very underdeveloped in others.

The Yucatán Peninsula, to the southeast, consists of a limestone table whose water supply is underground; the Mayas held its natural wells (*cenotes*) in reverence. The land itself is devoted primarily to *henequén* (sisal, or hemp). Given its fine beaches and its Mayan ruins, the Yucatán Peninsula has become a major destination for tourists, while parts of Mexico's more rugged western coast have been attracting tourists for years. On the Gulf coast the major town and port is Veracruz, whose climate is typical of Gulf towns: steamy and subtropical. The southern extremes of Mexico, close to Guatemala, are lush and warm.

Pacific bay near Huatulco, Oaxaca. Photo by Steven Bell.

POPULATION

As to population, that has grown exponentially during the twentieth century, as it has in other Latin American countries. At the end of the Revolution there were about 14 million Mexicans; by the 1950s there were more than twice as many. In part, the growth can be attributed to better health care and, in particular, to a decline in infant mortality. Also, a factor has been the lack of birth control, the latter being frowned upon by the dominant Catholic Church. By the 1970s the government was recognizing that the rapid expansion of Mexico's population was a serious problem; in 1973 a National Population Council was established and plans were made to reduce the rate of growth through education and family planning. In soap operas, for example, the actors talked openly about contraception. It proved to be one of the most successful state-coordinated family planning campaigns in the world. A 1980 census claimed that the annual population growth had been cut by about a third, as compared with 1970. Projections regarding the likely population level in 2000 were accordingly revised downwards, to 100 million. In fact, the present-day population is of the order of 90 million.

ETHNICITY AND LANGUAGE

Its history has led to Mexico being regarded as the standard-bearer, the most complete embodiment of the fusion and coexistence of American Indian and Spanish elements. As we have seen previously, it has even been called the birthplace of a new race (the mestizos). In fact the most fascinating—and troubling—aspect of Mexican culture is the way in which the country has retained so much of its cultural diversity, its social stratifications, and at the same time has achieved such a fusion of seemingly incompatible elements.

Mexico is the most populous Spanish-speaking nation in the world (though it will one day be eclipsed, ironically enough, by the United States). The early film star Cantinflas provides a stereotype of the Mexican style of speaking Spanish. As with all stereotypes, this one has some basis in fact, but it errs in its exaggeration and oversimplification. The intonation of many Mexican speakers is certainly recognizably different from those of other Spanish speakers. Given the strong indigenous substratum and the peculiarities of the country's flora and fauna, Mexican Spanish also has a large number of characteristic lexical items of indigenous origin still in everyday usage, such as *tianguis* (open-air market) and *escuincle* (child), just to name two. Quite how many dialects of Mexican Spanish there are depends on how finely one chooses to draw distinctions. Pedro Henríquez Ureña, a distinguished linguist from the Dominican Republic, once drew a map of broad dialect areas in Spanish America, one which identified two basic dialects for Mexico; people in the south were grouped with others in neighboring countries, while the rest of Mexico was lumped together as one dialect area. Other experts have argued for a more subtle identification of multiple dialects. This is not the place to enter into a detailed discussion of such possibilities, but two observations must be made with regard to changes in the language. The first concerns the homogenizing effect that comes from increased internal migration. The second relates to the outside influence of the United States, which is felt generally but is particularly significant in the northern border region.

Within its present-day territory, Mexico has great geographical and ethnic diversity, and this diversity, combined with historical factors, has made for linguistic diversity too. There are upwards of a million speakers of the main indigenous languages, such as Nahuatl (spoken by the Aztecs), Maya, Zapotec, and Mixtec (found in Oaxaca), and Tzotzil and Tzeltal (in Chiapas, close to Guatemala). And, across the country, predominantly in the central and southern regions, more than 50 indigenous languages are still used by at least a few speakers, with some 16 of these languages found in the state of Oaxaca alone. In the 1940s, folklorist Frances Toor mapped out 51 distinct and significant indigenous ethnic groupings, from the tribal, idiosyncratic, and fiercely independent Yaqui and Tarahumara in the north, to the Tarascos of Michoacán and the Otomí of the north-central provinces, to the more obscure Lacandones of Chiapas. The continuous and ongoing effects of miscegenation, changing government policies toward the Indians and, indeed, changing and uncertain definitions of the very concept of Indian identity in Mexico have made precise delimitations difficult at best. Political turmoil and processes and policies of cultural assimilation and indoctrination have worked to reduce the number of identifiable indigenous populations, while social stratification, geographic isolation, and marginalization have been among the factors favoring their survival. One recent, and fascinating, study by Aída Hernández Castillo documents how one small ethnic and linguistic group on the Chiapas-Guatemala border, the Mames, has disappeared and reappeared in government censuses and even on the radar screen of ethnographers and anthropologists over the course of the twentieth century, due to changes in government policy, daily practices, and changes in the way they identify themselves. This challenges both the idea that the Indians are passive and the idea of a pure Indian identity. The Mames have migrated between Guatemala and Chiapas, Mexico, and from the high sierras to the jungles; many have exchanged traditional Catholicism for the theology of liberation, and many have become Protestant members of the National Presbyterian Church or Jehovah's Witnesses. Most, under the pressure of post-Revolutionary government institutions, abandoned their traditional practices, dress, and language, later to readopt them in a conscious reconstitution of their identity.

Concern for and attention to Mexico's Indian heritage and indigenous peoples has never been higher than in the early post-Revolutionary period, both in terms of official rhetoric and actual government policy. Many have remarked upon the ironies surrounding the creation of Mexico's famous Museo Nacional de Antropología in the late 1950s and 1960s. At the same time as the government was collecting ethnographic data on the country's many indigenous groups for incorporation into the museum as a celebration of the nation's Indian heritage, government policy in the field was encouraging assimilation and the abandonment of traditional practices. Increasingly, since 1970, policies have shifted to emphasize greater respect for local and ethnically distinct communities, and this tendency gathered even greater impetus from the broad public support and international attention generated by the Zapatista rebellion in Chiapas in 1994.

However imprecise estimates may be, it is instructive to consider the general historical evolution of Mexico's ethnic composition. In 1570, after the destruction of Tenochtitlán but before the decimation of the Indian population by disease had reached its peak, there were perhaps more than 3 million Indians, compared with just 10,000 white Europeans, that is to say peninsulares (people born in Spain) and criollos (people of Spanish blood); there were

Supporters of the Zapatista rebellion, in Mexico City. Photo by April Brown.

some 15,000 persons of mixed blood, including mestizos (Indian/Spanish mix), mulattos (African/ European mix) and zambos (African/Indian mix), and perhaps 20,000 blacks. Through the mid-seventeenth and early eighteenth centuries, Indian numbers dwindled perhaps to as few as 1 million. But by the dawn of independence in 1810, the Indian population had recouped its numbers and stood at approximately 3.5 million. The numbers of peninsulares and criollos remained fairly constant at some 15,000, while the mixed population of mestizos and mulattos had grown to more than 2 million (Iturriaga, 90). In other words, at the dawn of independence Indians still constituted the majority of the population in Mexico, and it is estimated that more than half of the population still spoke indigenous languages, either monolingually or bilingually. By all estimates, and however Indian is defined, the Indian population as a percentage of the total steadily diminished in the nineteenth and twentieth centuries, reduced from perhaps some 60 percent to perhaps 35 percent by the dawn of the Revolution in 1910.

In view of the relatively large Indian labor force, Africans were brought to Mexico in smaller numbers than to other countries; it has been estimated that perhaps as many as 250,000 blacks were imported during the three centuries of the slave trade. But over those same centuries, the black African element to a large degree joined the mestizo mainstream due to miscegenation and acculturation. The mulatto element is seen principally on the Gulf coast in the vicinity of the port of Veracruz, and on the Pacific coast in the states of Guerrero and Oaxaca.

Most broad estimates today give figures for Mexico's ethnic composition in the region of 60–75 percent mestizo, 15–30 percent Indian or strongly Indian, 9 percent white, and 1 percent other. If the primary consideration is language, however, the figure for Indians would reduce to 10–12 percent (based on the number of monolingual and bilingual speakers of indigenous languages), with the mestizo percentage increasing accordingly. Mid-century authoritative scholars such as Toor and Wolf can paint widely divergent, but equally reasonable, pictures. Toor's focus on folk culture underscores the pervasive influence of the Indian substrata in shaping Mexican customs. Wolf's more historical and anthropological account, while highlighting the persistence of strong indigenous community traits and significant pockets of bilingual and even monolingual speakers of native languages, nonetheless concludes that by the mid-twentieth century there were no pure Indians, and certainly no pure Europeans in Mexico (with the exception of recent immigrants). The works of Mexican intellectuals Guillermo Bonfil Batalla and Octavio Paz present similarly contrasting views, with stronger ideological inflections. Bonfil, while recognizing that the population self-identifying as Indian would not likely exceed 10–12 percent, emphasizes the persistence among the great majority of the population of a "deep Mexico" rooted in pre-Columbian practice and outlook, including community ritual and harmony with nature, one that has continuously resisted the "imaginary Mexico" imposed by colonial domination. Paz, while recognizing considerable cultural continuity extending back into the pre-Columbian era, insists that the dominant and majority culture in Mexico since the conquest has been Western.

How far racial prejudice exists in Mexico today (or in Latin America generally) has been a matter of much debate. Perhaps the best conclusion one can draw is that many prejudices and discriminations exist in a host of subtle ways, but that these discriminations and prejudices are often social, political, and economic, rather than racial. For example, whether a person is regarded (or regards himself) as an Indian has to do with how far he is integrated into the modern nation and how far he has traditional Indian cultural habits (even if such habits are usually synthesized with Spanish ones).

It is interesting to note the degree to which there has been integration in Mexico, as contrasted with the segregation that is more characteristic of the United States. Compared with Mexico, the United States is racially divided. Yet, socially, the United States is homogenizing: it assimilates immigrants into the ethos of the American Dream, eliciting considerable conformity, and suffering the tyranny of the majority. In some ways it is Mexico, with its racial and cultural blending, that has been the real melting pot, and yet Mexico is also unevenly modernized, socially stratified, ethnically diverse, and fragmented.

REGIONALISM VERSUS CENTRALISM

Pressures towards national unity have been quite powerful; since approximately 1350 they have been applied continuously from the same place, the Zócalo (main square) in Mexico City, formerly the site of Tenochtitlán's main temple. Centralism, hierarchy, and authoritarianism have perhaps been an inevitable response to diversity and to disruption over the course of Mexico's history. The desire to establish an identity that is distinct from Spain's, and the need to defend itself against the challenge of U.S. authority in modern times, have strengthened Mexico's need for unity. All the same, the unity of today's Mexico is rather superficial; there are many local, regional, and subcultural allegiances and affiliations. And there are clear historical precedents for this. Even the Aztec empire was only a loose federation of subject peoples and did not require social or cultural unity. The Spanish system of granting titles to land and Indian labor during the colonial period favored the creation of large haciendas that sustained their own micro-societies, and it fostered the emergence of powerful local leaders (caciques and caudillos) who played key roles in nineteenth- and twentieth-century politics. The institutions of today have been built upon networks of alliance and patronage that the governing party established in collaboration with local strongmen. As a result, nowadays things such as health care, education, economic opportunity, and democratic freedoms penetrate to Mexico's regions extremely unevenly, often on a personal basis.

Tensions between regionalism and centralism have deep roots. In many respects, in fact, resistance to the powerful force of the centralism that has coursed through Mexican history has been regionalism's reason for being. At one geographical extreme Baja California, due to its sparse population, rugged terrain, and distance from major population and power centers, has been as much an outpost for wayward sailors and individualists as it has been an integral part of Mexico. At the other extreme, the Yucatán Peninsula has a strong sense of independence and a deeply ingrained pride in its autonomy, sustained by an improbable and tension-filled alliance between staunchly Hispanicized hacienda families and a large Maya peasant population. Throughout most of the colonial period, the colonizers in Yucatán gave their direct allegiance to Spain, not to the colonial authorities in Mexico City—at least until the Yucatán elite needed the national government to save them from defeat during a Mayan uprising in the middle of the nineteenth century. For anyone accustomed to breezy U.S. bi-coastalism, it might be difficult to imagine how poorly communicated and independently minded some parts of Mexico have been, how strongly differentiated the arid plains of northern Chihuahua and Sonora are from the fertile valleys and volcanic chain of the Valle Central, and these in turn from the forests and lowland jungle of the south.

There are many bases upon which to divide Mexico into different regions, but the fundamental regional distinction sets the north against the south, and each against the central authority that historically has sought to control them. The interaction between the north and the south has been minimal, such that in many ways they are different Mexicos. In the north, whose climate is harsh and where, at the time of the conquest, the Indian population was scattered and nomadic, criollos and mestizos are predominant (especially in the states of Durango, Zacatecas, Nuevo León, Coahuila, Chihuahua, and Sonora). In contrast, in the south, where the Indian population was more concentrated and more highly organized, an Indian or mestizo character predominates (in the states of Michoacán, Guerrero, Oaxaca, and Chiapas). Income, education, Spanish-language literacy, and many other indices are generally higher in the north, and the northerner is much more modernized and individualistic, whereas in the south traditional, community-based values are stronger. Most interpretations of Mexican history and culture have emphasized the uneasy coexistence of two Mexicos, though each analyst assesses them differently. The tradition-bound majority of Mexicans, whose culture traces back to remote pre-Hispanic origins, constitute the first Mexico. The second is composed of an elite minority that has sought to modernize or de-Indianize the country, often through the imitation of foreign models of development that do not apply well to Mexico.

THE MODERN ECONOMY

In Spanish colonial times, land was used primarily for plantation agriculture in the south, and livestock and cattle ranching in the north; there was silver mining in the central and north-central provinces. Today, however, Mexico has become one of the world's major oil producers, about half the production being destined for export. There is also a significant petrochemicals industry. Export manufacturing, in particular the products of the maquiladora industry in the U.S. border region, is important. Tourism, banking, and agriculture are also major economic activities. Beyond those there lies an extensive range of informal, unofficial, and quite often illegal activities, including the drug trade.

The oil industry, a nationalized operation under the name Pemex, has been somewhat inefficient and there have been attempts to privatize it, backed, of

Craft market at Mitla Ruins, Oaxaca. Photo by April Brown.

course, by the United States; but these have proved to be politically sensitive. The maquiladoras are mostly foreign-owned assembly plants and are the largest export earner. Maquiladoras were in part an answer to the problem of accommodating the bracero laborers returning from the U.S. guest workers program, but are clearly seen also as a response to Asian factory operations. There are well over 2,000 maquiladoras in the border region, and they employ well over half a million workers. In the early years they assembled consumer products from parts or materials made in the United States but increasingly they are manufacturing parts, and Japanese and Korean businesses also use the maquiladoras.

One significant fact about the informal sector, both its legal and illegal activities, is that it operates outside the tax system, bringing the government no tax revenue. It is, of course, difficult to know quite how extensive this sector is. It is, of course, difficult to know quite how extensive this sector is: according to estimates, between 25 and 38 percent of economic activity in Mexico is informal. Certainly the streets are filled with vendors of everything imaginable. Though informal in the sense of unofficial, the sector is formal in the sense that it is organized by groups, hierarchized, and territorial. Children who sell chewing gum are at the bottom of the pile, and the drug lords are at the top. There are thought to be 14 regional drug cartels and the U.S. government estimates that perhaps $25 billion in drug money is laundered annually through the banking system. It also estimates that 70 percent of the cocaine that reaches the United States enters via Mexico. The drug barons are even celebrated in song, in *corridos*. In an effort to legitimize themselves they invest in legal businesses such as the construction industry and tourism. Corruption of politicians and government officials by the drug trade rivals that of Colombia.

Another significant economic factor relates to increased migration to the United States, often on a seasonal basis, a phenomenon that the economic hardships of the 1980s increased. Indeed, not only the number but also the social and economic range of migrants widened at this time from the traditional rural peasant base. Migrants, whether legal or not, tend to send money back to Mexico. The College of Mexico estimates that in 1984 undocumented migrant workers alone took or sent as much as $2 billion back to Mexico as remittances (*remesas*), to help relatives get by at home. If this estimate is accurate (and, of course, figures for undocumented workers are hard to come by), then these monies are the fourth largest source of foreign exchange, and there is no doubt of their stimulating effect upon some local economies. The new PAN government of President Vicente Fox has made attention to the rights and problems of Mexican immigrants in the United States a strategic priority of his administration, not least because Mexican citizens residing in the United States can now cast absentee ballots in Mexican federal elections, and they constitute a significant base of conservative PAN support.

LAW AND ORDER

The Mexican police force is universally disliked and mistrusted. Partly because, like other public employees, they have been poorly paid, the police have not evolved a professional culture, and many officers have given in to corruption. Routinely, police officers expect *mordidas,* payoffs even for the most minor of offenses such as traffic violations, while police involvement with drug trafficking has been a major problem. Among the many divisions of the police force the most feared are the *madrinas* (the "godmothers"), who are agents of the Federal Judicial Police (PJF). In addition to such official police units, there are private strong-arm groups that look after the interests of the powerful. Unions have their bullies to keep people in line, as do many private companies, not to mention the terrorizing activities of rural bosses and drug dealers.

This scenario, in some ways a hangover from the times of Porfirio Díaz and the Revolution, leads to much abuse of human rights, and it influences the political process. By 1990 Human Rights Watch had declared that a human rights emergency existed in Mexico. During the 1990s President Salinas, who was keen to ingratiate himself with the United States, made some effort to improve things, but abuses continued and, in any case, the United States under Bush the First was more interested in economics than in human rights. It is not that the appropriate legislation has been lacking; it has been observed that "Mexican legislation is exemplary, and the country is a signatory to various important international human rights declarations."[3] The problem is that that legislation has not been enforced, and the legal system, when it does work, is slow moving. However, in recent years there has been some improvement. It is noticeable, for example, that after years of resistance against them, foreign observers were allowed to monitor the elections that brought Vicente Fox to power.

The military forces are more disciplined and more respected than the police, though they, too, have suffered from corruption in the higher ranks. The rank and file have tended to be drawn from the rural poor, and the officers from the lower middle class, a military career being seen as secure. While males under 40 years of age are required to register as eligible for service, enlistment itself is voluntary. The military forces are not large. At the beginning of the nineties, for example, Mexico was spending about half of 1 percent of its GNP on the military (while the United States was spending nearly 6.5 percent). Figures such as these, however, have to be taken with a pinch of salt, since the facts about military spending in Mexico are hard to come by,

Mexico City at night. Photo by April Brown.

and official appropriations are known to be supplemented by unpublicized discretionary allocations.

Statute requires that the military defend the nation's sovereignty (presumably against the United States) and assist with national projects such as disaster relief. Since the mid-twentieth century most military energy has, in fact, been spent on internal matters—narcotics, public unrest, even conservation. Acting on government orders, the military played an unfortunate role at Tlateloco in 1968 and has been at some pains to redeem its public image since. More than once, however, it has acted to suppress opposition to the government. It has been a frequent presence during elections, such as those of 1990, when troops in Guerrero broke up opposition meetings. In fact, the military forces have tended to protect the interests of the political elite, and in return the latter have tended not to interfere with them. Cynics see the military as another arm of government; there are modern-day rural volunteer reserves, for example, whose apparent role is to keep public order but who some believe act as government spies.

EDUCATION

In colonial times education was the private privilege of Spaniards and creoles, and to some degree of men rather than women. Whatever education was

Mexico City street scene. Photo by April Brown.

offered to other echelons of society was thanks to the Church, and particularly to the Jesuits. Federalists and liberals throughout the nineteenth century paid lip service to the importance of broad access to basic education, but political turmoil and lack of resources generally made improvements impossible. The reform governments of the 1860s and 1870s took steps to establish obligatory public education through the 1857 constitution and the 1867 Organic Law of Public Instruction in the Federal District; and in 1874 religious instruction was prohibited in public schools. Under Porfirio Díaz, educational policies took a positivist turn, and some significant advances were made in higher education for the minority, but primary education for the masses was largely neglected, and illiteracy for 1895 was still estimated at 86 percent. The Revolution in the early twentieth century sought to widen educational opportunities, and to secularize education. The Revolutionary ideal was to provide free public education; in fact, in this regard the new constitution of 1917 was more ambitious than those of other countries. Real advances were made under Vasconcelos, President Obregón's administrator of federal education in the 1920s, and later during the Cárdenas, Avila Camacho, and Alemán regimes. But, as in many other places, in modern Mexico there is a gulf between theory and practice. In principle, education remains secular and is provided free to all Mexican citizens between the ages of 6 and 14. Officially, parents are required to ensure that their children receive an education. But that last obligation is rarely enforced and the reality is that educational provision is very uneven, with glaring regional disparities. Today, educational opportunities are still lacking for those in remote rural areas, and young people face considerable pressure to enter directly into the work force, such that higher education remains the privilege of the well-to-do. Illiteracy is still a problem, though much lower than it once was, thanks to government initiatives; as an illustration, in 1990 literacy stood (at least officially) at 92 percent as compared to about 35 percent during the thirties. The average number of years spent in school increased from 1.5 to 6 over that same time span. There have been education campaigns designed to combat various diseases, but shortages of qualified teachers and medical personnel have hampered progress in those.

As in most countries, control of education has been very centralized. In Mexico the controlling body since its foundation in 1921 has been the Ministry of Public Education (Secretaría de Educación Pública). Changes in government every six years have often brought changes in educational programs, undermining continuity and long-term planning. In short, the system has not been efficient. Higher education expanded dramatically after the Tlatelolco debacle, when Echeverría's government was trying to buy off the malcontents. To some degree, it could be argued that the education reforms enacted by the post-Revolutionary PRI governments have come back to haunt them. Virtually free access to public university education at massive institutions such as the National University (UNAM), for those who can meet academic standards, have produced a burgeoning middle class which has taken to heart much of the Revolution's socialist rhetoric. Many people have been unable to find gainful employment commensurate with their skills, despite the erratic economy. It is from these sectors that the increasingly vocal opposition to the PRI in 1968 has since emerged. In the late 1990s, for example, when the PRI government proposed to introduce a modest tuition charge at the UNAM, to make the institution more self-sustaining and to enhance the quality of education, a massive and rather virulent strike by students and faculty shut the university down for more than a year.

During the 1980s it was recognized that quality had not kept pace with the expansion, but a reform plan proposed by President de la Madrid had little effect, having to deal with inflexible unions and the personal interests of certain powerful individuals. The economic crisis also took its toll on education in general: expenditures during the eighties declined by over 20 percent. By the end of the century Mexico was spending well below the 8 percent of GNP recommended by the United Nations. Teachers' salaries declined also and, as a result, they left for other jobs, or came to regard teaching as a part-time job to be combined, necessarily, with others. The loss of teachers has been matched by student attrition; by the end of the century about half would never finish primary school, while about a quarter of those who went on to the secondary level did not finish, and at the university level between half and two thirds of those who had begun were destined to drop out.

The system fails especially in serving those who need it most. The figures for literacy, years of schooling completed, and other measures are far worse for places such as Chiapas than for urban areas in the central valley. Those who have the personal means have essentially abandoned the public system and therefore, as far as education is concerned, society is increasingly divided between the haves and the have-nots. Although according to the constitution schools are supposed to be secular, religious schools are quite common and now they are often the places to which the wealthy send their offspring. This is not simply a matter of disaffection with the shortcomings of the state system, but it also reflects a more conservative, perhaps a more self-centered outlook, one that pays little attention to the egalitarian ideals of the past.

HEALTH

Comparable disparities of a regional and economic nature affect health care, in a country that must deal both with diseases related to modern industrialization and with issues such as bad housing, undrinkable water, malnutrition, and lack of prenatal care. Mexico also has the second highest incidence of AIDS in Latin America. Daunting though the prospects for the future are, there have been some improvements in health care, resulting, for example, in a marked reduction in death rates from 26 per 1,000 in 1930 to 5 per 1,000 in 1986.[4] In 1943 a Social Security Institute was founded and charged with responsibility for general health care; a separate institute followed later for the care of state employees. In 1983 it became the Mexican's right to receive health care, whether through these or other forms of provision, yet about a third of the population falls outside these nets and has to rely on charity. Somewhere between 5 and 10 percent of the population can afford private health schemes.

A surfeit of doctors and other medical personnel exists in the central valley, serving its major cities and, similarly, a large number of medical personnel work in the region bordering the United States, offering care to U.S. nationals at prices well below those in the United States itself. By contrast, the poorest rural states, plus some impoverished areas in the main cities, lack facilities and doctors. As many as 90 percent of the people in Chiapas have been described as malnourished, and three quarters of the people in some areas lack safe drinking water.[5] Improvements in the provision of primary care, sanitation, health education, and nutrition are certainly needed, but there is a further cause for concern in the effects of a polluted environment.

THE ENVIRONMENT

Mexico routinely uses all the agricultural chemicals that the United States considers most noxious. Foodstuffs are contaminated by agricultural practices, and industrial contaminants pollute the environment. The poor quality of Mexico City's air (only the most notorious example) is known to encourage a high incidence of such diseases as bronchitis, emphysema, and bronchial cancer. Eighty percent of the time the city's air is hazardous to the respiratory system. There is a high level of exposure to lead. About a quarter of all vegetables are contaminated with heavy metals. Some 30 percent of the capital's population live in places without a sewage system. In fact, water pollution from both

Food vendors set up in front of a Mexico City church. Photo by Steven Bell.

industrial and human waste encourages salmonellosis, typhoid, and cancer in many parts of the country. For example, the number of toxic substances in the New River, in the U.S. border region, has been estimated at 100. The maquiladoras alone produce about 20 million tons of waste a year.

In addition to pollution, the environment suffers from erosion, some 50 percent of the land being affected. Each year about 370,000 acres of land become useless. A further half-million acres turn to desert, and a million and a half are deforested. Mexico has already lost most of its tropical jungle. Some of its flora and fauna are under threat; for example, about 10 percent of its bird species are at risk. In all, environmentally, the prospects are bleak, but of course Mexico is not alone in this, nor is it entirely responsible for its woes. It is suffering the effects of rapid industrialization, poor management, and world economic pressures, like many other developing countries.

NOTES

1. Fanny Calderón de la Barca, *Life in Mexico,* p. 433.

2. It is tempting to compare the modern state of affairs in places like Cancún.

3. Barry, "Human Rights," in *Mexico: A Country Guide,* p. 67.

4. These are figures reported by President Salinas in a state of the nation speech delivered in 1990. In that same speech he admitted to a government tradition of censoring the facts regarding national health.

5. Figures reported by H. Nelson in "Pinpointing the Culprits," *World Health,* June 1989, p. 13.

2

Religion

PERHAPS THE MOST MEMORABLE SCENE in the 1990 feature film *Cabeza de Vaca* is its final one, which shows conquistadors marching across a barren plain and bearing an immense cross; their pace is brisk and purposeful. For, as we have seen, the Spaniards came to the Americas with the purpose of spreading Catholicism, and they were highly effective, if somewhat brutal, in doing so. The modern legacy of their endeavors is that 90 percent of Mexicans are Catholic. More generally, Mexico is overwhelmingly a Christian country, with Protestantism, which has made recent inroads (from 2 percent to nearly 10 percent since 1950), accounting for most of the remainder.

The secularizing impulses of governments seem sometimes to have hardly dented the religiosity that pervades present-day Mexican life. It is not that institutionalized religious practices and ideology are particularly important, because for most Mexicans what really matters is informal, everyday rituals. A taxi driver who may never attend mass except for funerals, baptisms, and weddings, may well have an image of the Virgin on his dashboard, and he may well cross himself every time his vehicle passes by a church. Evidence of religious habits such as this is widespread, but such practices are rarely pure: instead, what there is today is a blend of folk Catholicism and pre-Hispanic religious customs. The crowning example of this is the reverence for the Virgin de Guadalupe, patroness of the nation, to whom we shall return in a moment.

Many factors help account for the fusion that took place between things pre-Hispanic and Spanish in colonial times. In the first place, there were the sheer numbers—first handfuls and then hundreds of Spanish missionary priests in the midst of Indian populations numbering millions. At the open air chapels of the first Franciscan monasteries and churches in Huejotzingo, Tlaxcala, and near San Juan Teotihuacán, mass baptisms were conducted, inevitably more concerned with a show of power than with the depth of belief among the converts. Even before the arrival of the Spaniards, the indigenous peoples had become accustomed to the conquering group's pantheon of gods being superimposed on those they had conquered, so the real novelty of the Spanish conquest was that the new lords looked different. It happened that the popular Catholic veneration of saints and martyrs, together with manifestations of the Virgin Mary, meshed almost perfectly with pre-Hispanic polytheism. The early missionaries were not above exploiting these parallels and looking the other way when idolatry was present, though often Church authorities came to regret it. Moreover, in both the pre-Hispanic and Spanish Catholic worlds, religious power and political authority were inextricably linked. In both, ritual processions and public religious celebrations were basic to community organization.

The pre-Hispanic was essentially crushed by the Spanish conquest, but it is often observed that the native population found some comfort in the continuity, however modified, of many of their beliefs and daily practices. And it is essential to remember that the processes of acculturation over the course of

Plaza Xicoténcatl, in Tlaxcala, site of an early sixteenth-century Franciscan monastery, a chapel, and a cathedral, where some of the earliest Catholic rites and conversions of Indian nobility were performed. Photo by Steven Bell.

300 years of Spanish colonial rule, though certainly lopsided, worked both ways. It has been noted that, for example, "of all the native traditions, the healing arts had the greatest impact on colonial society" (Curcio-Nagy, *Oxford History of Mexico*, 163). Spaniards, criollos, and mestizos came quickly to trust and value New World herbs and medicinal practices for the treatment of their American ailments. In an ironic reversal of this, the lost and ship-wrecked Spanish explorer, Cabeza de Vaca, claims to have come to be regarded by some of his Indian hosts as a shaman. (Even today, it is impossible to find a public market in Mexico that does not have several stands purveying the most incredible array of natural medicines and herbal potions, usually accompanied by scribbled cardboard signs explaining their particular magic.)

Over the centuries, *cofradías* responsible for organizing the annual processions celebrating the local patron saint have thrived; these celebrations invariably mix pre-Hispanic and Catholic elements with more modern permutations, colored and modified for tourist consumption and ethnographic recreation; examples are the famous sacred games of Carnival at Chamula, the complex Day of the Dead ritual festivities in Tlaxcala, and the Carnival at Huejotzingo in which, among other oddities, a nineteenth-century historical battle between invading French troops and Mexican forces is reenacted using masks of pre-Hispanic origin.

CHURCH AND STATE

During colonial times the sway of the Catholic Church was unquestionable. While many tensions arose between the clerical hierarchy and those who manned the rural outposts and lived and worked with the Indian and mestizo populace, there was never any doubt that church and state worked hand in hand. The Church was not only powerful but rich, owning much of the land, and its influence shaped every facet of social life, particularly education. The Church built cathedrals, monasteries, and convents, but also schools and hospitals and orphanages, libraries and universities. Under the Bourbon dynasty in the late colonial period, some of the first significant measures were taken to restrict the influence of the clergy and bring them more under the control of the Spanish monarchy; most notably, in the middle of the eighteenth century, the Bourbons ordered the expulsion of the Jesuits from Spanish-controlled territories. Above all, Bourbon authorities focused their reform efforts, though mostly to little effect, on cleansing popular religious spectacles of their more profane, Indian- and African-tinged excesses; they imposed restrictions on music and dance.

The cathedral, on the Zócalo, in Mexico City. Photo by Steven Bell.

Precisely because the Church was so ubiquitous, most of the political debates and ideological struggles in colonial times drew on different factions within its ranks. Early missionary priests of the regular orders—Franciscans, Dominicans, and Jesuits—became fierce advocates for the native populations, and they worked to educate the indigenous nobility, and studied and recorded their languages, histories, and customs. Nuns and priests, most famously Sor Juana Inés de la Cruz and Carlos Sigüenza y Góngora, often challenged Church dogma, and religious officials figured prominently among the victims of the Inquisition, from whose authority the Indians themselves were exempt. Priests were also some of the most receptive to the new ideas of the Enlightenment; many watched the progress of the French and American revolutions with interest, and it was church figures such as Hidalgo and Morelos who first led the struggle for Mexican independence from Spain.

After independence, liberal statesmen aggressively tried to separate church and state, and they promulgated measures designed to limit the power and influence of the Catholic Church on Mexican life. But efforts to reduce the sway of the Catholic faith over the last 200 years have met with no more success than did the earlier efforts by conquerors and missionary priests to extirpate the paganism and idolatry of the Indians. To this day, anti-clerical measures meet with serious and often unbreakable resistance; it was so in the case of the Cristero Rebellion of 1926–29. While most of the modern liberal and post-Revolutionary governments have paid lip service to the separation of church and state, they have practiced a politics of compromise and accommodation with the Church, turned a blind eye to violations of the principle, and perpetuated the gap between (anti-clerical) rhetoric and (religious) reality.

Valentín Gómez Farías led efforts to curtail the privileges of the Church in the first half of the nineteenth century, initiating the so-called First Reform while standing in as interim president for Santa Anna. He introduced measures to secularize education and free people from the obligation to pay ecclesiastical tithes. Under the Reform Laws championed by Benito Juárez in the 1850s, and incorporated into the 1857 constitution, ecclesiastical privileges were drastically reduced, property was confiscated, and religious orders suppressed; clergymen were even prohibited from wearing religious garb in public. Juárez and his allies rewrote the federal calendar, reducing religious holidays and increasing civil ones. They also established a civil registry to record births, deaths, and marriages, signaling their wish that the state take over the social functions traditionally entrusted to the Church. So began the somewhat cumbersome dual system that still exists today, under which couples who want a church wedding, as most do, get married twice, once before civil authorities and once in church. When introduced, these reforms provoked a strong conservative reaction, involving some of the first, but far from last, serious armed conflicts between church and state. These Reform Laws of the mid-nineteenth century "should be seen more as the start of a process than an accomplished task," and "even today, much of the program is hardly realized and likely never will be" (Vanderwood, *Oxford History of Mexico*, 377). However imperfectly implemented, the Reform Laws had a chilling effect on Mexican relations with the Vatican. Even during the French occupation there were great difficulties; when Maximilian defended freedom of religion and lent support in 1864 to the establishment of a temple of the Church of Christ in Mexico City, the Vatican recalled its ambassador to Mexico.

The Reform Laws of the nineteenth century did open the door for religious freedom and diversity; in their wake, there were a number of sporadic, mostly short-lived schisms and, more significantly, Protestant denominations began to grow. Lutheran congregations, for example, date from 1850, Baptist congregations from 1860, Anglican (Episcopal) from 1869, and Methodist from 1873. Many factors have won the Protestant evangelists converts, especially among the disenfranchised in isolated rural and some indigenous communities, and primarily in the far reaches of the north and south. These include the social services that many Protestant missions have undertaken in education, health care, and housing; one must also take account of the lack of Protestant strictures against divorce and birth control, and the attractions of a close-knit community. Since most of the original founders and missionaries come from the United States, these denominations have frequently been treated with suspicion and even hostility, being dismissed as sects by some and attacked as agents of U.S. imperialism by others. In recent years, the growing influence of the Protestant denominations has undoubtedly alerted the Catholic majority, and Catholic hierarchs and government officials alike have seen the growth of Protestantism as a threat to the status quo. In the northern provinces, Mormons and Mennonites have established communities. In the southern states of Oaxaca, Chiapas, Yucatán, and Tabasco, such diverse groups as the National Presbyterian Church and the Jehovah's Witnesses have developed followings among the Indian communities where, after the fashion of the first Catholic missionaries in Mexico, they have translated the Bible into all of the local indigenous tongues. Some of the Protestant influence makes its way into Mexico via Guatemala, the most Protestant of the Latin American countries.

The gap between anti-clerical rhetoric and religious reality is exposed by the fact that successive modern constitutions in Mexico have had to reaffirm virtually the same restrictions on church power and influence, each time as if they were treading on new ground. The 1917 constitution extended the Juárez reforms, with new articles that affected all types of religion. These laws once again prohibited religious orders, guaranteed religious liberty but restricted public religious acts to designated buildings, prohibited religious groups from owning real estate, made marriage a civil matter, and, above all, limited the participation of churches and their representatives in matters of state. In the 1920s, President Calles launched one of the most drastic and concerted onslaughts on the powers of Catholicism; he supported an attempt to establish a separate, national Mexican Catholic and Apostolic Church, and ordered the occupation of churches and cathedrals. Needless to say, he provoked a visceral and violent reaction among conservative church leaders and their followers, particularly in the central-western and north-central states of Jalisco, Guanajuato, Michoacán, Colima, and Zacatecas. That became a religious civil war waged with the cry of "Viva Cristo Rey" ("Long live Christ the King") and known as the Cristero Rebellion (1926–29). After spending some 30–40 percent of the national budget to quash the uprising, Calles had to make concessions in order to bring the conflict to an end.

Calles's concessions ushered in an extended period which essentially returned church-state relations to the state of mutual tolerance that had prevailed for most of Porfirio Díaz's rule: a modus vivendi was reached in which the Church accepted the registration of priests in a civil registry, while the government agreed to stay out of the internal affairs of the church (*Milenios de México*, 1381). This kind of coexistence under separation of powers between the ostensibly revolutionary social policy of the government on the one hand and the Church on the other extended into the late 1970s and early 1980s, when a new era in the relations between the Mexican government and the Church (and the Vatican hierarchy) began to take shape. Pope John Paul II visited Mexico to inaugurate the Latin American Bishops' Conference held in Puebla in 1979. In the mid-1980s, however, the position of the Church shifted and the accommodation between church and state started to break down; the former became increasingly associated with forces of opposition and political and social change. Tensions grew palpable in 1988, when church leaders in the northern state of Chihuahua threw their support behind demonstrators protesting over electoral fraud on the part of the Institutional Revolutionary Party (PRI). Seen against this background, it was thought very significant that President Salinas appeared at his inauguration at the end of that decade flanked by five bishops plus the Vatican's representative in Mexico, a man known for his conservatism. Many assume that Salinas was using his rapprochement with the Church and the Vatican to bolster his authority in the wake of a disputed electoral victory.

A surprising and significant transformation of church-state relations has ensued. In 1992, with Salinas's support, Article 130 of the constitution was amended: churches could be legally registered, they could once again legally possess property, and priests were allowed to perform religious ceremonies in public. In that same year diplomatic relations with the Vatican were restored, and Pope John Paul II made repeated visits to Mexico in the 1990s. This process culminated in 1999 when President Zedillo, in a widely observed public act, attended the inauguration of a new cathedral in a suburb of Mexico City. Nonetheless, these recent changes have been more a matter of publicity than substance, and the Church has probably recouped less power than it might have hoped. Interestingly, though, from the conservative opposition party PAN, the new President Vicente Fox's divorce and subsequent remarriage to his former press secretary and campaign manager has been the cause of some renewed tension between him and the Church hierarchy.

That said, in modern times the Church is still highly influential, whether through its hierarchy or through pressure groups such as Catholic Action and the Christian Family Movement. Unlike most Latin American Catholic churches, Mexico's has been largely autonomous and financially self-sufficient, though closely tied to the Vatican. The importance of Mexico in the eyes of the latter is proved by the frequency of papal visits (some of which, despite the constitution, have been supported from the public purse). Representatives of the Catholic Church now range from conservative to liberal, from the intellectual to the pragmatic. Bishops in the southern states have been concerned about social conditions; those in the northern ones, as mentioned, have protested about corruption and electoral fraud. The Catholic hierarchy, however, has tended to be conservative and secretive. In contrast to the conservatism of the hierarchy, the lower ranks of the clergy have always done much to improve social justice; we may recall that it was a member of the clergy, Fray Bartolomé de las Casas, who drew attention to mistreatment of Indians in early colonial times; and if we look for evidence of social involvement by members of the Church closer to our own times, we find that in the late twentieth century, in central and southern Mexico, there were about 15,000 base communities devoted to religious social work, with about ten times as many activists supporting them. In the wake of the Zapatista rebellion in Chiapas that broke out in 1994, the diocese of San Cristóbal de las Casas has provided significant political support for the Indian rebels, and the local bishop has acted as mediator in peace negotiations between the rebels and the government.

THE VIRGIN OF GUADALUPE

Popular festivities in Mexico are frequently Catholic in inspiration, and invariably colored by indigenous practices. No figure better captures the power and reach of popular religiosity, or its fusion of pre-Hispanic and colonial ingredients, than the Virgin of Guadalupe. In the present day her image is ubiquitous; she is universally admired and venerated, by the pious and skeptical alike, and she serves as a focus for national pride and identity. No

Pilgrims on their knees ascending the Tepeyac hill toward the Basílica de Guadalupe. Photo by Steven Bell.

doubt for that very reason, the Virgin's popularity is particularly high among Mexican immigrants and Chicanos (Mexican Americans) in the southwestern United States.

It is estimated that the shrine to the Virgin of Guadalupe receives on average 10 million pilgrims a year. If so, then it is the most visited center for Christian pilgrimage in the world, easily exceeding Lourdes, and in fact rivaling Rome (*Fiestas, peregrinaciones, y santuarios en México,* 119–21). The pilgrims on her feast day alone, many making their final approach on their knees, can number in the tens of thousands. The site where the Basílica de Guadalupe now stands, on Tepeyac hill in the northern suburbs of Mexico City, was a site of religious devotion in pre-Hispanic times. Precisely because the site suggested idolatry in the eyes of the Spaniards, it was only in 1737 that authorities recognized Guadalupe officially as the patroness and protector of Mexico City, and not until 1756 that her status as patroness of New Spain was acknowledged by Pope Benedict XIV. Additional ceremonial titles have since been bestowed upon Guadalupe: in 1910 Pope Pius X declared her Celestial Patroness of Latin America, and in 1945 Pius XII elevated her to Empress of the Americas. Bold new construction has appeared as well. La Iglesia del Pocito was built in 1891 over the well at the foot of Tepeyac, whose waters are said to possess curative powers. An eighteenth-century basilica, which now houses a museum and has tilted and sunk into the ground, is flanked by an aggressively modern one with a striking, tarnished copper roof, built in 1976. Designed to accommodate as many as 20,000 people at mass, it is proof of the continuing importance of the Virgin of Guadalupe in the Mexican mind.

It is precisely her ability to be so many things and fulfill so many functions that accounts for the Virgin of Guadalupe's power of attraction. From the point of view of the indigenous population, the dark-skinned Virgin could be seen as a modified version of the earth goddess Tonantzín, who was worshiped at Tepeyac for many years prior to the arrival of the Spaniards. For some of the early Spanish colonial church officials who chose to acknowledge her miraculous apparition, Guadalupe's popularity among the indigenous and the popular classes seemed like proof of the success of their campaign to indoctrinate the natives. And, of course, for the growing numbers of criollos and mestizos born in Mexico, who would eventually wage a war for independence from Spain under her banner, she signified something uniquely Mexican, and marked them as a special or chosen race.

It is the mysteries in which the Guadalupe legend and early history are shrouded, and the long years of controversy and debate about her, that make her so fascinating a phenomenon. According to tradition, the Virgin appeared to a Christian Indian laborer, Juan Diego, in 1531 at the hill known as Tepeyac, near Mexico City. She is held to have spoken to him in Nahuatl (the Aztec language) and to have identified herself as the Virgin of Guadalupe. She appeared to him several times between December 9 and December 12, telling him to find the bishop and inform him of her wish to have a shrine to her built at that spot. Eventually the Indian managed to persuade the bishop to act, thanks to the graces of the Virgin. She gave Juan Diego a bunch of roses to carry to the bishop wrapped up in his humble cloak made of maguey fibers; when he unfolded the cloak before the Bishop, in place of the roses a beautiful mestiza image of the Virgin had miraculously appeared. The first small hermitage was erected on the Tepeyac hill, near where the Indians had had a temple to the goddess Tonantzin, in 1533, under Bishop Zumarraga, and the structure was expanded in 1557 under Archbishop Montúfar. But many early Church fathers remained skeptical, and objected that the Indians were simply venerating their own deity.

References to pilgrimages and worship at Tepeyac are found not only in the archives of the Church, but also in the sixteenth-century writings of Bernal Díaz del Castillo and Fray Bernardino de Sahagún, among others. There had, however, been a number of earlier debates and official inquiries into the nature of the image and the seemingly irrepressible cult it inspired. In 1556 a Franciscan called Francisco de Bustamante charged that it was all idolatrous superstition, and the viceroy of the time chastised the archbishop for encouraging belief in the divine powers of the image of Guadalupe, which the viceroy himself apparently considered to be simply a painting by an Indian artist. In 1648 a book by Miguel Sánchez did much to popularize the Virgin of Guadalupe among the better-educated castes in New Spain.

In any event, the growing symbolic importance of the Virgin of Guadalupe for the inhabitants of New Spain was such that officials could only jump on the bandwagon. New church construction and renovations at the Tepeyac site continued apace. In 1622, Archbishop de la Serna dedicated a new basílica that moved the main shrine down to the bottom of the hill. Still another, more elaborate colonial structure containing a seminary was begun in 1695, expanded in 1709, and consecrated as a collegiate church in 1750. The reverence of the masses has never waned, and discussion of the Guadalupe phenomenon among scholars periodically resurfaces. In 1756, the painter Miguel Cabrera examined the treasured image imprinted on Juan Diego's cloak and deemed that it could only be a work of divine origin. Rebel priest Servando Teresa de Mier, on the other hand, later in the eighteenth century, asserted that the Guadalupe legend was little more than a ruse perpetrated by authorities to attract the indigenous population to Catholicism.

As we have seen, the legend was helpful to the mission of the Church in colonial times, and it is representative of the sort of blending that has taken place between the indigenous and European; anthropologists have noted how the Catholic Marian (Mary) cult comes to be associated with the cult of the Aztec mother goddess, Tonantzín. As seen in chapter 1, Father Hidalgo, the first major figure of the movement for independence, appealed to the Virgin of Guadalupe and called for the fall of the Spanish colonial government in the same breath. While the forces that fought for independence rallied under the banner of Guadalupe, troops loyal to the Spanish monarch sought protection and inspiration in the Virgin de los Remedios, whose veneration had been popular among the first Spanish conquistadors under Cortés.

Nowadays the central place of the Virgin de Guadalupe in Mexico's idea of itself could hardly be more secure. Daily, the community at Tepeyac takes on a popular, carnival-like air, as busloads of curious visitors mingle with humble and reverent pilgrims who approach and climb the stairs of the Tepeyac hill on their knees, together with pickpockets and street vendors selling tamales, cotton candy, and all manner of religious artifacts. Félix Báez-Jorge has suggested the Guadalupe mystery is at once a "formidable ideological construction" and a social phenomenon whose ramifications and everyday manifestations continue to attract the curiosity of social scientists and art historians (Báez-Jorge, *Mitos mexicanos*, 144). In 1995, for example, a Jesuit scholar discovered a codex dating from 1548, signed by Fray Bernardino de Sahagún, that appears to predate Miguel Sánchez's book, previously thought to be the first documentary reference to the apparition story, by 100 years. At about the same time, two researchers, with the acquiescence of Church officials, examined the original Guadalupe image in detail. They determined, among other things, that the sun rays surrounding the Virgin were made of gold, and are peeling off; that the hands of the Virgin are the most retouched part of the painting, having been shortened, presumably to make them appear more Indian. They also found that the gold stars on the Virgin's blue cloak were added by human hands, sometime in the sixteenth century, but they concluded that an original image underlies these modifications and remains inexplicable (Musacchio, *Milenios de México*, 1212).

RELIGION AND MODERN LIFE

For Mexicans, as for most people, church attendance is a matter of sacred ritual, a private affair rather than a social one; unlike people in the United States, Mexicans do not tend to define their social circles in relation to particular church communities. Moreover, going to church is sometimes dismissed by men as women's business (*cosa de mujeres*). Even so, one cannot but be impressed by the everyday religiosity of ordinary Mexicans. Saints' days pepper the calendar, pilgrimages are legion, and altars, religious images, and artifacts clutter private homes. There is also a firm tradition of ex-votos, which are objects offered to a saint, Christ, or the Virgin Mary, as a public expression of gratitude for their miraculous intercession; the gratitude may be due to things like having survived an illness, having had a good harvest, or having found a lost item that is precious. They are very personal expressions of thanks, yet they are placed at altars and in churches for all to see. Hernán Cortés had an elaborate gold and emerald ex-voto made because he had survived a scorpion's sting. This last is an example of how they have sometimes become fashionable manifestations of wealth and influence, but ex-votos are in most cases an expression of humble folk art. Sometimes they are simply little charms representing an affected body part, a leg or an arm. There is a characteristic tradition of small, artisan-quality paintings on tin, depicting the miracle and including a captioned explanation; this tradition was widely practiced from the late colonial to the early modern periods. Nowadays, ex-votos may have photographs or photocopies attached, a story or an explanation, sometimes in verse. They can be commissioned of anonymous artisans who depend on them for their living, but many are designed and manufactured by those giving thanks. There is an impressive collection of painted ex-votos at the Museum of the Basílica de Guadalupe and the Frida Kahlo Museum also contains her private collection.

Ex-votos painted on tin, displayed at the Museo de la Basílica de Guadalupe. Photo by Steven Bell.

Religious artifacts in an antique shop, Puebla. Photo by Steven Bell.

The Virgen de Guadalupe phenomenon has been discussed. All over Mexico celebrations are held on December 12, the feast of the Virgin of Guadalupe, and pilgrims on their way to pay homage at the shrine in Tepeyac are traditionally offered food and drink by people who live along the road. December is a busy month. A few days after the feast of the Virgin of Guadalupe comes the start of a series of ritual reenactments known as the *posadas.* This word means "inns," for the posadas commemorate the search of Joseph and Mary for shelter during the Advent period. Over the course of nine nights and ending on Christmas Eve, people go from house to house; children dressed as angels and Joseph and Mary lead these pilgrims, carrying candles and singing. On arriving at a house the group divides and some people go in, leaving the others outside to beg for admittance. At that stage the religious side of the celebration fades away; each night culminates in a party whose star (sometimes quite literally) is the piñata.

Originally the Spanish missionaries would stuff a pot with colored paper and it would have seven protruding points to represent the seven deadly sins. Nowadays, though, sometimes in the form of a star (guiding the way to Bethlehem), piñatas come in all shapes and sizes. They are hollow, made of clay, covered with papier-mâché and filled with sweets and small toys, and of course are also very popular at birthday celebrations. Blindfolded children armed with poles lash about in the air trying to break the piñata that is hanging above them, and then there is a scramble for the contents. Traditionally, the last of the posadas, on Christmas Eve, would be followed by going to Midnight Mass, and it is Christmas Eve that has precedence over Christmas Day itself. The date in the Hispanic Christmas calendar when gifts are exchanged has always been the Feast of the Magi (January 6), an occasion when children put messages in shoes, requesting gifts. Largely because of commercial pressures and foreign influence, however, Christmas Day is becoming increasingly important in many households. On December 28 comes Los Santos Inocentes; this is the equivalent of April Fools' Day.

Other traditional Catholic holidays are celebrated much as they are in Spain and the rest of Latin America, with Mexican variations. Corpus Christi celebrations, solemn Holy Week processions, and festive Carnival rituals, as mentioned earlier, are full of props and choreography that come from the pre-Hispanic tradition. Easter is very much a religious feast, with no bunnies or egg hunt, but it has sometimes entailed one curious custom; on Easter Saturday children would be wakened by a tug on the ears and with the words "¡Feliz Sábado de Gloria!" ("Happy Easter Saturday"), after which they would be doused with water in the street. As our use of the past tense implies, this is a dying custom, possibly because water is so precious in Mexico.[1]

THE DAY OF THE DEAD

No festivity compares with Día de Difuntos, or Día de Muertos (Day of the Dead), which is especially of interest to anthropologists and tourists who are drawn to the darker mysteries of Mexican life. Deriving and much adapted from pre-Hispanic ritual, this is now an occasion when families remember the dead but also celebrate the continuity of life. The original celebration, honoring children and the dead, took place at the time in the Aztec calendar that was associated with the goddess Mictecachuatl, the "lady of the dead," a time that also saw ceremonies honoring the war god Huitzilopochtli.[2] In the post-conquest era the Spaniards tried to Christianize the celebration by moving it from July/August to coincide with All Saints' Day, in early November, and as a result the celebration became another hybrid one. The extent to which the Mexican celebration of the Day of the Dead should be considered unique and the degree to which its characteristics are truly of pre-Hispanic origin are matters that continue to generate lively debate among scholars, though most do agree that it embodies a peculiarly Mexican outlook on death.

Visiting the graves of one's departed relatives in order to pay homage to them on the first day of November is common practice in many countries,

Iglesia de la Santa Veracruz, Mexico City, tilted and sunken in
the dried bed of Lake Texcoco. Photo by Steven Bell.

especially among Catholics. But what makes the visits distinctive in Mexico is
their festive mood. Family members tell anecdotes about those who have
passed on; special meals are prepared; food, drink, even cigarettes are placed
beside graves, together with religious trinkets. Bright flowers are in profusion,
as is colored tissue paper. These visits are not morbid affairs but rather
moments of communion with the dead, and a sign of acceptance that while
death comes to everyone, life goes on. Quite often there are fireworks. Apart
from sprucing up graves, families make special preparations at home. These
include improvising altars, perhaps from upturned crates covered with sheets,
in rooms specially set aside for the purpose. Incense might be burned there,
and candles lit to guide the dead as they return to visit their relatives and feast
with them; a bowl and a towel are commonly placed close by so that the vis-

Large-scale Day of the Dead display on the Zócalo in Mexico
City, in front of cathedral. Photo by Juan León. Courtesy of
Imagen Latina.

iting dead can wash beforehand. Sometimes *cempasuchitl,* a flower said to
have four hundred lives, is placed at the altar.

November 1 (All Saints' Day) might be devoted to remembering children;
November 2 (All Souls' Day) to adults. Traditionally, there would be a meal
in the early hours of November 2. *Pan de muerto* ("bread of the dead") is
eaten; this is a sweet bread often topped with a representation of bones, and
good luck is thought to be in store for whoever happens to bite down on a
miniature skeleton hidden inside the loaf. Family members exchange gifts
featuring death motifs, such as sugar skulls and coffins, some of them personalized with names.

The festivities in celebration of the Day of the Dead vary somewhat from
region to region, and the religious side is stronger in rural areas than in the

Rural church in the state of Puebla, with traditional paper-cut banners. Photo by Steven Bell.

major cities, but all Mexico is involved. In some regions dark breads are made with human figures represented on them—the souls of the departed returned. One place that is famous for its Day of the Dead celebrations is Mixquic, once an Aztec farming community and nowadays a part of Mexico City that attracts large numbers of tourists with its festivities. Mexican artists have made much use of the images associated with the Day of the Dead, the most notable case being that of José Guadalupe Posada (see pages 99, 261–62).

A CAVEAT ON ETHNIC AND CULTURAL DIVERSITY

Inevitably, our account of religion in this chapter, and the one of social customs in the next, resort to generalizations that, like so much in Mexico itself, leave many cultural and ethnic groups out of the picture. In other words, what we are saying goes for the majority, for urban people and for the many in the provinces who have become largely assimilated to shared cultural patterns. Quite simply, it is impractical, beyond the scope of this book, to attempt to describe the customs of small minorities such as the Yaquis or the Seris in the north, to the Huaves and the Mixes in the south. Nonetheless, a coda to this chapter seems appropriate, a brief illustration of how one such minority, the Huichol people of Jalisco and Nayarit, have clung to their own animist beliefs and certain cultural habits. The Huichol people believe that the elements of nature can take a personal and a supernatural form, that gods can turn into plants or animals, and that they are revealed supernaturally in rituals. Thus, the rain god can assume the form of a snake, and the evocation of a snake image, for example in a vision, might herald rain or promise fertility. Each year the Huichol make a long and (traditionally) arduous pilgrimage of some 250 miles from their home territory across the central plateau, in search of a small, well-camouflaged cactus with a button-shaped growth at the top that yields *peyote,* a hallucinogen that is an essential part of their culture. Small amounts of peyote help them ward off hunger and fatigue, but larger ones, such as those taken by their shamans, bring visions that make sense of the world. Such visions also inspire Huichol paintings and designs. (These traditions have also been subject to the effects of modernity; it is not unheard of for the pilgrimage to be made by car, and for the artifacts to end up in the hands of tourists.) The use of peyote was documented by early Spanish chroniclers and had a very long tradition amongst Mexican Indian peoples before the Spaniards came. Needless to say, the colonial authorities tried to outlaw it, and so it went underground. Later visitors from abroad, such as the British writer Aldous Huxley, used peyote for more personal adventures. It is otherwise known as mescaline.

NOTES

1. For information on music and dances, see chapter 6, "Performing Arts."

2. The Aztecs believed that death in battle or by sacrifice was an honor that guaranteed the victim future blessings. The tears of sacrificed children were thought to ensure that rain would continue to fall.

3

Social Life, Leisure, and Food

RELIGION, AS WE SAW in the previous chapter, accounts for a number of festivities and affects social life in many ways. We turn now to secular celebrations and society, to matters such as family relations, the roles of men and women, leisure activities, and eating habits.

SECULAR CELEBRATIONS

Fiestas, says Octavio Paz, are the ordinary Mexican's only luxury. Certainly, few countries can claim such a full calendar of religious and civic holidays, national and regional festivities. In a book about the way in which ritual celebrations in Mexico inculcate and reinforce social values, while at the same time providing opportunities to express opposition or simply to let off steam, a 1977 survey is cited that identified 5,083 different civic and religious occasions that are celebrated during the year; the result is that "no more than nine days go by without a fiesta somewhere in Mexico" (Beezley et al., *Rituals,* xiv). The resources and energy devoted to them by people from all walks of life, and particularly by members of the lower classes, are extraordinary. As we have noted, many public and private celebrations are religious in origin. To these, under the influence of secularization, have been added the major civic holidays such as Cinco de Mayo and the Independence Day celebrations on September 15 and 16. These now rival the religious ones in their elaborate design, festive air, and mass appeal; in fact, they have become a kind of alternative civic religion.

As in most of the Hispanic world, one's saint's day is at least as important as one's birthday, though this too is changing. There is one birthday of special importance for women of the urban middle and upper classes; it is the *quinceañera* celebration given for the girl who has reached fifteen and is entering womanhood. The young lady first goes to church accompanied by close friends and family members, and there the priest addresses her on the subject of becoming a woman. There follows an extravagant party involving large numbers of people and much expense. Apart from the tiresome question of what to wear, preparation for the event involves her choosing the ladies and chamberlains who will attend her and accompany her in the dances. In the past, this celebration announced to the wider world that the young lady was ready to marry.

Understandably, civic holidays and fiestas have taken on great significance as a result of the nation-building and secularizing impulse. Modern statesmen and government officials have tapped into some of the religious passion and popular fervor with which religious celebrations are vested. The celebration of independence from Spain is Mexico's most important national holiday, becoming a huge party, with the advantage that the main festivities come at night on the eve of Independence Day itself, rather like New Year's Eve and New Year's Day. For the first year after independence, under Emperor Agustín de Itúrbide, September 27 was celebrated. Itúrbide was soon gone, however, and Independence Day was moved to September 16 by the Constitutional Congress of 1824, to commemorate the dramatic moment when Father Hidalgo first called for the people to rise up in arms against the Spaniards. President Guadalupe Victoria presided over the first Independence Day celebration on this date in 1825; he established a tradition of liberating slaves, and later prisoners convicted of minor offences, their release being considered a symbol of national freedom. In 1833, Gómez Farías added fireworks to the festivities. These early celebrations had a significant religious, as well as civic, component. Celebrations took place in churches as well as government buildings, with the joint participation of civic and religious authorities. Until 1857, when the celebration was secularized under the reform governments, a mass was traditionally celebrated on September 17 to remember fallen heroes of the armed struggle. Maximilian, the monarch put in by the French, was actually the first Mexican head of state to celebrate independence in Dolores; later, in the twentieth century, President Lázaro Cárdenas repeated the gesture, as have most presidents since. In 1896, Porfirio Díaz had the bell that Hidalgo rang to gather his parishioners brought to Mexico City from Dolores, and installed it atop the main entrance to the Palacio Nacional. In 1910, on the 100th anniversary of independence, Díaz set up a commission that organized events spanning the month of September, and that year the famous Angel of Independence monument, a gift from France, was inaugurated on the Paseo de la Reforma. Today, huge crowds still fill the main plazas of every city and town on the evening of September 15. Government officials reenact Hidalgo's Grito de Dolores with cries of "¡Viva!" to celebrate the nation and its heroes; the national anthem is sung and fireworks light up the sky in the colors of the flag. In homes, in bars and restaurants, and on the streets, there is music and dance, while traditional Mexican foods and drinks are consumed in abundance. On the day of September 16, the president usually presides over a military parade through downtown Mexico City.

After September 16, the May 5 (Cinco de Mayo) is probably the most recognized national holiday in Mexico; in recent years, it has become quite popular as well in parts of the United States (where its observance in fact dates back to 1922) and it is now taken as an occasion to celebrate the growing Mexican-American presence north of the border. Generally few people in the United States, however, know that the festivities commemorate a famous victory by the Mexicans over invading French troops on the outskirts of Puebla. Porfirio Díaz liked to make particular propagandistic use of Cinco de Mayo, often inaugurating new public works and monuments, or promulgating new laws on that date. Since 1931, festivities in Puebla have generally included a reenactment of the battle on the original site.

Before the late nineteenth century, the anniversary of the coming to the New World by Columbus—now known as the Día de la Raza (Day of the Race) or, with more profuse political correctness, the Fiesta de Indigenismo, Hispanismo y Mestizaje—was hardly celebrated in Mexico. Only in 1892 was it declared a holiday, and in that year Porfirio Díaz unveiled a statue of Columbus that still stands on Mexico City's Paseo de la Reforma. In subsequent years government officials took it as an occasion to affirm a sense of solidarity with other Spanish American nations and with Spain itself, since the wounds of the struggle for independence had had sufficient time to heal. The tone began to change, however, in the late 1930s under President Cárdenas's more socialist and *indigenista* government, particularly in the context of the rise of fascism in Europe and the dictatorship of Franco in Spain, which sent many Spanish citizens into exile in Mexico. Since then, and leading up to the quincentenary in 1992, celebrations have taken on a more radical and polemic character. Increasingly, the occasion has been used by intellectuals to invite reflection on the moral and political fiber of the Spanish conquest and colonization; among activist groups, it has inspired celebrations of the indigenous cultural heritage, demonstrations to vindicate indigenous rights and dignity, and protests against the poverty and marginalization suffered by contemporary indigenous communities.

These are only a few examples of the many civic holidays recognized today by the government. Others include the Day of the Constitution (February 5), Flag Day (February 24), and the birthday of Benito Juárez (March 21). The

Scene from parade celebrating the Mexican Revolution. Photo by Marco Antonio Cruz.

Revolution of 1910, of course, has added its own civic occasions to the calendar. Some have been elevated to prominence and have since faded, such as the celebration of the time in 1938 when President Cárdenas nationalized the petroleum industry. The Day of the Mexican Revolution (November 20), of course, is a major holiday; it was first held in 1929 and has generally been an occasion for parades and the celebration of sporting achievements. Since its completion, the Monumento a la Revolución, where the remains of the heroes of the Revolution are interred, has been a focal point of the festivities.

The shifting fortunes of May Day (Día del Trabajo) have mirrored the ongoing evolution of government dealings with organized labor. First celebrated in Mexico in 1913, in the early years it was simply the occasion for incipient labor organizers to hold meetings to discuss the latest international developments. Beginning in the 1920s and through to the 1960s and 1970s, the government on the whole exercised effective control over labor through the official unions tied to the governing party (PRI), and May Day marches and workers' demands remain well-orchestrated, largely peaceful, and festive affairs. Starting in the 1980s, the decline of the official unions and the increase in opportunities for opposition parties in the political system led to the emergence of significant independent labor organizations, and on several occasions they have clashed on the streets with members of the official unions, the latter protected by riot police.

Plaza de la Conchita, Mexico City. Photo by Steven Bell.

In addition to its own national civic and religious celebrations, under international influence and commercial pressures Mexico has adopted and produced its own versions of many holidays, from Valentine's Day (Día del Amor y la Amistad), to Mother's Day and Father's Day. There are also countless holidays dedicated to various occupations.

SPORTS AND ENTERTAINMENTS

Mexicans amuse themselves otherwise much as do people elsewhere, going to parks and country places, attending concerts and other performances, reading, playing games, wandering through street markets, dancing, watching television or going to the cinema, or playing video games and browsing the Internet. In Mexico City, the expansive Chapultepec Park, which dates back to pre-Hispanic times as a recreational retreat for the nobility, is still popular on weekends, and it offers vast green spaces, lakes, and springs. There are also numerous art and history museums, theaters, and auditoriums. The National Zoo, and even the presidential residence, Los Pinos, are there. Chapultepec also contains the Castillo de Chapultepec; once a military installation that was assaulted by invading United States forces in 1847 and defended by the Niños Héroes, it later served as a presidential palace for Maximilian and Porfirio Díaz. The more centrally located Alameda Central park, which is much

A typical day on the main square (Zócalo) in Mexico City. Photo by April Brown.

smaller, was popular among the well-to-do in the nineteenth century, and contains a famous marble monument to Benito Juárez, erected in 1910 on the centenary of national independence. We might also mention a place close to Mexico City, one that in fact consists of the vestiges of the lake on which the city was built; this is Xochimilco, site of the famous Aztec agricultural system of floating gardens, where today people take rides in flower-decorated boats, occasionally latching on to other boats carrying bands of musicians, who for a consideration will provide a serenade. It is a popular place with lovers. These days, in urban environments people may spend time in shopping malls or, in the case of Mexico City, stroll through the fashionable area known as the Zona Rosa, the more recently trendy Polanco area, or the arts districts in the Colonia Condesa or colonial Coyoacán.

Playing cards and dominoes are popular in some quarters. As one can observe while riding the subway or bus, there is a lively interest in comic books, as well as in television soaps, and in their spin-off photonovels (see page 99–101). Especially in small towns and provincial capitals, the real leisure tradition centers on the plazas, particularly the focal point of the main square (*plaza mayor*), where people go to have a drink, to walk about, to watch other people, and to meet friends. It is in the main squares that much of the entertainment takes place, such as bands and dancing.

Organized team sports do not have a long tradition in Mexico, though of course the pre-Hispanic civilizations had constructed impressive courts for

Children in a town square (plaza). Photo by Steven Bell.

their ball games. Traditional Mexican spectator and athletic activities tend to be tied to rural livestock and hacienda cultures and are individualistic arts, many of them of Spanish origin. Bullfighting came to Mexico as early as 1526; it was first practiced primarily on horseback. During the colonial period bullfighting grew in popularity across the country, particularly in the central western and northern provinces. Bullfights (*corridas*) were generally held in public plazas, for many years primarily at the Plaza del Volador, a short distance from the Zócalo in Mexico City. In the late colonial period, under the Bourbons, interest in bullfighting among the elite declined somewhat, and this provided something of an opening for others to take part, amateurs who had no access to horses and who increasingly entered the ring on foot; bullfighting became common at local fairs and on holidays. Meanwhile, the popularity of the bullfights at the Plaza del Volador increasingly inconvenienced the urban population. Officials of the nearby university complained, and government officials ordered construction of the first permanent bullring (Plaza de Toros) in 1788. In the late eighteenth century, immigrant bullfighters from Spain, such as Tomás Venegas, alias el Gachupín Toreador, introduced the latest Spanish techniques. Father Hidalgo, the leader of the movement toward independence, is said to have owned three haciendas dedicated to raising fighting bulls; but the popularity of bullfighting diminished in the early nineteenth century in proportion to the rise of anti-Spanish sentiment. Ever since, the fortunes of bullfighting have tended to rise and fall according to the whims of national leaders. Juárez in the nineteenth century and Carranza in the twentieth are among those who at one time attempted to shut down the corridas. Bullfighting is still important to certain sectors of the population. The main rings in Mexico City today, La Plaza México and El Toreo, both date from the twentieth century, and there are more than 200 permanent rings across the country.

Another significant sporting and cultural tradition, also tied to hacienda traditions inherited from Spain and influenced by the Arabs, is the *charrería* or *charreada,* which is very much like a rodeo insofar as it involves equestrian and roping skills in the handling of livestock. Horses first came to Mexico with Cortés, and early viceroys encouraged the development of livestock culture in the vast arid expanses of the northern provinces that were being explored and colonized. Some suggest that the idea of the *fiesta charra* originated in Salamanca, in Spain, where it is also a celebration of country ways, with plenty of food and traditional folk dancing. But Mexico has its own spin on it, and by the early- and mid-twentieth century, the *charro* (see below) tradition had taken on a life of its own, quite removed from its original basis in livestock culture and horsemanship.

Starting in the 1930s, the popular ranch comedy musicals of Mexican cinema consolidated the place of the *charro* and his female counterpart, the *charra* or *china poblana,* in the popular imagination; they became the very embodiment of national identity and patriotic honor. These stereotypes extended beyond Mexican borders, and the charro and the china poblana still find their way into many Mexican tourist promotions. In the course of a typical movie, by the time the fiesta is in full swing the charro has abandoned his work outfit in favor of the fancy braided dress suit and he has joined the dancing; the music is played by mariachis—whose standard costume is itself a variation on the semi-formal charro outfit—and the signature dance is the jarabe (see pages 177–78). Real charros were not always pleased with this rather romantic idealization of their image. In fact, rugged and independent-spirited Mexican cowboys and hacienda owners from the central and northern states had been an important force in the struggle for independence; many served as military leaders.

Emperor Maximilian, with his penchant for Mexican popular culture, is said to have played a role in popularizing the more formal black charro outfit. Porfirio Díaz also exploited, urbanized, and formalized the charro tradition. In the late nineteenth century, professional charro companies began to tour not only Mexico, but also Europe and North and South America. Charro outfits were also common among the various factions and troops during the Revolution that broke out in 1910. Emiliano Zapata's preference for charro dress did much to lend more humble, working class and campesino associations to the charro figure. In fact, in the early years of the post-Revolution a kind of unspoken debate played out among the Revolution's cultural and political leaders as to what figure should emerge as the embodiment of post-Revolutionary society.

The actor Cantinflas's popularization of the working-class *pelado* figure, through the vaudeville-type Teatro de Revista in the 1920s, might have suggested an alternative that was in consonance with Revolutionary rhetoric. But, in the end, it was the charro figure popularized first through musical theater and then the movies that won. Ironically, the rather aristocratic figure of the charro of the northern ranches, representing the colonial past, was elevated to preeminence at a time when post-Revolutionary governments were talking of their commitment to Indians, campesinos, and the working class. At about this same time, charrerías turned into competitive sporting spectacles combining deft horsemanship and refined costumes. The first charro association was formed in Guadalajara in 1919; a national one was established in Mexico City in 1921; and in 1933 the Mexican Sports Confederation gave charrerías official recognition.

Another popular pastime in Mexico of rural origins is the much-ballyhooed cockfighting (*pelea de gallos*), legal not only in Mexico but also in a number of other countries, and in some states in the United States. It is resolutely a male affair, attracting men of all classes. Spectators place bets on roosters who fight to the death with special blades strapped to their feet. The pelea de gallos was reportedly a favorite entertainment of President Santa Anna, in the first half of the nineteenth century. The Mexican film *Amores perros* (2000) exposes a variant, dog fighting, a clandestine activity that apparently is popular in certain working class neighborhoods. More mainstream gambling is available in such places as the Hipódromo de las Américas, first established for elite patrons in the early twentieth century, and at the urban *frontones*. These are courts where jai alai, a game that came to Mexico in the 1920s from the Basque country in Spain, is played; it is somewhat like racquetball or squash, played against walls but in the open air, and with scoop-like bats. Jai alai is also played professionally.

Interest in developing team sports grew during the late nineteenth century, at a time when Mexico's leaders wanted to emulate the social and economic success of Britain and North America. Baseball first came to Mexico in the 1880s, and the first league was formed in 1899, primarily composed of company teams. The presence of many North American workers in the expanding industrial sector under Porfirio Díaz served to boost interest in the game. The Chicago White Sox played the first exhibition game by a U.S. team in 1910. A Mexican baseball league was founded in 1925, and 30 years later it became affiliated to the U.S. minor league system, with the first Mexican players reaching the major leagues in 1958. The Los Angeles Dodgers pitcher Fernando Valenzuela, who rose to fame in the 1980s, has been the most celebrated player to do so. Despite various ups and downs, Mexican baseball has remained popular. With the advent first of radio and then of television, many Mexicans have become avid fans of U.S. professional baseball.

Of course, as in all Latin American countries, the dominant team sport, and the one that fires the most extreme nationalistic passions, is soccer (*fútbol*). As was the case with baseball, it first came to Mexico thanks to the presence of foreign industrial workers, this time from Britain at the end of the nineteenth century. Once again, many of the early teams were company affiliated. Pachuca was one of the most famous of the early clubs; América (1917) and Necaxa (1923) were among the first nationally recognized clubs. Other popular teams include Cruz Azul, Atlas (from Guadalajara), and the Pumas (of the Universidad Autónoma). (North Americans will be surprised to know that university-affiliated soccer teams in Mexico are professional.) Soccer quickly became the number one sport for Mexican boys across the country. The Mexican Soccer Federation of 1927 affiliated with the International Soccer Federation. Mexico played in the first World Cup, held in 1930 in Uruguay. It has qualified for numerous other World Cups since; its best showing to date came when the country hosted the World Cup for the second time in 1986. The palaces of Mexican soccer are the Estadio Olímpico, inaugurated in 1946, and the imposing Estadio Azteca; built for the 1968 Summer Olympics, and for the 1970 World Soccer Cup, it opened in 1966 and it holds upwards of 100,000 fans. Mexico's best soccer players today are under contract to teams throughout the world; the greatest aspiration is to sign with a European team, the salaries and international attention being greater. Probably Mexico's most famous player of all times was Hugo Sánchez, who captained the national team in the 1986 World Cup and went on to play for many years in Spain; today he is a commentator for Mexican broadcasts of the World Cup. As elsewhere, the passions of Mexico's soccer fans can get out of control at times. A riot in 1985 at the Estadio Universitario left eight people dead and many more injured. In recent years, fans have taken to gathering in the vicinity of the Angel de la Independencia monument on Paseo de la Reforma in Mexico City, to celebrate international victories and to vent their frustration over losses. Riot troops now come out in full force on these occasions.

As a participatory sport, American football has had little appeal so far. A small amateur league has been dominated by two well-endowed private universities, the Instituto Tecnológico de Monterrey and the Universidad de las Américas on the outskirts of Puebla. As a spectator sport, however, thanks to

Azteca Stadium. Photo by Peter Standish.

virtually universal access to television, American professional football is attracting larger and larger audiences. In recent years, the National Football League has put on an exhibition game, filling the Azteca Stadium.

Two other spectator sports have won a significant, working class following, and for different reasons. One is boxing. Boxing has been viewed as a sign of the Darwinian struggle for survival; for many working-class youths it offers a glimmer of hope of escaping from poverty (Monsiváis, Del rancho al internet, 76–77). This is exactly the gist of a feature film titled Pepe el Toro. For young aspiring boxers, and for the sport's many fans as well, the success of Mexican boxers abroad is a source of national pride. As has been noted, the combination of nationalistic pride and a wish to make a mark in (and on) the United States is encapsulated in the ring name of Mexico's most famous early-twentieth-century boxer, el Kid Azteca (who also crossed over into acting in such films as El gran campeón). Many Mexican boxers have excelled, especially in the lightweight divisions. Julio César Chávez has won several world titles at different weights; for his first title in 1984, he defeated another Mexican boxer, Mario Martínez.

Professional wrestling (lucha libre) has a rather different kind of attraction for its audiences, and it is hardly a path to wealth and notoriety, since its heroes appear before their public disguised with masks. The appeal of professional wrestling can be seen to lie largely in its soap opera–like melodrama, and in the way it seems to mirror the average Mexican's cynical view of the workings of Mexico's social and political systems, in such a way that the audience easily identifies with it and finds it cathartic. For example, the outcome is preordained and the appearance of open and fair competition is just a ruse; rules exist, but they are arbitrarily enforced, and the officials can be bribed; the wrestlers are unmistakably divided into good and evil, but it turns out they are all part of the same show (Rubenstein, *Oxford History of Mexico,* 661–62). Like boxing, wrestling has enjoyed a successful partnership with television and film, since both have marketed their products to the anonymous masses. The most famous Mexican wrestler of all time, Santo, el Enmascarado de Plata (The Saint of the Silver Mask) became the star of a series of popular, B-grade movies, the first of which was *Santo contra Cerebro del Mal* (*Santo versus the Evil Mind,* 1958).

FAMILY, FRIENDS, SOCIAL ETIQUETTE

Migration is taking its toll on traditional Mexican social structures, including the family. However, we can say that in addition to immediate blood relatives, the dominant Mexican idea of family normally encompasses more distant relatives as well as unrelated individuals (often referred to as cousins or uncles and aunts) who have grown close, and who may live in the same household. Indeed, households quite often include more than one nuclear family. If single, a grown-up son or daughter may well stay on living with parents rather than finding independent housing, and even married sons and daughters are quite likely to live with parents, at least for a time. Extended families often gather together socially, for example to eat on Sundays.

An important aspect of the social scenario is godparenthood (*compadrazgo*). Apart from fulfilling genuinely religious functions associated with such ceremonies as baptism and first communion, a compadre may participate in other life events regarded as significant, including those of a wholly material nature, such as moving into a new house, getting a new car, even having one's first haircut. Compadrazgo formally associates a person with a family, and it brings with it an obligation of mutual respect and support.

Another important part of social relations is *cuatismo;* this word, deriving from a Nahuatl one meaning "twin brother," refers to a close bond between two or more male friends who may socialize together and confide in each other—"best buddies," so to speak. Extending from this we come to the more general phenomenon of *amiguismo,* which is a reliance on personal connections and mutual favors in order to achieve things in social life and the workplace. Of course, this phenomenon exists in other countries but, if we are comparing Mexico with the United States, we should note that there is an important difference in the way in which society regards it. In the United

States it is recognized as widespread but somewhat frowned upon, while in Mexico it is simply what people normally do.

In many ways Mexicans are quite formal, and politeness is important; one sees this in the way they dress in the business place and on social occasions and, above all, in their forms of address. Titles matter; knowing that one's interlocutor is an architect, one would address him as Arquitecto Sánchez, and if a woman is known to have a degree (or if in doubt and anxious to play safe), one would address her as Licenciada González. In general, the use of first names is reserved, as in most countries, for close acquaintances and friends. Doing business of any sort is normally preceded by a period of socializing. Many observers have noted that people in Mexico and the United States have a different attitude toward work, and some have suggested that puritanism is responsible for the U.S. way. It is often said that Mexicans work to live (enjoy their leisure), while people in the United States live for work.

MEN AND WOMEN

If one is to believe the scenario painted by *Like Water for Chocolate* (*Como agua para chocolate*), Mexican women can be perfectly independent and assertive, and men are wimps. The mother in that picture is dictatorial, one daughter so rebellious and liberated as to ride about naked and join a revolutionary band, and the other, though apparently submissive and dutiful, is capable of quietly manipulating others with her cuisine!

The truth is that there is indeed a popular tradition of culinary rituals designed to keep husbands in order, and there is evidence of female participation in the Revolution, not to mention the early days of industrialization. In general, however, women have had influence within the home over certain matters, but their authority and especially their freedom have been severely curtailed once across the threshold and into the outside world. Women's access to education was opened up under Porfirio Díaz in the late nineteenth century. The 1917 constitution, for all its laudable reforms (for example, its acknowledgment of the right to divorce and its provision of certain labor rights), did not give women full political rights. Mexican women did not win the right to vote until 1954, which was later than a good number of Latin American countries.

Social attitudes are changing but they sometimes lag behind legal provisions. Women are expected to behave and dress in certain ways. They can now be found in virtually every walk of life and their organizations are increasingly influential, but women are still at a disadvantage as compared with men, and often subject to various forms of exploitation and abuse. It is significant, for example, that the operators of the maquiladoras prefer women workers because they cost less and are less unionized, due in part to family commitments that draw them away. More generally, machismo, a widespread phenomenon in the Hispanic world, and one that some people think has its roots in Spain's long-term occupation by Muslim peoples, still runs deep, even in an era of rapid change. Surely the fact that the term *machismo* has made its way into English reflects the pervasiveness of the phenomenon in the Hispanic world. Interestingly, machismo is stronger in Latin America than in Spain.

Traditional attitudes are sometimes bolstered by the projection of national stereotypes, in particular the china poblana and the charro, to which we referred previously. The latter, a sort of Mexican cowboy figure complete with sombrero, high-heeled boots, and braid-trimmed costume, is quite easy to describe, and well known. The former is more complex. *China* in Spanish suggests Chinese or Chinawoman, but the word as applied here derives from an Indian term that was in general use in early colonial times to refer to a domestic servant. Some confusion arises because one early china, who was known as Catarina de San Juan and who became famous for her devotion to good works, happened to be of Asian origin (though probably not Chinese). Furthermore, the word *poblana* is open to two interpretations, meaning either "from Puebla" or "from the pueblo" (from [among] the village [folk]). As luck had it, Catarina de San Juan worked in Puebla, and so the first of the two meanings has sometimes been thought to be the main one. In fact, though, china poblana really denotes a servant girl from the country, of modest means but honorable. A traditional garb has become associated with the china poblana: off-the-shoulder white blouse with heavy embroidery, full green skirt, shawl, hair swept back, silk shoes. Frequently the colors of the Mexican flag have been reflected in her costume, but by now it has infinite variations, from something quite simple to the bold and elaborate.[1]

The china poblana has been converted into an archetype of Mexican womanhood. At first, the association with Catarina de San Juan led to her being viewed as the very essence of virtue and humility, indeed, as saintly. It served the colonial establishment to foster such an archetype. However, in the nineteenth century the image changed, became less saintly, more modish, and rather risqué, to such a degree that when Fanny Calderón, the wife of Spain's first ambassador to Mexico, was contemplating wearing a china poblana costume she was firmly advised that doing so would give quite the wrong impression. By then the china poblana was a liberated woman, though she was on her way to being exploited in another way, like her partner the charro, for commercial purposes. In modern times, for example, there is a product line

Dancers from Oaxaca at a festival, wearing *china problana* costumes. Photo by Natalia Fregoso. Courtesy of Imagen Latina.

known as El Charro, while the china poblana has appeared in Corona beer advertisements and on cans of processed food. As time has passed, her oriental association has been forgotten, her image transformed into that of a light-skinned mestiza.

By the 1940s, recognizing the importance of the archetype, Puebla had established a china poblana day. Organized by a committee of women, when first held it included a competition to design a monument to Catarina de San Juan, composing a hymn in her honor, the issuing of commemorative postage stamps, financing a movie starring María Félix, arts and crafts exhibitions, the selling of local products and, of course, a marketing campaign to bring in tourists.

This information comes from a description of the event by Luis Andrade. Writing in a government publication, Andrade conveys an official impression of the strong nationalistic sentiment that the china poblana is supposed to evoke:

[Her image] moves and captivates us at all the national celebrations, and she is the one who has created waves of enthusiasm abroad, the one who has made tears of deep emotion flow from our eyes when we have seen her at festivals and in theaters in North America and Europe, marvelously performing the footwork of the *jarabe tapatío* in her silk slippers [. . .] under the proud wing of her *charro's* braided sombrero.[2]

Mexican history is full of powerful female archetypes. Octavio Paz has criticized the tendency among Mexican men to see women as either the pure, vir-
ginal mother, or the treacherous whore (the Virgin or Malinche). Not that
this tendency is exclusive to the men of Mexico. It has been analyzed by social
psychologists, in the context of Latin machismo, as a defensive response of
insecure or victimized males caught in an authoritarian and patriarchal society, a response directed at women who are perceived as stronger and more
self-secure.

The *soldadera* has come to be another stock figure of Mexican womanhood, and a quite malleable image she has, too. The term denotes a female
camp follower of armed bands and military troops. This is a role that today is
almost exclusively associated with the Revolution, when soldaderas seemed to
have been very common, or at least particularly visible, serving both with federal troops and with revolutionary contingents. Scholars and feminist historians, however, have traced their participation in armed conflicts in Mexico
back before the conquest. The soldadera encompasses a whole range of functions and qualities in the popular imagination; she can be invoked to connote
the rough and uneducated easy woman who services the troops, but much
more frequently she is the humble yet noble country girl, the rugged and self-
sacrificing servant and patriot, or the tirelessly loving and faithful wife or mistress. Soldaderas have been protagonists of many of the most famous popular
narrative ballads (*corridos*) of the Revolution; thanks to one of them, Adelita
has come to serve as a kind of generic proper name for the soldadera figure.
She has been immortalized in some of most dramatic and unforgettable photographs of the Revolution from the portfolio of Agustín Casasola. The
extent to which the soldadera has been idealized as one of the myths of post-
Revolutionary culture is apparent in the role played by actress María Félix in
the Golden Age film *Enamorada.* A much more authentic and realistic portrait of the life of the soldadera is in *Hasta no verte, Jesús mío,* the novelized
memoir of a soldadera, based on taped interviews and written by Elena
Poniatowska (1969).

Not surprisingly, the roles of men and women in society have frequently
been the theme of works of art, especially in modern times. There is, when all
is said and done, some truth underlying *Como agua para chocolate.* There is
probably more underlying Berman's film *Entre Pancho Villa y una mujer
desnuda,* 1994 (discussed on page 160) and in a highly successful novel of the
1980s by Angeles Mastretta, *Arráncame la vida.* Mastretta's protagonist is a
girl who is swept off her feet by an older man; the girl becomes a woman, and
her comfortable enjoyment of the material benefits her husband provides
does battle with her realization that he is ruthless and unscrupulous, while he
treats her patronizingly, stifling her potential. As the role of the dutiful

daughter in *Como agua para chocolate* seems to imply, one appropriate place for a woman to be is in the kitchen. Rosario Castellanos, an early feminist writer, has a famous short story called "Cooking Lesson" ("Lección de cocina"), in which she portrays an intelligent, well-educated modern woman struggling to come to grips with the expectations placed upon her by society in general, and marriage in particular.

FOOD AND DRINK

One of the many anomalies brought about as U.S. commercial and cultural tentacles reach abroad is the selling of Taco Bell food south of the border. Two observations can be made about this. In the first place, Mexico is knowingly swallowing a version of its own food that is rather less than authentic, food that is really a corruption of the already homogenized fare that is thought of as Mexican north of the border. Second, some of those same Mexican consumers would undoubtedly wax eloquent and passionate, if given the chance, in protest against U.S. imperialism. (Even at good Mexican restaurants in the United States, the fare typically features northern Mexican and Tex-Mex dishes, such as burritos and fajitas, not Mexican cuisine from the heartland. In other words, rather like the local guides and vendors at pre-Hispanic ruins in Mexico, Mexicans operating restaurants in the United States often capitulate to the expectations of their customers, rounding down towards a stereotypical, bottom-end-of-the-market formula, rather than offering food that reflects the true variety and interest that is Mexican.) Not everything is refried beans and salsa.

The fact that Mexicans occasionally indulge in American fast food should not raise the least fear that their unique traditional cuisine is in any danger of disappearing. They are not making hamburgers and pizza at home. Mexicans relish their typical dishes and the fine art of their proper preparation. Mexican cuisine, in fact, has a great deal to offer, beginning with the vast range of natural products that comes with having such a varied climate and terrain and two long coastlines. As a general rule, though modern supermarkets now abound, Mexicans prefer to use fresh rather than processed ingredients, and they may still feel more comfortable shopping at traditional open-air or covered markets comprising numerous, individual stands organized by product type. Fresh, warm, corn tortillas are purchased daily for the mid-afternoon meal, fresh off the machine at the corner tortilla stand. Breads too, particularly the staple French-styled *bolillo*, are usually bought daily at the neighborhood bakery. In many Mexico City neighborhoods, vendors still come on a designated day of the week to set up a temporary, tarp-covered booths to service the demand among household chefs and servants for fresh ingredients.

A number of the products of nature that we outside have long since taken for granted and used on a daily basis came (and come) from Mexico. Mexico gave us the tomato and the avocado, it gave us corn and chocolate (an indulgence of the Aztec nobility). Mexico before the Spaniards arrived had about 50 different species of vegetables and grain, and about twice as many varieties of fruit, including mango, papaya, and guanábana. To the land's own products were added others from Europe. As in everything, in its cuisine Mexico is hybrid, the product of indigenous and European practices, not only those of the Spaniards but those of other Europeans, especially the French, who became so influential in the nineteenth century.

Maize, the revered staple of the Indians, is still ubiquitous, and it is prepared in many ways, not only as tortillas. *Atole* is a drink made from maize, usually drunk hot. *Pozole* is a corn-based stew made with white hominy and pork or, traditionally, meat from a pig's head. *Menudo* is similarly based, but uses offal. Tamales are cornmeal based, with spicy or sweet scrapple wrapped either in corn husks (in the northern and central regions) or banana leaves (in Yucatán). *Huitlacoche* is a fungus that grows on corn, used to make a sauce or in tacos and quesadillas. Maize is traditionally ground on a concave stone bed called a metate. Another native cooking utensil that is still in use in many places is the *comal*, a simple form of hotplate made of clay, on which tortillas are prepared.

Other distinctive characteristics of the cuisine include the widespread use of cilantro as an herb, together with herbs that are less widely known outside Mexico, such as epazote, and the use of squash blossoms (*flor de calabaza*) for flavoring or decoration. One of the many flavored water drinks (*aguas frescas*) served to accompany a meal is *agua de Jamaica:* it is an infusion made from Jamaica blossoms and has a burgundy color. The lime (*limón*) is at least as frequent in Mexican dishes as is the lemon (*limón real*). Dozens of different peppers are used in cooking. Not all of them are hot, but the ubiquitous jalapeño is definitely mild in comparison, say, to the serrano or the habanero. Large poblano peppers can be stuffed with cheese or other ingredients to produce *chiles rellenos*, which are generally nothing like those found at Mexican restaurants outside of Mexico. Poblano peppers are also used in the famous seasonal dish from Puebla, *chiles en nogada*. Certain cactuses or cactus-like plants are edible, or provide fruit: diced leaves of the prickly pear cactus are cooked and served as a vegetable, known as *nopales*. The agave (*maguey*) is used to make fermented drinks, including the sometimes crude, moonshine-grade *pulque* and, of course, the more refined tequila, named after the place where it is produced. Pulque, though the name comes from no known indigenous language, dates back to pre-conquest times. It is popular among the rural poor and the urban working class, because it can be had cheap in often-clandestine *pulquerías*, where it is likely to be served from a wooden barrel. But pulque also might be shared among other classes, in special shallow vessels, at wedding receptions or on special gatherings, for those seeking connection with pre-Hispanic roots or when seeking to invoke the aura of ancient, pre-Hispanic deities. One 1986 survey counted some 1,200 pulquerías in the Mexico City metropolitan area, though the average tourist would be hard-pressed to find them. Pulquerías are known for their odd names, like Everybody's House, The Hen of the Golden Eggs, or The Atomic Bomb.

A fierce relative of tequila is *mezcal*, which can come in several flavors, sometimes with a worm in the bottle. *Damiana* is an herb-based liquor from Baja and Sinaloa, reputedly having aphrodisiacal properties. *Xtabentún* is another liquor, derived from anise and honey and coming from Yucatán. Mexico's beer is now widely known abroad; less well known is its rum, though it can be of good quality. Not so Mexican wine. Although Hernán Cortés ordered settlers in the sixteenth century to plant vines, and although some of these were later transplanted to Chile and Argentina, where highly successful wine industries have developed, Mexico's own grapes have largely been given over to producing the popular brandy, and its wine has been poor in quality. There are many fruit-based drinks, a common one being *sangrita*, which combines orange and pomegranate juices with tequila and is often spiced with pepper. A variant of coffee is *café de olla*, made by adding cinnamon and brown sugar. The traditional Mexican version of drinking chocolate involves mixing grated chocolate with milk, using a simple wooden whisk that is spun between the palms rather as one does when trying to make fire with a stick; the drink is spiced up with cinnamon and cloves.

Chocolate flavors some savory dishes and is the key ingredient in one national dish eaten on special occasions: *mole de guajolote*. *Guajolote* is an example of a typically Mexican word of Indian origin, and it means "turkey"; other Hispanic countries call turkey "pavo." A typical recipe involves a long list of ingredients to make the mole sauce: three or four kinds of chiles, onion, tomato, sesame, pumpkin and anise seeds, peanuts, raisins, garlic, cinnamon, black pepper, cloves, and, of course, chocolate. Mole sauce is often associated with Puebla, but there are regional variants; in Yucatán it can come with banana added. Ceviche is a popular dish, one that has spread to other parts of Latin America. It is made by marinating raw fish or seafood in lime juice, with peppers, tomatoes, olive oil, and herbs. As one would anticipate, regional dishes reflect what is available locally. Thus, fish in Yucatán might well come baked in palm leaves, and tortillas might be made of wheat flour rather than maize in Sonora, where wheat is grown. The recipe for a famous dish from Yucatán, *cochinita pibil*, goes something like this: banana leaves are laid in a casserole dish and ribbed pork is placed on top; *achiote* (annatto seed) paste is mixed with bitter orange juice, cumin, oregano, cinnamon, black pepper, salt, garlic, and chiles, and the whole is poured over the meat, which is then left to marinate before it is cooked slowly until the meat falls off the bone; a sauce accompanies this dish, made of radishes, onion, chiles, and either more juice or vinegar; it is eaten with tortillas.

Many dishes, ingredients, and eating habits are comparable to those found in parts of Spain. For example, raisins, olives, almonds, and cumin are all common in the dishes of both countries. Many of the desserts are variants on Spanish ones, adapted to local products, in particular fruits. *Arroz con leche* (rice pudding) for example, is a popular dessert. As in Spain, *buñuelos* (sweet fritters) are consumed in Oaxaca just before Christmas, served on earthen-ware dishes which are then broken; and, similarly, in Mexico one eats baked *huachinango* (red snapper) at Christmas, just as one does *besugo,* a similar fish, in Spain.

Everyday eating patterns vary and are changing, but for most, the day might begin early with coffee or chocolate, perhaps with some form of pastry. Then might come a more substantial mid-morning brunch—for example *chilaquiles* (tortillas with tomato sauce, chicken, cheese, and cream) or *huevos con machaca* (scrambled eggs with shredded beef). The main meal, called simply *la comida,* is taken any time after 1:00 P.M. and often runs quite late. Meals do tend to be long and relaxed, sociable affairs. The attentiveness and hospitality of the staff at restaurants, even fairly modest ones, can be extraordinary. The main meal may be followed by a late evening snack, perhaps hot chocolate with pastries (*pan dulce*) or perhaps something from the corner *taquería* or street stand. On the streets there are many temporary and semi-permanent stands set up by food vendors, hawking all manner of snacks. Though public health and tourism officials often try to get rid of them, they are an essential, if chaotic, part of the vibrant street life that most Mexicans would sorely miss.

We began this section by referring to the influence of U.S. fast food in Mexico. It is therefore fitting to close it with a word about urban Mexico's own favorite fast food items: the tacos and *tortas* sold on street stands and at many late night taquerías. Tortas (the word means "sandwich" only in Mexico) are made with a toasted hoagie-type bun, the obligatory garnish ingredients being sliced avocado, a thin layer of refried beans, sliced onion and jalapeños, and sometimes tomato. The main ingredients might be chopped grilled chicken, eggs scrambled and fried, eggs and ham, or a pork, ham, and egg combination (known as *la cubana*). The real Mexican taco is not hard but made with a small, soft, warm, corn tortilla, folded in half over what is usually some kind of sliced meat filling. It is garnished with a mixture of chopped cilantro and onion, optionally a small slice of pineapple, and topped off with a spoonful of spicy chile sauce, either red and tomato based, or green and tomatillo based. The choices for filling may run from the mysterious contents of the *taco al pastor*, to beef flank steak or pork rib meat, to cow brains or tongue. The chefs who produce these tacos operate at breathtaking speed. The layered taco al pastor meat is continuously cooking on a huge upright turning spittle; with one slice of the knife, the meat falls into the tortilla held in the other hand, the garnish is quickly added, and the whole concoction tossed onto the waiting plate, the pineapple slice being added with a flourish.

NOTES

1. Similar costumes are found in parts of Spain.

2. Luís Andrade, "Se levantará un monumento a la china poblana," in Carrasco Puente, ed. *Bibliografía de Catarina de San Juan y de la china poblana.* The *jarabe tapatío* is otherwise known as the "Mexican Hat Dance."

4

The Media

IT WOULD BE AN understatement to say that the modern mass media have been a powerful force in Mexican culture. Their role has always been controversial and yet they have been central to the process of modernization. They have served to unify the country, but they have also subjected it to challenges. On the one hand, radio and television (along with cinema, to a lesser degree) have overcome the isolation of rural provinces, going beyond local and regional concerns. They have armed vast numbers of citizens with a set of common issues that have fostered an almost mythological sense of shared identity. On the other hand, the growing national mass media network has facilitated the penetration into Mexico of foreign styles and ideas, of individualism and consumerism. Bluntly speaking, the media have helped make possible the cultural imperialism of Hollywood and other U.S. industries.

It has been suggested that the mass media are promulgators of an "official mythology." (Monsiváis, *Del rancho al internet*. See also Monsiváis and Bonfil, *A traves del espejo*, 49–97.) They often celebrate traditional customs, and do so by using the quaint and colorful discourse of sentimental nationalism; yet these are the very things that one expects the media to render obsolete. The Mexican media have played a paternalistic, quasi-religious role in providing Mexico with a reassuring means of self-identification. The result, as Monsiváis sees it, is that Mexicans may accept as their own the stereotypical images that radio and television ceaselessly mock and yet surreptitiously enshrine. Thus we arrive at the paradoxical situation in which a prosperous, worldly elite is the most staunch defender of traditional mores and picturesque local color, even though these are things that the members of the elite never actually experience for themselves. Meanwhile, those on the margins abandon the traditional life—witness the massive domestic and international migrations, or the very effective exploitation of new electronic and digital communications networks by the leaders of the Indian rebels in remote Chiapas jungles.

Mexico can boast of having had the first periodicals, as well as the first daily newspaper in the New World. Radio came early to Mexico, too, and established a strong foothold. And Mexico was a pioneer in early experimental television, becoming the sixth country in the world to have formal broadcasts. All the same, the mass media have been limited by many of the structural weaknesses and contradictions that have affected the rest of Latin America. Though the media came to Mexico, as to the rest of Latin America, at about the same time as they did to Europe and North America, their importance, their development, and their functions have depended on politics and on social factors such as levels of education and literacy. In print media, Mexico still lags behind some other Latin American countries (such as Argentina and Chile), where literacy and affluence are more broadly based.

Even now, the operation of the media is colored by antiquated practices inherited from the colonial period: centralism, authoritarianism, patronage, the cult of personality, corruption, and collusion. While some observers suggest that the press is free and critically more independent than in almost any other Latin American country, it still obeys an unwritten set of complex strictures. In both radio and television a highly efficient apparatus of control is carefully disguised behind a shiny veneer of open access and competition. The Peruvian author Mario Vargas Llosa once characterized the Mexican post-Revolutionary political machine as a "perfect dictatorship" because it had such an effective democratic appearance. Extending that idea, one might say that the Mexican media world, whose radio and television production are so dominated by the Azcárraga empire, has well nigh been a perfect monopoly.

Viewed against a background of dependency and underdevelopment, print media have been fiery, combative, and partisan. It was in print that political and intellectual elites debated ideas that led to independence from Spain, the birth of the Revolution, and, most recently, the 2000 transition from one-party rule to a more truly participatory democracy.[1] But, in contrast to most Western European countries and the United States, where the processes of nation building and modernization are linked to the growth of print as a mass medium, in Mexico even today printed matter has not really reached the masses. Reading magazines and newspapers has always been a minority activity; formal education has spread slowly, and as late as 1950 the level of literacy stood at only 50 percent. That said, it is to the print media that the powerful elite pays closest attention, and it is print media that have historically been the most carefully controlled and harshly censored.

Radio and television, in contrast, have been truly mass media, and despite their greater reach and influence have been subjected to less explicit vigilance by government authorities. This is largely due to the fact that, whereas print arose in the wake of independence when the political and intellectual elites were fighting for change, the appearance of radio and television coincided with the consolidation of the post-Revolutionary political apparatus. In other words, radio and television came at a time when clearly it was in the mutual interest of political leaders and media entrepreneurs to establish working relationships based on complicity. The media magnate Emilio Azcárraga once famously and frankly declared that "we are part of the system" (see Trejo Delarbe, 84).

Media development and production involves a complex and very Mexican mixture of antagonism and compliance among foreign (U.S.) corporate and government interests, powerful Mexican media entrepreneurs, the Mexican government, and (to a much lesser extent) Mexican audiences and leaders of public opinion. A thick layer of populist, even socialist, rhetoric hides a structure that is basically capitalist and authoritarian. The system is not easily fathomed from the outside, and even within Mexico it has had contradictory interpretations. Intellectual critics may denounce the lack of government involvement to ensure competition and public access, while at the same time decrying the omnipotent hand of covert government intervention. The system is sometimes denounced as a pawn of Hollywood and foreign interests; yet it has effectively defended the cause of Mexican cultural sovereignty and made possible the creation of a powerful Mexican media empire that in many respects has successfully resisted U.S. control. In this, as in other things, Mexico has a unique position among the Latin American nations, being both beneficiary and victim of its proximity to the United States. To a significant degree Mexico has successfully assimilated and adapted the styles and forms of the U.S. mass media and, to some extent, it has turned these into weapons of self-defense. In fact, Mexico has exerted its own media dominance, its own form of cultural imperialism, in the rest of Spanish-speaking Latin America (and increasingly it does so in the Hispanic United States).

JOURNALISM IN COLONIAL TIMES

In keeping with its role as the principal seat of Spanish authority in the Americas, Mexico not only had the first printing press, but also the first newspapers in the New World. Although the spreading of news obviously predates colonial times, Francisco González can be considered the modern journalist's earliest relative. He is the first official town crier about whom we have some information. Not unlike today's journalists in Mexico, González's principal charge, in 1524 and 1525, was to broadcast the official edicts and pronouncements of the Mexico City town council. As for the printed word, Juan Pablos (whose name still graces a publishing house) was the first to publish European-language texts in New World; he obtained permission to import and operate New Spain's first printing press in 1539. Other printing presses slowly followed: in Puebla by 1640, but in Oaxaca not until 1720, and then, in more rapid succession, in Guadalajara in 1792, in Veracruz in 1794, and in Mérida in 1813. These dates reflect the strict control that the central authorities of church and state exercised, for the most part successfully, over the printed word. But the rising tide of news and public opinion could never be completely stemmed, certainly not as transmitted by word of mouth, or even entirely in its various written forms. Throughout the colonial period, and particularly as the push for independence from Spain gained force, colonial authorities issued edicts and imposed increasingly severe penalties in an attempt to put an end to the popular and satirical anonymous broadsides—*pasquines*—that would surface overnight, pasted onto public walls. Often these took the form of ingenious poems or epigrams, laced with double meanings, colorful gossip, and cutting allusions to local authorities. Far more than any official pronouncements, these satirical broadsides became an important precursor of the often personalized and wildly partisan liberal press that criollo intellectuals would unleash in the nineteenth century.

Soon after the arrival of the printing press, it became common to print occasional news sheets and flyers (*hojas volantes*), after the European fashion. At first many had a narrative flavor. They carried international as well as local and regional news, and dealt especially with official, civic, religious, and military events, as well as providing accounts of more lively scandals, horrors, and acts of sacrilege. Clearly, they had a vital function at a time when news and contact with the wider world were hard to come by. The earliest example we have of an hoja volante from New Spain presents accounts, some of them eyewitness, of a terrible earthquake that occurred in Guatemala in 1541.

Starting in 1666, these occasional news sheets became more frequent and were called *gacetas* (gazettes). The first gaceta known to have been produced in a numbered series started in Puebla in 1667. A trend toward more or less regular installments culminated in what is considered to be the first true newspaper in the New World, the *Gaceta de México y Noticias de la Nueva España*. This ran to six consecutive monthly issues, comprising some eight pages each, and earned for its editor, Juan Ignacio de Castorena y Ursúa, a reputation as the father of Mexican journalism. The precedent that Castorena established was followed and refined by the editor of the second *Gaceta de México,* Father Juan Francisco Sahagún de Arévalo. This newspaper appeared monthly, between 1728 and 1739, as licensed by the viceroyalty. After a two-year hiatus occasioned by a shortage of newsprint, Sahagún resumed publication in 1742 under a new title, *Mercurio de México,* but the undertaking did not last beyond the end of that year. The third and final colonial version of the *Gaceta de México* was not launched until 1784, and its editor was Manuel Antonio Valdés.

Each successive incarnation of the *Gaceta de México* brought refinements in terms of its gathering, selection, organization, and timely presentation of the news. But all three had a common format, and they all espoused the same ideas regarding the nature and purpose of the news. All three concerned themselves with the past as much as the present. They set out to document the achievements of their times for the benefit of posterity, as indicated by the fact that they were invariably indexed and bound into annual volumes. All three *Gacetas* were emulating their counterparts in Europe, trying to display their own cultural refinement and show pride in America's novelty and newsworthiness. All the editors were criollos, none was a peninsular, but all three drew their international news primarily from newspapers that had been printed in Spain, with the inevitable time lag that this implied. For local and regional news coverage, beyond the accounts of strange and colorful incidents, these papers focused on official news of civic, military, and especially religious events. They covered ceremonies celebrating the arrival from Spain of new colonial officials, news of continuing pacifications and indoctrinations of the indigenous population, baptisms and miracles and ecclesiastical martyrdoms and canonizations, inaugurations of architectural monuments, and official proclamations. Rarely was the news organized into any kind of hierarchy of importance; it tended to be grouped according to geography. And always, the function was purely informative, with nothing like what we would expect today by way of contextualization or expression of political opinion. These colonial journalists were essentially bureaucrats whose task was to feed a passive populace that was subject to virtually absolute church and state authority. If anything, this subordination of the colonial press to the state's authority became even more pronounced as the end of colonial rule approached. In fact, between 1810 and 1821, Valdés's *Gaceta de México* became the *Gaceta del Gobierno.* Though a dramatic change took place in the nineteenth century, the influence of the colonial inheritance on the Mexican press is still felt nowadays; today, *gacetilla* is the word used to describe reporting controlled by under-the-table payments by the government.

The First Daily Paper

Mexico's first modern-style daily newspaper appeared in 1805, when Carlos María de Bustamante and Jacobo de Villaurrutia received permission to publish the *Diario de México.* The *Diario* did much to help shepherd the country through the transition from a closed, colonial society, to a newly enlightened, more populist one. Though much shorter lived than its competitors the *Gacetas,* the *Diario* survived as long as it did (twelve years) because it acquiesced to the constraints of colonial authority. The editors declared their intention of following the laws of decorum, they steered clear of attacks on prominent figures of authority, and they avoided matters of politics. (In any case, only the official *Gaceta del Gobierno* had access to real information on such matters.) Though the editors' sympathies, when legible between the lines, often appeared to lie with the independence-minded criollo elite, rarely did the paper have significant coverage of the uprisings that were being led by the likes of Hidalgo and Morelos. Yet the *Diario,* with its ephemeral four-page daily issues, did provide immediate and practical information, enlightenment, and entertainment for a broad-based readership, not only for the criollo elite. As the paper itself declared, it sought to inspire the habit of reading (and writing) to foster open communication. It opened up its pages to contributions by aspiring poets, politicians, journalists, and historians who previously had had no outlet for expression. Frequently, the editors were swamped with material. Most of the paper's articles went under pseudonyms, initials, or anagrams; from the safety provided by such anonymity, and for the first time in Mexico, the *Diario* carried critical analyses and commentaries on various social and economic issues. Arguably, its miscellaneous section made it Mexico's first significant literary publication. The *Diario de México* stands halfway between the safe, historically conscious *Gacetas* of the colonial period, and the rampantly partisan press of the nineteenth century. In certain respects, it set a standard for the objective transmission of useful public information that would not again be duplicated until the emergence of the fully industrialized press, toward the end of the nineteenth century.

THE NINETEENTH CENTURY

Low levels of general education and literacy continued to limit the audience, and consequently the impact, of the printed word throughout the nineteenth century. But the times were ebullient, intoxicated, chaotic, and uncertain ones, as the press raced to catch up with the freedom of expression enjoyed by Europeans and other North Americans. Throughout at least the first two thirds of the century, censorship alternated with a militant and libelous press and on occasions even seemed to inspire it. Governments came and went as if on an endlessly revolving carousel, conservative and liberal journalists did battle, and allegiances among the various factions seemed to change as quickly as the political landscape.

As in politics, a free-for-all in journalism followed the withering of Spanish control; after 300 years of paternalistic rule, Mexico was ill-prepared suddenly to run itself as a modern republic. When the presses were liberated by independence, it was as if the children (that is to say the criollo elite) had been turned loose in the candy store. Newspapers proliferated, in the capital as well as in the provinces, most proving short-lived victims of the constantly shifting political tides. From the colonial extreme in which political analysis and commentary in the press were essentially taboo, the pendulum had suddenly swung to the opposite extreme; journalism became ideological and polemic, and it was often laced with the most rabid and unsubstantiated rumors and personal attacks. Harsh censorship often resulted, newspapers were summarily shut down, editors heavily fined, and journalists jailed. But the fact was that once the principles of freedom of expression and self-government had been established, the players and the fields of information multiplied so rapidly that it was rarely possible for governments, whose own existence was at best precarious, to exercise anything but partial control. Judged by modern journalistic ideals of objective analysis and well-substantiated reporting, the nineteenth century was not a high point in Mexican journalism. Still, perhaps at no other time in Mexican history has freedom of expression been less proscribed. Newspapers and magazines in the nineteenth century provided the principal forum in which intellectual leaders and major criollo and mestizo statesmen debated the destiny of the nation, albeit largely among themselves and absent the participation of the masses.

The principle of equal access to a free press, of course, went hand in glove with the overthrow of the colonial regime. Consider the fact that, when his ragtag army took control of the regional capital of Guadalajara in late 1810, Father Miguel Hidalgo, the first and perhaps the most radical campaigner for independence, immediately founded the aptly named *El Despertador Americano* (*The American Awakener*). Just seven issues appeared before Guadalajara was retaken by troops loyal to the viceroyalty, and the paper shut down and issues confiscated. Before its demise it achieved circulation figures that were unprecedented, of as many as 2,000 copies per issue. *El Despertador Americano* was just the first and most famous of several upstart newspaper ventures that championed the cause for independence from Spain. In support of the insurrection led by José María Morelos, liberal theologian José María Cos founded the weekly *Ilustrador Nacional* (*National Enlightener*) in 1812. The paper's appearance immediately provoked the wrath of the Spanish viceroy, but even before it was shut down, Cos had helped launch another insurgent periodical, the biweekly *Ilustrador Americano,* which lasted a year. It also came under attack by the Spanish colonial authorities. Cos's collaborator, another prominent intellectual author of independence, Andrés Quintana Roo, also produced his own insurgent publication, the weekly *Semanario Patriótico Americano,* in whose pages the writings of the rebel priest Fray Servando Teresa de Mier found a home.

Intellectuals loyal to Spain, encouraged by government authorities, responded with newspapers supporting the royalist cause, such as the *Verdadero Ilustrador Americano* (*The True American Enlightener*). Though in 1812 Spain proclaimed the freedom of the press throughout the colonies, this had little practical effect. However, the proclamation did inspire audacious intellectuals to undertake new journalistic ventures, many in Mexico's capital, and many more that became the first independent newspapers to appear in the provinces, such as the *Despertador de Michoacán,* the *Correo Americano del Sur* in Oaxaca, the *Gaceta del Gobierno Americano en el Departamento del Norte* in Guanajuato, and *El Misceláneo* in Yucatán. Indeed, it was a newspaper from the provinces, Puebla's *La Abeja Poblana,* that in 1920 dared to print the crucial Plan de Iguala, Agustín de Itúrbide's manifesto outlining the path that would finally lead to independence.

Without doubt the most significant and famous of the enlightened liberal reformers was José Joaquín Fernández de Lizardi, commonly considered to be the author of the first fully fledged novel produced in Spanish America (*El Periquillo Sarniento,* 1816/1831). Fernández de Lizardi launched the first of his numerous journalistic endeavors in 1812, employing what would become his universally recognized pseudonym, *El pensador mexicano* (The Mexican Reflector) for its title. The paper continued to be published, but softened the tone of its criticisms of the viceroyalty after Fernández de Lizardi was jailed; he was finally released by a new viceroy in 1814, having served a six-month sentence. Fernández de Lizardi was a prolific editor and author, but as so much of this work was anonymous or produced under a pseudonym, and so sketchy is the historical record of periodical publications of this period, that historians still argue about the authorship of several of them. It is presumed that Lizardi first turned to the novel because he thought it less readily censurable. He advocated freedom of expression, religious tolerance, the growth of industry and the arts, and the more effective and egalitarian administration of education, the economy, and social relations. When independence finally came, Fernández de Lizardi at first supported Itúrbide's so-called empire, but soon he became disenchanted with the suppression of the Constitutional Congress and of dissidents, and many of his writings foreshadowed the empire's downfall.

In the nineteenth century, Mexico's leading statesmen were also men of letters. While they were members of a cultural and economic elite, they were not men of exclusively European stock. Two of the leading political figures of the time, Benito Juárez and Porfirio Díaz, as well as two of the leading literary and intellectual figures, Ignacio Ramírez and Ignacio M. Altamirano, were "Hispanicized" individuals from provincial families, and of Indian blood.[2] Díaz, for example, who was predominantly Indian, was arguably the most Francophile, the most Europeanized, of all of Mexico's modern political leaders, in certain attitudes even more European than Maximilian of Hapsburg, the monarch imported into Mexico during the French intervention. This demonstrates that, while racial prejudices certainly have existed in Mexico, there has also been a strong tradition of openness to cooperation and assimilation among criollos, mestizos, and Indians (at least those of a certain nobility).

Magazines and newspapers, after the European fashion, proliferated in the early- and mid-nineteenth century, with the unleashing of pent-up passions made possible by independence. Besides providing a relatively stable and reliable source of news and information, newspapers and magazines took on the larger task of modernizing the country and bringing it in step with the outside world, of educating and enlightening the populace. Newspapers were the major, often the only, forum available for public debate and literary, cultural, and academic expression. Furthermore, most literary works, before they appeared in book form—if they appeared at all in book form—came out in serialized installments. In the capital, the press was dominated by a relatively small circle of journalists and intellectuals, who often wrote simultaneously for competing publications, under a variety of well-known and widely recognized pseudonyms. To judge by the print runs that are known, these men argued and exchanged ideas mostly among themselves, though the readership was constantly growing. Countless small and short-lived pamphlets, flyers, occasional papers, and newspapers arose and fell. They served the interests of particular parties, factions, or splinter groups in a chaotic and constantly changing political environment. Over the course of the nineteenth century, journalism was a means of defining the new nation's image.

Illustrated magazines at first took the form of miscellanies that were ostensibly addressed to women—as most radio and television programming would be—but the material was invariably penned by men. They provided light instruction in morals and manners, and sketches of customs and traditions, in the Romantic, costumbrista spirit, with an implicit message that all things Mexican were worthy of literary portrayal. Early, popular examples of such publications, sold by subscription, included the *Calendario de las Señoritas Mexicanas* (1838–41), and the *Semanario de las Señoritas Mexicanas* (1841–42). Eventually, such magazines evolved towards more serious-minded publications, no longer addressed solely to a female audience, and they combined literary and scientific texts; such is the case with the *Revista Científica y Literaria* (1845–46), and *La Ilustración Mexicana* (1851–55). At times when censorship became harsh and allegiances were shifting, these apparently innocuous magazines served as important outlets for the creative energies of journalists and intellectuals.

As for the newspapers of the mid-nineteenth century, two stood out far above the rest for their popularity, durability, comprehensiveness, and reliability. *El Siglo XIX* and *El Monitor Republicano* were both mouthpieces for liberal ideologues, though the particular faction they served, and their degree of openness to more conservative writers, changed over time. *El Siglo XIX*, published in Mexico City and the more consistently liberal of the two, was the brainchild of Ignacio Cumplido but it is most closely associated with its longtime, if intermittent, editor Francisco Zarco. Zarco launched many other mostly ephemeral ventures over the course of his long career, from the satirical *Las Cosquillas* (*Tickles*) to the ideological *El Demócrata*. He was perhaps the most renowned professional journalist of nineteenth century Mexico, a man who excelled at passionate editorial writing, reporting, and lighter sketches of local color. *El Siglo XIX* first appeared on October 8, 1841—during the second period of rule by Santa Anna, of whom the paper was often openly critical—and with a few hiatuses it was published until 1896. *El Monitor Republicano,* launched in 1844 by Vicente García Torres, was the other major daily newspaper of the middle of the nineteenth century. All the famous liberal authors and journalists of the time, as well as many of the conservatives, wrote for these two papers.

Most of the small and regional newspapers that managed to stay afloat were of a liberal, federalist persuasion, but the conservatives, who favored centralism and monarchy, also had their editorial outlets. The most important of these was probably *El Tiempo,* edited by the powerful, conservative ideologue don Lucas Alamán. Others included *El Católico* and the *El Universal,* a title that would last into the next century. Alamán was reputedly an important influence in the creation of the Lares Law, brought in under Santa Anna's last government, in 1853; this law provided for the most oppressive restrictions on press freedom that Mexico had ever seen. Other laws, the Leyes de Reforma (Reform Laws, 1856 and 1857), generated one of the most fierce ideological debates ever seen in the Mexican press. *El Siglo XIX,* among many others, defended the liberal ideals that included freedom of expression and separation of church and state, while the weekly *La Cruz* (*The Cross*) eloquently argued the conservative case. *El Monitor Republicano,* for its part, did some rather astonishing ideological about-faces, but to its credit it opened its pages to editorial opinions of all sorts.

Following the North American invasion of 1847–48, Mexico saw the publication of its first English-language newspaper, *The American Star.* After the war with the United States, the political situation in Mexico was extremely volatile; in response to the triumph of Benito Juárez and the Reform Laws, and the support the liberals received from the United States, the conservatives fixed their sights on potential alliances with European interests. This had predictable consequences for journalism. Small, short-lived, narrowly partisan journals proliferated. The Juárez government, in exile after the French invasion, produced its *Diario del Gobierno de la República Mexicana* in 1863, while Zarco, hidden in Mexico City, produced the underground *Boletín clandestino* in defense of the reform movement; the French interventionist interests were represented by *La Crónica del Ejército Expedicionario,* and a bilingual *Periódico Oficial del Imperio* was published in Spanish and French, eventually to become simply the *Diario del Imperio.* In 1861 the conservatives brought out *La Prensa,* which was concerned primarily with the defense of church interests, while famous liberals in the capital, like Manuel Payno, founded the satirical *El Monarca,* which was poking fun at the European emperor even before his arrival.

With the defeat of the French and the restoration of the liberal republic in 1867, Mexico's political future became more settled, and the press entered a period of refinement, growth, and modernization. There were publications of every conceivable political persuasion, and journalism thrived on vehement partisanship and narrow factionalism; together with personal attacks and impressionistic and anecdotal reporting, there was impassioned ideological criticism. For the next ten to twenty years, Mexican journalism enjoyed one of its periods of greatest freedom, a period in which a vigilant eye was kept on the government in power. Two developments perhaps best characterize journalism during this early period of the restored republic. The first is Manuel Altamirano's literary review *El Renacimiento* (*The Renaissance*) which exemplified the progress made in journalism. The second is the gradual but radical swing in the relationship between leader Porfirio Díaz and the press, which showed how alliances could change and exploitation increase.

With Altamirano's *El Renacimiento,* founded in 1869, cultural journalism took a quantum leap forward; in essence, it was the first magazine in Mexico to be devoted exclusively to intellectual and literary issues, standing above the political fray. Altamirano's intention was to promote a culture of mature and sophisticated literary expression, which he saw as part of the national project of social and political modernization. The fact is that the nationalistic aspect of his program had largely already been achieved, so that his real contribution was an aesthetic one, involving mastery of formal design and refinement of expression. Altamirano secured the collaboration of all of the leading intellectuals and literary figures of the day, both established and upcoming authors, and from all colors of the political spectrum. Without the work of Altamirano and *El Renacimiento,* it is hard to imagine the subsequent appearance of major literary reviews that came to rival the literary quality of their counterparts in Europe—reviews like the *Revista Azul* (1894) and the *Revista Moderna* (1898–1903).

It is ironic, and frequently forgotten, that General Porfirio Díaz originally rose to power thanks in part to the considerable and often vociferous support he received from the liberal press. Later, after his paternalistic, French-flavored style developed during his second term of office (1884–88), he would exercise strict control over the print media, which he effectively co-opted by means of government subsidies. (He thus established a precedent that would be followed after the Revolution and throughout the twentieth century.) By 1885–86 the pressures on independent newspapers were such that few—only three liberal and three conservative papers—dared oppose Díaz's reelection. By 1888, there were 30 official newspapers subsidized by the government, and many more in the provinces. The repression of independent journalism, involving prison and even assassination, led many journalists to flee into exile.

Among the most significant and daring newspapers to stand up in opposition to Díaz were *Regeneración,* and *El Demócrata*. Started in 1893 by a particularly bold group of students, *El Demócrata* is best known for having published excerpts of a novelized account of the Díaz army's violent repression of the Indian rebellion in Tomochic. The government immediately closed the newspaper, and most of the staff were jailed. The Flores Magón brothers associated with *Regeneración* were among the most radical and persistent intellectual precursors of the Mexican Revolution that would finally overthrow the Díaz regime in 1910. They fled into exile in 1903 and restarted *Regeneración* in San Antonio in 1904, later moving it to Saint Louis, Missouri. At its peak, *Regeneración* reached press runs as high as 30,000 copies, most of which were circulated underground in Mexico. But more typically, the majority of Mexican journalists and intellectuals during the Porfiriato had little choice but to suppress their keener critical instincts and remain on the payroll of the official publications of the Díaz regime.[3]

Particularly in the tumultuous, post-independence years of the nineteenth century, newspapers and magazines had been an essential vehicle for discussion and dissemination of liberal ideas. But overall, the printed press's effectiveness as a modernizing agent has been limited. If any silver lining is to be found in its clouded history, it is that it has generated a healthy level of skepticism among Mexicans vis-à-vis what journalists present as the truth.

SINCE THE REVOLUTION

During the Revolution of 1910 the press once again was the means by which ideas were spread, and it served to rally support and maintain morale among politically active members of the population. Once the political situation after the Revolution became relatively stable, the press returned to a familiar pattern of operation; though ostensibly free, it was in fact subject to many subtle and not-so-subtle forms of censorship. If anything, post-Revolutionary behavior vis-à-vis the press resembled the pattern of government-press relations during the immediately preceding Díaz regime—a rather ironic, if unsurprising, turn of events, in that it was precisely that more repressive regime that the Revolution had set out to overthrow.

Today, as throughout the twentieth century, governments maintain control over the press through a complex web of concessions and permissions, and particularly by manipulating what amount to government subsidies, without which few newspapers could survive. The government has monopolized the paper and newsprint industry; in the tradition of the gacetilla; it makes unofficial payments to journalists and newspapers in exchange for the publication of press releases; and it grants or withholds income from advertising through its extensive network of local, state, and federal agencies. The end result has been a largely unspoken but rather transparent culture of collusion, a well-oiled machine in which government control masquerades as self-censorship on the part, of newspaper owners, journalists, and editors. Over the course of the twentieth century the press voiced opposition on many occasions, but for the most part, the major national dailies that emerged in the twentieth century reflected the prevailing ethos and served as vehicles for the powerful.

Two newspapers stand out as the standard-bearers of the twentieth-century press: *El Universal* and *Excelsior.* Founded in their current form in 1916 and 1917, respectively, they can boast today of having the greatest longevity of Mexico's current national dailies. They thus occupy in the twentieth century a position analogous to that of *El Siglo XIX* and *El Monitor Republicano* in the nineteenth. Both were comprehensive newspapers modeled after the modern format employed at the time in major U.S. dailies; and they moved Mexico in the direction of a professionalized industry, with many innovations in typesetting, production, and formatting. Both as well considerably expanded the scope and variety of information provided; they made extensive use of wire services and other sources—including some articles in English—and enlivened their pages with abundant illustrations. For many years the two papers dominated the market and were locked in fierce competition. *Excelsior* generally had the upper hand, in part because of editor Rafael Alducín's ingenuity in marketing and public relations: he is credited with having introduced Mother's Day to Mexico, and he ran promotional contests such as the best photo of a newborn baby, or the best Nativity display.

Excelsior and *El Universal* have gone through several ideological phases and political ups and downs. *El Universal,* according to Fernández Christlieb, made a name for itself as a supporter of Carranza and as a defender of the Allied cause in World War I, a stance which earned it the tacit backing of the American Embassy in Mexico and private U.S. financial support. The paper remained strong financially well into the Alemán administration in the 1940s, but it later declined when faced with new competition from *Novedades*. It has since been revived, thanks to the introduction of modern equipment and more lively formatting; it appears today under the punning slogan, "the news as viewed from left to right."

Excelsior originally rose to prominence as a vehicle of the conservative wing of the Constitutional Assembly of 1917, including the powerful faction from Sonora headed up by presidents-to-be Obregón and Calles. Its express sympathies with the Cristero revolt, however, earned it Calles's disfavor, which precipitated a series of ownership and labor disputes that eventually placed control of the paper under a worker's cooperative in 1932. This precedent of union governance would later also be followed in the creation of *Unomásuno* (1977) and *La Jornada* (1984). *Excelsior* endured through the 1930s, 1940s, and 1950s, sustained by its original reputation. Its second period of prominence came in the late 1960s and 1970s, when it became central to a crucial moment in the history of Mexican journalism.

Each modern Mexican president has established his own style of managing the press. In the early post-Revolutionary years, President Alvaro Obregón is said to have maintained an easy complicity with journalists, thus furthering a kind of old-boy network in government-press relations. Obregón would hold off the record meetings and favor journalists with inside information, and reportedly he relished interviews which gave the appearance of openness but which he carefully controlled by asking and answering his own questions (Reed Torres, 290). This established a precedent for the kind of complicity between the government and the press that has held sway, to a greater or lesser degree, through all subsequent presidencies in the twentieth century. In this relationship, high government officials and the executive branch pay attention to what appears in the newspapers, because they know that journalists are one of the select social groups with the awareness and understanding to evaluate public policy. One could say that government officials and the bureaucracy provide newspapers' primary audience. But at the same time, high government mostly stands back and encourages the appearance of an open press, as long as a certain line is not crossed, first because the government is confident of its control, but mostly because it views journalists and intellectuals as generally quite innocuous, since what they write has so few readers.

In contrast to Obregón's more laissez-faire attitude toward the press, Presidents Calles and Cárdenas were each in different ways primarily responsible for crafting and imposing the post-Revolutionary political machine. Calles attempted to exercise more direct control, while Cárdenas sought to enlist the press, as he did radio, as a vehicle of his more "authentically" Revolutionary program of national socialism. He established the state-owned newsprint monopoly, PIPSA, in 1935. Ever since, PIPSA has served as a double-edged institution; while it has kept newsprint available to editors at subsidized costs, it has often also been a useful tool for the exercise of government control.

One product of this period was *El Nacional,* a daily founded in 1929, originally as *El Nacional Revolucionario,* the official organ of Calles's National Revolutionary Party. Later, under Cárdenas, it was appended more directly to the federal government, and its title was shortened. Ever since, *El Nacional* has endured as a prototypical "paper without readers," reliably uncontroversial, sustained by direct and indirect government subsidies. Its independent Sunday cultural supplement, *La Revista Mexicana de Cultura,* nonetheless, has had many distinguished editors over the years.

For all the control the government exercised over the press, the 1920s, 1930s, and early 1940s were still an ebullient time in which intellectuals of all stripes found hope and inspiration in the cause of the Mexican Revolution. Martín Luis Guzmán, for example, remained a thorn in the government's side and a major conservative force in journalism. In 1920 Guzmán returned from the United States to run the editorial page of *El Heraldo de México,* and he founded the evening paper *El Mundo* in 1922. An opponent of Obregón, Guzmán was exiled once again (this time in Spain) from 1925 to 1936; after his return to Mexico, he directed the political magazine *Tiempo,* founded in 1942.

Younger, avant-garde intellectuals rallied around Vasconcelos, himself the editor of his own intrepid periodical, *La Antorcha* (1924). Led by the charismatic muralists Diego Rivera and David Alfaro Siqueiros, many artists took on the role of the workers' party intellectual. In response to conservative, Catholic periodicals favoring the Cristero Revolt, such as *El País,* they expressed their views through such organs as *El Machete,* founded in 1924. *El Machete* soon became the official newspaper of the Communist Party in Mexico; it had to go underground for a time starting in 1929, but it fared better under the Cárdenas administration, and kept going until 1938. Many of *El Machete's* contributors went on the write for *El Popular,* which was founded in 1938, and originally directed by Vicente Lombardo Toledano as the newspaper of the Confederación Mexicana de Trabajadores (Workers' Confederation).

More cosmopolitan intellectuals came together as a group and produced an outstanding literary review, *Contemporáneos,* which appeared monthly between 1928 and 1931. It picked up and refined the tradition of quality literary periodicals handed down by the late-nineteenth-century *Revista Azul* and the *Revista Moderna.* This tradition would later be continued by *El Hijo Pródigo* and *Tierra Nueva,* to which Octavio Paz contributed, and later by the *Revista Mexicana de Literatura, Cuadernos del Viento, Plural, Vuelta, Nexos,* and, most recently, *Letras Libres.* There have also been cultural extension reviews attached to the two major Mexico City universities: these are the *Revista de la Universidad* and *Casa del Tiempo.* Finally, no discussion of cultural journalism in the early post-Revolutionary years would be complete without recognition of the role played by *El Universal Gráfico.* Launched in 1922, it was possibly the first evening daily newspaper to appear in Latin America. But its real historical importance derived from the intellectual and artistic quality to which it aspired, and its ideological pluralism.

Many of Mexico's major periodical publications had their origins in the first half of the twentieth century; this includes weekly magazines and supplements of long standing, such as the *Revista de Revistas,* first established in 1910, and *Jueves de Excelsior,* which appeared continuously from 1922 to 1996. *Ovaciones,* for its part, broke ground when it appeared in 1947 because it employed a tabloid-like format, and because it specialized in sports reporting and entertainment, addressing itself to a mass audience. Following the example of *El Universal Gráfico,* evening extras and supplemental editions became more popular beginning in the late 1930s and 1940s. The *Excelsior* offshoot *Ultimas Noticias,* for example, launched in 1939, was renowned for reporting the latest news from World War II. In 1962, *Ovaciones* also added a mildly salacious and sensational afternoon edition, featuring a girlie photo; it is reputed to have reached an almost unheard of periodical circulation of 300,000. Today *Ovaciones's* two daily editions are owned and managed by the Televisa media empire.

Two significant national dailies emerged in the 1960s. *El Día,* founded by Enrique Ramírez y Ramírez, is known for its anti-imperialist posture and its support for the more left-leaning factions within the PRI. *El Heraldo de México,* since its revival in 1965, has defended a more conservative, anti-communist and anti-populist position.

The history of *Novedades* exemplifies well the enduring links between politics and print journalism in Mexico. Founded in 1939 by Ignacio Herreras, it soon came to rival *Excelsior* and *El Universal* for prominence among major national dailies. *Novedades* reached its pinnacle of power and political influence in the mid-1940s when, under new editors, it put itself at the service of the presidential campaign of Miguel Alemán. It remained vital throughout the Alemán administration and beyond, under the general editorship of Rómulo O'Farrill, Sr., giving tacit support of the government's pro-business policies. In 1950, the parent company Novedades Editores added *The News* to its burgeoning repertoire of publications, and this is still Mexico's major English-language daily. After the end of Alemán's presidential term, he and O'Farrill became partners, not just in Novedades Editores but also in the growing Mexican tourism industry and in the emerging television industry; in the latter realm they joined forces with the Azcárraga family as partners in the Televisa media empire.

In recent decades, *Novedades* has lost most of its political significance; it is one of the few major dailies that still includes prominent color photos of social events organized by the political and business elite and their children. As with many periodical publications, however, *Novedades*'s Sunday cultural supplement has maintained an independent reputation, through several incarnations, particularly when it was known as *México en la Cultura*, and directed by Fernando Benítez between 1949 and 1961.

Benítez is widely credited with having transformed cultural journalism in contemporary Mexico. He vastly enhanced its effectiveness in the diffusion of the arts and literature, with lively reporting and other promotional events and techniques. For much of the second half of the twentieth century, the most important cultural supplement at any given moment was the one where Benítez and his team were employed: first it was *El Nacional*'s *La Semana en la Cultura*, then *Novedades*, then *La Cultura en México*, which appeared in the political weekly *Siempre*, then the *Unomásuno* supplement entitled *Sábado*, and finally *La Jornada Semanal*.

As a print empire, in the 1960s and 1970s Novedades Editores sought to expand into regional markets, with such offshoots as *Novedades de Acapulco* and *Novedades de Cancún*. But its efforts in this area pale in comparison to the earlier achievements of José García Valseca, who pioneered the print media network in Mexico in the 1940s, 1950s, and 1960s. He remains the only example of a media mogul enthroned exclusively in the realm of Mexican print media; his chain of national and regional publications was wildly successful. A veteran of the Revolution with little formal education, and a remarkable independent entrepreneur (said to be fictionally portrayed in Carlos Fuentes's novel, *The Death of Artemio Cruz*), García Valseca endured many early trials and tribulations in his efforts to break into the newspaper and publishing industry. His fortunes changed dramatically when he decided to print comic books (*historietas*) not on glossy paper but on cheap newsprint. His comics, beginning with *Paquito* (1935) and *Pepín* (1936), were devoured by their marginally literate audiences, with daily circulation figures of some 300,000 copies. With the capital thus accumulated, García Valseca launched *Esto* in 1941, Mexico's first sports daily. García Valseca then turned his attention to the paucity of quality new coverage in Mexico's regional capitals and provinces, producing papers such as *El Fronterizo* in Ciudad Juárez, founded in 1943, and *El Heraldo de Chihuahua* and *El Sol de Puebla* in 1944. Through the 1940s, 1950s, and 1960s, he continued to add a Sun (*Sol*) to regional capitals, and constantly worked to make the distribution of the news more profitable and efficient. When he inaugurated *El Sol de Guadalajara* in 1948, for example, it was said to rival the major national dailies in quality, and it was printing 1 copy daily for every 4 Guadalajara residents (as compared with the rate in Mexico City of 1 copy for every 30). By the late 1960s, the chain was publishing some 37 newspapers that accounted for some 22 percent of the total newspaper circulation in the country. Such independent power and influence, however, apparently became more than the government in Mexico would tolerate; ostensibly because of credit problems, García Valseca was forced to sell his newspaper holdings to the government, which in turn passed them on to other private financial interests.

The *Excelsior* Breakup

Throughout the student demonstrations in 1968 that culminated in the Tlatelolco massacre, *Excelsior,* under the editorship of Julio Scherer García, stood out among all other dailies for its support of the protesters and its criticism of government actions. When Luis Echeverría took over the presidency in 1970, in his effort to rehabilitate the government's fallen public image, he decided to favor the upstart *Excelsior* with exclusive news bulletins and interviews. In retrospect, this prospective alliance of convenience between a spirited newspaper and an authoritarian political machine proved to be volatile. When *Excelsior* went too far in challenging the taboo on personal criticism of the president, and when it had accumulated too many enemies, a coup from within the newspaper's union was orchestrated in 1976. Scherer García was deposed as editor-in-chief and many journalists left with him. Vicente Leñero, for one, has chronicled these events in his nonfictional novel, *Los periodistas* (*The Journalists,* 1976).

The government's role in bringing about the coup is still not publicly acknowledged, but for journalists and intellectuals this incident is a defining moment and a bitter pill to swallow. It did away with any illusions they might have had about full press freedom in Mexico, or of any possible collaboration based in mutual respect between independent journalists and the government. Still, in retrospect, it is possible to suggest that the coup had a silver lining, for when Scherer García and his supporters left, they created two new publications that throughout the 1970s and 1980s admirably championed the cause of a critical press. With one group of banished journalists, Manuel Becerra Acosta set up *Unomásuno,* while Scherer García and others began the political weekly *Proceso,* which ever since has occupied a prominent position in Mexican journalism as a watchdog specializing in investigative reporting. At the same time, *Excelsior's* outstanding literary review, *Plural,* was closed down. Many of its collaborators signed on with its editor, Octavio Paz, and launched a monthly literary magazine called *Vuelta.* Another group, with leanings less toward high art than popular culture, launched the rival cultural and political monthly, *Nexos,* under the leadership first of Carlos Monsiváis and, later, Enrique Florescano and Héctor Aguilar Camín. Since the death of Octavio Paz in 1998, *Vuelta* has been replaced by *Letras Libres,* directed by Enrique Krause. *Nexos* and now *Letras Libres* represent the left and the right political wings of the literary and cultural establishment.

The Mexican press has often provided proof of the country's close relationship with Europe and the United States—indeed, it has frequently been a channel for foreign influence. Besides, there have always been small groups of intellectuals who have been aware of foreign standards of journalism and hoped for a Mexican press that would match them. Before 1900 the press was primarily an instrument by which other institutions achieved their ends; in the twentieth century, however, it began to develop an identity of its own, separate from political, religious, and economic institutions, and the rise in the number of different newspapers in the latter part of the century was of the order of 50 percent.

The Present State of Print Journalism

Unlike other Spanish American countries, where a single newspaper tends to be dominant, Mexico has several. But Mexico could be said to be a land of too many newspapers without readers. Circulations for serious newspapers and magazines are remarkably low, even in light of the estimated 10 percent rate of illiteracy. Newspapers that have had their day manage to survive thanks to political patronage and the aforementioned government subsidies. Serious periodicals in fact compete poorly with adult comics (*historietas* and *fotonovelas*) and mass-marketed magazines tied to the electronic media, such as *Teleguía* (*TV Guide*) and *Vanidades,* and other Spanish-language versions of foreign (U.S.) trade magazines produced by media conglomerates, particularly Televisa. Something like a third of the country's population is concentrated in Mexico City, so it is not surprising that the main national newspapers are based there. Yet in the Mexico City of today, a vast metropolis, only the sports tabloid *Esto* claims a circulation of more than 300,000 copies. The three best national dailies—*Reforma, La Jornada,* and *El Financiero*—each claim to have a circulation of about 130,000. Despite the dominance of newspapers from the capital, the various provinces have their own, among them Monterrey's *El Norte,* the only regional paper to rival the circulation figures of those produced in Mexico City.

Some newspapers, *Excelsior* for example, almost went out of business in the late 1990s, as the old system of government financing began to fall away and readers turned to independent papers. The late twentieth century was a period of change; journalists tried to break with the forms of patronage and graft that had often marred the history of the Mexican press. There had been little communication between journalists in different regions, no overarching body that could bring them together and represent their interests. In fact, the press was marked by ideological and personal feuds, and by insularity. Not that all journalists wanted to see changes made to a system that had provided them with such things as hospitality, free entertainment, and access to prostitutes, besides generous payments if they kept certain stories under wraps. What happened when President Salinas sought to do away with the government's monopolisitic control over the press's access to newsprint is illustrative of these difficulties. The monopoly had been widely criticized as a mechanism of indirect censorship by partisans of greater journalistic independence, but when the change was proposed, journalists and newspaper editors themselves shot the initiative down, for fear that removal of the government subsidy would bring financial collapse and endanger their livelihood.

There has been a rising tide of violence against journalists. The assassination of journalist Manuel Buendía in 1984, gunned down on a Mexico City street, drew renewed attention to the limitations on press freedom. (The director of federal security at the time, José Antonio Zorilla Pérez, was eventually charged and convicted of the crime.) Statistics for 1998 provided by the Fundación Manuel Buendía report 202 incidents of aggression against journalists during that year, ranging from threats to homicide. Most of the threats were directed at political and crime reporters, with the great majority occurring outside of Mexico City.

The difficulties faced by those who were brave enough to speak out against corruption are illustrated by the story of Jesús Blancornelas, who founded a muckraking weekly, *Zeta,* in 1980. In November of 1996 he was about to fly to New York to receive an international press award when he was visited by a Tijuana police chief who warned him that if he did so he would be risking his life. About a year later the prophecy almost came true: a car in which Blancornelas was being driven was ambushed, his bodyguard was killed, and Blancornelas himself was struck by four bullets. He had reason to have a bodyguard; *Zeta* had run stories about corrupt politicians, about the relationship between drug lords and the police, and about killings related to the drug trade. It had also run a story implicating an eminent politician in the murder of the co-founder of *Zeta,* Héctor Félix. In 1987 *Zeta's* offices had been riddled by gunfire.

The Committee to Protect Journalists, based in New York, had chosen to honor Blancornelas, not only in recognition of his achievements as editor of one of Mexico's most independent newspapers, but also to highlight the dramatic transformation that was taking place in the Mexican press. *Zeta* was one of the first Mexican newspapers to challenge the decades-old system of bribes, kickbacks, and distribution of government advertising that had been used by the ruling Institutional Revolutionary Party (PRI) to keep the Mexican press in line. *Zeta* reporters were expressly forbidden to accept gratuities from government officials, and the paper made a concerted effort to cover opposition parties fairly. Ironically, as the quality of journalism improved in Mexico, the risks to journalists increased, as powerful figures, unaccustomed to public scrutiny, lashed out violently.

About three weeks before the attack on Blancornelas and his bodyguard, a workshop entitled "¿Cómo se defiende la libertad de prensa?" ("How Can Freedom of the Press Be Safeguarded?") had taken place in Mexico City. Raymundo Riva Palacio, one of the people who addressed this gathering of about 30 of Mexico's top journalists, pointed out that governments had made a concerted effort to undermine and co-opt any press group that challenged the status quo, yet the press had generally been compliant with the system. "The collusion of the press is so complete that the government does not have to resort to direct censorship to suppress ideas and information," wrote Riva Palacio, "the press cannot bear the idea of unbridled competition" (Orme, 22).

Yet the mechanisms of state control that Riva Palacio described have begun to break down. In the mid-nineties, with the onset of NAFTA, access to information by journalists improved, and there was a lessening of the old corrupt methods of control and a move towards more subtle and modern spin-doctoring. Most observers trace the beginnings of the struggle toward greater journalistic independence back to the Scherer García editorship of *Excelsior* between 1968 and 1976. His tradition has been sustained through the byproducts of the *Excelsior* breakup, most notably by the political weekly *Proceso,* and later by the most respected mainstream organ of Mexico's poltical left, the newspaper *La Jornada. La Jornada's* extensive coverage of the Chiapas rebellion in 1994 gave a notable boost to its circulation figures. Courage and independence have also been shown by local and regional publications, most notably the aforementioned Monterrey daily *El Norte;* it has won numerous prizes for its quality, and it has grown steadily since it was established by members of the Junco de la Vega family in 1922.

1993 saw the founding, by the same Junco de la Vega family, of the national daily *Reforma,* which has also challenged the long-standing system of intimidation and collusion. Indeed, right from the start, it bucked the system, refusing to submit to the traditional, PRI-linked, periodical distribution union, and so having to be hawked by independent vendors on street corners. Yet still its popularity soared. *Reforma,* and a few other papers, have set up a barrier between the business and editorial sides of their operations. For example, *Reforma*'s reporters are not allowed to get advertising from the sources they are reporting, a practice that is common in other newspapers.

By the time President Salinas handed over power to Ernesto Zedillo in late 1994, the very ethos of Mexican journalism had changed. Journalists who once might have tried to make a career by cozying up to powerful politicians now built their reputations on exposés of the latest political scandal. Mexicans had access to dozens of print outlets spanning the ideological spectrum. The new generation of young reporters was better educated, more independent, and more highly paid. (Ironically, Salinas found himself the target of forces he had unwittingly unleashed: an emboldened press published stories accusing the ex-president of everything from corruption to murder.) Mexico's press continued to move toward independence under Zedillo, who seemed to lack both the skills and inclination to manage the media. Also a factor was the near collapse of the Mexican economy in early 1995, which greatly limited the PRI's ability to buy off journalists. The emergence of political competition has further undermined the system, as rival political parties have purged journalists from government payrolls. A real nail in the coffin of the old political system was the midterm election in which the PRI lost its majority control of the Congress and, hence, of the nation's purse strings.

As we have seen, however, freer investigative journalism has brought new risks. Some powerful figures inside and outside the government have come under increased scrutiny and some have reacted violently. The Blancornelas case is illustrative of many like it. For example, the bullet-ridden body of the editor of the weekly *7 Días* was found in his burnt-out car; several months earlier, *7 Días* had published a story on a government investigation of the former secretary of the state of Guerrero, who had been accused of framing his ex-girlfriend on drug charges and ordering the murder of her attorney. While journalists in Guerrero demanded a government investigation into the murder, the case generated little coverage in Mexico City, whose journalists felt isolated from the violence that afflicted the provinces; between 1986 and 1996 ten journalists were murdered in Mexico and only one was from Mexico City. But a series of attacks on Mexico City journalists made it clear that no one was immune to the growing violence. For instance, two reporters for *Reforma* and another for the Mexico City daily *El Universal* were also attacked; all had been reporting on crime or police corruption. A police reporter with the Mexico City magazine *Cómo* was also murdered. Lawlessness had become an overriding concern, but journalists were also being subjected to a proliferation of lawsuits, and Mexico's libel law—written in 1917—which did not allow truth as a defense, granted special protection to public officials.

There is a coda to the story about Blancornelas. While the murders of three Mexican journalists at about the same time had received little attention, the attack on Blancornelas was covered on television and radio and was on the front page of virtually every newspaper in Mexico. This fueled international coverage. In the United States, the Blancornelas attack was covered on national TV news programs as well as in *The New York Times, The Los Angeles Times, The San Diego Union-Tribune,* and on National Public Radio. A public outcry ensued, demonstrating that reporting is an effective defense against an attack on reporting. Mexican authorities, feeling forced to take action, referred the investigation into the attack on Blancornelas to the federal prosecutor's office, which had greater resources, experience, and independence than the state prosecutor who normally handles such investigations. Federal authorities explained they were taking over the case because the crime was committed by a drug cartel, and trafficking is a federal offense. Despite this decision, the fact remains that those responsible for crimes against journalists have rarely been apprehended. In investigating and denouncing corruption, journalists in Mexico do take great risks, but it is also true that protection has increased thanks to freer and wider dissemination of information. The kind of journalism that once set *Zeta* apart is becoming more common in Mexico; bribes are no longer routine, and the press has become more aggressive, professional, and independent.[4]

The Illustrated Press

The readership for printed matter has always been limited by levels of literacy, which explains why illustrated print forms have played so important a role over the history of Mexico. The late-nineteenth and early-twentieth-century engraver José Guadalupe Posada is at the core of this important tradition. In the early decades of the twentieth century, Posada reached a mass audience with his etchings, which used skeleton motifs for satirical purposes, poking fun at the Church and the landowners. Posada's cartoon style influenced artists and cartoonists such as José Clemente Orozco and Miguel Covarrubias. Perhaps no one has done more than Posada to bridge the gap between popular culture and the world of high art, between the visual arts and printed media such as newspapers and magazines.[5] But the tradition itself reaches back at least to early-nineteenth-century forms of illustrated political satire and caricature—perhaps even to the lampoons of colonial days—and it remains strong today in the popular political caricatures of cartoonists such as Rius, and in the still flourishing market for adult cartoon narratives (*historietas* or *fotonovelas*). The exaggerated conventions for portraying emotions that became common in the 1940s under the influence of Disney can be seen in the magazine *Siempre,* in cartoons by Rius (Eduardo García del Río) that ridicule superpower politics. Mexico City magazines, especially the independents, are great masters at using cartoons to satirize the political establishment. Masters of the political cartoon from the ideological left, like Rius and El Fisgón (Rafael Barajas Durán), have even deployed their art in what might be considered a new, and quite entertaining, hybrid form—deft contemporary political analysis brought out by serious publishers such as Grijalbo, but in comic book form. Examples range from Rius's *Marx para principiantes* (1972) to his *El supermercado de las sectas* (1999) and *El sexenio me da risa* (1994) by El Fisgón.

Comics began to appear in Mexico at around the turn of the twentieth century. As early as 1902, U.S. comic strips appeared and within a year the first Mexican one, *Don Lupito,* a humorous strip cartoon by Andrés Audifred. For the next three decades, comics more or less aped U.S. trends and were often simply translations of U.S. originals. The period from the late 1930s through the 1940s was a time when Mexican artists—and not just graphic artists—took a well-tried formula from the United States, Mexicanized it, and watched it take off. Thus, in 1936 Germán Oliver Butze first published the humorous *Los supersabios* (*The Superbrains*) and in the following year Gabriel Vargas brought out *La familia burrón* (*The Donkeyson Family*). Adventure strips became even more popular than humorous ones, and thus was born the comic book in the mid-1930s. Throughout Spanish America, political satire, underground publications, and Marvel superhero comics have flourished since the mid-twentieth century. In the 1950s Manuel de Landa created the mini-comic book; this was a pocket-size comic book that sold at a low price. The most well known mini-comics come from Editorial Argumentos, which publishes Mexico's best-selling romance comic *Lágrimas, risas y amor* (*Tears, Laughter, and Love*). Comic strips are very popular reading material in Mexico.

After comic books, *fotonovelas* (photonovels, or romantic stories told in balloon-captioned pictures) are the most widely distributed printed material in Latin America. Initially they came from Spain to northern parts of Latin America and from Italy to the Southern Cone, where they flourished in the 1950s. With the rise of television there came dual productions of *fotonovelas* and *telenovelas* (soap operas). Mexico now controls much of the market in both Central America and the Caribbean. Mexican photonovels are distributed via a tier system; they go first to major cities, then minor ones, then rural ones in Mexico, then work their way down the Central American isthmus.

According to Cornelia Butler Flora, there are several standard types. The *fotonovela rosa* (pink photonovel) is full of poor, innocent women who face rich, evil women in a struggle for the love of rich, cynical men who are torn between their base instincts (the seductive appeal of the evil, rich female) and their noble ones (marriage to the virtuous, poor heroine). Beginning in the late-1960s, but only becoming the norm by the mid-1970s, there emerged a new version of the photonovel called the *fotonovela suave* (soft photonovel) which, though based on the sort of dilemma found in the pink photonovel, took a less Manichaean, more middle-class view, suggesting that the two options (money versus love, for example) could be reconciled. A third type of photonovel is the *fotonovela roja* (red photonovel) which is more down to earth in theme and orientation than the pink photonovel; middle-class people are hardly seen in the former; in fact, the characters rarely have stable jobs, and they tend to be darker skinned, less well dressed, and from poorer areas. The covers and titles (for example, *Secretos del corazón*) of the fotonovela rosa and the fotonovela suave strike a romantic and tender note. In contrast, the fotonovela roja covers usually feature full-length shots of scantily dressed women, and their titles are more down to earth (for example, *Casos de la vida*). Female sexuality is portrayed as an irresistible temptation to men, leading them into sin and tragedy, and so the roja genre manages to emphasize the importance of keeping on the straight and narrow and at the same time to provide something close to soft-core pornography. It is a genre that tells of violence, family disintegration, and the destructive powers of sexuality, often entailing rape and incest; and it is the best-selling genre. A fourth type is called the *fotonovela picaresca* (picaresque photonovel) and it too exploits sexuality, though more exclusively and overtly, eschewing questions of love. Typically, its story deals with a heroic adolescent whose recently discovered sexual prowess sends women wild. The latter are usually well-endowed and barely clothed, false blondes who are married to older, impotent men; typical titles are *Sexy risas* (*Sexy Laughs*) and *Fiebre de pasiones* (*Fever of Passions*). It is common to find passengers engrossed in their reading on every form of public transportation.

ELECTRONIC MEDIA

The impact of radio and television is greatest where literacy and education have penetrated least; in Mexico, perhaps nothing has so affected the development of the modern nation. What the printed press could not achieve in its almost 500 years of existence, the broadcast media have done in about 70: they have united a diverse population under the banner of nationalism, backed by a set of shared myths, and they have brought Mexico into greater contact with the rest of the world. However, as elsewhere in Latin America, the electronic broadcast media have also favored the intrusion of foreign cultural and commercial influences. Mexico has also used the media for the exercise of its own influence abroad.

Television and radio have a lot in common in terms of their genesis, their development, their structure of ownership and administration, their program content, and their social effects. Both, like cinema, came to prominence in the context of post-Revolutionary nationalism. Both functioned in the service of a state apparatus that, for all its socialist rhetoric, was basically capitalist, authoritarian, and paternalistic. Both were the product of mutually beneficial collaboration by three partners: U.S. corporate and government interests, Mexican entrepreneurs, and Mexican government institutions. Both radio and television emulated the North American model of private investment unfettered, at least on the surface, by government control and regulation. They adapted the U.S. model successfully, introducing programming full of popular, quintessentially Mexican contents. As a result, they served both the desire for profit and the national need to stand up to imperialist cultural domination. Following the U.S. model, they tapped into the same stable of popular stars as the film industry, drawing on the wildly successful world of vaudeville. And finally, both radio and television in Mexico have been dominated from the start by a small group of powerful families—most notably, the Azcárraga family, creators of Televisa media empire. If anything, the concentration of ownership and control of the electronic media have been even more remarkable and pronounced in Mexico than in the United States, no doubt partly because of relatively scarce capital resources.

Radio

Like other new media in the modern era, radio quickly reached Mexico, sparking interest on the part of government officials, entrepreneurs, and international agents eager to exploit its possibilities. The first Mexican radio transmissions took place in 1921, scarcely a year after the inauguration of radio itself. But while the early excitement and fascination were high, it took time to grasp the potential of radio and to provide the infrastructure that was required in order to exploit it. Whereas in the United States some 700 radio stations were already in operation in 1921, in Mexico by 1929 there were only some 15. It was after 1930, with the launching of Emilio Azcárraga Vidaurreta's XEW station, that the mass-media potential was realized.

For practical purposes, radio was officially launched in 1923. Early that year, short-lived experimental stations came on line; later the government authorized the first non-experimental radio stations to be operated; and by the end of 1923 at least four commercial and three public radio stations had begun. Most were in Mexico City, with the remainder scattered throughout the northern provinces and the border region, particularly in Monterrey, where there was a powerful and largely independent entrepreneurial class that had had some success both in resisting challenges of foreign capital from the United States, and in maintaining a degree of autonomy in the face of centralist pressures from Mexico City. It was from this environment that the most powerful family in Mexican radio and telecommunications, the Azcárragas, would emerge. This central and northern dominance of the radio and telecommunications industries established a pattern of uneven access to information, an imbalance that extends to many aspects of Mexican life.

The government established a Department of Radio in 1923. In the early days several branches of the federal government had a hand in the radio industry; in 1923, for example, the Department of Agriculture proposed an extensive network of the transmitters to cover the country with news and meteorological data, a proposal that could not be funded. Also in 1923, the Department of Defense took over an early experimental station, and the Department of Education, of course, was in general actively involved in public radio. Radio aficionados and engineers with technical interests, together with private entrepreneurs, soon organized themselves into clubs to promote their interests: first the Liga de Radiodifusores, soon afterwards the Liga Central Mexicana de Radio. Judging by their public pronouncements and petitions, this group quickly came to represent the interests of private Mexican entrepreneurs; for example, they tried to limit the airtime of government stations. Under the leadership of Azcárraga, these groups would evolve in the late 1930s and 1940s into powerful lobbying organizations: the Asociación Mexicana de Estaciones Radiodifusoras Comerciales (AMERC), and the Cámara Nacional de la Industria de la Radiodifusión (CIR)—to which "y la Televisión" would soon be added, making it CIRT. The interests of the United States were represented by government officials during the 1924 Conferencia Interamericana de Comunicaciones, held in Mexico City. (U.S. incursion into the Mexican market is evident in the existence of CYJ, a station used in the early days by General Electric, primarily for technical experimentation and corporate promotion.) Rivalries between the various interests involved led to regulations governing radio broadcasting known as the Ley de Comunicaciones Eléctricas (1926). Ever since the start, radio has been a mixed medium, the result of serious competition between commercial and noncommercial stations, and it evolved toward a complex and often covert collaboration between the government and powerful private interests.

Because of the considerable capital required to purchase transmitters and other equipment, the earliest commercial stations could be financed only by private entrepreneurs who had accumulated capital in other areas (in Azcárraga's case, the automobile industry) and/or people who had a direct interest in the expansion of the new medium (for example, retail distributors of radio receivers and equipment). There was also collaboration with manufacturers of other consumer goods, both foreign and domestic, manufacturers who were eager to exploit the advertising potential of the new medium, following the U.S. pattern. And finally there was collaboration with capital interests accumulated in related media, particularly newspapers.

The 1920s were also significant for the development of programming. There was a slow evolution of the entertainment formats and genres which would eventually characterize Mexican radio, and which were largely borrowed, talent and all, from popular theatrical reviews. The air was filled with commercial music (at first largely highbrow), commercial advertising (following the North American model), and news programs (indicative of the affiliation with parent companies from the print media). Much like the early cinema, radio's early programs were dominated by transmissions of official events and ceremonies.

Critics of radio and television in Mexico, particularly those on the left, have always complained about the lack or the poor quality of cultural and educational broadcasting, and about the preponderance of commercial, essentially monopolistic, interests. They have ascribed the failures of the system to the turbulence of the post-Revolutionary times in which these industries emerged, and to the purported neglect, shortsightedness, or sheer ineptitude of central governments, which failed to oversee these industries in the public interest. There is some irony in the fact that many of the very critics who decry the stifling hand of governmental censorship also call upon that same government to take control. More scrupulous scholars, however, have argued instead that the facts clearly demonstrate that successive governments did have an active role in shaping the early development of the media. But their measures led to a system thoroughly dominated by a small group of media magnates, closely allied with the interests of the Institutionalized Revolutionary Party (PRI). Mejía Barquera, for example, says that the Obregón- and Calles-controlled governments of the 1920s and early 1930s, in particular, had neither the capital resources nor the know-how and administrative efficiency with which to develop a national communications network that would unify and modernize the nation. Instead, the government tried to use concessions of broadcasting rights and privileges in pursuit of three goals: curtailing the participation by foreign (U.S.) interests (while being careful not to alienate those who were bringing in advertising dollars), encouraging Mexican entrepreneurs, and reinforcing the government's ownership and control of the Mexican airwaves.

Radio took a leap forward with the inauguration in August 1930 of radio station XEW, the property of Emilio Azcárraga Vidaurreta, whose brothers had founded one of the first commercial radio stations in Mexico back in 1923. Suddenly XEW became the most powerful radio station in the Western Hemisphere, with a signal reaching all corners of Mexico (at least those corners where people had radios), but also well beyond the country's borders. This station would become the flagship for the dominant radio network of regional affiliates, and also the seed from which the television giant Televisa would eventually grow. For a long time Televisa would exercise an almost monopolistic control of the Mexican television industry; it would be one of the most successful and influential family-owned media empires in the world.

Azcárraga Vidaurreta, from a family of deft entrepreneurs with links to the Monterrey business elite, had independent capital resources accumulated in other business ventures and international connections that gave him access to further resources. It was the lack of such resources that frustrated and ultimately doomed the Mexican government's ambition of setting up its own national radio network. Significantly, Azcárraga's wealth had been accumulated by exploiting a relationship with U.S. industrial interests, first as a distributor for a Boston footwear manufacturer, and subsequently through a highly successful network of Ford automobile distributorships. His marriage into the Milmo family, which was in control of French banking resources, no doubt contributed further to his privileged financial position. His success was also due to connections with U.S. media networks and other commercial interests. Early on he obtained distribution rights for Mexico from the Victor Co. (soon to be merged into RCA-Victor), and he set up the Mexico Music Company to sell sheet music, phonographs and records, and radio receivers. Azcárraga played off U.S. capital interests against the national and international political interests of Mexico's post-Revolutionary governments, in ways that were beneficial to all parties involved, and most particularly to himself and his burgeoning media empire. As long as he facilitated U.S. access to the Mexican market for electronic equipment and provided a outlet for commercial advertising, U.S. interests were happy to provide him with financial backing and technical assistance. As long as he did not challenge government authority and complied with requirements for public service airtime for government propaganda, and safe, nationalistic entertainment, the government was happy to extend his authorizations and facilitate his near monopoly.

Azcárraga was by no means the only entrepreneur during the Golden Age of Radio in Mexico (roughly 1930 to 1950). Starting in 1930, the number of stations, both commercial and government-run, multiplied dramatically. But Azcárraga's XEW was undoubtedly dominant and, if not always in the vanguard, was quick to poach, mimic, and adapt seductive program formats—such as the musical variety show, radio drama, and serials—from the powerful North American networks. In the early days, no doubt the sheer novelty of the medium was sufficient to ensure a captive audience, but at bottom XEW's longevity as the industry leader must also be ascribed to its successful production of popular programs that managed simultaneously to satisfy the desire of commercial advertisers—U.S. concerns such as Colgate-Palmolive and Proctor and Gamble, and Mexican ones such as those that made beer and cigarettes—to reach large audiences, and to meet the government's requirement of rallying the nation.

In the United States, drama and comedy were common on radio, but in Mexico music set the tone and became the centerpiece of programming, even on some of the noncommercial stations. During primetime, musical programs generally accounted for 70–90 percent of the fare. At least half of the airtime devoted to music was normally given over to Mexican songwriters and performers, with most of the rest devoted to music from other Latin American countries. Rare indeed was attention to musical forms that were fashionable outside the Spanish-speaking world, though there were some notable exceptions, such as Alberto Domínguez's program "Míster Jazz." Non-Azcárraga stations were much more open to foreign forms and performers, indicating, once again, how far he was hand in glove with the government.

Musical performers passed through radio's live musical variety shows on their way to fame and fortune, and many of them had their own shows.[6] Radio plays, both (melo)dramatic and comedic, together with talk shows, generally rounded out the prime time lineup. The theatrical part of all this was soon to evolve into the immensely popular melodramatic serials (*radionovelas*), forerunner of the Mexican television soap operas (*telenovelas*). At first most of these programs were done live, but soon many were taped for distribution to network affiliates across the country and throughout the hemisphere. Following the North American model, many of these programs had permanent commercial sponsors. On station XEW, for example, Vicks VapoRub sponsored the advice and talk show "La Doctora Corazón," while the Mexican cigarette manufacturer El Aguila underwrote the musical variety show "Mi Album Musical." Sample titles of early radionovelas, clearly suggesting their melodramatic bent, include "Secreto de Confesión" ("Confessional Secret"), "Un Angel en el Fango" ("An Angel Amid the Slime"), "Aves sin Nido" ("Birds Without a Nest") and "El Derecho de Nacer" ("The Right to Be Born"). Azcárraga, nothing if not the astute businessman, clearly saw the money to be made in the cost-effective production and distribution of programming, as indicated by the formation in 1941 of the production company Radio Programas de México (RPM), a forerunner of his later television production company. By the mid-1940s, Radio Programas de México had arrangements with almost half of the radio stations in Mexico, and distributed taped programs to affiliates in at least ten other Latin American countries (Hayes, 69–70).

Mexico's Golden Age of Radio corresponded exactly to its Golden Age of Cinema. Throughout the 1930s and 1940s, and well into the 1950s, the allied industries of sheet and recorded music, sound cinema, and radio—all initially drawing on the same talent—operated a revolving door. Azcárraga had a strong hand in all of them. Examples of this symbiosis abound: "Santa," based on the best-selling naturalist novel by Federico Gamboa, was produced as a theater review (1920), as radio drama, and in several film versions; or one could cite the numerous reviews of the ranch comedy variety, such as "Rayando el Sol," which provided direct inspiration for popular film versions of the same name.

Musicians from across the country flocked to the capital city hoping to make their mark. Many of the most successful would continue on to the New York recording studios of the Columbia Broadcasting Corporation and NBC/RCA-Victor (to which the Azcárraga empire was also affiliated). There was a flowering of Mexican popular music of all sorts. More fundamentally, there was codification, standardization, and institutionalization of an official Mexican musical culture, from traditional song forms, to marimba bands and balladeers, to dances such as the jarabes and corridos. Soon to become famous were the mariachi bands, which had previously been a rather unknown, regional phenomenon; they migrated in droves to the capital city from the Jalisco region. Today, of course, largely thanks to the influence of Golden Age radio and cinema, they have become virtually synonymous with Mexican popular music. Of all the popular music types promoted by the new media, two came to dominate radio and movies. One was the Mexican *bolero*, a sentimental, romantic ballad often associated with a legendary brothel musician called Agustín Lara. The other was the *canción ranchera*, which was inextricably associated with the ranch comedy movie genre and mariachi music, and with traditional charro and china poblana regional costumes; its most famous interpreters were Jorge Negrete, Lucha Reyes, Chucho Monge, and Lola Beltrán. Lara's music, even when at its most seductive, was frequently a source of controversy, denounced by conservative sectors of society as un-Mexican and immoral, and held responsible for the death of authentic popular musical traditions. (Ironically, Lara's music would come to be considered a relic of the past under the onslaught, starting in the 1950s, of new international musical fashions like the mambo and the rumba, salsa, and rock and roll.) The canción ranchera, in contrast, worked in the other direction; it tended to comfort and reassure, giving hope to the burgeoning urban masses, making them feel that the music and traditions they had known would endure.

By the late 1930s Azcárraga's radio empire had become the quasi-official representative of Mexico's national interests in broadcasting. This situation must be understood against the background of post-Revolutionary government policy. The 1917 constitution provided protection against foreign interests and encouraged Mexicans to accumulate wealth. Several other key measures adopted by the official bureaucracy sent clear signals to potential media entrepreneurs regarding the government's intention to influence radio content. For example, there were strict prohibitions of political content that might threaten national security. By the 1930s commercial stations were required to carry to 30 minutes per day of government programming, and they had to ensure that a minimum of 25 percent of all music broadcast was typically Mexican. But as we saw earlier, the percentage of Mexican music carried on the major commercial stations usually exceeded this level anyway. In fact, the commercial stations tended to be much more popular and populist, and arguably much more nationalistic, than the more highbrow government stations. The latter would offer concerts by the famous new wave classical composers of post-Revolutionary nationalism, like Carlos Chávez and Silvestre Revueltas, together with poetry recitals and lectures by Mexico's leading intellectuals. When it came down to it, the private sector had more success in modernizing and unifying the country than did the government, for all the latter's nationalistic ideology.

Radio's influence over public tastes and opinion has long since been eclipsed by the mesmerizing power of television, yet it is still a vibrant medium in Mexico, still reaches more people. Indeed, the rise of television breathed new life into Mexican radio; it allowed structures of ownership and control of radio to be freer, and it gave radio an incentive to play a different role in the Mexican media mix. During the 1980s and 1990s, radio enjoyed a significant resurgence, particularly with the popularity of talk shows and news programs. Here was an alternative to the largely homogeneous, apologetic, and discredited television coverage of events such as the Zapatista rebellion in Chiapas and a rash of high-level political assassinations, not to mention the political reforms that swept the country as the century closed.

Television

One cannot but see radio as a kind of proving ground for the media magnates who would come to dominate television and the rest of the electronic mass media in Mexico; it was in radio that they honed their business acumen and flexed their monopolistic muscles, and in radio that they established the parameters of an idiosyncratic media system in which entertainment values and commercial interests have always predominated.

The precedent of radio influenced the development of television in Mexico in virtually every respect. An initial period of vigorous experimentation quickly gave way to pressures for international standardization and to the dominance of U.S. equipment manufacturers. As in radio, a predominantly commercial system emphasizing entertainment took root early on and flourished. This system, again like radio, copied U.S. styles and formats but added a Mexican flavor, was largely Mexican owned, and was staunchly protected by the government. The Mexican industry became powerful throughout the Spanish-speaking world. In television, real diversity of offerings and competition have been even rarer than in radio, and the Azcárraga family has been very dominant.

All the evidence points to the fact that the Mexican government took a much more direct, immediate, and overt interest in the establishment of television than it had radio. The truth, however, is that there was much less to be understood, legislated upon, and decided. By the time the first commercial television station was inaugurated in 1950, the country had already had some 25 years of experience in the establishment and regulation of mass media, and the patterns and structures of ownership and administration, the possibilities and constraints that were in place would essentially be applied to the new medium. As had happened in the case of radio, television was inaugurated with transmissions of major public events. It would then simply transfer the talent and adapt the basic array of programs that had been established in radio: news, sports, talk, and variety shows, and the stock theatrical forms, especially comedy and melodrama (the telenovela).

This does not mean that there was no fanfare and ceremony. In 1947 President Miguel Alemán Valdes announced the creation of a blue-ribbon panel (under the auspices of the Instituto Nacional de Bellas Artes, whose head was the composer Carlos Chávez), and he charged it with studying the different ways in which television networks were taking shape around the world. Mexican television's technical pioneer, Enrique González Camarena, and the prominent intellectual Salvador Novo headed the panel. They focused primarily on the contrast between Great Britain's BBC, a publicly funded system, and the U.S. system, in which the revenues from commercial advertising sustain privately owned networks. Novo favored the British system, while González Camarena threw his considerable weight behind the push for a U.S.-styled system. González Camarena was a precocious technician in the television field. He had begun television experiments with his own equipment as early as 1933. By 1940 he had even patented his own system of color television reception, which he employed for closed-circuit transmissions in Mexico City. He continued his experiments while in the employ of the Azcárraga radio empire as a technical advisor. In 1948, he received authorization to operate his GON-CAM laboratories, and in 1949 he was named technical advisor to the National Commission charged by the Secretaría de Comunicaciones y Obras Públicas with regulating television operations in Mexico. For all González Camarena's efforts, the equipment used for the first commercial television transmission in Mexico, in 1949, was purchased from RCA.

Some scholars suggest that the INBA report commissioned by President Alemán was part of an elaborate series of maneuvers by which Alemán, whose administration was very pro-business and patently unconcerned with any conflict of interests, tried to make sure that his family had a significant financial stake in the new television industry and to curtail the growing and seemingly unstoppable power of the Azcárraga media empire. Several developments would appear to bear this out. The very first authorization to operate a commercial television station in Mexico was handed not to Azcárraga but to Rómulo O'Farril and his son, who had been key but discreet supporters of Alemán's presidential candidacy. (Interestingly enough, the O'Farril family had made its money in the automobile industry, as had Azcárraga originally). And it was Alemán who, as president, had first encouraged and facilitated the O'Farril family's entry into the media: first, with the pro-Alemán newspaper *Novedades,* and subsequently with permission to operate a radio station.

Mexico's first commercial television station, Channel 4, XHTV, was inaugurated on August 31, 1950, with a special musical program transmitted from the Jockey Club of the Hipódromo de las Américas. Among this station's very first major broadcasts there is, perhaps not coincidentally, an address by President Alemán to the nation. Azcárraga Vidaurreta, in the corporate person of Televimex, received the government's third commercial concession, and his XEW-TV, Channel 2, began to broadcast in March 1951. Channel 2's first transmission was of a baseball game from Mexico City. Azcárraga's television studios, in Televicentro, were formally inaugurated on January 12, 1952, with a professional wrestling show; the building has been a landmark ever since.

Television was, of course, costly, so that initially it was slow to develop. Mejía Barquera reports that in 1951 scarcely 5,000 television sets had been sold to Mexican homes, compared with some 10 million in the United States. Though the numbers grew, the competition between the three existing stations proved to be harmful to them: in 1952, radio was attracting some 40 percent of the available advertising revenues in the country, print media some 30 percent, while television won over but a small portion of the rest, in competition with billboards and other forms of direct access to the consumer. Competition for these revenues left the three major commercial stations in difficult financial straits. In response to this, throughout the early 1950s representatives of the three conducted a series of negotiations to explore various merger arrangements. These negotiations culminated in March 1955 with the merger of the three stations into Telesistema Mexicano, S.A. (TSM), jointly owned by the three entrepreneurs, Azcárraga, O'Farril, and González Camarena, but with Azcárraga as president. All three stations moved their operations to Azcárraga's newly constructed Televicentro on the Avenida Chapultepec, resulting in significant savings in infrastructure and overheads. Moreover, the three stations arranged to share the programming for which they previously competed, and to divide up the programming spectrum into three separate menus. Thus, for example, in one of their first such successful programming arrangements, they purchased together the rights to the Second Pan-American Games, held in Mexico City: Azcárraga's Channel 2 took swimming and basketball; O'Farril's Channel 4 took baseball, tennis, and football; while González Camarena's Channel 5 broadcast all of the evening events. Eventually each channel came to address the program needs of a different segment of the market. Channel 5 focused primarily on children's programs, cartoons, and foreign-made action adventure series; Channel 4 specialized in soap operas and foreign feature films; Azcárraga's flagship Channel 2 carried most of the special events, international news, and the best home-grown programs—variety shows, game shows, sitcoms, and dramas—featuring Mexico's stars. Obviously, such an arrangement, in which direct competition was replaced with an efficient pooling of resources and equipment, greatly increased profitability and provided the means and the incentives for accelerated expansion of the industry. With this major merger, and competition effectively eliminated, commercial television in Mexico moved forward by leaps and bounds in the late 1950s and 1960s.

A word should be said about television soap operas, which are immensely popular in Latin America. *Telenovelas,* as they are called, tend to have simple, often black-and-white sociopolitical messages (e.g., landowners are evil, peasants are good); they tend to involve prosperous people and the action tends to take place indoors; they are usually structured around a scene of discovery or revelation in which the main character finds out such things as the true identity of a parent or that he or she is of a higher class than previously thought. A favorite pattern has a protagonist born into one social class, raised in another, and returning to his or her true home. Telenovelas are not often subversive but they do allow space for viewers' dreams and for their voyeuristic instincts. *Rosa salvaje,* which starred Verónica Castro in the 1980s, exemplifies one frequent fantasy element in the telenovelas: that of the young woman from the poorest sectors of Mexico City who marries a gallant socialite after a chance encounter. Mexico has been a major producer and exporter of soap operas, and its formulas have been imitated by other countries, such as Argentina. Mexico's telenovelas often focus on the trials and tribulations of the rich. A highly successful if somewhat atypical example, produced by Televisa, was *Cuna de lobos* (*Cradle of Wolves*). In the late eighties this soap opera was watched by about half the population of the country, the largest audience ever known for a telenovela. When the final episode was transmitted, Mexico City came to a standstill while everyone stayed at home to watch. The number of soap operas broadcast daily on television in Mexico is impressive, and there is even one channel devoted exclusively to them.

Only in 1959 did the government take a direct hand in television production and transmission, with the inauguration of Channel 11. Responsibility for this channel was delegated to a major vocational institution, the Instituto Politécnico Nacional (IPN). From the start, the reach and influence of this station were hampered by a low budget—it has never accepted commercial advertising—and a very weak transmission signal, but over the years it has performed an invaluable public service. In 1969, the station's status and budget were enhanced when its technical operations were assigned to the Secretariat of Communications and Tranportations (Secretaría de Comunicaciones y Transportes), though programming remained under the direction of the IPN. Quality cultural programs were bought from Europe, and the station began production of its own cultural news programs. Even so, the signal remained very weak, barely covering Mexico City. The station's operations were strengthened in 1989, when new regulations allowed the channel to profit from sponsorships by government agencies and private enterprises. With this new source of funding, it became possible to extend the transmission signal to nearby states, and to produce series on history and geography, art and anthropology. For a long time artists and intellectuals in Mexico City have prized the station for the quality of its daily news program "Hoy en la Cultura."

In the 1990s, the government divested itself of its major television holdings, and Channel 11 became one of its last bastions of direct involvement. When the sale of government interests into private hands became imminent, in 1992, many in the intellectual community raised concerns about the future of quality cultural programming. As a concession to them, the VHF Channel 22 was withheld from the sale, and instead transferred to the dominion of the all-encompassing Consejo Nacional para la Cultura y las Artes (National Council for Culture and the Arts). Throughout most of its nearly 10 years of existence, Channel 22 has provided very high quality cultural programs. Its critics' major complaint is that it does not produce enough programs that are truly Mexican, though the fact is that budget limitations compel the station to purchase most of its programs abroad.

The early 1970s had been a time of readjustment and considerable tension, in the national television industry as in all facets of social and political life. In the wake of the 1968 Tlatelolco tragedy, Mexico was faced with far-reaching social unrest and a serious crisis of political legitimacy. Critical decisions were made that would change the face of television in Mexico for the next 20 years. At the very moment (1972) when another major merger in the telecommunications industry was giving rise to a powerful new corporate entity, Televisa, S.A., that further consolidated the Azcárraga family's virtual monopoly of the private television industry, the new administration of President Luis Echeverría challenged the Azcárraga empire, now run largely by son Emilio Azcárraga Milmo, by deciding to bring the government into the television field in a serious way, providing an alternative voice. Now, in contrast to the largely pro-business attitude that had characterized previous administrations, Echeverría's had adopted a much more leftist approach in an attempt to renew and update populist ideals. The government would be socially and culturally more proactive, and try to make Mexico a leader among developing nations. In the aftermath of the events of 1968, Echeverría had hoped to give the government a way of projecting a better image and of responding to the many critics who were arguing that it had abandoned its social, cultural, and educational obligations, had turned over control of the mass media to private interests, and had given free reign to crass commercial products.

First, Echeverría created a new division of the Secretaría de Comunicaciones y Transporte (SCT), to oversee the broadcasting industry. Several commercial programs were censored for excessive violence, and when administration representatives continued to attack the excessive commercialization of television, and its pernicious social effects, rumors of an impending state takeover of the industry became rampant. Though no wholesale nationalization took place, the government did announce in 1972 its purchase of the struggling, independent commercial Channel 13. Shortly thereafter, the Echeverría administration made public an ambitious plan—later known as Televisión de la República Mexicana—to extend government television signals into remote rural areas, particularly in southern Mexico, to which even commercial signals had still not penetrated. Enrique González Pedrero, an emerging intellectual and future PRI politician, was named the first director of Channel 13. His plan was to establish a mixed operation in which major productions could be centralized for efficiency, while opening up the way for local programming that would give a voice to inhabitants of the provinces. Significantly, however, from the very start González Pedrero openly acknowledged that the new government-owned television operations would have to rely on revenues from commercial advertising.

State-owned television in the 1970s did see important advances in the scope and coverage of television signals across the country. By 1976, Televisión de la República Mexicana (TRM) could boast a network of some 100 local stations scattered across the provinces. Channel 13, too, slowly but surely extended its coverage—first to encompass as much as 70 percent of the Mexico City metropolitan area and later extending to 3.8 million homes across 26 Mexican states (*Apuntes* 107, 112). But the investment required to achieve this, together with problems of financial mismanagement, strapped the government's television operations with a debt from which it would never fully recover. As the next 20 years would demonstrate, the enterprise was doomed to fail, because the government had neither the financial resources, nor the technical infrastructure and know-how, nor the administrative skill to efficiently produce and distribute its own television programs.

With the arrival of the new administration of President López Portillo in 1976, government administration of the mass media underwent a wholesale revision. Channel 13 was placed more directly under the executive branch, in the Secretaría de Gobernación, and a new regulatory entity, the Dirección de Radio, Televisión, y Cinematografía (RTC) was created, with the president's sister, Margarita López Portillo, installed as director. During her tenure the government's shepherding of the mass media and cultural industries foundered miserably. Programming on the government stations suffered from erratic policy making, and ranged from fairly traditional cultural and educational fare, transmitted mostly over the local and regional networks, to the kind of commercial fare that predominated on the major commercial channels. The object of the latter was to draw audiences away from Televisa, but the attempt failed. Some noteworthy programs were developed, such as a game show called *Las trece preguntas del trece*, and particularly the news program *Siete días* which, starting in 1978, was anchored by the popular Televisa personality Joaquín López Dóriga, and which managed to provide a refreshing alternative to the paternalistic omnipresence of Jacobo Zabludovsky and his *24 Horas*. But in general, Channel 13's most successful programs amounted to second-class imitations of Televisa's. Part of the difficulty that Channel 13 had in differentiating its programming arose from the fact that Televisa's own offerings were themselves already thoroughly in tune with the government.

Under the administration of López Portillo's successor, Miguel de la Madrid, the government's television operations were once again thoroughly reorganized, with limited success. The administration of radio, television, and film were separated, and the government's various television enterprises, among which there had frequently been tension, were brought together in 1983 under the umbrella of the Instituto Mexicano de Televisión, or "Imevisión." In an attempt to resolve tensions between the more cultural and educationally oriented programming of the regional network, and the commercial fare of Channel 13 in Mexico City, a new national station, Channel 7, was added to the government lineup in 1985; 70–80 percent of its programming was to be directed toward a wider audience, with sports and popular cultural programs.

Somewhat ironically, perhaps the most significant and enduring legacy of Mexican governments' 20-year venture into commercial television, of the effort to counterbalance Televisa, was that it awakened the media giant to the need to more carefully cultivate its public relations and image, to address its public service commitment and its larger social, cultural, and educational responsibilities.

At the same time that the print media were being transformed by the growing demand for information, Mexican television was experiencing the birth of competition. In 1993, in accordance with its economic liberalization program, the Salinas government sold off state-owned television assets, including a station that went to a businessman named Ricardo Salinas Pliego (no relation). Few observers expected this station, rechristened Televisión Azteca, to pose any real challenge to Televisa. The latter's nightly newscast was the sole source of news for the vast majority of Mexicans, and the news it featured was stale and larded with respectful interviews with prominent politicians. While Televisión Azteca's nightly news program was still favorable to the PRI, it took more risks than Televisa's. Azteca found that its ratings soared when it aired controversial stories, such as an interview with Subcommander Marcos, the charismatic leader of the Chiapas rebels. Within a few years, Televisión Azteca had siphoned off 40 percent of the prime-time audience. Televisa fought back by upgrading its coverage, trying to reinvent itself; Mexico's television war had begun.[7]

Cable television, though it still enters a very limited number of Mexican homes, is a rapidly growing force, and for this it raises increasingly urgent social and cultural concerns. Cable has been available since 1954, but it was not until 1974 that Cablevisión received a formal concession from authorities and permission to operate 12 channels. In Mexico, cable television has targeted only a limited audience; it was focused first on the northern states and along the border, and in the more affluent neighborhoods of Mexico City. In 1991, premium channels were added, and in 1997, the number of basic channels available increased to 33. Cablevisión was launched as a subsidiary of Televisa; in 1995, 49 percent of the stock was acquired by a subsidiary of TELMEX.

During the 1970s, 1980s, and most of the 1990s, cable offerings were composed almost exclusively of English-language programs available in the United States. This naturally fed fears in some quarters related to dramatically increasing penetration by the U.S. and English-language cultural industries, even though access to cable was so limited and costs prohibitive for the majority of the population. Change on the supply side of the industry is so rapid at present, however, that the debate has been transformed before it ever really got started. Increasingly, cable channels such as CNN and Discovery provide original Spanish-language programs, many of them directed at an international rather than a specifically Mexican audience. Cablevisión shares the market in Mexico City with Multivisión, and across the country the technology continues to expand through a number of providers. No doubt the programming, and thus the terms of the critical debate about cable in Mexico, will have shifted several more times before access to cable becomes feasible for the majority of Mexican homes.

A NEW ERA

Though the media, particularly television and radio broadcasters, were biased in favor of the PRI, they were important in the 2000 presidential election. They made a significant contribution toward making the electoral process transparent, by monitoring possible irregularities on election day, and announcing the results of exit polls. Journalists noted, however, that as the race tightened between Fox and PRI candidate Francisco Labastida, Fox's press coverage turned negative while there was support for Labastida. On June 19, the president of the Federal Electoral Institute issued a statement saying that media coverage of presidential candidates was no longer balanced. The election of Vicente Fox (the PAN candidate) to the presidency ended the PRI's 71-year hold on power, a period during which most media had unabashedly supported the regime. Fox's new government quickly pledged that it would respect freedom of the press. Mexico now has an active professional media community, represented by organizations such as the Academia Mexicana de Derechos Humanos (Mexican Academy of Human Rights), the Centro Nacional de Comunicación Social (National Center for Communication Across Society), and the Sociedad de Periodistas (Association of Journalists). The First Mexican Congress on the Right to Information was held late in 2000, and it established the need for a code of ethics devised by journalists, media owners, and representatives of the public.

NOTES

1. Note that one of Vicente Fox's declared aims in coming to power after decades of PRI control was to open up the media to greater competition and freer debate.

2. Racial prejudice exists to this day in many complex and subtle forms—witness the clearly disproportionate and unrepresentative presence of blondes and light-skinned people in Mexican television programs and commercials.

3. It is a commonplace among journalists of our own day to speak of "newspapers without readers" in Mexico, by which they mean papers that to all intents and purposes consist of government advertising and public service announcements.

4. Full details of this and other instances of violence have been documented by the Committee to Protect Journalists and are available at their Web site. *Zeta* takes its name from the final letter of the alphabet. The fact that an actress in the feature film *Traffic* also has that name is surely coincidental, but it is interesting to note that the film gives a picture of precisely the sort of web of corruption that underlies the Blancornelas investigation.

5. The work of Posada is discussed in chapter 8, "Visual Arts."

6. To President Lázaro Cárdenas is attributed the statement that the Mexican people "are profoundly auditory and radio can be a factor of inestimable effectiveness for the integration of a national mentality" (Hayes, 88).

7. The most egregious abuse of the libel laws was perpetrated by Televisión Azteca owner Ricardo Salinas Pliego; he used lawsuits to quash reports linking him to a money-laundering scheme.

5

Cinema

MEXICO HAS A VERY STRONG cinematic tradition. Early attempts at filming coincided with the Revolution of 1910, which supplied dramatic events and larger-than-life figures that seemed to have been made for the movies. A Golden Age came in the 1940s and 1950s, when to speak of movies in Spanish virtually became synonymous with speaking of Mexican movies, and in recent decades, after a period during which production-line, formula films proliferated, there has been a resurgence of creativity and renewed international interest. Ranging from standard B-grade formulas featuring show girls and wrestling superheroes, through melodramas, comedies, and musical shows, to boldly experimental and esoteric art films, Mexican cinema exemplifies every conceivable genre.

Variable quality and rises and falls in international recognition are explained, in part, by the size of Mexico's internal markets and the degree to which its film industry has been autonomous. Despite its ups and downs, Mexico has developed one of the largest infrastructures for film production in the world, one that among Spanish-speaking countries has been rivaled only by Argentina and Spain (and in recent times, Cuba). Even in some of the industry's grimmest years, assembly-line productions have helped satisfy the demands of Hispanic American audiences across the continent. Mexico's ability to provide an authentic Hispanic alternative to dubbed or subtitled Hollywood fare has made it a source of pride, but visibility and influence have also made it an easy target for criticism, and paradoxically have opened it up to charges of engaging in its own kind of cultural imperialism. Much as Hollywood shaped and fed the world's appetite for glamorous images, so Mexican cinema produced a set of stock images, values, and behaviors that Spanish-speaking audiences around the world took to heart.

Cinema has been dependent on foreign models, influence, and investment (largely from Hollywood), but it has also been relatively autonomous. Especially through the first half of the twentieth century, cinema had a crucial role in nation building. The critic Carlos Monsiváis has eloquently summarized some of the many and sometimes contradictory social functions that cinema has had: it has sidestepped barriers of illiteracy and supplanted many traditional functions of the oral culture. For Monsiváis, film has systematically produced approved and sharable versions of reality, ideas as to what nation, family, and society should be. It has destroyed, even while mystifying and enshrining, what once seemed to be immutable traditions; and it has set new models of conduct. It has often criticized the very modernity it had a hand in introducing, favoring the local and the provincial, and offering up to its audiences new and more complex visions of the nation and the world (*A través del espejo*, 67–92).

In the Golden Age of Mexican cinema, there was a remarkable convergence of popular enthusiasm and critical acclaim. In stark contrast, cinema in the contemporary period has most often been characterized by a decisive split between the popular appeal of commercial formula films (and of Hollywood blockbusters), and independent, formally experimental art films. Moreover, it has been the underlying aim of most new cinema in Mexico not to build up but rather to question basic myths of the nation, and to explore alternative ways of being Mexican.

EARLY DEVELOPMENTS: SILENT FILMS, DOCUMENTARIES

Moving pictures became an instant novelty in Mexico when introduced just before the turn of the twentieth century. A U.S. national first brought one of Edison's kinetoscopes to Mexico in 1895, and a Frenchman, Gabriel Vayre, is thought to have established the first projection salon in Mexico City in 1896. Mexican entrepreneurs quickly got in on the action themselves, with equipment purchased from abroad. A keen rivalry arose between the two preeminent Mexican filmmakers of the time, Salvador Toscano Barragán and Enrique Rosas. By 1902, a number of permanent cinemas had been installed in Mexico City, and soon the taste for movies had spread to almost every part of the country.

As happened in other countries, photographers began by filming scenes of daily life and public events. Representative titles from 1896–97 are *Riña de hombres en el Zócalo* (*Men in Scuffle on the Main Square*) and *Rurales mexicanos al galope* (*Rural Police Riding Their Horses*). Early documentary shorts made Mexican audiences aware of their own country, and they brought people and places from Europe and North America to life. Mexico's president at the time, Porfirio Díaz, quickly learned to exploit the new technology for propaganda purposes, using documentary shorts of a sort we might call photo-ops today, such as *El General Díaz paseando por el bosque de Chapultepec (General Díaz on a Stroll Through Chapultepec Park).*

French-made silent features became dominant, in Mexico as elsewhere, at least until 1914, when first Italian and then American-made features moved to the forefront. The first Mexican fictional feature from an original script had its premiere in 1908. *El grito de Dolores (The Cry for Independence at Dolores)* starred and was directed by Felipe de Jesús Haro. It made a valiant attempt at recreating the historical highlights of the struggle for independence; nonetheless, it received some rather harsh reviews that criticized its errors of fact and its convoluted plot, its anachronisms and lack of verisimilitude.

Among the more prolific early entrepreneurs, Salvador Toscano stands out, thanks in part to the efforts of his daughter Carmen Toscano, who in the late 1940s established a film archive in her father's honor and organized a good deal of his documentary footage into a feature-length memoir entitled *Memorias de un mexicano (A Mexican Memoir, 1950)*. This film captures the outbreak of the Revolution against the backdrop of the Díaz regime's modernization initiatives, and the grand celebration Díaz had organized to mark the centennial of Mexican independence. Like many historical documentaries, this film has a huge impact on viewers today, since it offers access to the style and flavor of a time past. At times the scenes surprise one with the triviality of daily life, or the portrayal of prefabricated public rites and rituals, or by self-conscious posing for the camera. Just as often, however, they are overwhelming because of the sheer scale and degree of involvement in public events. Salvador Toscano was heavily involved in all aspects of the industry: he made films, bought films, and exhibited them at his movie salons. He even created some of Mexico's first fiction films. But Toscano's greatest achievement is the extensive documentary footage that he shot throughout his lifetime, only a fraction of which survives today.

The Revolution's photogenic qualities gave much impetus to film production in Mexico. Film technology brought the dramatic events to the attention of moviegoers throughout the world, and gave such vivid and charismatic figures as Pancho Villa unprecedented notoriety. Many people, only half tongue-in-cheek, consider Villa to be Mexico's first true movie star. He may prove to be its most enduring star as well, since one of the more interesting recent films from Mexico, *Entre Pancho Villa y una mujer desnuda,* playfully explores the significance of Villa's film-enhanced legend for Mexican life today. In 1914 Villa in fact signed an exclusive contract with the Mutual Film Corporation of the United States; not only did he give exclusive rights to Mutual to document (and glorify) his exploits, he also agreed to engage in his major battles when the light was good, and even to reenact them for the cameras whenever it had been impossible to capture the originals on film.

Critics have discovered a particular Mexican style and a remarkable narrative complexity in such early newsreel productions as Toscano's film covering President Díaz's *Viaje a Yucatán* (*Trip to the Yucatán*, 1906), and in *La entrevista Díaz-Taft* (*The Díaz-Taft Conference*, 1908), which was shot by the Alva brothers for Enrique Rosas. The crowning achievement of the silent era in Mexican cinema was *El automóvil gris* (*The Grey Automobile*, 1919), directed by Rosas for his company, Azteca Films. This hybrid feature, part fiction, part documentary, reenacted a recent incident, incorporating newsreel footage into its final scenes. Shot at locations where the actual events occurred, *El automóvil gris* reconstructs in 12 serialized episodes an incident in which uniformed Carranza army officials carried out a series of burglaries of urban mansions, using the gray sedan of the movie's title as a getaway vehicle. Against a background of public indignation, several members of the band of criminals were arrested and executed; Rosas incorporated his own documentary footage of their execution. *El automóvil gris,* with its sensational depiction of events, heralded something that was to become characteristic of much of Mexico's early sound cinema: melodrama. *El automóvil gris* was twice re-edited, a soundtrack was added, and it was re-released as a commercial feature, first in 1933 and again in 1937.

THE GENESIS OF THE GOLDEN AGE

At the end of the 1920s, Mexico could hardly claim any major successes in feature film production, but a substantial pool of talent and experience, as well as the makings of a significant infrastructure for film production, had been in the making. Many of the artists and technicians of the Mexican industry had been drawn to Hollywood in the early years, Dolores del Río being the most notorious case. Born of a well-to-do Mexican family and married at 15 to a wealthy lawyer and rancher, del Río was discovered on a visit to Mexico by the American director Edwin Carewe. Presented to the American public as a Spanish, rather than a Mexican, starlet, she starred in some 30 Hollywood films, both silent and sound, before finally appearing in her first Mexican film in 1943.

The advent of the soundtrack, with the new language and culture issues it raised, complicated the international market dominance that Hollywood films had enjoyed throughout the 1920s. Film historians have suggested a

Pedro Armendáriz and Dolores del Río, stars from the Golden Age of Mexican cinema.

number of explanations for Hollywood's less-than-resounding success in Spanish-language productions. Whatever the causes, Hollywood's shortcomings drove the nascent film industry in Mexico to resist foreign dominance and win international recognition. Mexico became a natural outlet for some of the surplus talent Hollywood had trained, from actors and directors to cameramen and stage technicians.

The Russian avant-garde director Sergei Eisenstein was the most famous international film figure to make his way to Mexico in these formative years. Having crossed from Europe to America, Eisenstein eventually arrived in

Mexico by way of Hollywood in 1930, to undertake work on an epic master-piece of the Mexican Revolution, titled *¡Que viva México!* (a title that became *Thunder Over Mexico* in English). Eisenstein himself never saw the project through to final editing (though its status as an unfinished masterpiece has probably enhanced its reputation). But Eisenstein's presence in Mexico clearly stirred up interest in the creative and critical possibilities of the new medium, and his work became a key influence on the films of Emilio Fernández (see below). Such infusions of international talent and influence contributed to a rich artistic and intellectual ferment in the avant-garde and early post-Revo-lutionary 1930s, and not only in cinema.

So much has been made of the classic films of the Mexican Golden Age that one recent trend has been to revive interest in the major precursor films of the 1930s. Though rarely as polished as later efforts, a number of competent fea-ture films were produced in the 1930s. They cover an amazing range of styles, genres, and themes, and they map out basic parameters for the future. One thing that gives the major titles from the 1930s a remarkable freshness is the fact that they were treading on largely uncharted terrain. Since the politics of the 1930s were dominated by the populist presidency of Lázaro Cárdenas, one useful way to categorize the major features of the period is according to their stance, implicit or explicit, vis-à-vis the institutionalized Revolution. A con-siderable group of 1930s films effectively ignored the Revolution, or simply held it as a given or an inconsequential backdrop. Amongst these are the early Mexican adaptations of steamy film noir–type urban melodramas as well as the first examples of a rural genre, the *comedia ranchera.* At one political extreme is *En tiempos de don Porfirio* (*In the Days of don Porfirio,* 1939). This film's nostalgia for the stable hierarchies of pre-Revolutionary days arguably provided some comfort to the sectors of society that felt most threatened by the Cárdenas government's land redistribution and nationalization programs. The opposite extreme is to be found in *Redes* and *Janitzio,* two films that sought directly to explore the rationale behind the Revolution's more radical reforms, particularly those that recognized the role of the Indian and the campesino in Mexico history. These films were the ones most attuned to the populist tenor of the Cárdenas administration's reforms, and they were those most influenced by the presence in Eisenstein and other partisans of the socialist international vanguard. Finally, two outstanding films directed by Fernando de Fuentes, *El compadre Mendoza* and *¡Vámonos con Pancho Villa!,* fall somewhere between the two extremes. While supportive of the ideals of the Revolution, these last two films did not hesitate to criticize its shortcom-ings and limitations, or the hypocrisy and corruption that found their way into its practical implementation. Each of these three types of film had its

counterpart in the prose fiction of the day: the escapist type in the popular, colonialist fictions of Artemio del Valle Arizpe; the *Redes* and *Janitzio* type in the socialist realism of writers like Jorge Ferretis and José Mancisidor; and the Fernando de Fuentes type in the classic novels of the Revolution by Mariano Azuela and Martín Luis Guzmán.

Urban Melodramas

Sound cinema in Mexico was launched with a melodrama titled *Santa* (*Saint,* 1931), directed by Antonio Moreno. It was the second of some six different film versions that have been made of Federico Gamboa's wildly popular novel of the same name, which first appeared in 1902. (Film versions range from a 1918 silent feature, to Paul Leduc's freely adapted *Latino Bar* of 1990.) Its lachrymose story line has become so well known that any schoolchild in Mexico could recite it by heart. While still an innocent country girl, Santa is seduced and dishonored by a soldier. She flees in disgrace to a Mexico City brothel, where she falls for a famous bullfighter and becomes his lover. Victimized as a pawn in the rivalry between her current and former lovers she falls ill and dies. Santa nonetheless has a kind of spiritual redemption thanks to the pure and disinterested devotion of the brothel's blind piano player. *Santa* enshrines a number of key archetypes of the national cinema: the fallen or victimized prostitute who appears as an object, in varying measures, of pity or fascination, of empathy or condescension. Also present in this film is the myth of rural innocence, contrasted with the all-consuming moral decadence found in the urban environment. Though popular commercially, Moreno's *Santa* has rarely been considered an intrinsically meritorious film. It deserves recognition, nonetheless, for single-handedly jump-starting the expansion of the national industry, with the new standards it set for the investment of time, money, and artistic talent. Its stars and its director were all brought back to Mexico from Hollywood, along with Canadian-born cinematographer, Alex Phillips, who thereafter had a long and distinguished Mexican career. The film also enlisted the talent of Mexican musical giants Miguel Lerdo de Tejada and Agustín Lara.

This same international flavor, in both style and personnel, is evident in another, more accomplished urban melodrama from the 1930s, which some consider Mexico's outstanding film of the decade, *La mujer del puerto* (*Woman of the Port,* 1933). Based on a French story, *La mujer del puerto* in a sense takes the *Santa* storyline of the innocent country girl seduced several steps further, through the addition of sordid detail, scandal-enticing incest, and some intense film-noir atmospherics. In a climax in the best melodra-

matic tradition, the protagonist commits suicide in a brothel when she realizes she has unknowingly slept with her brother. The directors were Arcady Boytler and Raphael Sevilla.

The Beginnings of Ranch Comedy

Allá en el Rancho Grande (*Over on the Big Ranch,* 1936), however, was the real milestone. Directed by Fernando de Fuentes, and starring yet another Mexican actor who had made his name in Hollywood (Tito Guizar), it became the prototype of a new and quintessentially Mexican genre, the comedia ranchera (ranch comedy). The film's popularity, at home and abroad, was to prove Mexican cinema's potential for export and drive it to the forefront of Spanish-language filmmaking.

The basic ingredients that *Rancho Grande* establishes are not too difficult to describe, but its immense and immediate popularity are more difficult to explain. It follows a loose, episodic structure, in which song freely substitutes for spoken dialogue. It fills the screen with typical scenes of local color: corrals, cantinas, cockfights, fiestas, and dances. And it populates its world with an inviolable set of stock characters: strong, proud, loyal, and honor-driven men, beautiful and virtuous young women, worldly-wise and tradition-preserving elders. The movie's plot turns on a series of ostensibly class-based, but ultimately superficial, misunderstandings and conflicts of honor. It thus avoids the social tensions that had been sparked by the Revolution and were still very much on the surface during this early post-Revolutionary period. Rather, like the famous gaucho literature which had swept Argentina, the ranch comedy genre extolled an idyllic, even mythical world of shared values, at a time when people were confronted with the onslaught of modernity.

Rancho Grande premiered in 1936 at the elegant Alameda Theater, recently built by the rising media mogul Emilio Azcárraga. But fire damage there cut short the film's initial run, and this is something that has made it more difficult to assess the film's initial reception in Mexico. No doubt exists, however, about the resounding success the film enjoyed internationally—it won Mexican cinema's first significant international prize, in Venice (for Gabriel Figueroa's camera work)—and as a consequence Mexican audiences flocked to the theaters, to discover for themselves what magic the film possessed and to pay homage to its success. To some degree, then, as had occurred with the novel of the Mexican Revolution, it appears that the ranch comedy genre did not truly take hold at home until it had been validated by foreign audiences. Perhaps the crucial revelation that came from *Rancho Grande*'s success was that, no matter how quaintly stereotypical Mexican films turned out to be, Spanish-language audiences preferred authentic Mexican cultural products to

the generic Hispanic productions that were coming from Hollywood. From 1937 to 1939, as overall film production in Mexico steadily increased, approximately half of all films made followed the ranch comedy model. The stock role of the singing charro became the vehicle through which Mexican box-office legends such as Jorge Negrete (1911–1953) rose to fame.

A New Social Consciousness

As with radio, television, and other twentieth-century technologies, Mexican officials often reacted slowly and ineffectively, if not indifferently, to the film medium, leaving the way open for monopolistic exploitation of it. But in the 1930s governments showed interest in the possibilities of film. The Cárdenas government, particularly, saw its potential not just as a revenue producer, but as a means of social and political influence. *Janitzio* (1934) and *Redes* (*Nets*, 1934). The latter, produced under the auspices of the Ministry of Public Education, expressed the new social consciousness that the Revolution in theory represented: an overturning of long-standing injustice and exploitation, a celebration of the common man, and a vindication of the Indian as central to Mexico's national identity. Both films embody the hope, which was widespread in the avant-garde 1930s, that a quality art cinema might develop and serve Revolutionary ends. Both were the work of international teams, and both showed the influence of Eisenstein, with their slow-moving, poetically inspired, and dramatically framed images. *Redes,* shot on location on the Caribbean coast of Veracruz province, employed local villagers as amateur actors and recreated a historical incident involving labor organization, solidarity, and resistance. *Janitzio,* set in the Lake Pátzcuaro region of Michoacán, tends more toward the commercial and melodramatic. It fleshes out a local legend focusing on a young Indian girl whose somewhat misguided efforts to help her people are misunderstood, only earning her repudiation by the villagers, who stone her, after which she is carried off into the sunset by her grief-stricken fiancé. The latter role was played by the young actor, soon-to-be major director, Emilio Fernández. Fernández's classic film *María Candelaria* (1943), in fact, would turn on the same central motif as *Janitzio,* and also be influenced by Eisenstein.

Fernando de Fuentes

Perhaps no one was more surprised by the runaway success of *Allá en el Rancho Grande* than its director, Fernando de Fuentes. Alongside Emilio Fernández, de Fuentes was a prime mover behind the achievements of the Mexican Golden Age. Though in their day they did not attract the same degree of attention as *Allá en el Rancho Grande,* two other films that he directed in the 1930s are more highly regarded by critics. Indeed, it was not *Allá en el Rancho Grande* but *¡Vámonos con Pancho Villa!,* one of the first films produced at the new government-sponsored, state-of-the-art CLASA studios, that was intended by its producers to be Mexico's breakthrough, and for that reason no expense was spared in making it. In the end, the movie's less-than-stellar reception only confirmed the vagaries of Mexican government involvement in the industry; the government supplied trains, equipment, and troops to serve as extras in the film, and yet its own censors rejected de Fuentes's final cut, and imposed a more optimistic conclusion. The losses sustained by the film contributed to CLASA (Cinematográfica Latinoamericana, S.A.) studios' financial difficulties for years to come. Similar in their ideological thrust, *El compadre Mendoza* (1933) and *¡Vámonos con Pancho Villa!* (*Let's Ride with Pancho Villa,* 1935) are a far cry from the apoliticism of the urban melodramas and the ranch comedies, and from the socialist agenda behind the realism of *Redes* and *Janitzio.* What *El compadre* and *Vámonos* bravely offered instead was a new critical realism that plugged into the heritage of the documentary newsreel.

El compadre Mendoza, a film that lay forgotten until critics rediscovered it in the 1960s, delves into the moral dilemmas posed by the Revolution, and it puts on display the crass opportunism and cynicism of the landowning classes (a subject that abounds in the narrative of the Revolution). Mendoza, a hacienda owner, plays off one Revolutionary faction against another, switching his allegiances as best fits his interests. In the process, he betrays the Zapatista general he once befriended and who has saved him from death. The film communicates a number of subtle, yet penetrating, insights, of which the title itself is evidence: *compadre,* besides literally denoting "godfather," more broadly connotes "bosom buddy."

Though a film that audiences of the time evidently did not appreciate, *¡Vámonos con Pancho Villa!* was a monumental undertaking that raised the tradition of the narrative of the Mexican Revolution to a new level. De Fuentes himself was clearly disappointed that its success paled in comparison with the notoriety enjoyed by *Allá en el Rancho Grande. ¡Vámonos con Pancho Villa!* further illustrates the kind of intellectual energy and artistic talent that went into early Mexican cinema. Xavier Villaurrutia, one of the group of writers known as the Contemporáneos (and also one of Mexico's first serious film critics) collaborated on the screenplay, which was adapted from a novel by Rafael Muñoz, while the renowned Mexican composer Silvestre Revueltas contributed the music. Basically, *Vámonos* follows a recurring pattern in narratives of the Revolution. A group of young provincial friends, inspired by the ideals of the Revolution and the charisma of people like Pancho Villa, join a Revolutionary band soon after deserting from the federal army. Little by little the young idealists lose their illusions as they face the harsh, anarchic realities of the Revolution and of those who claim to represent it. De Fuentes's original ending, which remained expunged from all publicly available copies of the movie until 1982, had the legendary Pancho Villa carrying out the mad and vengeful slaughter of an innocent family. Apparently, such an ending treated the icons of the Revolution with too much sacrilege, even for the progressive presidency of Lázaro Cárdenas.

In all, the 1930s are a key period in the development of Mexican cinema. All of the essential ingredients of the Golden Age were put in place. These included an expanding but constantly shifting alliance between the private sector, the state, and foreign investment. Financial support was always susceptible to being sabotaged as one presidential term gave way to another. At the close of the decade, the Mexican industry was on the verge of an era of high achievement, and the films of Emilio Fernández would seem for a time to offer a perfect synthesis of the developments that had taken place in the major films of the 1930s.

Most historians date the beginnings of the Golden Age of Mexican cinema from 1936 or 1938, and from the appearance of *Allá en el Rancho Grande*. It was during the 1940s that the Golden Age reached its peak, while in the two decades that followed, its tried and true formulas lost their luster and the star system decayed. The Golden Age was as much a commercial as an artistic phenomenon. Comedies and melodramas with a recognizably Mexican flavor were produced in sufficient quantity and with sufficient quality and professionalism that the industry was able for a time to approach the unthinkable: to challenge the dominance of Hollywood. Even at the height of World War II (of which, more to follow) Mexican movies never outdid Hollywood films at the box office, but the progress was nonetheless considerable. In 1930 only about 2 percent of the films shown in Mexican theaters had been Mexican, as against some 80 percent that came from Hollywood. By the mid-1940s, Mexico had become the world's largest Spanish-language film producer, its prominence in the international Spanish-language market was unquestionable, and nearly 50 percent of the movies distributed to theaters across the country were Mexican. While the overall quality of Mexican films would quickly diminish, the commercial footing that Mexico established at this time would never quite be lost.

Many factors, both internal and external, account for the rise of Mexican cinema in its Golden Age. Externally, the outbreak of World War II gave a huge boost to the Mexican industry, while reducing Hollywood competition. Since Spain and Argentina aligned with the Axis powers, U.S. producers threw their full support behind Mexico, both indirectly, by curtailing the export of raw film stock to its rivals, and directly, by greatly increasing investment in the Mexican industry. Mexican producers responded by hoisting the banner of the Allied cause and pan-American solidarity. This shows in rather blatant propaganda vehicles such as *La liga de las canciones* (*The League of Songs*, 1942), *Canto a las Américas* (*Song to the Americas*, 1942), and *Cadetes de la naval* (*Naval Cadets*, 1944). It also carries over and echoes in the background of major films such as *Salón México* (1948), in which a Mexican veteran from the war plays an important role.

As for internal factors, beginning in 1940, the institutionalized Revolution turned the presidency over from the radical populist Lázaro Cárdenas to new leaders who, though ever faithful to Revolutionary rhetoric and the corporatist political machine, emphasized modernization and capitalist development. This shift assuaged fears among investors that there might be a full nationalization of the film industry (in 1938 Cárdenas had provoked the wrath of foreign governments and international corporations when he nationalized Mexican oil). A mixed financial structure evolved, in which the initiatives of private producers were encouraged, but also influenced, by the government, through its control of loans from the Banco Nacional Cinematográfico (National Cinema Bank), created in 1942.

The government also maintained some control over the industry through state-controlled unions; these extended to virtually every aspect of society and the economy, including the cultural and artistic realms. A single, state-controlled union (the Sindicato de Trabajadores de la Industria Cinematográfica [STIC]) held sway in the film industry, from 1919 into the 1950s. But the shining stars who emerged during the Golden Age were hardly going to be content with union-scale wages that in effect equated their work with that of lowly technicians and stagehands. Led by Mario Moreno (Cantinflas) and Jorge Negrete, the more prominent actors, directors, and cameramen broke off to form their own union (the Sindicato de Trabajadores de la Producción Cinematográfica [STPC]). This development exposed some of the contradictions underlying the Mexican system. While the government publicly reaffirmed its allegiance to the original workers' party union, behind the scenes it made many concessions to the big-name stars with whom, in any case, the presidents liked to hobnob. Though it protected vested interests, this split within the industry would also prove to be a serious impediment to its continued health and development.

Despite such factors, the Golden Age brought steadily improving production values and strategies and a Mexican replication of the Hollywood system. The industry was able to combine popular appeal with artistic creativity. It also came up with a set of predictable generic formulas. At first these genres were the ranch comedy, the urban melodrama, the Cantinflas vehicle, and the Fernández-Figueroa–style allegory of national history and identity. Later, the *cine de arrabal* (the urban-slum melodrama, or working-class soap opera) and the *cine de ficheras* (the brothel melodrama) would also become immensely popular. Above all, the achievements of the Golden Age were predicated on the successful maintenance of a stable of stars, figures with whom the public could identify but whom it could also set upon a pedestal. There were some good actors, such as Miguel Inclán, but the industry was really sustained by a handful of figures who became revered icons and are still national idols.

Cantinflas was the first Mexican actor to have star appeal, and others were groomed to follow quickly on his heels. The tenor Jorge Negrete excelled in the ranch comedy's singing cowboy role. Dolores del Río and Pedro Armendáriz, in the Fernández-Figueroa films, became a legendary and inseparable team; he was the virtuous, homegrown man for all seasons; she has often been said to embody both the Virgin of Guadalupe and the archetypal Mexican woman—loyal, humble, pure, dignified, and self-effacing to the end. Pedro Infante and María Félix, who were among the last to emerge, became the outstanding national idols. Interestingly enough, each broke to some degree with the dominant, stereotypical Mexican gender roles, if only to reaffirm the norm all the more effectively. María Félix, throughout her career, excelled in the role of the feisty, wild-spirited, even emasculating female, but that only made her final conquest by the man all the more impressive and reaffirming of the gendered pecking order. Pedro Infante exploited working-class roles that entailed showing considerable humility and compassion. So central to the success of Golden Age film was the public's identification with these stars that some observers go so far as to suggest that the premature deaths of Negrete and Infante in the 1950s, rather than being incidental symptons of the Golden Age's decline, were causes of it.

CANTINFLAS

Mario Moreno, better known as Cantinflas, was not only the first Mexican actor to show the kind of star appeal that could draw large audiences to the theater, he also became an industry unto himself, starring in some 50 films over five decades, including some in English during the 1950s. He is still Mexico's most identifiable film figure of all time. The name Cantinflas is derived for an apocope of the phrase "en la cantina inflas" ("you inflate [yourself] in the cantina").

In contrast to the Hollywood apprenticeship of much of the talent that went into the Golden Age, Cantinflas worked his way up through the national ranks and migrated to film from the popular, vaudeville-type tent theaters that traveled the country. He began his film career with a small part in *Ne te engañes, corazón* (1936) and refined his skills in the company of a sidekick called Manuel Medel in two 1937 films directed by Arcady Boytler, films full of local color and patriotic implications, and ranging in tone from the tender to the mildly satirical. In one of these films, *Aguila o sol* (*Heads or Tails*), the two characters produce sketches for a tent show, as if to document the origins of Cantinflas's humor. *Así es mi tierra* (*That's the Way My Home-land Is*), the other film, is something of a spoof of the then recently estab-lished ranch comedy genre. Though none of these early films did particularly well at the box office, Cantinflas's work began to receive favorable critical attention, as evidenced by the quality of the collaborators enticed to con-tribute to his next film, *El signo de la muerte* (*The Sign of Death*, 1939); they included the writer Salvador Novo and the composer Silvestre Revueltas.

Cantinflas's real breakthrough came when he teamed up with veteran film-maker Juan Bustillo Oro for *Ahí está el detalle* (*That's the Thing*, 1940). This film consecrates Cantinflas's brand of humor, as well as the picaresque-style character he adapted from the comic strip *Chupamirto*. He plays a nobody who insinuates himself into a well-to-do household. First he seduces the ser-vant girl and cleans out the patrons' pantry. Later, he pretends to be the wife's long-lost brother, so as to live at the expense of the naive husband. The film concludes with a celebrated scene that finds Cantinflas in court to answer for the death of a local gangster, though since he is innocent of the crime he thinks he is being interrogated about the death of a dog, of which he is guilty.

The resounding success of *Ahí está el detalle* opened the door to comic film-making in Mexico, and through it passed a number of fine comedians. According to the critic Gustavo García, Cantinflas's success is due to his knack for embodying the popular class's own particular style; "What the larger public sought and found in him was, for the first time, to see their strategies for daily survival displayed before their eyes on the big screen" (*Epoca de oro,* 19). Cantinflas made an art of speaking incessantly while say-ing nothing of substance, in recognition of which two new words entered the Mexican lexicon: the verb *cantinflear* and the noun *cantinflada*. His hyperac-tive talk is replete with double meanings and not-so-veiled allusions. Much of his humor, as in the trial scene mentioned above, derives from complications and misunderstandings. He is not the only Mexican with a flair for small talk and the verbal dexterity one needs in order to escape a thorny predicament or turn a situation on its head!

Despite his continuing popularity, after these early films Cantinflas gradu-ally lost his creative and critical edge. In later films he turned away from this cunningly mischievous *peladito* character toward a more ambiguous portrayal of humble and anonymous types from the working classes. This process began with a spoof of the police: *El gendarme desconocido* (*The Unknown Policeman*, 1941). It then ran through a series of gentle and predictable parodies, such as *Soy un prófugo* (*The Escaped Criminal,* 1946), *El supersabio* (*The Genius,* 1948), *Si yo fuera diputado* (*If I Were a Congressman,* 1951), *El extra* (*The Extra,* 1962), *El padrecito* (*The Priest,* 1964), and many more. The fact that his handpicked director, Miguel Delgado, orchestrated virtually every one of his Mexican films from the 1940s through the 1980s did little to save the situation. In the process of going mainstream Cantinflas gained an international reputation but betrayed his original character.

As Cantinflas's humor became more predictable, many came to prefer the more modern comedy of his contemporary and main rival, Germán Valdés (Tin Tan), who got a later start in the cinema, but proved equally prolific. Valdés broke ground with a greaser (*pachuco*) character evocative of the U.S.-Mexico borderlands. His humor, spiced with "Spanglish" and alluding to cross-cultural issues, touched a nerve and captured the flavor of an increasingly important aspect of Mexican experience. Valdés also excelled at a more frank sexual allusiveness, and often appeared surrounded by show girls, for example in *Calabacitas tiernas* (*Tender Pumpkins,* 1948).

EMILIO (EL INDIO) FERNÁNDEZ FUENTES AND GABRIEL FIGUEROA

The year 1933 was a big year for Mexican cinema, marked by the appearance of both a quality urban melodrama, *La mujer del puerto,* and an outstanding political film, *El compadre Mendoza.* But it was 10 years later that Mexican cinema truly came of age. In 1943 Fernando de Fuentes produced his outstanding film adaptation of the Venezuelan author Rómulo Gallegos's classic novel *Doña Bárbara,* starring María Félix in one of her first leading roles. This film showed how the expectations of Mexican cinema had broadened considerably; no longer content to be simply a national phenomenon, it would now aspire to subcontinental, even Pan-American stature, and try to conquer the whole Latin American market. The year 1943 also saw Julio Bracho burst onto the scene with a sophisticated urban melodrama, *Distinto amanecer* (*A Different Dawn*). But the real critical acclaim and notoriety went to two films directed that year by Emilio Fernández, *Flor silvestre* and *María Candelaria.* They swept through Europe and took home several prizes, including a Golden Palm from the first post-war Cannes Festival, in 1946. Fernández was also the first director to develop a significant reputation in the United States, as is corroborated by the invitation he received to collaborate with John Ford on *The Fugitive* (1946).

In the later years of a career that spanned four decades and included some 40 films, Fernández produced some less-than-spectacular efforts and found himself shut out of the industry, but throughout the decade of the 1940s, teamed with the cinematographer Gabriel Figueroa, Fernández defined a distinctive Mexican style of filmmaking. His achievement was to bring together various elements of the outstanding films of the 1930s: the flair for melodramatic seduction of the audience found in, say, *Santa* and *La mujer del puerto;* the critical edge in the treatment of historical and political themes that had been so evident in *El compadre Mendoza* and *¡Vámonos con Pancho Villa!;* and, above all, the lyricism and social didacticism of *Redes* and *Janitzio.*

One could speculate that Fernández's drive was fueled in part by his less-than-secure origins. Born of an Indian mother in the northern state of Coahuila, Emilio "el Indio" Fernández went to California in the 1920s and played small roles in a number of Hollywood films. No doubt his Hollywood sojourn gave him some of the keys to successful feature filmmaking, such as adherence to simple, archetypal, and melodramatic plots. But Fernández returned to Mexico in 1933 determined to create a new cinema made by Mexicans for Mexicans, reflecting Mexican themes and values. One of his films was titled, eloquently enough, *Soy puro mexicano* (*A Mexican Through and Through*, 1942).

Never shy about aggrandizing his own legendary status, Fernández once famously declared that "el cine mexicano soy yo" ("I am Mexican cinema"). With his bravado and his relish for the spotlight, Fernández resembled the muralist Diego Rivera, and indeed in many respects he sought and succeeded in doing with film what Rivera had achieved with paint. Both offered a lyrical vision of epic proportions, one that sought to capture the historical essence of Mexico. Both were steeped in the socialist fervor of the international avant-garde, which in Mexico coincided with the early post-Revolutionary period. Both took inspiration from the ground-breaking work of two highly original Mexican bodies of art from the turn of the century: the satirical engravings of José Guadalupe Posada and the landscapes of Gerardo Murillo (otherwise known as Dr. Atl). On the downside, both Fernández and Rivera have been accused of presenting a highly stylized and idealized, tourist's view of Mexico that bought into the myths of the Revolution and unwittingly served the government's propaganda machine. Nonetheless, both offered a new perspective that put Mexico's Indian heritage in a positive light, celebrated Mexico's mestizo character, and vindicated the common folk for their enduring struggle against exploitation and injustice.

Fernández and his famous cinematographer Gabriel Figueroa drew extensively on so-called native imagery and established a set of stereotypical Mexican images, motifs, and landscapes: deep blue skies dotted with distant, feathery white clouds; barren, seemingly endless horizons punctuated by the dramatic vertical lines of the maguey cactus or a solitary and isolated church tower; dramatic native facial features and human forms set against a backdrop of ancient, pre-Hispanic ruins. In their underlying messages, were these films radical or reactionary? Whatever one concludes, there is no doubt that their techniques were innovative.

Flor silvestre (1943), the Fernández-Figueroa team's first acknowledged masterpiece, combines a melodramatic tale of impossible love with a political drama that captures the essential elements of the Mexican Revolution. Speaking from the narrative present as a widow, Dolores del Río (in her first Mexican movie ever, after many years in Hollywood) tells her son, a young military cadet, the tragic story of the brave and principled father he never knew. The story is told as an extended flashback, and it takes place in a rural area dominated by the patriarch of a large hacienda, where everyone knows everyone else. In its own rather quaint and melodramatic fashion, *Flor silvestre* gives equal time to both the admirable principles of the Revolution and the unfortunate excesses that plagued its execution. Though the film clearly rejects rigid class divisions, it still places the hopes of the nation in the offspring of the land-owning classes.

María Candelaria was even more celebrated than *Flor silvestre,* and it has similar ideological tensions and ambiguities. It rewrites the story told in the 1935 production *Janitzio,* the first Mexican film in which Fernández had a leading role as an actor. It shifts the action to the famous Floating Gardens of Xochimilco, which provide Fernández with an ideal microcosm in which to express symbolically his vision of Mexicanness. (The Floating Gardens, called *chinampas,* were a pre-Hispanic invention, and though today they have been engulfed by the southern expansion of Mexico City, at the time of the film they were still a rural backwater.) The film revives the tragic story of the young Indian peasant woman who is unjustly ostracized by her local community, a plot that betrays the peasants' narrow adherence to traditional mores and their failure to understand the larger structures of power in which their community is enmeshed. Dolores del Río and Pedro Armendáriz once again appear together as the humble yet principled Indian villagers and star-crossed young lovers. The film dramatizes social prejudice, exploitation, and injustice, and it clearly sympathizes with its Indian protagonists. But for many critics this comes at the cost of a rather naive and simplistic representation of the indigenous. Fernández himself was perhaps unaware of the irony involved even in the framing of the film; the young Indian heroine's tragic story is introduced by the very artist whose dishonest and exploitative portrait of her, undertaken because he considered her to represent the essence of Mexican beauty, provoked the scandal which led to her dishonor.

Fernández's other major films from the 1940s are less important than *Flor silvestre* and *María Candelaria,* but they are often more focused in style and ideology, and each highlights a particular aspect of the Fernández-Figueroa team's filmmaking. Most leave behind some of the earlier films' syrupy sentimentalism to branch out in new directions. *Enamorada,* for example, shows Fernández's lighter side. It was the first of many Fernández films that helped make María Félix a star. Playing the daughter of a well-to-do provincial family, she sustains an entertaining tête-à-tête with co-star Pedro Armendáriz, the latter in the role of a slightly coarse, stubborn, and proud Revolutionary, complete with fancy charro outfit. The story develops as a kind of Mexican *Taming of the Shrew,* and in the end María Félix marches off to battle walking behind her man as he rides his horse, acceding patriotically to the popular Revolutionary role of soldadera (female camp follower).

Río Escondido is sometimes criticized for its didacticism, for toeing the party line. It displays the characteristic visual motifs and camera techniques of the Fernández-Figueroa team in perhaps their purest form. María Félix again stars, this time as a young schoolteacher, improbably called upon by the president himself to carry the Revolutionary principle of universal education to the countryside, and to help overcome the dark forces that would impede the progress of the Revolution. As she travels on foot across the parched and barren landscape to reach the isolated village of Río Escondido, she succumbs to a heart condition. On the way she is rescued and befriended by a young medical student, who has also been sent to the countryside on a social mission. Meanwhile, the town boss is introduced; he is a former Revolutionary, a man of violence and cruelty. Once she arrives, the beautiful young schoolteacher confronts the town boss fearlessly, and exploits his desire for her—without compromising her principles—so as to obtain his support for her social and education reforms, which duly begin to mobilize and raise the consciousness of the local peasant population. Then her confrontation with the town boss comes to a head; he rapes her and she shoots him. With the peasants thus liberated, she succumbs once again to her heart ailment. From her deathbed she sends off a report to the president, and she lives just long enough to receive his reply, which consecrates her status as a national heroine. Playing melodramatically on every possible patriotic emotion, *Río Escondido* clearly would rally and unite the Mexican people.

In one of his last films of the 1940s, Fernández finally turned his patriotic and moral didacticism from the rural countryside to an urban setting, but his vision of Mexico City nightclub culture, in this shadowy black-and-white film, is bleak. *Salón Mexico* (1948) takes its title from the name of the famous Mexico City dance hall, a title that was also used by composer Aaron Copeland for one of his musical pieces. This film is a melodrama of the sort known as the *cabaretera* (cabaret film) or *cine de ficheras* (from *fichas,* the tokens used in such dance halls to divvy up the women for hire). This genre of films would be extensively and often cheaply exploited throughout the 1950s. *Salón México* once again involves a noble and chaste friendship in a tragically doomed scenario. Here, a virtuous, gentle-hearted policeman seeks to protect a fallen heroine both from the abuse and exploitation of her pimp (in which he fails) and from the dishonor of her family in the eyes of society (in which he succeeds).

OTHER GOLDEN AGE DIRECTORS AND GENRES

One should not assume that the Fernández-Figueroa films were the be all and end all of the Golden Age; the director Julio Bracho, for example, also established a considerable reputation for urban and urbane filmmaking. Bracho's roots could hardly have been more different than those of Fernández. He came from a prominent Durango family that was closely associated with the fortunes of Mexican cinema. Dolores del Río was a cousin; his sister, Andrea Palma, was a leading actress; and his daughter, Diana Bracho, became one of Mexican cinema's greatest stars.

In 1943, Bracho directed one of his most acclaimed films, *Distinto amanecer* (*A Different Dawn*), which paired his sister with Pedro Armendáriz in leading roles. Everything about the film provides a refreshing contrast to the typical Fernández-Figueroa fare. The action unfolds in a thoroughly modern Mexico City, and it traces events occurring in the course of a single night. A chance encounter with an old college classmate draws a sophisticated but bored couple, trapped in a routine and disillusioned existence, into crime and political intrigue involving union leaders, government officials, and campus radicals. The film is well regarded for the quality of its acting, its film noir atmospherics, its realistic depictions of Mexico City locations, and its frank treatment of urbanization and modernization and of the kinds of moral bankruptcy and alienation they can breed. *Distinto amanecer* was meant to capture the disillusionment of a generation of intellectuals who had come of age in the midst of Education Minister José Vasconcelos's original Revolutionary cultural programs; nowadays, it seems to anticipate the problems and concerns that would resurface during the large-scale student protests of 1968. Bracho would go on to make many other movies, among them a key political one that proved to be too hot for its time. Based on a 1929 novel by Martín Luis Guzmán, *La sombra del caudillo* (*The Shadow of the Dictator,* 1960) is famous today not because many Mexicans have seen it, but because its distribution was blocked by the Mexican government for nearly 30 years.

Many other quality films were produced and shown in the 1940s. Though most break far less ground than the films of Fernández and Bracho, and have little of their polish and critical edge, they nonetheless demonstrate the general level of sophistication that Mexican cinema had attained. During the 1940s, the family melodrama came into its own. Complacent and superficial, syrupy and sentimental, melodramatic and even voyeuristic, deftly sublimating wider social issues and acceding to the status quo, the family melodrama captivated large moviegoing audiences as had few genres before. At first, melodramas focused on the relatively stable lives of the typical middle-class family to which so many Mexicans wished to belong; their jealousies, rivalries, and scandals provided a foretaste of soap opera entertainment (see chapter 4). The decade opened with Juan Bustillo Oro's wildly popular *Cuando los hijos se van* (*When the Children Leave the Nest*, 1941), which was not only twice remade as a movie (1957, 1969), but also later adapted into a television soap opera (*telenovela*). The film lacked the artistic camera work of a Fernández-Figueroa film, but it did star Sara García as the all-knowing and self-sacrificing mother, a role she would repeat so many times that she came to be called "the mother of Mexico."

Another director, Alejandro Galindo, insistently tackled thorny social issues while generally managing to retain a popular appeal. For example, his *Una familia de tantas* (*A Family Like So Many Others*, 1948) takes quite a cynical view of the out-of-touch yet stubbornly authoritarian middle-class patriarch. The subtext of this film deals with the growing tensions in 1940s Mexican society between the traditional order (represented by the father) and the ever-increasing pace of modernization and the American way of life (represented by a young appliance salesman who wins the heart of his daughter).

Galindo pursued his interest in the social and cultural implications of U.S.-Mexican relations in several other popular and critically acclaimed films. One was *Campeón sin corona* (*Champion without a Title*, 1945), an important early example of the working-class focus of urban filmmaking in Mexico. The film chronicles the rise and fall of an inner-city boxer who is ill prepared to handle his success and notoriety when he goes on to triumph in the United States. The subtheme explores the insecurity that the boxer feels in a confrontation with a Mexican-American rival, who speaks fluent English and knows the ropes north of the border. Another Galindo film would tackle the issue of U.S.-Mexican relations even more directly. *Espaldas mojadas* (*Wetbacks*, 1953) presents a stark, even sensationalized and alarmist vision of the horrors visited upon Mexican immigrants to the United States. It was one of very few films at the time, and for many years to come, to deal directly with this subject, one that many Mexicans, especially those living away from the border, have often preferred to ignore.

Pedro Infante and the *Cine De Arrabal*

Increasingly, the family melodrama shifted its focus from the self-contained middle-class family, to the larger, extended family of the so-called popular neighborhoods, and the urban slums. This sub-branch of the genre was dubbed the *cine de arrabal,* and in the hands of its acknowledged master, Ismael Rodríguez, it bowled over the competition. Rodríguez produced a trilogy of films in the 1940s that, though scarcely known outside the Spanish-speaking world, made their star, Pedro Infante, into an idol with whom the whole Mexican nation seemed to be able to identify. *Nosotros los pobres* (*We, the Poor,* 1947) is still thought to be the most widely viewed Mexican movie of all time. Along with its sequels, *Ustedes los ricos* (*You, the Rich,* 1948) and *Pepe el toro* (*Pepe the Bull,* 1952), it was recycled for years in theaters and later in television reruns.

Clearly, the wider public appreciated the frank, if very stylized, representation of their lives in films like *Nosotros los pobres.* Its plot follows a series of complications and intrigues. Betrayal and deception never seem sufficient to impede expressions of unwavering tenderness, compassion, and solidarity, while singing and celebration alternate with cruelty and exploitation. Most view the film as one that makes palatable or sidesteps the inescapable poverty, degradation, and injustice to which these working-class figures are subject; it extols their sacrifice and pain. In films such as this, women are generally saints or sinners. The singing role of Pepe el Toro, the humble carpenter whose life is chronicled in *Nosotros los pobres,* presents an interesting contrast to machismo: he is generous and tender, sincerely romantic, and compassionate to a fault. Through the most unimaginable tragedies he steadfastly maintains his faith in people and his passion for life.

To judge by the success of this sequence of films, no Mexican director was ever as adept as Ismael Rodríguez at tapping into the collective unconscious. Later, when the Golden Age was losing its shine, Rodríguez directed a super-production in color that made a last attempt to pull together the myths and icons of classic cinema. *La cucaracha* (*The Cockroach,* 1958)—its title came from the best known of all the popular Revolutionary ballads—brought Mexico's most famous actresses, Dolores del Río and María Félix, together for the first and only time on screen, and cast the celebrated Emilio Fernández in the role of a sinister colonel. The film was meant to be the crowning epic of the Revolution, but even the presence of these aging stars could not save it from coming over as a sad parody, as proof that the strategies of the Golden Age were exhausted.

FADING LIGHTS OF THE GOLDEN AGE

Throughout the 1950s, the number of features produced annually in Mexico frequently exceeded 100, reaching a high mark of 136 in 1958. But at the same time, quality and creativity—and, in some people's opinion, even the standards of common decency—slowly but steadily declined. Film budgets shrank, production times were often drastically curtailed, and, not unexpectedly, cheap and tawdry B-grade films began to proliferate.

The majority of films now had a clear urban flavor and reflected the changing sexual and moral values of mainstream Mexican society. This shift is most evident in the cabareteras—the night-club melodramas, or brothel/cabaret films. Such films had antecedents, with very different moral subtexts, in films such as *Santa* and *Salón México*. These earlier films generally featured prostitutes whose hearts of gold and suffering as victims of circumstance made them vehicles for the expression of traditional moral standards. In contrast, the immensely popular cabaretera films of the 1950s most commonly testified to the erosion of such values. The cabaretera films easily became the dominant and most marketable genre of the period, alongside movies designed to exploit the latest dance-hall crazes like the mambo and the rumba. With their more cosmopolitan and Pan-Hispanic flavor, these films not only reflected ongoing changes in Mexican society, but they also showed the industry's desperation to keep pace and hold onto the gains it had made among Latin American audiences, and that at a time when Hollywood competition had returned with a vengeance.

Not all of the cabaretera films were purely exploitative and opportunistic. Two outstanding instances were *Sensualidad* (*Sensuality*, 1950) and *Aventurera* (*Adventuress*, 1949), both directed by Alberto Gout. These films made Ninón Sevilla the most successful of several Cuban-born actresses who popularized the genre and its sensual Caribbean rhythms in Mexico. In both films, Sevilla plays a prostitute, traditional portrayals of saintly mothers as the pillars of virtue having long since been abandoned. In these films it is the upper crust of society that comes in for the harshest, if implicit, condemnation—the corrupt public officials and local elites who sustain and exploit the underworld. Both films acknowledge the darker side of the social system, while spinning involved tales of secret lives and family breakdowns, of sordid passions and ruthless acts of vengance, that may, or may not, go punished. Both films were of the kind that most moviegoers would condemn in public, yet flock to see.

Driven by the competition from the new television medium, the first artistic nudes appeared in Mexican films like *La fuerza del deseo* (*The Power of Desire*, 1955) and *La virtud desnuda* (*Naked Virtue*, 1955). This growing liberalization of standards would later dovetail with the student movements of the 1960s and be revalued not as moral decay but as a necessary liberation from unhealthy taboos and repression. One noteworthy 1974 film, *Tivoli,* would parody and recreate nostalgically the cabaret scene of the 1950s, and spark a new, even more permissive round of cabaretera films in the late 1970s.

LUIS BUÑUEL IN MEXICO

At a time when production values and creative energy were on the wane, Luis Buñuel cast a bright light on the Mexican cinema scene. Debates still are waged about which country, if any, should stake claim to the reflected glory of Buñuel's work. Born in Spain, he began his filmmaking career there and in France before the Spanish Civil War. In exile during the Franco years, he passed through New York and Hollywood for a time, and he arrived in Mexico rather accidentally in 1946. Between 1946 in 1964, Buñuel directed some 20 Spanish-language films in Mexico, before returning to Europe in the 1960s.

As an internationally renowned figure, Buñuel kept Mexico on the world cinematographic map, but he also overshadowed his Mexican contemporaries. Critics have complained that Buñuel's characters, even in his films with a thoroughly Mexican focus and subject matter, lacked essential ingredients of the authentic Mexican tradition, and showed little real understanding of the people and society in which he was working. But like Spanish Civil War exiles in other artistic fields, Buñuel gave the Mexican cinema industry a rich infusion of technical expertise and creative inspiration at a time when these things were lacking. Above all, Buñuel's work in Mexico broke ground in the area of professionalism. He overcame technical and financial limitations (limited budgets, hurried production schedules, a limited pool of acting talent, and producer-imposed restrictions on artistic freedom and creativity). He produced—on time and within budget—an extensive filmography that rarely compromised his basic themes and ideas. Such a lesson was not lost on the young, experimental directors who emerged in Mexico in the 1960s and who often had to finance their efforts by any means available.

Just how refreshingly un-Mexican Buñuel's films were becomes evident in the comparison between two films with similar themes: the Mexican classic *Nosotros los pobres* (discussed on p. 139) and Buñuel's best-known Mexican film, *Los olvidados* (*The Young and the Damned,* 1950). Rather than a sentimental sublimation of poverty, *Los olvidados* painted a visceral, totally unromantic picture of the street children in Mexico City's poorest neighborhoods. It was shot on location and without major stars (though Roberto Cobo would go on to become one). Buñuel's street children, however ruthless, are complex beings touched by the whole range of human emotions, and Buñuel treated them with honest sympathy rather than condecension. *Los olvidados* won a prize for best direction at the 1951 Cannes festival, and it is still considered by many to be the greatest film made in Spanish up to that time. But, not surprisingly, the film proved troublesome for both the moviegoing public and government officials, and it enjoyed some success at the box office only after it had met with the approval of international audiences and critics.[1]

THE 1960s: CRISIS AND NEW BEGINNINGS

By the early 1960s, the extent to which Mexican cinema had lost touch not only with its own society but also with the larger world of cinema had become palpable. The industry had been reduced for the most part to the cheapest kinds of commercial formulas appealing to lowest common denominators. One example is provided by the series of superhero films starring the immensely popular Santo, a masked wrestling figure, which began in 1961 with *Santo contra el cerebro diabólico* (*Santo Versus the Evil Brain*). This basic formula would be endlessly recycled over the next 25 years, through some 50 films.

The general situation to which some 40 years of post-Revolutionary government had led the nation was accurately reflected in the Mexican film industry in the 1960s. On the one hand, the industry had been built on an uncertain mix of state involvement, private interests, and foreign investment that, in areas such as distribution and exhibition, was monopolistic. On the other hand, the Revolution's political machinery had created huge, state-controlled unions that engaged in fratricidal struggles. While union protectionism had perhaps had some benefits in a capital-intensive industry that faced stiff foreign competition, it had become a hindrance to the apprenticeship of new talent. The crisis, which extended into all aspects of Mexican life, arose in the widening gap between dynastic post-Revolutionary institutions and the expectations and aspirations of the ever-changing Mexican society they ostensibly served. This is what would come to a tragic head in the infamous events of 1968 now known as Tlatelolco.

The seeds of renewal were sown starting in the early 1960s, in a handful of cinematic experiments that came not from within the established industry or the closed ranks of the official film unions, but from a group of young and staunchly independent intellectuals. Many were one-time students of the National University, and they had been brought loosely together by their work on certain projects, among them a short-lived but ground-breaking film magazine, *Nuevo Cine,* which appeared in installments between April 1961 and August 1962. Paul Leduc was one of very few members of the *Nuevo Cine* group who went on to a solid career as a filmmaker. *Nuevo Cine*'s mostly self-produced and financed incursions into filmmaking were more like audacious projects than finished products, though the point was precisely to demonstrate that there were alternatives to the stale and outdated formulas of the established industry. Their impact on Mexican cultural life was immeasurable, and it went far beyond the realm of film. Almost all of them would go on to make substantial contributions in one or several fields: José de la Colina and Salvador Elizondo as writers and editorialists; Emilio García Riera as Mexico's leading film historian; Carlos Monsiváis as one of the country's most irreverent and incisive social and cultural commentators. Other participants included the future film critic Jorge Ayala Blanco, and Manuel González Casanova, who became the first Director of the Centro Universitario de Estudios Cinematográficos (CEUC), the new cinema department at the National University. Founded in 1963, the CEUC would see a number of the key directors of the new Mexican cinema pass through it.

The *Nuevo Cine* group drew inspiration from the presence of Buñuel, mediated by the likes of the author Carlos Fuentes and the artist José Luis Cuevas, both of them confidants of the exiled Spanish filmmaker. The basic tenet was a new and insistent cosmopolitanism, following Octavio Paz's famous declaration in *The Labyrinth of Solitude* (1950) that "we [Mexicans] are now the contemporaries of all men." Reviving the spirit of the Contemporáneos avant-garde group of the 1930s, they rejected most established forms of cultural nationalism, such as the Indianism of the famous murals of Diego Rivera or even the classic Fernández-Figueroa films, because they regarded these as perpetuations of colonial dependence. They claimed the right to treat universal, modern and postmodern themes that were of significant social, psychological, philosophical, and political complexity. They also insisted that Mexican artists had a duty to pursue the kind of bold formal experimentation that was to be found in recent European and North American literature and film, and in certain key works of Latin American literature.

Their first accomplishment of note, and it was indicative of this group's brash independence, was Jomi García Ascot's *En el balcón vacío* (*On the Empty Balcony*, 1961). Based on the biography of García Ascot's wife (exiled in Mexico as a young girl due to the Civil War in Spain) and adapted for the screen by García Riera, the film was financed by contributions from friends, and shot over the course of a year on weekends. It involves an intimate evocation of the woman's traumatic childhood memories of flight from her birthplace. Though rejected by most distributors in Mexico, the film outperformed several official Mexican entries at the Locarno Film Festival in Switzerland.

In 1964, the film union that had broken off to represent the leading Golden Age actors (the STPC) sponsored a new event, the First Experimental Film Contest. The very idea of the contest tacitly acknowledged the decline of commercial filmmaking, as well as the increasing tensions between the young mavericks and the old guard. Though its effects were primarily symbolic, the contest provided a further incentive to several aspiring young directors. First prize went to a boldly sardonic anthology of offbeat and surrealistic image sequences by Rubén Gámez, with the provocative title of *La fórmula secreta, o Coca Cola en la sangre* (*The Secret Formula, or Coca-Cola in One's Blood*, 1964). In one scene, a patient receives a transfusion of Coca-Cola, an obvious allusion to U.S. imperialism and to the blind admiration on the part of some Mexicans for all things from the United States. Mostly, however, the film develops a highly stylized parody of stereotypical images of Mexico. Gámez himself has said that his goal was not so much to denounce the government or the system, but rather the Mexican people themselves for their passive acquiescence and lack of higher aspirations. *La fórmula secreta, o Coca-Cola en la sangre* uses original texts by the novelist Juan Rulfo, read by the poet Jaime Sabines, along with a wide-ranging musical score. It has become something of an underground legend, a status no doubt enhanced by the fact that Gámez always considered the project unfinished (he ran out of money) and did not produce another film for more than 20 years.

Two other films that came out of the *Nuevo Cine* movement charted a somewhat different course and also underscored the fact that at the time there was significant interaction in Latin America between the new literature and the new filmmaking. Both *En este pueblo no hay ladrones* (*There Are No Thieves in This Town*, 1964), directed by Alberto Isaac, and *Tiempo de morir* (*A Time to Die*, 1965) directed by 21-year-old Arturo Ripstein, were based on adaptations of early stories by Gabriel García Márquez. (García Márquez was shortly to become the leading figure in the boom of Latin American literature, and he has remained a major force, as a source for scripts and behind the scenes, in the push for a new cinema in Latin America.) Like the works of literature upon which they were based, both of these films are set in isolated, barren, provincial towns where time seems frozen. In worlds where change seems impossible and destiny oppressive, they deal with elemental and submerged passions, pride and honor, vengeance and resentment. *En este pueblo no hay ladrones* won second prize in the First Experimental Film Contest. It has the added attraction of cameo appearances by an amazing list of key figures in the artistic and intellectual changes then taking place in Mexico: the authors Rulfo and García Márquez, the artists José Luis Cuevas and Leonora Carrington, *Nuevo Cine* group members García Riera and Monsiváis, and even the young directors themselves, Isaacs and Ripstein.

One of Rulfo's stories was successfully brought to the screen by veteran director Roberto Gavaldón: *El gallo de oro* (*The Golden Cockerel*, 1964). Carlos Velo's adaptation of Rulfo's novel *Pedro Páramo* (1966) did not receive as much favorable critical attention, but it does boast the curiosity of starring a North American actor of Hispanic extraction, John Gavin, who would later become Ronald Reagan's controversial U.S. ambassador to Mexico.

The events of 1968 had a chilling effect on the various independent artistic and intellectual initiatives that had blossomed in Mexico during the early 1960s. Many students and intellectual leaders were rounded up and imprisoned, and the nation was left in shock. Tlatelolco soon became the subject of a whole range of literary treatments, so much so that the literature of Tlatelolco has become a category in itself. In film, however, it was a different story. Whether due to self-censorship or more blatant means of suppression, direct and even indirect treatments on film of the events of 1968 have been few and far between.

A group of students from the National University's Centro Universitario de Estudios Cinematográficos (CUEC), including Paul Leduc, produced a rare documentary of the Tlatelolco events, *El grito* (*The Shout*, 1968). It was quickly edited from footage shot between July and October 1968, and it includes an eyewitness account by the noted Italian journalist Orianna Fallaci. Two other university productions, *El cambio* (*The Change*, 1971) and *Crates* (1971), dealt with the disillusionment and alienation felt by many of the youthful participants in the events. For a long time, the outstanding treatment on film of the events of 1968 would be Felipe Cazals's *Canoa* (1975), though he chose not to deal with the massacre itself but with the general climate of fear and anxiety provoked throughout Mexican society. Apart from this, no full-length feature film on Tlatelolco was distributed until 1990, when Jorge Fons's *Rojo amanecer* (*Red Dawn*) appeared.

When the new president, Luis Echeverría, took office in 1970, in the wake of Tlatclolco, his initiatives included a concerted effort to repair the damaged relations between the government and the nation's artists and intellectuals, and he instituted sweeping reforms in the film industry. He created a government film school, the Centro de Capacitación Cinematográfica (CCC) and finally built premises for the Cineteca Nacional (National Film Institute) on the site of the former Churrubusco studios. He dramatically increased state financing and support, restructuring the Banco Cinematográfico. The ultimate goal was to boost Mexico's standing in the international community, and the strategy was to foster unprecedented critical freedom among filmmakers and to encourage frank treatment of significant (and sensitive) social and political issues. Even today, informed opinion varies widely as regards both the underlying motivation and ultimate effectiveness of Echeverría's new policies. Certainly, during the 1970s and 1980s Mexican cinema continued to face a steep uphill battle in its search for effective promotion and distribution and for international recognition. The fact is that then and since, private production companies, sometimes with state support, kept supplying theaters with assembly-line genre films.

Exploiting Echeverría's new openness, nudity and soft porn suddenly proliferated in commercial features, both in wild youth-culture orgies (Gabriel Retes's *Fin de fiesta,* 1971) and in newly emboldened cabaret films, filled with street slang and double-entendres. Films such as *Noches de cabaret* (*Cabaret Nights,* 1977) and *Muñecas de medianoche* (*Midnight Dolls,* 1978) enthroned starlets like Sasha Montenegro and left little to the imagination (a far cry from the rumba divas of the early fifties and the artistic nudity of the late fifties). Many of these titillating films were directed by people who had established a reputation for quality during the Golden Age. Commercial producers also continued to recycle the ranch comedy formula, with appropriate updates for the times.

In the late 1970s and early 1980s, as migration made the commercial and cultural frontier between Mexico and the United States increasingly porous, a new B-grade genre, the "narcofilm," appeared. Generally set in a stereotypical north of Mexico fought over by the drug lords and their corrupt accomplices among the federal police and judiciary, and by U.S. undercover agents operating outside the law, these films fed their audiences large doses of violence, tough and sexy women, and truck-driving men. By the time of *Lola la trailera* (*Lola the Truck Driver,* 1984), the genre was reaping astonishing profits; from an initial investment of $150,000, this film is said to have grossed $2.5 million in U.S. Hispanic markets, and $1 million in Mexico. Later, the genre gravitated toward a sensational, docudrama mode; producers adapted the hottest stories from police reports and the afternoon scandal sheets.

Certainly some progress was made during the Echeverría years, progress that the efforts of subsequent presidential administrations could not entirely reverse. García Riera provides statistics that document the degree to which Echeverría effectively re-nationalized the industry. The Echeverría policies did facilitate the kind of independent, experimental filmmaking that had tentatively surfaced in the 1960s. The resulting list of accomplished directors must include, among its older ranks, Luis Alcoriza, Paul Leduc, Felipe Cazals, Arturo Ripstein, Jaime Humberto Hermosillo, Jorge Fons, and Alfonso Arau. Others, like Nicolás Echevarría, Alberto Cortés, Alfonso Cuarón, María Novaro, and Guillermo del Toro, have followed in their footsteps. Their major films enlivened Mexican cinema through the 1970s and 1980s and into the 1990s, despite having to weather endless political, social, and economic crises.

It was, above all, the work of Luis Alcoriza who kept quality cinema alive through the industry's darkest period of crisis. Almost single-handedly, he carried forward the biting satire and quirky symbolism of the more European-style work of his mentor, Buñuel. An exile to Mexico from the Spanish Civil War as a young boy, Alcoriza began as an actor and then became an assistant to Buñuel and worked with him on many of the scripts for his Mexican films, including *Los olvidados*. Once on his own, Alcoriza made several interesting films in the 1960s, of which *Tiburoneros* (*Shark Hunters*, 1963) is probably the best known. Without eschewing commercial values or traditional realism, the film sensitively explores the effects of modernization, from the city to the provinces, as manifest in the divided loyalties of the protagonist, who leaves behind his family and busy life in the city to become a shark hunter on the coast.

Alcoriza's *Mecánica nacional* (*National Body Shop*, 1971) reflected the changing tenor of mainstream filmmaking in Mexico. Although *Mecánica nacional*'s distinctive 1960s air now gives it the feel of a period piece, it is an entertaining reflection of Mexico's new sophistication, and its implied critique of the characters' vulgarity and coarseness, of the absence of any semblance of dignity or moral high ground, is hard to miss. (The title has a double meaning: "national body shop" and "the mechanics of the nation.") As the film opens, the protagonist (the owner of a body shop) gets caught up with his wife and family in a huge traffic jam on the highway, on their way out of town to catch the finish of a road race. Typical macho invective is hurled from car to car as the hot and frustrated race-goers are forced by the traffic to pull off the road. With people ready to make the best of the situation (the road race was perhaps only a pretext for a family outing anyway), a stereotypically Mexican festive mood takes over; everyone has their picnic then and there, with a captive audience before which they can parade their pretensions and dirty linen. The scenes and images approach an absurd crescendo. In its final blow, the film depicts the mother/grandmother of the mechanic, who has stuffed herself with food all night, as suffering a heart attack, or perhaps just a terrible bout of indigestion. In its mechanical rush to progress, the Mexico that Alcoriza portrays seems to have lost its moorings. As if to erase any lingering doubt about this message, two U.S. tourists who have taken the whole scene in provide a biting caption to the images with their voiced-over declaration in English: "There's nothing Mexican here."

The success of *Mecánica nacional* was followed by a similarly styled national satire directed by Gustavo Alatriste, entitled *México, México, ra, ra, ra* (1974). Opening with a deafening soccer-match cheer of unbridled nationalistic pride, the film exposes the venality that cut across early 1970s Mexican society. Nothing and no one is spared as the film's critical gaze ranges across the contemporary Mexican landscape: the culture of poverty studied by Oscar Lewis, the kickbacks and servile flattery that grease the socioeconomic and political pecking order at every level, the complicity between business and government sectors, the impractical rhetoric of radicalized students and intellectuals. The film denounces the way powerlessness and arbitrary personal authority beget resentment and violence.

México, México, ra, ra, ra, like *Mecánica nacional,* stars the comic actor Héctor Suárez, who deftly handles multiple roles. Suárez has specialized in working-class roles ranging from the do-gooder, to the picaroon, to the good-for-nothing bum. He has applied his comic talents to a number of projects, both marginal and mainstream, ranging from Paul Leduc's underground exposé, *¿Cómo ves?,* to the blockbuster commercial features, *El milusos* (*The Jack of All Trades,* 1981) and *El milusos 2* (1983), which gently exposed the harsh realities awaiting impoverished provincial immigrants who flock to Mexico City in pursuit of a better life. (This success translated into a famous Televisa television program, *¿Qué nos pasa?* (*What's Going On with Us?*), in which he presented entertaining, if somewhat didactic, comic sketches dramatizing an array of Mexican vices and self-defeating institutions and behaviors).

Felipe Cazals established a solid reputation for *auteur* cinema with three powerful of films in the mid-1970s. Cazals has had a long and distinguished career that demonstrates how hard the choices are that independently minded directors are forced to make. He began with a series of short documentaries in the late 1960s. He then attempted an unsuccessful historical epic, *Emiliano Zapata* (1971), before defining a characteristic style with *Canoa* (1975), *El apando* (1976), and *Las Poquianchis* (1977). These last three films contain many rich ambiguities, but also convey some of contemporary Mexican cinema's darkest and most sobering sociopolitical criticism. Critics and film historians still regard Cazals most highly for the bold achievements of *Canoa,* the first feature film to treat events surrounding the 1968 student movement in a critical manner. It narrates the story of a group of students from a state university that at the time was notorious for its radicalism (the BUAP in Puebla); these students pass through the small town of San Miguel Canoa during a camping trip. Though their activities have been innocent, the students are on the verge of being lynched by the local citizenry when federal troops arrive. *Canoa* was produced by CONACINE (Corporación Nacional Cinematográfica), an organization created by the Echeverría administration. Some observers have expressed surprise that such a critical film was distributed, and conclude that this fact confirms the Echeverría administration's commitment to creative freedom and critical realism. Others, however, take note of how Cazals's film shifts the main focus away from the main events in Mexico City.

Like *Rojo amanecer,* this film emphasizes sharpening cultural and generational gaps, seen here in the fanatical conservatism of a small-town mob, whipped into a frenzy by the local priest; in the film's climax, it is government troops that ride in to save the students from the wrath of the local mob. None of this negates the incisive social analysis Cazals's film contains, but it may help explain his success in obtaining government sponsorship and immediate national distribution. Cazals's other two films from the mid-1970s are fact-based dramas drawing a critical portrait contemporary Mexican life. *El apando* is a film version of a very difficult novel by the writer and political activist José Revueltas, and it gives a rather hyperrealist or surrealist account of Revueltas's experience of prison life. Like *Canoa,* Cazals's *Las poquianchis* was based on a infamous scandal: innocent young girls from the provinces were purchased from their rural families to work as virtual slaves, in horrifying conditions, in distant brothels. The story can be difficult to follow, because Cazals jumps back and forth between the historical incidents and their journalistic discovery, and freely interweaves the story of the daughters sold into prostitution with the plight of their peasant families. The dark atmospherics and the denunciation of unimaginable human degradation and exploitation give the movie an eerie, surreal feeling, in stark contrast to the soft-porn, call-girl films being made by other people at that time.

After studying film in France in the 1960s, Paul Leduc returned to Mexico and worked on a number of documentaries. This experience was reflected in his first major feature, *Reed: México Insurgente* (1971) which tries to take a balanced look at the Revolution, such as had rarely been taken since de Fuentes's *¡Vámonos con Pancho Villa!.* Leduc used hand-held cameras to bring about an effect of pseudo-documentary realism; the film was even colored sepia when it was blown up to a 35-mm format. Leduc's *Frida, naturaleza viva* (*Frida, A Vibrant Still Life,* 1984) did even more to bring the attention of international art film aficionados back to Mexico, and it won several international awards. While *Frida* shares a number of historical and formal features with *Reed: México insurgente,* its style and flavor are basically different; it shifts from linear, objective realism to a fragmented, subjective surrealism. The film presents a somewhat ponderous sequence of poetic, visual scenes, from a wandering camera angle, almost entirely without dialogue. Many of these establish a narrative present in which we see the famous painter during her later years, surrounded by her paintings and her collections of Mexican artifacts, suffering excruciating pain of the kind that had become the subject of much of her work. These scenes alternate with unordered flashbacks, some pseudo-documentary and in black and white, that recreate key situations and events in her life—her childhood; her tempestuous relationship with her husband, the famous muralist Diego Rivera; and their involvement with the

Mexican and international Communist parties. Clearly, the overall thrust of the film is to celebrate Kahlo's reverence for all things Mexican, and her dedication to the Mexican people. But the tragedy of her emotional and physical suffering, and the way in which she challenged viewers of her paintings to confront the harsher aspects of women's reality, are captured with particular eloquence. (The film's Spanish title contains a play on words: "still life" in Spanish is *naturaleza muerta*, literally "dead life"; this is turned on its head by substituting the adjective *viva* and the result is an expression that suggests not only vibrant life but also sharp intelligence.)[2]

Each of Leduc's films makes a distinctive and provocative cinematic statement. In two of his more recent efforts, he has used a kind of carnavalesque, musical format as a vehicle for his social and political criticism. *Latino Bar* (1990) is a loose adaptation of the classic *Santa* story, focused on working-class violence and exploitation. In *Dollar Mambo* (1993), which deals with a rape committed by U.S. GIs during the 1990 Panama invasion, he turns his critical gaze on the subject of U.S. intervention in Latin America, and in *Concierto barroco* (1989) he gives a rendering of the story of the Cuban Alejo Carpentier's novella, in a film in which music plays a prominent part, but dialogue, once again, is noticeable for its absence.

Among directors of the new cinema, Arturo Ripstein has most consistently been able to make commercially successful films despite the topsy-turvy nature of the Mexican film industry. Ripstein's ability to obtain sponsorship throughout the unsettling reversals in the industry during the López Portillo administration (1976–82) led some critics to charge that his independence was compromised. Ripstein himself, however, has insisted that he seeks to move his audiences, that he is not a director with a message.

Most recently, he has been known for large-scale productions that update classic dramatic and melodramatic structures, but his early films frequently highlighted characters beset by futile compulsions to escape destinies through obsessive controls, isolation, or confinement. After his precocious debut with *Tiempo de morir* (*Time to Die*, 1965), Ripstein directed *El castillo de la pureza* (*The Castle of Purity*, 1972). Based on a true story, the latter paints a disturbing picture of a man who locks up his wife and children, ostensibly to protect them from the impurities of the outside world and who, ironically enough, manufactures and sells rat poison to make a living. *Cadena perpetua* (*Life Imprisonment*, 1978), also a well-regarded film, tells an equally disturbing story of a petty thief who, try as he might, cannot escape the vicious web of urban crime and corruption as a police officer blackmails and exploits him. (This dark picture of life in the city is still relevant, given the perpetual problem of crime and police corruption in Mexico City.)

It was Ripstein's adaptation of the Chilean novelist José Donoso's *El lugar sin límites* (*A Place Without Limits,* 1977), with uncredited script work by the Argentine writer Manuel Puig, that did most to help return Mexican cinema to the Latin American and international spotlights. *El lugar sin límites* was one of the last films still made in Mexico with state funding from the Echeverría administration. Though the film evades any direct critical treatment of political issues, it clearly displays a new openness in its treatment of gender roles and sexual identity. It is full of delightfully extravagant performances and sexual tensions involving homoeroticism and homophobia. A typical, provincial macho type finds himself seduced by La Manuela, a transvestite homosexual prostitute (played by Roberto Cobo, of *Los olvidados* fame). Later, egged on by his brother, the man violently beats his seducer to death. Though far from being Ripstein's most representative work, the film met with critical acclaim.

Ripstein directed some rather uninspired efforts in the late years of the López Portillo administration, among them a vehicle for Televisa star Lucía Méndez, titled *La ilegal.* He made a comeback, however, with *El imperio de la fortuna* (*The Empire of Fortune,* 1985), a second film version of Juan Rulfo's screenplay, *El gallo de oro* (*The Golden Cockerel*). He also scored a big box office hit with *Principio y fin* (*Beginning and End,* 1993), a melodramatic family saga with an urban setting adapted, like Fons's *El callejón de los milagros* (*The Alley of Miracles,* distributed in the United States as *Midaq Alley*) from a novel by the Egyptian author Naguib Mafouz. A recent film of note is *Profundo carmesí* (*Deep Crimson,* 1996), in which a gigolo armed with a matinée idol persona and a Spanish accent, who makes a living seducing aging and well-to-do women, enters into an unlikely but obsessive and ultimately destructive relationship with a single mother. In a very different vein, in 1999 Ripstein brought García Márquez's novella *El coronel no tiene quien le escriba* (*No One Writes to the Colonel*) to the silver screen.

A very different kind of filmmaker emerged in the person of Jaime Humberto Hermosillo. Whereas Ripstein, a "movie brat" and son of the producer Alfredo Ripstein, has shown a predilection for large-scale works, Hermosillo remained content to direct understated films of more modest scope. He has also been more concerned to protect his independence. Early in his career, like Leduc, he shot several films in 16-mm format in order to save money, though later obtained backing for them to be blown up to 35 mm; in more recent times, Hermosillo has worked directly with video. From the start, Hermosillo has excelled at tender comedies and off-beat satires, keeping a tight focus on personal relationships and challenging traditional gender roles.

Hermosillo's best-known films from the 1970s all focus squarely on female protagonists. Ramírez Berg calls *La pasión según Berenice* (*The Passion Accord-*

ing to Berenice, 1976), *Naufragio* (*Shipwreck,* 1977), and *María de mi corazón* (*Mary My Dearest,* 1979) the "madwoman trilogy" because together they amount to a compelling critique of "a patriarchal system that badgers women into insanity" (87). *María de mi corazón,* particularly, has developed a strong following on the international art film and video club circuits. The screenplay was adapted from a García Márquez story (yet another of many contributions to Mexican cinema made by this famous Colombian novelist and long-time Mexico City resident). The first part of *María de mi corazón* traces the relationship that develops between the protagonist (the ubiquitous new cinema actress María Rojo) and Héctor, a former lover and now a small-time burglar. María makes her living performing magic at parties for children. But rather than being sleight of hand, María's magic is real, and she uses it with a zest and natural innocence to which Héctor quickly succumbs; he leaves behind his life of crime and becomes María's assistant in a traveling magic show. This upbeat opening only makes more potent the sad reversal that then unfolds.

Hermosillo's films are not without their darker moments, but on the whole, his characters are tender figures, refreshingly unencumbered by taboos and psycho-social neuroses, and they are drawn sympathetically, without judgment. The fact that at the time most Mexican films with a critical edge painted a harshly cynical picture of Mexico makes this aspect of Hermosillo's films all the more remarkable. Hermosillo has continued to direct refreshing films that consistently break new ground, many of his projects having been supported by producer Manuel Barbachano Ponce, a staunch defender of independent filmmaking in Mexico. In 1984, Hermosillo completed *Doña Herlinda y su hijo* (*Doña Herlinda and Her Son*), which was certainly the most unselfconscious treatment of homosexuality in Mexican cinema up to that time. Indeed, the kind of rampant homophobia tolerated, if not celebrated, in so many mainstream Mexican films (witness even Jorge Fons's 1993 film, *El callejón de los milagros*), might make Hermosillo's treatment of the subject matter appear to be full-blown fantasy. At first, government officials hindered distribution of Hermosillo's film in Mexico, until pressure was felt from the acclaim he was receiving internationally.

Doña Herlinda deals with four sensible, upper-middle class characters in the regional capital of Guadalajara: a physician, his young homosexual lover, his widowed mother, and the woman to whom his mother manages to marry him (so that she might have a grandchild). Through love and mutual respect, tolerance and understanding, tact and discretion, the characters manage to harmonize their divergent interests and desires and actively shape the world around them, as they prepare to share life together. Interestingly, some critics have seen in this a possible metaphor for the way the PRI government negotiated the conflicting forces in twentieth-century Mexican society. Hermosillo covered still more new terrain with another film, distributed in 1991, that did surprisingly well in Mexican theaters. A kind of *Sex, Lies, and Videotape,* the movie *La tarea* (*Homework*) was in fact a remake of one that Hermosillo had originally made in video format. Here, Hermosillo's innovations were more formal than thematic: *La tarea* is shot from a single, fixed viewpoint and sets itself up like a series of Chinese boxes.

The career of director Jorge Fons, one of the first new talents to come out of the film school that had been created at the National University in 1963, illustrates the difficulties that have confronted many filmmakers. His list of credits remains sparse, and a gap of more than ten years separates his first individually directed feature film from his second. In 1976, his first full-length feature, *Los albañiles* (*The Stonemasons*) appeared, based on a novel by Vicente Leñero. It combines a nuanced portrait of contemporary urban life with a murder mystery.

The subject of Fons's next feature *Rojo amanecer* (*Red Dawn*, 1989) was bound to generate controversy, and he staked his reputation on it. *Rojo amanecer* is virtually the only Mexican feature film to focus more or less directly on the Tlatelolco massacre of October 2, 1968. Ever since the film appeared there has been speculation as to whether the director made any concessions to government censors in order to get it distributed. It is perhaps the closest thing the new Mexican cinema has to a modern classic, and it won several Ariel awards (the Mexican equivalent of the Oscars). Due in part to budgetary limitations, Fons chose not to attempt to recreate the mass mobilizations that had taken place in 1968. Instead, all of the action is shot in an apartment in the large public-housing project that overlooks Tlatelolco Square where the massacre occurred. The film skillfully uses the "day in the life of" format to explore attitudes to and the effects of the 1968 student movement in a representative middle-class family. From petty family conflicts and typical generational tensions the story moves on to a newfound solidarity in the face of invasive government authority. Some critics, inevitably, were disappointed that this film, appearing some 20 years after the event, did not provide more complete documentation of the complex historical circumstances that led up to the Tlatelolco massacre. Critics also found some of the plot melodramatic and the dialogue stilted. Yet the film's chosen format effectively gives the larger-scale public events a particular, human face. It dramatizes how the older generations were jolted out of their comforting illusions about government benevolence, while the younger generations woke up to the flesh-and-blood dangers of their idealism.

In 1994, Fons followed *Rojo amanecer* with a film we have already referred to, one with strong commercial appeal, using a screenplay by Vicente Leñero based on a work by the Egyptian novelist Naguib Mahfouz. *El callejón de los milagros* boasts an impressive cast of stars, including María Rojo, Ernesto Gómez Cruz, and the young Salma Hayek. This film updates the classic *cine de arrabal* (the melodramatic saga of the inner-city neighborhood); it deals with a varied group of characters whose lives intertwine in the vicinity of a single street in an old section of downtown Mexico City. With its emphasis on social scandal *El callejón* has the air of a polished and liberalized soap opera. In the best (or worst) tradition of the formula, it enshrines the misery and mediocrity of lives it portrays in a largely realistic and sympathetic manner; while for young men, the best option is illegal immigration to the United States, for beautiful young girls without prospects, the only escape is to be ushered, by ruthless pimps in flashy cars, into a life of high-class prostitution. The use of an anthology-type structure lends some interest to the otherwise rather predictable material; each segment of the film successively focuses on the life and point of view of each of the main characters, so that often viewers see the same incidents and events from different perspectives. In cultural terms, the film captures how in Mexico City, one of the largest cities in the world, each street and each neighborhood can still have the characteristics of a small and close-knit community.

TRENDS IN CONTEMPORARY CINEMA

The López Portillo presidential administration (1976–82) was by all accounts a difficult period for most independent producers and directors. López Portillo installed his sister, Margarita, as head of a newly created branch of the executive, the Directorate of Radio, Television, and Cinema. In principle, the new administration favored private initiatives and commercial value rather than the kind of state support for quality filmmaking that had been favored by Echeverría. Incentives were provided to attract foreign producers and directors to Mexico. Favoritism, scandal, and ineptitude plagued management of the new office. In 1982, a tragic, preventable fire consumed the Cineteca Nacional and the National Film Archives, one of Latin America's most extensive film collections. Some saw the fire as a price that the nation sadly had to pay for such mismanagement of the industry.

In response to continued economic crises, the next two presidential administrations, of Miguel de la Madrid (1982–88) and particularly Carlos Salinas de Gortari (1988–94), followed a course of economic liberalization and privatization, in the cinema industry as in most areas in which the government had substantial involvement. Tacitly, however, government policy recognized that it would prove impracticable, indeed disastrous, to pull the state-sponsorship rug completely out from under the industry. That is why, in 1983, the de la Madrid administration created the Instituto Mexicano de Cinematografía

(IMCINE); IMCINE lent its support, in conjunction with other public and private sources of funding, to most of the significant film projects of the 1980s and 1990s.

Alongside IMCINE, TELEVICINE (Telvisa's film production company) has emerged as the other major force in the contemporary industry. Created in 1978 as the film branch of the Azcárraga family television conglomerate, Televisa, TELEVICINE has sought to exploit the growing international, and particularly U.S. Hispanic, markets for Spanish-language television and video; it has proved to be a powerful force, given its economic weight and its established stable of writers, directors, and actors. TELEVICINE's original mission was to create a family cinema that could be promoted over the television airwaves and exploit its stars. Such was the case with *El chanfle* (*The Soccer Boot*, 1978), starring the well-known television comedian Chespirito, and with *La ilegal* (*The Illegal Immigrant*, 1979), starring pop star Lucía Mendez. (Film vehicles for the latest female pop stars have consistently been popular.)

Among TELEVICINE's greatest commercial successes was the series of vehicles it created for "la India María" (María Elena Velazco), a character originally developed on the popular television variety show *Siempre en domingo* (*Always on Sunday*). In classic comic style she is a country bumpkin whose endearing, down-to-earth wit and practical wiles allow her to get the best of her city-slicker antagonists. This made her into a popular heroine with whom moviegoers readily identified. Her early films include *Tonta tonta pero no tanto* (*Not as Foolish as You Think*, 1971) and *La presidenta municipal* (*The Municipal President*, 1974), in which she plays a role reminiscent of those of Cantinflas. In 1987 she starred in *Ni de aquí, ni de allá* (*Neither from Here nor There*) in which she carried her beguiling wit and humor across the border, playing an illegal domestic in Los Angeles. The popularity of the India María figure has provoked considerable discussion; for some, she epitomizes the demeaning stereotype of the Indian, yet for others, her dark skin and braided black hair have provided of refreshing contrast to the blond and fair-skinned models that dominate Mexican advertising and television.

In an effort to make the most of the surprising commercial success and critical attention that some recent independent and state-sponsored films have achieved, in the 1990s TELEVICINE added some quality, artistic films to its repertoire of glossy commercial fare. Occasionally, films such as *Entre Pancho Villa y una mujer desnuda* (*Caught Between Pancho Villa and a Naked Woman*, 1994) have managed to combine substance with entertainment value to a degree rarely seen since the heyday of the Golden Age.

With the implementation of the North American Free Trade Agreement in the early 1990s, privatization and commercialization of the film industry have continued at a pace that alarms nationalist partisans who fear foreign and particularly U.S. domination, and with good reason. Old film industry regulations, though never strictly observed, required theaters to show Mexican films 50 percent of the time. These regulations were replaced in 1992 with new ones that reduced that requirement substantially. The state-owned distribution monopoly, the Compañía Operadora de Teatros, the last nationalist stronghold, was put up for sale. Since then private, national and international theater chains like Cinemex, Cinemark, and Cinépolis have opened up all over the country. (With ticket prices in Mexico still low by international standards, cinemas have so far held their own against the ever-rising tide of home video and DVD.)

One should make no bones about the difficult challenges facing aspiring producers and directors. However, worthwhile and interesting films have appeared, not only by established directors of the New Cinema like Cazals, Ripstein, Hermosillo, and Leduc, but also by a new generation of young producers and directors. Below we discuss some of them, in addition to which the following deserve a mention: Alberto Cortés's *Amor a la vuelta de la esquina* (*Love Around the Corner,* 1985), Carlos García Agraz's *Mi querido Tom Mix* (*My Dear Tom Mix,* 1991), Carlos Carrera's *La mujer de Benjamin* (*Benjamin's Wife,* 1991), Alfonso Cuarón's *Sólo con tu pareja* (*Only with Your Partner,* 1991), and his more recent *Y tu mamá también* (*And Your Mom Too,* 2002).

The prophets of doom have been hard pressed to explain the success that films such as these have enjoyed among the growing ranks of university-educated, middle-class Mexican filmgoers. That this success has come just when many measures that protected Mexico's cinema from competition are being lifted makes their perplexity even greater. As if strengthened by adversity, the new directors have shown themselves to be adept at devising ways of financing their projects. Today, in Mexico as in many countries, complex coproduction arrangements involving private, government, university, and nonprofit foundation support, both foreign and domestic, underwrite many quality projects.

The complex gestation of filmmaker Nicolás Echevarría's historical film, *Cabeza de Vaca* (1990), illustrates well both the height of the hurdles to be overcome and the kind of perseverance that has been employed to overcome them. The film was originally launched as an exclusive IMCINE production in the mid-1980s, but for reasons never fully explained the state withdrew its financial backing while the project was still in pre-production. Undaunted, Echevarría aggressively sought backing from a broad mix of international sources that included both Spanish and British television, and he was able finally to complete work on the film in 1990. *Cabeza de Vaca's* international backing assured it a broad and effective distribution. Echevarría responded with a hermetic tour de force which, together with Paul Leduc's *Frida* and one or two other films, brought Mexican cinema a level of international recognition rarely seen since the classic Fernández-Figueroa films broke onto the European film festival circuit in the mid-1940s.

Cabeza de Vaca is freely based on the published memoirs of its legendary title figure, a member of a sixteenth-century Spanish expedition led by Pánfilo Narváez that was shipwrecked off the coast of Florida in 1527. Cabeza de Vaca's memoirs recount how he wandered lost among the Indians of the southern United States for several years before making his way back to the north of Mexico, where he finally stumbled upon another Spanish expedition. Though Echevarría had worked mostly with documentaries, the finished product in this instance is nothing like an objective, authoritative, historical re-creation. Rather, through inventive use of imagery and sparse and garbled dialogue in a variety of tongues, the film attempts to convey the subjective and archly New World experience of the individuals involved. Some of it is heavy-handed and the acting can be ponderous. We see how, in his struggle to survive, Cabeza de Vaca essentially went native. Much of the action is shrouded in dark ritual and mystery. It deliberately leaves much to the viewer's imagination, and each new screening can reveal new symbols and deeper meanings; thus, by means of this heuristic quality, the viewer's experience parallels that of the historical figures. Only the powerful and eloquent opening and closing scenes, in which we see Spaniards interacting with Spaniards, lend themselves to conventional interpretation. In the opening scene, as the explorers march inland through the jungle, their desperate hope that their Christian cross will protect them is as patent as their fear is palpable. But by the end of the film, when the long-forgotten Cabeza de Vaca is rescued by the Spanish explorers, a remarkable inversion of perspective has been achieved. Suddenly we see, as the natives must have, and as Cabeza de Vaca himself surely did, how the Spanish conquerors, mounted on their powerful horses and clad in shining armor, could seem to be equally mysterious and barbaric.

The kind of artistically ambitious and revisionist look at pre-Hispanic America that Echevarría provided in *Cabeza de Vaca* has appeared in other noteworthy contemporary films as well.[3] Juan Mora Catlett's *Retorno a Aztlán/In Necuepalitzli in Aztlán* (*Return to Aztlán,* 1990) is visually stunning and perhaps Mexico's only feature length film to have dealt exclusively with pre-Hispanic Mexico. It weaves a magical tale around the Aztec legend of the group's mythic origins in lands to the north of Mexico, and paints a polychromatic picture of Aztec culture. In recognition of the vigor and difference of Mexico's indigenous cultures, the film uses the Nahuatl language in its dialogue and pre-Hispanic instruments in its score. The 1994 Zapatista rebellion in Chiapas has also inspired renewed attention to indigenous subjects among practitioners of the so-called militant cinema in Mexico.

Two closely related trends have stood out in recent Mexican cinema. One has been the powerful upsurge of women's issues, women's perspectives, and women directors. The other has been the return to prominence in Hollywood of Mexican themes, directors, and stars. These trends came together most visibly in the huge international success of *Como agua para chocolate* (*Like Water for Chocolate*, 1991), based on the novel by Laura Esquivel and directed by the veteran of Mexican theater and film, Alfonso Arau.

Historically, women have found it virtually impossible to make their way into the higher power circles of the Mexican cinema industry, the cases of Matilde Landeta and Marcela Fernández Violante being rather exceptional. Interest in the handful of films that Landeta directed in the late 1940s and early 1950s was revived when she returned, after an exile from the industry of some 40 years, to direct *Nocturno a Rosario* in 1990. As for Fernández Violante, having directed films such as *De todos modos Juan te llamas* (*Whatever You Do It Makes No Difference*, 1975) and *Misterio* (1980), in 1985 she was appointed director of CUEC. The position of women can hardly have been helped by the disastrous experience under President López Portillo's sister, Margarita, as head of the Radio, Television, and Cinema Directorate. But since at least the mid-1970s, the new Mexican cinema has frequently championed the overturning of traditional male-centered perspectives and shown greater sensitivity to women's issues (most notably, in the films of Jaime Humberto Hermosillo). Beginning in the mid- to late-1980s, new female directors have met with significant support and encouragement. Their films have tapped into rapidly changing sensibilities, in Mexico and across the globe, without restricting themselves to feminism. Often favoring the intuitive and natural/supernatural over the rational and objective, women directors have also proved to be extremely adept at reviving and exploiting, not without some controversy, the attractions of magical realism.

Several young female directors have come out of Mexico's film schools, either the state's Centro de Capacitación Cinematográfica or the National University's Centro Universitario de Estudios Cinematográficos. Noteworthy debuts have been made by Busi Cortés and Dana Rothberg, among others. Cortés' *El secreto de Romelia* (*Romelia's Secret*, 1988) was adapted from a text by the noted author and feminist Rosario Castellanos, and explores the lives of three generations of women in a single family. Rothberg, in her second film, *Angel de fuego* (*Angel of Fire*, 1992), follows the life of a protagonist who earns her living as a fire-eater. This film examines the plight of working-class women caught up in a vortex of temptations and seduction on the fringes, literally and figuratively, of Mexico City.

Among new women directors, María Novaro has unquestionably developed the most solid international reputation. Most of Novaro's films have followed scripts co-written with her sister, Beatriz. Their first film, *Lola* (1989), takes a penetrating look at the prospects of young working women in Mexico City, and it won several Latin American prizes. The protagonist is a single mother, recently separated from an aspiring rock musician, who supports herself and her young daughter by selling black-market clothing at a street stand. In a role that has little in common with the two female archetypes of classic Mexican cinema (the pure and self-sacrificing mother, and the vice-ridden prostitute) Lola succumbs to the pressures of her existence and abandons her daughter, but later comes to terms with her responsibilities. Novaro's second film, *Danzón* (1991), also features a single mother in a search for personal fulfillment and identity, but it follows a softer and more ambiguous story line, centered on the protagonist's passion for ballroom dancing. Her routine existence as a telephone operator is disrupted when her long-time dance partner, whom she depends on emotionally, one day fails to appear. The search she undertakes becomes a voyage of self-discovery and affirmation.

One of Novaro's more interesting and recent films, *El jardín del Edén* (*The Garden of Eden*, 1994), continues to explore the theme of women's search for meaning and identity in a chaotic, globalized, and media-overloaded world where traditional moorings no longer hold firm. This film, however, branches out from the tightly drawn focus on the life story of one representative woman. It moves the setting to the border town of Tijuana, a multilingual and multicultural crossroads. It loosens structurally to follow an ensemble cast of marginalized or alienated figures. Most of them have crossed or hope to cross the border in one direction or the other. Eventually, out of their intersection, they discover some meaning in their lives, however partial or temporary. At the core are two contrasting young female figures. There is a Mexican American girl who can barely speak Spanish but seeks awkwardly to find her Mexican roots, though helplessly lost and unfulfilled in both worlds. And her counterpart is a stereotypical air-headed, blonde *gringa* who has come in search of her brother, a latter-day hippie. With similar awkwardness, but natural spontaneity, she discovers feelings of compassion and finds purpose in her involvement in the disordered lives of those around her. These diverse North American and Mexican characters attempt to come to terms with the complex web of complicity and interdependence that binds together the people of the two nations. To further complicate this cultural and linguistic hodge-podge, in the background indigenous communities eke out an existence on both sides of the border. Whatever *El jardín del Edén* may lack in overall coherence, it easily makes up in its provocative portrayal of the kind of cultural hybridity that has long characterized the border region, and increasingly encroaches into the heartlands of both countries.

In recent years Mexican cinema has shown signs of once again transcending the divide between the popular audiences that frequent mass-produced films and the latest Hollywood movies, and the discerning audiences that prefer international art-house fare. *Entre Pancho Villa y una mujer desnuda* (1994) ties together several interesting threads in Mexican cinema in an original way, and it also brings a bold vision of shifting and revalued gender roles to a mainstream, commercial production. The film was adapted from Sabina Berman's successful stage play and co-directed by Isabelle Tardán.

Entre Pancho Villa y una mujer desnuda opens with a scene of two apparently self-assured executive women at work, giving orders to their male subordinates and sharing the latest details of their sex lives. As the film unfolds, however, their power and independence undergo a thorough reexamination. The protagonist has an affair with a history professor who is hard at work on a new biography of Pancho Villa, but the relationship is skin-deep at best and does little to address her emotional needs. The film excoriates the leading male figure, though it is softened by a good deal of humor. The history professor likes to project the image of a self-assured don Juan, but at bottom he is extremely insecure; his struggles as a writer show that, at least figuratively, he is impotent, and he draws what inspiration he can from his alter ego, Pancho Villa. In a series of hilarious scenes, Villa appears as a ghost at the pair's side, or when the historian is alone, at moments of crisis in his love life or his writing. Villa constantly implores him to lift his flagging spirits, in the desperate hope that he will do no dishonor to his gender or to traditional Mexican machismo. To further emphasize the continuity between the Villa archetype and the contemporary male, the film also shows Villa in a series of historical flashbacks as a mama's boy—an aspect of his character glossed over in the standard historical texts. In a final twist, it is suggested that not just the male but the female figure too feeds her fantasy on the legendary masculinity of Villa. In all, the film skillfully relates contemporary gender issues to stigmas deriving from Mexico's cultural heritage. It wraps a complex social and historical portrait in a highly entertaining package.

Many Mexicans are now exploiting the possibilities of Hollywood as much as they are being exploited by it. They are tempted to flee the economic constraints and cumbersome bureaucracy of filmmaking in Mexico, attracted by carte blanche budgets and massive publicity and distribution networks. Hollywood, for its part, has recognized the economic potential of the growing Hispanic population of the United States and the fashionableness of all things (sensuously) Latin among the younger generation. *Como agua para chocolate* was the trailblazer, yet no one anticipated its immense success, in Mexico, in the United States, and worldwide. It tells a melodramatic love story, intensified by absolute adherence to arcane traditions; the suitor of the youngest daughter cannot consummate his impassioned love (until the very end of the movie, replete with fireworks and engulfing flames), because convention dictates that the eldest daughter marry first. The thoroughgoing focus on a household of women suggests the prospect of a feminist subtext, but the characters' generally conservative acceptance of tradition minimizes the threat they pose to traditional values and manners. Like other products of the so-called feminine boom that has swept through Latin American art and literature in recent decades, this film thoroughly exploits the attractions of magical realism. The most striking example is the way in which the emotions the young daughter feels are suffused into the foods she prepares, with amazing physical effects on those who consume them. One might almost conclude that with such unlikely scenarios the film (like the novel) is presenting a gentle, tongue-in-cheek parody of such soupy, magical realist hyperbole, but in fact there is no unambiguous evidence for such a conclusion.

Like certain other Mexican manifestations of the feminine boom, *Como agua para chocolate* appears to take refuge from the present through a nostalgic revival of that most legendary of recent pasts, the Revolution. But in spite of the historical focus, the Revolution is little more than a backdrop, and the film has a strangely atemporal, rather incongruously enlightened and contemporary air. The movie does speak of the long-standing ties that have bound the United States and Mexico, but it seems intent on defusing their historical tensions. The heart-broken young daughter finds solace and comfort in her marriage to a young American doctor from the Southwest, a kind of benevolent father figure for her (though quite white, he too claims some Hispanic heritage). Rather like the screen adaptation of Carlos Fuentes's novel *Gringo viejo* (*The Old Gringo*), the film appears to be bent on suggesting an improbable mutually respectful relationship that might serve as a model for more fruitful and humane relations between the two nations. U.S. and European audiences no doubt are attracted by the way the film highlights the features that Latin cultures are supposed to have, features that are missing in the coldly capitalist and technologically efficient Anglo-American way of life—comforting traditions combined with ardent passion, and time to enjoy the sensuality of the smell of rose petals.

The success of *Como agua para chocolate* opened the door for Arau to direct a Hollywood film in a similar vein. In *A Walk in the Clouds* (*Un paseo por las nubes,* 1994), the main action shifts from northern Mexico to California, but the formula and basic premises remain the same; it is nostalgic for simpler times (World War II), when traditional values of hard work and sacrifice, of integrity and loyalty, still mattered. It also presents a positive model for intercultural relations, in which traditional prejudices and class divisions might be overcome thanks to adhering to core values.

Other, younger directors have crossed over with aggressively contemporary updates of genre films that have enjoyed a vigorous cult following. Rather than exploiting Mexico's stereotypical differences, these films emphasize how conversant Mexico has become with the latest vices of popular culture. Richard Rodríguez, for example, made *El Mariachi* (1992) in Mexico on a shoestring budget, apparently with little thought of possible profit; but his film was picked up for international distribution and it turned out to be a smash commercial, and even critical, hit. Drawing on the popular narco-film genre, it acquired a kind of stylized, bare-bones realism, a postmodern aura. The hero, a young innocent seeking only to eke out an honest living as a traditional, itinerant musician, gets caught up in the war between rival drug lords through a case of mistaken identity. His sense of pride and principle lead him not only to win the girl, but also to stand up to the drug lords with unlikely courage and amazing dexterity. *El Mariachi's* success led Rodríguez to Hollywood, where he directed the frightfully violent and wildly chaotic *From Dusk Till Dawn*.

A similar cult following has also grown up around an accomplished horror film directed by Guillermo del Toro. *Cronos* (1992) follows the fortunes of an elderly Mexican antiques dealer who discovers, hidden in an ancient statue in his possession, an ancient alchemist's device that gives vampire-type immortality. A darkly obsessed U.S. industrial magnate plays the antagonist who is in desperate pursuit of this magical but bloodthirsty device. On the basis of this, del Toro was entrusted with a $30 million budget by Miramax films to direct the English-language film *Mimic* (1997), which is in the same vein.

The underlying issues of cultural politics that have always been present in Mexican cinema's relations with Hollywood have not been expunged. Salma Hayek today, like Dolores del Río several generations before her, may well wonder whether her cultural capital and identity are being compromised when in the service of Hollywood and cosmetic companies. Still, there can be little question that in the midst of grave uncertainties about the country's future, Mexico's cinema has regained a level of quality and interest that does its strong tradition proud. Consider the quality of such recent films as *Del olvido al no me acuerdo* (*From Forgetting to Not Remembering*, 1999) by Juan Carlos Rulfo, the famous writer's son, and of *Amores perros* (*Love's a Bitch*, 2000). The latter, for example, having caught people's attention at several film festivals, was quickly picked up for wide international distribution, even gracing the shelves of small-town branches of Blockbuster Video in the United States.

Amores perros was the first full-length feature film by Alejandro González Iñárritu, who had previously worked in television; its screenplay is by the young novelist Guillermo Arriaga. The film is based on the old idea of several lives that cross; in fact, the structural nexus of the plot is literally a crossroads, where a serious car accident occurs. In ensuing sections of the film, we follow the lives of different people implicated in the accident: a working-class family, one of whose members stakes his future on his fighting dog; a young to middle-aged pair of lovers who set up house together only to find that their life is ruined by the accident; and finally an alienated upper-middle-class man who has turned hired assassin and tramp. Among other things, this film deals with different social strata, their weaknesses and foibles. For example, the woman in the second section is a model whose publicity images loom large in the background in contrast with the reality of her shattered life (and body); the fact that she is (a false) blonde, and Spanish, reflects a certain Mexican preference for the foreign, its continuing dependence on imperial, colonial models. A number of themes and motifs run through these episodes: dogs play a role in each case, always given to unquestioning loyalty and inspiring genuine affection in their owners; there are also recurrent suggestions of an underworld; and the theme of Cain and Abel is evident more than once. In the concluding scene the hired assassin sells his vehicle and heads off on foot with his dog across a barren landscape. Is he redeemed, turning over a new leaf? Is the sale of his vehicle (an SUV) a symbol of his rejection of a certain set of values? As he heads off across the wasteland towards a distant glow, the film seems to speak of the ugliness of modernization and industrialization, but perhaps there is a hint of some desirable and different future, or even a mythical El Dorado. Whatever the ending may imply, like many fine films, this one can be enjoyed at face value; it is skillfully put together, moves at a brisk pace, is well acted, and intrigues the viewer. It is proof that Mexican cinema is still very much alive.

NOTES

1. Our account of Buñuel is deliberately brief, notwithstanding his importance in Mexico. The reason is that so much has been written about him elsewhere.

2. 2002 saw the release of another *Frida*, a biopic directed by Julie Taymor. It stars Salma Hayek, who also was producer. This film is based on a biography written by Hayden Herrera.

3. This and other films mentioned here were released at about the time of the 500th anniversary of the Spanish discovery of the New World—in other words, at a time when it became politically correct to talk not of discovery but encounter.

6

Performing Arts

MUSIC, DANCE, AND THEATER are often closely linked, and they were inextricably so in pre-Hispanic and early colonial Mexico. In fact, their close association in the performance of Aztec rituals was exploited by the Spaniards, whose own performance practices of the time were in any case mixed. Consider that theater begins as verbal artifact, but is only fully realized when performed; it is a communal activity rather than one engaged in by individuals in private settings.

The evolution of things distinctively Mexican began in colonial times and naturally gained impetus during the nineteenth-century movement towards independence and especially at the time of the Mexican Revolution. Neither independence nor the Revolution, however, brought cultural independence; by the early twentieth century, after centuries spent emulating European models, Mexicans began to find a voice of their own, but even then they were steeped in the latest foreign techniques. They infused their works with local, indigenous, and folkloric elements and then, ironically, their work began to attract the attention of Europe and the United States. In dance and especially in music (much as in the areas of painting and sculpture) international attention was drawn to Mexico in the wake of its Revolution, a time when, as it happened, there was also a reaction in Europe against its own traditions, and instead a pursuit of the exotic, the primitive and native.

During the course of this chapter we shall adopt a broadly historical approach, and particularly in its early sections we shall move freely from one genre to another. We may begin our account with some illustrative comments focused largely on music. There is something paradoxical about music; it is the purest of art forms, one that rarely attempts to represent anything but itself, its own sounds and rhythms, and yet it is almost inseparable from social events, celebrations, and rituals. Dance is closely entwined with the forms of musical accompaniment upon which it is dependent, and with the setting or stage on which it is performed. (Interestingly, however, while the history of Mexican popular and fine art music is full of cross-fertilizations, dance is more clearly divided into folkloric, high art, and popular forms.)

Mexico is now famous for certain distinctive musical practices and forms, such as the mariachi band, *norteño* music, and the canción ranchera that rose to popularity during Mexican cinema's Golden Age. Music, particularly popular music, is ubiquitous in Mexico; the mariachi band, for example, can be heard at all kinds of festivities and events, even during masses. Most of the distinctive music that we associate with Mexico is popular. Yet this Mexican music has grown primarily from European roots; while there are Indian and African elements in parts of it, such elements are less prominent than in the music of some other Latin American cultures.

The European sources can be divided into two categories, partly corresponding to historical phases. First came the popular and religious medieval and Renaissance forms brought to Mexico by the Spaniards. The predominant flavor of these forms was southern, the flavor of the Spanish provinces of Extremadura and Andalucía, from which the majority of the early colonizers and missionaries came. Such music drew on the confluence of Islamic, Jew-

Mariachis perform at a family celebration. Photo by Steven Bell.

ish, and Christian cultures. Later, especially in the eighteenth and nineteenth centuries, there were other European influences: from the works of Romanticism, from opera, and from the dances of elegant salons. Brought to Mexico by immigrants and visiting musicians, these things were copied and adapted by Mexicans. Twentieth-century influences, particularly on popular music, included such crazes as the fox-trot and the cake-walk from the United States, and the rumba, mambo, and other forms from the Caribbean.

COLONIAL TIMES

To judge by the chronicles left by the Spanish conquerors and missionaries, music, dance and theater were important in many pre-conquest Meso-American ceremonies and festivities. The early missionaries exploited analogies between Christian and pagan practices as they set about the task of converting the natives. Most historians believe that as far as music is concerned, many pre-Hispanic practices were effectively supplanted by orthodox Spanish religious ones. If so, then what of the pre-Hispanic did survive? Although the evidence on which to base an opinion is not particularly solid or plentiful, it has been asserted that "from pre-Cortesian music we have received not a single melody, not a single beat"; whatever is assumed to have survived is of doubtful authenticity, and has been colored by European influences (Mayer-Serra, 120–21). And so the indigenous exoticism for which Carlos Chávez made Mexico famous in the early twentieth century boils down to a speculative invention of what might have been pre-Hispanic music, conceived from a thoroughly European, avant-garde standpoint, and it is as strange and exotic for modern Mexicans (except possibly for those in the most isolated indigenous communities) as it is for foreigners (161–62). If pre-conquest music has not survived, neither has there been the kind of determined attempt to reconstruct, revive, and exploit it in Mexico that there has been in modern times with Andean music. The simple fact is that we do not really know what pre-conquest music in Mexico was like.

Somewhat more identifiable is the African contribution to colonial music. There are several explanations of the origins of that contribution: importation of slaves (though this was never done on the scale found elsewhere in Latin America), or the fact that numbers of slaves escaped during colonial times from the Caribbean islands to the Mexican coast. (We might add that in the twentieth century there was commercial exploitation of Caribbean musical forms.) One curious instance of African influence has nothing to do with drums, or with characteristic rhythms, or with call-and-response patterns: the marimba, an instrument common in Meso-America and (even held to be the national instrument of Guatemala) is generally thought to derive from an African xylophone. That said, there is no doubt that the main formative influences on Mexican music are European, though not only Spanish. There is certainly hybridization in music, but it is not the thorough hybridization one finds in other parts of Latin America.

Especially in colonial times, the rituals of the Catholic Church exerted a pervasive influence on music. Churches, and cathedrals in particular, required singers, instrumentalists, composers, and teachers who could ensure that music was available and of adequate quality. Organs and more portable instruments were brought over from Spain. In the colonies, natives were trained in Spanish musical ways, and a number became quite distinguished performers and composers. The archives of Latin American cathedrals are rich with proof of the level and style of musical activity; they show us that, in addition to the works of local musicians, distinguished European composers of polyphony had their music performed in the New World.

After 1700 music in Spanish America gradually moved toward the secular, and with that there came a decline in quality and quantity. For the most part, the viceregal court appears to have paid little attention to refined musical composition—so much so that by the dawn of independence Mexico was sorely lacking in musical instruction and skilled musicians, a fact noted by many foreign travelers and observers, and one regretted throughout the nineteenth century by nationalist partisans and liberal-minded statesmen.

Due to their very nature, popular forms are extremely difficult to trace and document, and a confusing proliferation of names and terms, some referring to both songs and dances, further complicates the task. Contemporary descriptions of early popular music and dance in New Spain, as in Spain itself and Europe, are few and far between, and the best testimony to their popularity comes, paradoxically, in the form of the official edicts expressing moral outrage and seeking to prevent them. Spanish popular forms from Andalusia completely dominated early Mexican popular music. To perhaps a surprising degree, the flow of musical inspiration and influence between Spain and its American colonies proved to be two-way.

Apart from songs of religious praise and the many ritual, didactic, and allegorical dances that were employed in the process of evangelization during the first century of Spanish colonial rule, almost all of the court and popular songs and dances practiced in Spain in the sixteenth century found their way to Mexico. These were already hybrids—the products of Gypsy, European, and Moorish (North African) influences. Perhaps it was because effective networks of social control took some time to establish that sixteenth century colonial authorities were surprisingly tolerant of songs and dances, and of the inevitable confusion of forms in an American society that brought together Spanish, indigenous, and African peoples. Such tolerance would diminish

considerably when in the seventeenth century the Church's role changed
from guardian of the natives to accomplice of the dominant Spanish and creole castes. As early as 1569, the Viceroy Luis de Velasco felt compelled to
impose limits on African exuberance, decreeing that blacks could only dance
in the main square in Mexico City on Sundays and holidays, between noon
and 6 P.M. During the seventeenth and into the eighteenth centuries, Spanish
colonial authorities increasingly denounced, censored, or otherwise sought to
restrict the lasciviousness of the dances and music of blacks, mulattos, and
mestizos—the people of the lower classes. But in the late colonial period popular song lyrics became more and more critical of the Church and other
authorities. During the battle for independence from Spain, Mexican popular ballads played almost as important a role in bolstering nationalist, anti-
Spanish sentiment as did the Virgin of Guadalupe.

   Something of the style and spirit of pre-Hispanic ritual dance did survive
in semi-disguised form in the religious festivities and rituals of the colonial
period, much more than was the case with music. The radical differences of
instrumentation and style between pre-Hispanic and European music must
have been a serious impediment to the survival of indigenous forms. This is
not to say that Indian performers were not an important part of religious festivities and rituals in colonial times; and surely their ways must have colored
colonial performances, even when they were performing on the European-
styled instruments on which they had received training from missionaries.
Maya Ramos Smith cites an example: in the festivities organized by the
Regent of Mexico City in 1600, it was decreed that Indian performers be
brought from outlying, missionary-dominated areas so that they might sing
and perform on their *vihuelas* (a *vihuela* being a Spanish stringed instrument
like a guitar) (*La danza*, 24).

   Ritual dance was a key ingredient in pre-Hispanic rites and celebrations,
and it seems to have been the form of artistic expression that Spanish colonial
authorities found least exotic and incomprehensible, most malleable and
compatible with Spanish medieval religious practices. Though always controversial and opposed by many moralists, Spanish religious festivities had themselves seen a resurgence in the sixteenth century, particularly in the form of
the religious plays known as *autos sacramentales* and the celebration of the
feast of Corpus Christi, which were brought early on to New Spain and celebrated continuously between 1526 and 1866 in Mexico City, no doubt with
ample participation of people of all sorts. The Jesuit Father Acosta's *Historia
natural y moral de las Indias* contains some quite explicit suggestions relating
to how the indigenous proclivity for ceremonial dance might be exploited for
the purpose of acculturation and evangelization. He calls for a permissive attitude to the practice of native dances by indigenous people (cited by Ramos

Smith, *La danza*, 20). Besides, no doubt the Spanish colonial authorities were entertained by the curious gyrations of their newly discovered subjects. The Spaniards' power to command performances by their Indian subjects must have encouraged a patronizing sense of having unearthed curiosities. Hernán Cortés returned to Spain in 1527 with a group of Indians to display to the European authorities; so much did their acrobatics delight the court of Carlos V that this dance troupe continued on to the Vatican to entertain Pope Clemente VII. Back in New Spain, one sign of tolerance, even of explicit support for dance as an outlet for Indian expression and as a mode of entertainment for the Spaniards, was to be found in the square beside the Viceregal Palace: the Plaza del Volador, outfitted specially for the practice of the famous pre-Hispanic flying dance.

The Spanish authorities had set their cathedrals directly upon the ruins of pre-Hispanic temples and places of pilgrimage and, as a result, Indian pilgrims continued to visit these sites as they had done in the past. (Today, one can see the flying dance reenacted outside the Museo Nacional de Antropología. Modern, amateur dancers dressed in Aztec garb, perform for the benefit of tourists in the Zócalo in Mexico City, between the cathedral and the excavation of the Templo Mayor, but their performances are of dubious authenticity; perhaps they are attempting to evoke the spiritual qualities

Aztec dance re-creation in front of the Palacio Nacional (National Palace), Mexico City. Photo by Steven Bell.

associated with the site, but there is little evidence that their activities derive in any direct way from pre-conquest practices.)

Other, more concrete links connecting pre-conquest and post-conquest religious dance can be found. There are similarities between, on the one hand, medieval Spain's long-standing battle for Catholic re-conquest of the peninsula and defeat of the infidel Moors, and, on the other, the process of conversion and evangelization of the Indians in the New World territories. The latter was an obvious and direct continuation of the former. In support of the military and spiritual confrontation in Spain, there had emerged theatrical performances, based heavily on dance and mime, known as *moros y cristianos* ("Moors and Christians"). Such performances were brought to New Spain in the early days and there they enjoyed considerable popularity. There was even a local variant that developed, known as the *danza de la conquista* (dance of the conquest), in which the Moors were, of course, replaced by the Indians in the role of vanquished villains. Theater and dance historians have speculated that the importance of war dances among the pre-conquest civilizations made the Spanish forms particularly accessible for the native population and a particularly effective means of indoctrinating them. Regionally, the danza de moros y cristianos developed strong, local traditions in many parts of central Mexico, traditions that remained virtually unchanged until very recently. There is, of course, some irony in the fact that Indians were joyously celebrating reenactments of the conquest of their own civilizations. Generally, the pagan ceremonies and dances of the Meso-American Indians found their primary means of expression in the context of Spanish religious pageantry. A more radical picture of one culture supplanting another is found in the evolution of secular dance, both of the popular and refined varieties; they show little, if any, recognizable indigenous influence, and were entirely of Spanish and European derivation, regardless of the racial characteristics of the dancers.

Looking back on the colonial era, Rodolfo Usigli writes that together with firearms and horses, theater was "one of the most vigorous elements of persuasion employed by the conquerors" (Usigli, 60). It was an instrument of indoctrination, a way of bringing the Indians to the faith and of keeping the colony in order. The colonial authorities, particularly during the Counter-Reformation and the time of the Inquisition, kept a tight rein on what was to be performed: Bishop Zumárraga instituted formal censorship in 1574. Drama in New Spain closely followed the fashions of the mother country and the popular Spanish theater of the times, in contrast to the more refined opera and ballet that were in vogue in France and Italy. As soon as theatrical production had a foothold in Mexico, popular, courtly, and hybrid forms of song and dance were used before, during, and after plays, and these numbers (*fan-*

dangos, entremeses, and *mojigangas* or *fines de fiesta*) became an increasingly important and welcome part of the experience. The repertoire of songs and dances during such performances presents us with a confusing array of names, and little detailed description exists of the forms involved. It is clear that they were Spanish, but they resulted from an eclectic range of influences, and the exact origins of many of them are subject to debate. Interestingly, according to the references to the songs and dances of the sixteenth and seventeenth centuries that we find in Spanish documents of the time, such as the plays of Lope de Vega and Cervantes, many songs and dances, particularly the more openly sensual ones, were due to the corrupting influence of the pagan and barbarous Indies. In all, secular music was apparently of least concern to the colonial authorities, and provided it was not seen as subversive, it was the least controlled, especially in remote places. With time, there was greater freedom of expression. Dances and songs brought over from Europe began to change in the process of acculturation. In 1785 the Spanish colonial viceroy acceded to the first officially approved public presentation in New Spain of popular airs and dances.

As to particular playwrights, two Mexicans from the colonial period deserve special mention. One was Juan Ruiz de Alarcón, born in 1580 to a well-to-do family; after twenty years in Mexico he became a student at the University of Salamanca (Spain's oldest), later occupying an important position in the Consejo de Indias, the advisory body to the Crown on matters relating to the New World. Alarcón, who was physically deformed, suffered the cruel derision of some of his contemporaries. In one of his plays, he turned this into a theme; *Las paredes oyen* (*Walls Have Ears*) deals with a hunchback writer who rebels against people who mock him. But, in fact, Ruiz de Alarcón was vindicated by his works, and his 25 plays have given him a reputation as one of the major dramatists of Spain's Golden Age. Alarcón's plays, which often deal with moral or ethical issues, are carefully constructed and strong on character; in some respects his work anticipates that of later, satirical Spanish dramatists. His most famous play, *La verdad sospechosa* (*The Doubtful Truth*), about an engaging but mendacious young man involved with two sisters, served as inspiration for Corneille's *Le Menteur* (*The Liar*). Though Alarcón's work was produced in Spain for the Spanish stage, Mexican literary historians still claim him as their own, and they suggest that the keen insight he showed into the plight of the social outcast may have related not only to his deformity, but also to his status as an *indiano* among peninsulares.

The second famous dramatist, though somewhat better known for her poetry, is Sor Juana Inés de la Cruz. Born as Juana Inés de Asbaje y Ramírez in 1648, she became so well known for her intellectual acumen that she was invited to live at the court of the viceroy. For reasons that are not entirely clear—perhaps an unhappy love affair or disaffection with the material ways of the world about her, and surely her wish to devote time to her studies and writing—she entered a convent and became Sor Juana Inés de la Cruz. Despite some difficult moments with the Church hierarchy, she wrote scientific, mystical, erotic, even feminist works, and these have made her the most celebrated and daring of all Spanish American creative writers during colonial times. Her plays include three autos sacramentales (allegorical illustrations of the meaning of the sacraments) with their accompanying prologues (*loas*)—the latter being especially interesting, not to say explosive, for the times. In them, instead of the stock panegyrics in support of the status quo, she presents Aztec women characters, attacks the strictures of antiquated dogma (which for good measure she associates with men) and suggests that doubt is the foundation for knowledge! *Divino Narciso* is one of the autos sacramentales; it links the mythological Narcissus with Christ, and Echo with the Devil, and in the loa she makes America an allegorical figure. There are also two secular plays in the style of Lope de Vega. One of them, *Los empeños de una casa* (*The Labors of a Household*), appears to be partly autobiographical; it has a strong leading female figure, and also a brown-skinned servant character called Castaño (Chestnut) who pokes fun at the machismo of white men; the style of the play is itself parodic. Notwithstanding the value of their works, both Alarcón and Sor Juana provide proof not only of the recognition to be won in the Spanish metropolis by colonial authors, but also of the influence of Spain's theatrical styles on colonial Mexico. In fact, Spanish styles and Spanish dramatists would be favored and officially supported for many years to come, and they would dominate the Mexican theater scene even into the early twentieth century, while Mexican dramatists often faced real impediments.

Early religious and missionary theater was performed outside of churches, in atriums, and in squares, in Spanish as well as in Náhuatl and other indigenous languages, as early as the 1530s. There is evidence that the very first *corral de comedias* (a Spanish courtyard–style theater) in Spanish America was built by Francisco de León in Mexico City in 1597. About a century later, next to the Hospital Real de Naturales, long a focal point for theatrical activity, the first Mexican coliseum theater was opened. It was destroyed by fire in 1722, but it was soon replaced, and more were built in other cities, with the result that the eighteenth century is sometimes called the Age of the Coliseum. As to the fare offered, it remained basically Spanish, in form and conception if not in actual authorship, and it was some time before the neoclassical and *costumbrista* styles took a hold. (*Costumbrista* refers to art that emphasizes local customs or human types; it provided a way for a nation anxious to highlight its own identity to do so through local color.)

FROM INDEPENDENCE TO THE REVOLUTION

In the nineteenth century, with its newly acquired independence, Mexico was trying to redefine its national identity. In the latter part of the century, it opened up to new European influences, Italian and French in particular. As these were brought to bear on older Spanish styles, music best described as Mexican began to appear. The popularity of Italian opera and the Spanish *zarzuela* (a form of light opera, full of local color) led to the development of the lyrical *canción mexicana*.[1] The poetic and musical properties of European dances such as the waltz and the polka, and musical forms such as the Italian aria, were more faithfully preserved in sophisticated urban centers than in distant rural areas. The ornamentation of the virtuoso *bel canto* style of singing, for example, appealed to the urban elite, but the tastes of ranchers and cowhands were less refined. The intricate poetic and musical forms characteristic of literate musicians were of less interest to rural people than were simplified, straightforward songs. And so songs were commonly reduced to two rhymed verses of four lines plus a refrain that typically repeated part of the verses. Musical elements (melody, harmony, and rhythm) were also simplified. Melodies were confined to a moderate range and emphasized harmonic tones; harmony was reduced to two or three chords; rhythms were based on European traditions, but a characteristic alternation or simultaneous use of 3/4 and 6/8 time made for a lively mix.

After the Revolution, a surge of nationalism led to greater appreciation of rural genres of music, such as the corrido and the canción mexicana. It was in this period that the latter's main type, the canción ranchera developed, rising to fame thanks to performances by Pedro Infante, Jorge Negrete, and others in radio broadcasts, recordings, and films. The ranchera has been featured in numerous motion pictures produced by the Mexican industry, serving not only to entertain, but also to emphasize national cultural values.

Historically derived from the Spanish *romance,* the corrido is one of the most popular and best known genres of Mexican music. Corridos and other song forms of the early nineteenth century told stories of the lives of settlers in northern Mexico. The violence, survival, and tragedies of frontier life were related in narrative ballads. The establishment of the Republic of Texas in 1836 and its admission as the 28th state in 1845 encouraged an influx into the border area of Germans, Czechs, and others who brought their own musical traditions, as well as cultural attitudes that produced social conflict with the native Mexican population. Towards the end of the century, the corrido, more than any other song genre, focused on struggles resulting from racial and class oppression. Resistance—the individual with his pistol, defending his rights—became the heroic topic of the genre and further distanced it from its origins in the romance. The Revolution of 1910 drew the corrido from Texas and the northern border deep into Mexico proper, where it recounted the adventures of bandits.

It came into its own at the time of the Revolution, and has remained closely associated with that ever since. The corrido clearly reflects the Mexican people's love of music, and is an example of functional exploitation of art. In fact, it is unlikely that the corrido would have achieved such popularity were it not for the Revolution, which somehow not only encouraged the use of the corrido but even demanded it. The Revolution was a fragmented, confused, and confusing historical event that advanced and receded by fits and starts, and on several fronts. It dragged on for the better part of ten years, sporadically affecting the daily lives of people throughout the country. Its heroes were an amazing cast of popular figures, eccentrics, and villains. The anonymous corrido provided the perfect medium through which to share and transmit news of the Revolution to a still largely illiterate populace. But above all, the corrido provided a way to take solace and establish a certain distance, however temporary and artificial, from the tragic uncertainties of the never-ending Revolution; one could celebrate the courage and triumphs of such popular heroes as Zapata and especially Villa, and poke fun at traitors like Victoriano Huerta or at perennial rivals such as the gringos. The corrido was largely a creation of the north and the central west—extending, with variants, down into the state of Morelos (the home of Zapata), but little known or practiced in the south. (It is another example of the frequent dominance of the culture of northern Mexico.) After the upheavals of the Revolution, the topics of the corrido were broadened to include other events: natural disasters, passionate love affairs, even happy occasions. In the end, it was a means of informing, relating, and remembering.

Approximately ten different types of corridos are recognized by experts. The characteristics that distinguish each type are neither musical nor formal, but rather focus on the subject matter or the intention of the text. The *balada romántica* is the universally popular sentimental ballad; the *historia* relates a criminal, disastrous, or sensational event; the *narración* is a dramatic narration; the *relato* is a statement or narration; the *ejemplo* is a lesson in morality; the *tragedia* relates an accident or violent death; *mañanitas* is a variety that thrives on rude language and humor; *recuerdos* are recollections of events, people, or times past; *versos* and *coplas* are vehicles for venting one's anger or frustration, or simply setting things straight. Almost all of the most popular corridos follow the same structure. The corrido singer (*corridista*) opens with a variation on the standard introduction, in which the singer humbly presents himself before his audience and announces the event he is about to narrate, and often the specific date on which it occurred. Then, after the story has been told, the ballad concludes with an affirmation of the lesson or moral of the story. Sometimes the singer will add a brief leave-taking to close the story, in symmetrical fashion. Corridos can be performed by more than one singer and there is a variety of instrumental accompaniments. Solo singers may accompany themselves on guitar or be accompanied by other instrumentalists, but the most prominent association is with the mariachi.

As noted earlier, the corrido derives from the romance, a popular and anonymous, eight-syllable verse ballad that narrated historical and epic feats. Bernal Díaz del Castillo makes reference to the romances in his famous chronicle of the conquest of Mexico. There is evidence that Cortés's soldiers used anonymous songs to express their protests and opinions (Mendoza, *El romance español y el corrido mexicano*). But the recognizably Mexican corrido did not emerge until the nineteenth century, after independence. The essential requirement for its appearance and popularity was the tension between a national consciousness of freedom and independence, and the existence of restrictions and limitations upon such things. The restrictions came in various guises: the U.S. invasion force of 1846–47, the intervention by the French under Maximilian of Hapsburg in the 1860s, and the oppressive and arbitrary injustice of authoritarian national governments, such as the one headed by Porfirio Díaz before the Revolution. With the outbreak of the Revolution, the corrido was at its peak; such was its power and popularity that it was also exploited in a printed form by people like Vanegas Arroyo, who happened to have the popular engraver José Guadalupe Posada in his employ. Printed sheets, emblazoned with the latest anonymous, satirical, or legendary corrido, and illustrated with a Posada caricature employing his characteristic skeleton figures, are said to have sold like hotcakes. Few artifacts can rival these documents for the way in which they capture the flavor and inventiveness of Mexican popular culture.

When the Revolution concluded, there were some efforts to exploit the popularity of the corridos for commercial ends. Some composers attempted to extend the tradition to cover contemporary events, abandoning the anonymity; but they met with little success. It seems that the essential ingredients of the corrido are popular origins, anonymity, and legendary subject matter. Although nowadays the corrido is primarily of academic and historical interest, it is a key element in Mexican folklore and still part of the repertoire of many so-called *orquestas típicas* (typical bands), especially those that play norteño music. Thus, while the corrido was originally the product of a single, itinerant musician, nowadays it is most commonly performed by groups and with accordion accompaniment (see below).

Mariachi is widely thought to be a corruption of the French word *mariage*; the theory is that it comes from the time of the French occupation of Mexico in the middle of the nineteenth century, when strolling musicians would entertain guests at weddings. A more nationalistic explanation of the name has it coming from the Coca Indian language of Jalisco, from a word for the wooden platforms on which dancers performed. There appears to be little disagreement, however, about the fact that the origins of the folk music traditions of mariachi are in Jalisco and its neighboring states.

The original mariachi ensemble appears to have consisted of a harp, a *guitarra de golpe,* a vihuela, and several violins. In Latin America in general instruments have been adapted or modified according to available materials and to performance needs. A case in point is the *guitarrón,* another common mariachi instrument; as its name suggests, it is an oversized guitar, and it evolved in Mexico because of the need to have a portable instrument to replace the harp. The modern guitarrón has six strings, allowing it to be played in octaves, and its sonority and function are comparable to those of the double-bass in other ensembles. In the 1920s a trumpet was added to the mariachi ensemble, and a second one joined it some 20 years later, completing the basic instrumentation that is used today. A major part of the mariachi repertoire consists of songs that may be interpreted by one of the instrumentalists or by a featured vocalist, traditionally male. The typical repertoire of mariachi ensembles focuses on songs and dances from the various regions of Mexico. Among the songs, *sones,* canciones rancheras, and corridos are predominant. Practically every city, town, and village can boast of having at least one song written in its honor.

Few aspects of Mexican popular culture seem more stereotypically Mexican or readily parodied than the mariachi band. They frequently don the huge round-brimmed sombreros, and a fancy, silver emblazoned charro outfit is *de rigueur* for any self-respecting ensemble. But, in fact, the mariachi band is a key component of everyday social life. Bands gather every evening downtown, waiting to be hired and driven off in taxi to perform for special celebrations and private parties for anyone who can afford them. They are often found in restaurants, moving from table to table, charging patrons by the song.

With Jalisco still in mind, a word might be added about the Mexican Hat Dance which is also associated with it—its name in Spanish being the jarabe tapatío (jarabe, "from Jalisco"). Although the dance can be traced to the fifteenth century, the name appeared in the eighteenth, in *jarabe gitano* ("gypsy jarabe") to identify the licentious lyrics applied to the Spanish *seguidilla manchega* (*seguidilla,* "from La Mancha"). Despite various attempts by Church and state authorities to suppress the jarabe in Mexico during the colonial period, its popularity grew, as did its variety, especially following independence from Spain. In the process of acculturation, regional character-istics were added, as in dance gestures from indigenous groups such as the pantomimes of Huichol Indians in the Jalisco area.

Another important dance is the *habanera.* Starting early in the nineteenth century the habanera, a dance that came via Cuba, had become the most pop-ular one in the Americas, and it remained so for many years, especially in Mexico. It was the peculiar combination of elements from opera, zarzuela, Mexican song, and the habanera that produced the lyrical Mexican variety of the romantic song known as the *bolero* (not to be confused with the unrelated Spanish bolero dance). Agustín Lara is the most famous of composers of Mexican boleros, but surely the most famous example of all is Consuelo Velásquez's "Bésame mucho."

The term *norteño* refers to musical styles in the north of Mexico and the border along the Río Grande river. Norteño music preserves vestiges of musi-cal traditions that developed when the southwestern United States belonged to Mexico. Songs and dances of the colonial period such as the jarabe, the *jarana,* and the romance were joined by the Revolution-inspired corrido, the waltz, and the polka. The nineteenth-century German and Czech emigration to Mexico also brought about a profound change in the basic instrumenta-tion and performance of borderland music. The introduction of the German accordion resulted in a new ensemble, the *conjunto,* consisting basically of a traditional guitar, a 12-string guitar, a double bass, and the *bandoneón,* an accordion-like instrument that features buttons instead of the keyboard. In the typical conjunto, the singer plays the bandoneón. When he—the singer is typically male—sings the lyrics, simple chordal accompaniments are played, allowing concentration on the verses. Between the verses the bandoneón pro-vides a florid, ornamental interlude. The *polca* became the principal genre of the new conjunto. The lyrics of its songs dealt with border problems, and over the border the music would travel, through California and Texas to New York and Florida.

AFTER INDEPENDENCE

As with music, nineteenth-century theater came to assimilate other Euro-pean trends, while still mostly acquiescing to Spanish ones. Notable among romantic dramatists were Ignacio Rodríguez Galván (1816–42) and Fer-nando Calderón (1809–45). Calderón's most enduring work, however, is in the neoclassical costumbrista tradition, and its title echoes that of a work by one of Spain's most famous comedians of manners, Bretón de los Herreros. The latter wrote a play called *Marcela o ¿Cuál de las tres?* (*Marcela, or Which of the Three?*) to which Calderón responds with *A ninguna de las tres* (*None of Them*). Calderón's play is a satire on the quality of women's education that also aims a few blows at over-sentimental romanticism, affectation, and, in particular, self-conscious Frenchification. France, during the brief reign of Maximilian, had become all the rage, and Mexico was becoming passionate about Offenbach. (All the same, Molière had probably influenced Calderón's play, albeit indirectly). Another dramatist who is more firmly in the same vein is Manuel Eduardo de Gorostiza (1789–1851), whose best-known play is *Contigo pan y cebolla* (*With You Bread and Onions*).

The nineteenth-century theater had its ups and downs, almost to the point of extinction, when the can-can and opera became the rage. In 1875 the government began giving subventions to productions of plays by Mexican dramatists, but it also imposed censorship. One result, for example, was that Alberto Bianchi (1850–1904) was imprisoned for a play that took issue with press-ganging. As a consequence of government policy, theater may have been plentiful but it tended to be unadventurous, with heavy romances and slight comedies predominant. The most important dramatist of the period was José Peón y Contreras (1843–1907), a doctor and a conservative politician; as a writer he was a realist who eschewed the excesses of Romanticism, and respected what was historically factual, though his characters lack depth. According to Dauster, his best play is *La hija del rey* (*The King's Daughter*), in which the problem of a father and son both being in love with the same woman is resolved in true Romantic style by having the father kill the son, and the girl go mad.

By the end of the nineteenth century theater was again in the doldrums, except for touring foreign companies that went under the name of their leading actors. Mexican actors were even having to speak with Spanish accents. With World War I and the Revolution in Mexico, that flow all but dried up. However, the popularity of zarzuela had led to the rise of some home-grown products in that light operatic style, especially those of José Elizondo; his zarzuela called *Chin-Chun-Chan* (1904) was the first Mexican work to enjoy a run of 1,000 perfomances. Another successful genre in the second decade of the twentieth century was the review, and once again Elizondo was a significant contributor to it. The stock country yokel character that emerged in such reviews later metamorphosed into the sort of picaroon made famous by the actor Cantinflas.

In the nineteenth century, art music had become freer from Church control but more dependent on the patronage of a tiny bourgeoisie. Mexico's first independent music academy was founded in 1825, but it was short-lived. In 1857, a Sociedad Filarmónica briefly appeared, and in 1877 the first Conservatorio Nacional de Mexico was established. Mexican adaptations and productions of popular Italian operas met with a good deal of success; an outstanding home-grown product was Aniceto Ortega's one act musical episode, *Guatimotzin*. Otherwise, most efforts focused on the development of a national piano virtuoso tradition; there were dances such as the waltz and the polka, there were potpourris and fantasias, nocturnes and serenades, exotic oriental and Moorish pieces, and military marches, all given a Mexican spin. Juvenal Rosas's *Sobre las olas* is a famous example of this sort of composition. For many years, public performances called upon mixtures of professional and amateur musicians, many of them women. Women composers of salon forms published their work in such mediums as the innocuously named *Semanario de las señoritas mexicanas* (*Mexican Young Ladies' Weekly*).

Although there has been a quite sharp divide between popular and classical music since the Renaissance, the Mexican popular tradition has provided a continuous source of native inspiration for classical composers. Throughout the century, as we have seen, there was a rich cross-fertilization between popular Mexican songs and refined, European forms and techniques of composition. When the first waves of foreign virtuosos visited Mexico in the 1840s, many performed arrangements of Mexican popular songs to satisfy the demands, and the pride, of their local audiences. Julio Ituarte, with his *Ecos de México* (1880), is often credited with writing the first truly accomplished and complexly structured stylization of popular Mexican songs, in a work that included arrangements of such standard fare as "Las mañanitas" and "El palomo." But he was just one of a number of composers "admired by a public who fully identified with a late Romanticism 'a la mexicana,' defined by its ornamental values, lightness of style, brevity, elegance, and a Modernism of attitude rather than of concept" (Moreno Rivas, *La composición...*, 23–24). Another man who deserves recognition is Ricardo Castro, who studied for four years in Europe, and achieved a high level of technical mastery in composition. Though a few tentative efforts had been made to compose symphonic works in the style of Romantic greats such as Beethoven (most notably, by Aniceto Ortega and Melesio Morales), it was only after Manuel Ponce's arrangements for the piano that nationalist elements made their way into the symphonic literature (in works by Ponce himself, by Chávez, and by Revueltas).

By late in the century we have the romantic nationalism of this pivotal figure, Manuel Ponce. One of the auditoriums in the National Palace of Fine Arts bears his name, and justly so, for he is widely recognized as the founding figure of classical music in Mexico. No less a figure than the eccentric painter Dr. Atl, in his groundbreaking treatise on *Las artes populares en México,* once reproached Ponce's work for having Europeanized and therefore diluted the authentic spirit of Mexican popular and folk melodies. But, in fact, Ponce's contributions provide a striking parallel to the achievements of such key figures as José María Velasco and Dr. Atl himself in the plastic arts. These men all brought professionalism and a concern for methodological rigor to the task of rescuing, documenting, and preserving what was uniquely Mexican: Velasco through his attention to Mexican flora, geology, and geography in his paintings, Atl with such diverse endeavors as his study of Mexican popular art and his scientific fascination with Mexico's volcanos, and Ponce with his rigorous analysis and annotation of Mexican popular song. What probably underlies Atl's criticism of Ponce is the ideological distance that separated the two. Atl was an eccentric and anarchic figure, given to wild impulses, reversals, and extremes, attracted by avant-garde messianism and fascism; Ponce, despite his time in Europe, was always a much more homespun nationalist, attracted to local traditions and simple values, with a marked conservative, even reactionary, disposition.

Ponce and his aristocratic friends were torn between the Romantic and modernist spirits, and so they are key transitional figures; they do go beyond the slavish emulation of European models that had characterized both the colonial period and the nineteenth century. Theirs was, in the estimation of Moreno Rivas, a "peculiar" modernity; they fell into step with modern experimental techniques, but they were also concerned to preserve the virtues and style of provincial life, the "heart and soul of Mexico" (Moreno-Rivas, *La composición...,* 27–29). This conservatism provided a defense against what some saw as the threat of contamination from abroad.

In 1913, Ponce published the results of his studies as *La música y la canción mexicana,* together with his own arrangements of such traditional tunes as "Cielito lindo," "Mañanitas mexicanas," and "La Valentina." Ponce aimed to identify and preserve the compositional formulas of what he considered to be the most valuable and authentic Mexican folk songs. His careful studies yielded useful classifications of Mexican traditional melodies. He recognized, for example, that the songs of the north (*canciones norteñas*) were generally characterized by rapid tempo and decisive rythms, and by biting, ironic lyrics, which he interpreted as a reflection of an audacious frontier spirit. Coastal Caribbean melodies from Veracruz, with their African influence, embodied the sensuality and voluptuousness of the tropics, while in the music of the central western highlands and valleys of the Bajío region (Jalisco, Guanajuato, Queretaro, Aguascalientes, and Michoacán) more languid amorous laments were frequent. However, because his investigation overlooked many significant regional styles and variations that he considered less authentically Mexican, Ponce's studies contributed to the canonization of the songs and ballads of the northern and central-western provinces of Mexico (the least multicultural regions of Mexico), and helped make them the stereotypical music of Mexico.

For the first time Ponce brought a truly refined understanding of European techniques and phraseology to bear on traditional forms and melodies of Mexico. Once his inventory was complete, the way was open for a vigorous and confident musical nationalism. Ponce himself, after 1925, would move in this direction, not only in an attempt to transcend the romantic folklorism of his early efforts, but also in order to replace the piano with the symphony orchestra; he was the author of some of the first successful Mexican symphonic compositions. In his later years Ponce tried to substitute modernist features for the sentimentalism that had characterized his early work, but his success in this was mixed. His techniques at this time included calculated dissonances, archaisms, and obvious folkloric allusions. Some of the more acomplished and successful of his compositions in this new vein were *Canto y danza de los antiguos mexicanos* (1933), *Tres poemas arcaicos,* and the *Concierto del sur* (1941). But in the view of many historians Ponce was more at home with his early expressions of romantic nationalism.

Shortly after the turn of the twentieth century, the divide between popular and high-art forms of music becomes more apparent. On the one hand, Mexico cultivated its own tradition of classical and symphonic composition; on the other, popular and traditional music underwent a dramatic process of standardization, urbanization, and commercialization through the mass media. To both of these processes the work of Manuel M. Ponce was a decisive contributor; his fame as the founding father of modern Mexican music is therefore fully justified.

Art Music Since the Revolution

Mexico emerged as a presence on the world high-art music scene only in the twentieth century, with the work of the leaders of the so-called Mexican National School of Composition, particularly Carlos Chávez and Silvestre Revueltas, whose triumphant, epic compositions with a native flavor drew international acclaim and provided the musical counterpart to the grandiose murals created by members of the Mexican School of Painting. Like the painters, the musicians were officially approved and underwritten by early post-Revolutionary governments. But nationalism in Mexican music, despite the conscious evocation of pre-Hispanic motifs, has its roots in contemporary European music. In fact, what distinguishes Mexican music of all types is the extent to which they are European based: Spanish and European influences far outweigh the African and Indian, and this despite the strength of Indian elements in other aspects of the culture.

Like Diego Rivera in painting, Chávez casts an imposing shadow over the field of Mexican music, which he dominated from 1920 to at least 1950 as a composer, conductor, theorist, administrator, and teacher. He is far and away the most famous Mexican composer of all time; in fact, his is the only name known to many people. The premises, practices, and ideologies of Rivera and Chávez are strikingly similar; they draw on the avant-garde and post-Revolutionary cultural climate and have a number of influences in common. Each led a renaissance in his field, but neither truly reached his declared goal of creating an art both of and for the people. However, both individually and in tandem they attracted attention and quickly won international recognition for Mexican artistic activity. Thanks to a thoroughly modern stylization of ancient pre-Hispanic motifs and elements, they created what came to be termed variously as Indianist (*indigenista*), or Mexicanist, art forms. Their work was promoted by the early post-Revolutionary governments, which saw it as emblematic of the post-Revolutionary ideological vision of social, cultural, and artistic progress. This official backing, however, tainted their work in the eyes of many of their detractors. It created a dogma and a set of stereotypes that would effectively stifle creativity, making it difficult for artists of subsequent generations to break away.

Chávez's principal model and source of inspiration was the Russian-born composer Igor Stravinsky, and throughout his career he maintained contact with leading world composers of his time, such as France's Edgard Varèse and Aaron Copeland.[2] Though today Chávez's reputation is based almost solely on his Indianist compositions, and particularly on the *Sinfonía india* (1935–36), his oeuvre includes numerous compositions of a purely abstract, international, avante-garde kind. *Energía* (*Energy,* 1925), for example, expresses the seemingly obligatory avant-garde celebration of advanced technology and employs the machine in movement as a metaphor, as does the "Danza de los hombres y las máquinas," one of the episodes in *H.P., Caballos de vapor* (*H.P., Horsepower,* 1925–26).[3] Other early Chávez compositions, such as the six *Exágonos* (*Hexagons,* 1923–24), have a geometric abstraction that parallels the style of Cubism; they endeavor to translate into sound the poetic and surrealistic images of the Carlos Pellicer poems upon which they were based. Critics note that most of the musical features associated with Chávez's Indianist compositions also characterize his non-Indianist works, and are probably linked to the modernist wish to break with Romantic principles of harmony and expression: there are rythmic and metric complexities and irregularities, and there is liberal use of dissonance.

Chávez began to develop his modernist/primitivist Indianism in 1921, when Diego Rivera had just returned from Europe to initiate the program of public mural art fostered by José Vasconcelos. The first work by Chávez in this new direction was the ballet *El fuego nuevo* (1921). In letters between intellectuals and collaborators associated with the avant-garde group known as the Contemporáneos, the work is referred to as Chávez's "Aztec ballet," and the correspondence reveals a wide range of attitudes toward it, ranging from excited anticipation of its premier in Paris, where exotic topics had become all the rage, to serious concern that it might only further fuel European preconceptions about Mexico.

Not only is Chávez's *Indian Symphony* the crowning work of the composer's Indianist vein, it is also the most universally recognized of all Mexican orchestral works. Today, all scholars and critics see it as a modern invention and re-creation of the indigenous spirit, and a thoroughly foreign one at that; it is in no way a direct or authentic manifestation of pre-Hispanic culture. As Moreno Rivas puts it, "[it] can seem as naive and disingenuous as the Mayan style on some of the buildings in Los Angeles, or the anachronistic Aztec colossalism of Diego Rivera's Anahuacalli Museum in...Mexico City" (*La composición*, 34–35). Moreover, in his attempt to evoke the pre-Hispanic past, Chávez did not use melodies from the great civilizations, since none had been preserved, but instead versions of melodies as they had evolved among isolated, northern, nomadic tribes. Thus, the first allegro derives from a Cara Indian melody, the second theme from a Yaqui melody; the middle section is of Sonoran Indian provenance, while the powerful finale borrows from the Seri Indian heritage. Nonetheless, despite the questionable authenticity of Chávez's indigenous sources, his originality itself is not in question. Even many of his critics acknowledge that Chávez's use of alternative instrumentation, his unusual mixtures of woodwinds and strings and horns, his radical dislocations of Romantic harmonies, his emphasis on melody and rhythm and linear, polyphonic texture, do effectively conjure up an impression of the grandeur of the ancient Mexican past.

Besides his many Indianist works, Chávez also produced a number of populist works, intended to embody the principles of the Revolution. These, however, generally met with less critical success. In later years, with the more polemic, programmatic, and embattled work behind him, Chávez refined his personal style and produced some of his most mature, balanced, ambitious, and accomplished works. Among these are several chamber works, his last four symphonies, an opera called *The Visitors,* and the ballet *Pyramid.*

Perhaps no other single figure so changed the face of a particular artistic activity as did Chávez the face of music. He dominated every aspect of classical music in Mexico. To mention only two more of his many official posts, he served as musical director and conductor of the Orquesta Sinfónica de México, from its foundation in 1928 until 1949, and as the director of the National Conservatory from 1928 to 1934. In this last capacity he conducted workshops that proved crucial in the training of new generations of Mexican composers and musicians. He was also an active participant in such international organizations as the Pan-American Association of Composers and the International Composers' Guild.

Silvestre Revueltas's brief career unfolded somewhat in the shadow of his contemporary Chávez. In their youth, Revueltas on violin and Chávez on piano often appeared together in public. Revueltas spent many years in the United States training and practicing as a musician, not, like Chávez, in the metropolis of New York, but primarily in the cities of Austin and Chicago. Later, Revueltas was named assistant conductor of Chávez's Orquesta Sinfónica de México, and it was in part thanks to Chávez's encouragement that Revueltas rededicated himself to composition in the 1930s. For many, Revueltas's outstanding works from the 1930s rival and perhaps outclass those of Chávez, in quality, originality, and interest. Revueltas came from a fairly humble but truly remarkable middle-class family that gave Mexico a whole cluster of rebel artistic talents; in addition to Silvestre, there were José the writer, Fermín the muralist painter, and Rosaura the actress. Silvestre's untimely death in 1940, and the many anecdotes that grew around his rather tumultuous and politically active life, have contributed to his legendary aura and cult following.

There is a somber, solemn quality about many of Chávez's best-known compositions. Revueltas's compositions, while sharing Chávez's nationalistic spirit and while using several of his techniques (such as sudden dissonances and an implacable beat), seem bent on capturing the vitality of contemporary Mexican life and its rich cultural mixture; they are upbeat. Invariably, critics highlight the way Revueltas's music expresses what seems to be a spontaneous and intuitive understanding, and a genuine sympathy for the culture of daily life in Mexico: the vibrancy of the sounds and colors of street life, of the fairs and marketplaces, of dance halls and public celebrations. Most of Revueltas's music is strongly grounded in the rhythms and harmonies of contemporary popular music and the folk tradition; for example, he includes the sounds of the mariachi band and the characteristic features of the corrido. But rather than simply borrowed or stylized, his melodies show uncanny signs of inventiveness. During the decade of the 1930s, his period of greatest productivity, Revueltas composed a number of ensemble pieces whose very titles indicate their roots in everday life: *Feria* (*Fair*), *Esquinas* (*Corners*), *Caminos* (*Roads*), and *Alcanías* (*Collection Boxes*). Revueltas also wrote scores for several major films of the Golden Age of Mexican cinema, such as *Redes* and *¡Vámonos con*

Pancho Villa! Revueltas's lighter side, and his interest in linking high-art music with popular forms and even new mass media, is evident in his *Ocho por Radio* (*Eight for/on the Radio,* 1933), a medley written for an eight-part chamber orchestra. His various symphonic compositions are among his most lauded works. The first of these, *Cuauhnahuac* (1930), established many of the features that would mark his musical style. Another, the symphonic poem *Janitzio,* produced for the Emilio Fernández film of the same name, takes its inspiration from the famous island on Lake Pátzcuaro in Michoacán, first settled by Indian fishermen.

Revueltas did not restrict himself to Mexican sources, a fact that accounts in part for the originality and influence of his music. Several of his compositions were inspired by the famous Spanish poet Federico García Lorca; one of his mature chamber works is in fact his *Homenaje a García Lorca,* which was performed on a visit to Spain in 1937, in the middle of its Civil War, shortly after the poet's violent death. (Revueltas actively supported the republican cause in the Spanish Civil War.) Similarly, the most famous of all Revueltas compositions, the symphonic poem *Sensemayá* (1938), while still very much a characteristic Revueltas work, was based on a poem of the same name by the Afro-Cuban poet Nicolás Guillén; Revueltas thus explicitly recognizes the influence of Africa on the rhythms of Mexican popular music. This dense and highly accomplished construct is reminiscent of Ravel and Stravinsky; it exemplifies Revueltas's fondness for crescendos.

Revueltas's work is still highly regarded today; it is perhaps the best and most unique achievement of twentieth-century art music in Mexico, the importance of Carlos Chávez notwithstanding. Revueltas assimilated but never simply imitated the works of the foreign composers of the time (Debussy, Ravel, Bartok, and Stravinsky); he added a powerful and intuitive understanding of the expressive possibilities of Mexican popular music. His style was very individual. More than anyone, he modernized Mexican music by freeing it from traditional forms and the requirement of a sublime message, and he did so without falling prey to the clichés to which musical nationalism was susceptible.

The National School of Composition, founded and led by Chávez, dominated Mexican art music between 1930 and 1950. Either in calculated and quickly conventionalized evocations of the pre-Hispanic past, or in new arrangements and orchestrations of the rhythms and melodies of traditional popular songs, the new music presented a remarkably unified front—reflecting the leadership and overwhelming influence of Chávez—as it evolved from an avant-garde attempt at breaking with Romanticism toward an American kind of neoclassicism. Both older and younger composers contributed to the rise of the nationalist movement, tempering the programmatic severity of

Chávez. Among the older composers born before Chávez and Revueltas, most notably José Rolón and Candelario Huízar, a lingering Romanticism generally colored their works, which were often historical in substance and inspiration, as in Rolón's *Cuauhtémoc* (1930) and Huízar's mystical symphonies *Oxpaniztli* (1935) and *Sinfonía cora* (1942). Luis Sandi, caught between generations, became a leading figure of Mexican nationalism and made many contributions as a composer, conductor, and arts administrator; he was best known for arrangements of Indian music, such as *El venado* (1936) and *Música yaqui* (1941), that emphasized flutes and percussion and employed pentatonic themes that were presumed to be characteristic of pre-Hispanic music. However, above all the success of four of Chávez's prize students at the Conservatory—Daniel Ayala, Salvador Contreras, José Pablo Moncayo, and Blas Galindo—ensured the dominance of the National School for many years to come. After a joint concert in 1935 at the Teatro Orientación, they came to be known as the Grupo de los Cuatro (Gang of Four). Their work had neither the dramatic stridency of Chávez nor the originality of Revueltas, but with considerable skill and technical accomplishment they extended the standard repertoire of Indianist motifs and nationalistic, folkloric themes. It was works by Sandi, the Grupo de los Cuatro, and Chávez, rather than the more elaborate and idiosyncratic compositions of Revueltas, that were featured at concerts of Mexican music given in New York City in 1940 at the Museum of Modern Art, to accompany an exhibition entitled Twenty Centuries of Mexican Art. While Ayala exemplified the continuing exploitation of the Indianist vein of composition, becoming increasingly decorative, even touristic, Galindo and Moncayo exploited in the populist/folkloric vein. These last two produced what have become far and away the most widely known works produced by the Grupo de los Cuatro: Galindo's *Sones de mariachi* (1940) and Moncayo's *Huapango* (1941). These highly accomplished orchestral arrangements and free improvisations on themes from the Mexican popular tradition are modern classics, and playing them is virtually obligatory at civic ceremonies; they are hymns to joy and simplicity, qualities that by implication are embodied in the Mexican people. Both works use multiple rhythms and meters, with the popular 6/8 notation dominant. In both, strings carry the pulsating rhythms of the traditional guitars and harps, while the trumpets evoke the mariachi tradition, and woodwinds suggest the sounds of pre-Columbian instrumentation and rural village bands.

Though the attraction of nationalistic music, particularly the exoticism of Indianist themes, endured into the 1950s and beyond, most of its creative energy had run dry by the early 1940s. Musical nationalism got something of a second wind when supporting the significant revitalization of classical dance and nationalist ballet that occurred in the 1940s. Not only were many

of the classics from the early years of the National School revived and choreographed, such as Chávez's *Los cuatro soles* (which in fact had been the original post-Revolutionary piece commissioned by Vasconcelos) and Revueltas's
Sensemayá, but also many new pieces were composed expressly for the ballet
at this time.

As happened with painting, art music in the 1950s began to explore more
abstract and experimental modes. With little nationalist baggage, Rodolfo
Halffter (1900–87), originally from Spain, experimented with dodecaphony,
and received some support from Chávez in this; Chávez gave a lecture on the
subject at the Colegio Nacional in 1955. Rafael Elizondo (1930–) and
Manuel Enríquez (1926–94), together with Mario Kuri-Aldana (1935–) are
members of a group known as Nueva Música de México, though many of the
latter's compositions, such as *Xilofonías* (1963), have neo-nationalist features
in their rhythms and instrumentation. A key development in the new direction was the composition workshop conducted by Chávez at the National
Conservatory between 1960 and 1964; most of Mexico's best-known contemporary composers attended this workshop, including Mario Lavista
(1943–), Héctor Quintanar (1936–), and Eduardo Mata (1942–95), who
would direct the Philharmonic Orchestra of the National University between
1966 and 1976, and the Instituto Nacional de Bellas Artes's Opera Company
from 1972 to 1985. These new radicals, under the influence of composers
like John Cage, increasingly incorporated chance into their compositional
technique, and they moved away from rhythm and meter, away from melody
and harmony, toward pure sound. Lavista established an experimental group
called Quanta, which emphasized improvisation; his works include *Diacronía*
(1969), *Diálogos* (1974), and an opera based on a Carlos Fuentes text, *Aura*
(1988). Beginning in the 1970s, Mexican composers also experimented with
electronic synthesizers. After visits to New York and Paris, Héctor Quintanar
directed the electronic studio at the National Conservatory. Indeed, many of
Mexico's youngest composers today have studied for extended periods
abroad. Such is the case with Daniel Catán, who has produced several compositions—*Mariposa de obsidiana* (1984) and *La hija de Rapopaccini* (1988)
—inspired by literary works by Octavio Paz.

Contemporary Popular Music and the Recording Industry

Mexico is the second largest music market in Latin America, and the first
among the Spanish-speaking countries. While international companies dominate the market overall, they function largely as national subsidiaries in Mexico, so that in 1996 only Sony had a slightly higher share of the market than
did the national record company Fonovisa, owned by the Televisa group

(Yúdice, 190–193). Moreover, in Mexico, as in most of Latin America, in recent years English-language popular music has actually lost part of its market share to Spanish-language popular music. The growing international popularity of Latin music, and the expansion of international Spanish-language television broadcasts, have certainly contributed to this shift. In 1996, 47 percent of record sales were by Mexican artists, with the rest taken up by other Latin American artists (20 percent) and English-language pop (33 percent). A similar array of popular musical preferences is indicated by studies of radio. In 1990, a survey of radio stations along the northern border found that 28 stations featured a mix of Spanish language music, 20 featured traditional Mexican tropical and ranchera music, while only 5 stations programmed English-language pop and rock (Lozano, 38).

Popular music in Mexico is full of variety, from tropical Latin American salsa to social protest ballads, to contemporary artists performing the whole range of traditional Mexican ranchera and mariachi music (first popularized by the likes of Los Panchos and Vicente Fernández), to Spanish-language pop songs whose popularity largely hinges on media exposure, and even to countercultural, Spanish-language rock and roll. Much as Golden Age cinema and radio once made singers like Jorge Negrete household names, so today television assures the star value of Mexican pop singers, who constantly and quickly adapt their music to the latest styles; examples are José José, Juan Gabriel, Lucía Méndez, Luis Miguel, Daniela Romo, Mijares, and the titillating Gloria Trevi. Music tailored for and marketed directly to teens has been another result of television's impact on the music industry.

Mexico is one of only a handful Spanish-speaking countries to have a significant tradition of original Spanish-language rock-and-roll music; this grew out of youth counterculture of the 1960s. Much as happened at Woodstock, the goings-on at a massive 1971 Mexican outdoor rock festival known as Avándaro captured the attention of, and scandalized, most of the nation. Mexico's oldest and still best Spanish-language rock band was called Three Souls on My Mind; today it is known simply as El Tri. Other Spanish-language rock bands of some notoriety are Café Tacuba, Caifanes, and Maldita Vecindad. The filmmaker Paul Leduc offers an interesting portrait of this facet of the so-called Mexican counterculture movement, in his 1986 film ¿Cómo ves? (What Do You Think?).

Dance in the Twentieth Century

The United States gives rather less state support to the arts than do many countries, Mexico among them. As we have seen, successive governments in Mexico have supported national and provincial theater, music, and dance activities, sometimes to further their own political ends. The Instituto

Nacional de Bellas Artes has played a major role in supporting the arts; significant national companies have been established to foment and project Mexican artistic activity; universities have also been a source of development of such activity.

Under Porfirio Díaz, and beginning around 1900, there were two parallel developments in dance: recognition of classical ballet as a professional activity requiring specialized training, and a more open and universal recognition of popular dance in theater. Díaz supported the construction of elaborate fine arts theaters: the Teatro Juárez in Guanajuato (1903), the Teatro Degollado in Guadalajara (1906), and what eventually became the Palacio de Bellas Artes. Late in the Porfiriato, and extending into the early twentieth century, theatrical spectacles, nightlife, and restaurants, served by both foreign and national artistic groups, were flourishing. The growing ranks of theatergoers began to develop an appreciation for the techniques exhibited by foreign touring companies presenting classical and European works. This reached a crescendo when world-famous ballerina Anna Pavlova visited Mexico in 1919 and captured the fancy of a broad Mexican audience. The fact that she incorporated a jarabe tapatío and a Fantasía mexicana complete with china poblana and charro costumes no doubt increased her Mexican following; her ardent fans included the poets Tablada and López Velarde.

The Orquesta Sinfónica Nacional de México was founded in 1923 and Chávez was appointed its first conductor; the corresponding step for dance was the foundation of the Escuela Nacional de Danza (National School of Dance) in 1932, as part of the Secretaría de Educación Pública's Departamento de Bellas Artes, with Carlos Mérida as its first director. The School of Dance became the domain and project of the Campobello sisters, originally from Durango, who first appeared as dancers in Mexico City in 1927, and had already established their own private dance school. All of the great Mexican artists and musicians of the time contributed to their programs at Bellas Artes, from Rivera and Chávez to Orozco and Montenegro. With Gloria Campobello teaching Mexican dances, and her sister Nellie, also an important writer, serving as assistant director, the Escuela Nacional de Danza emphasized nationalistic art, but tried to incorporate classical techniques and discipline and international influences. Guillermina Bravo, who would go on to break crucial ground in the dance field, was a young student at the school in the 1930s.

In the mid 1930s, two U.S. ballerinas, Waldeen Feldenkrais (commonly known simply as Waldeen) and Ana Sokolow, brought Martha Graham–styled modern dance techniques to Mexico. The formation of a new state-sponsored dance company in 1948, the Ballet Nacional de México led by Guillermina Bravo, took dance in Mexico to new heights. Bravo had studied with Feldenkrais (1913–93) and had previously co-founded the Ballet Waldeen, the aims of which were to leave behind the strictures of classical ballet and make use of indigenous elements. Despite an agenda that often brought her into conflict with authorities (she choreographed works on such things as guerrilla struggles, union shenanigans, and U.S. exploitation of Mexican workers), Bravo managed to win considerable government support for the Ballet Nacional, and to improve the working conditions of its dancers. In the 1960s the Ballet Nacional began sending people to and being influenced by the Martha Graham School in New York, and this gave rise to some controversy relating to the question of whether it was truly a national company.

With these precedents established, Mexico has maintained a fairly consistent level of quality and originality in its major artistic dance troupes. The Ballet Nacional de Mexico, headquartered in Querétaro since 1991, continues to conduct world tours. The state has also underwritten other contemporary dance companies: the Ballet Independiente de Mexico, established in 1966, and the Ballet Teatro del Espacio, founded in 1979 by Gladiola Orozco and Michel Descombey. *La muerte del cisne* (1982) and the *Sinfonía fantástica* (1989) were just two of many innovative Descombey chorcographics.

Mexico was the first of the Latin American countries to set up a folk dance company, establishing its Ballet Folklórico de México in 1952, under the direction of Amalia Hernández, who had been associated with the Ballet Nacional. The Ballet Folklórico is now based at Bellas Artes in Mexico City, and since 1960 it has given four or five performances a week, largely for the benefit of tourists. This company has toured the world several times, and its success has inspired the formation of many other, smaller regional troupes.

Theater in the Twentieth Century

As we saw when discussing theatre in the colonial period, the fact that it is close to daily life and is an activity that can be engaged in and appreciated even if one has no training or is illiterate, makes it extremely useful to powers that be. But theater can also function subversively against them. So it is that ever since colonial times theater has been more severely censored and controlled than any other art form; its development in Mexico has been hindered at every conceivable level. Two of the three outstanding dramatists of the twentieth century, for example, suffered constant harassment during their efforts to create a politically and historically critical theater. Still, perhaps nowhere is the theatricality of life more fully visible, more celebrated and exploited, than in Mexico. It is thus extremely appropriate that the best known of all modern Mexican plays, Rodolfo Usigli's *El gesticulador,* centers on the threatricality of life in general and more specifically on the theatricality of post-Revolutionary politics.

For all the impediments, it would be true to say that among Latin American countries, Mexico now boasts the most solid theatrical infrastructure, rivaled only by that of Argentina. Real steps towards developing that infrastructure were taken after the Revolution. In 1919 the government established the Teatro Folklórico with the express intention of boosting theater that was popular in style and Indian in theme. In 1924 the Teatro de Muciélago was set up, with a repertoire consisting largely of lyric and folkloric treatments of indigenous dances and ceremonies. Finally, in 1929 the Secretaría de Educación Pública (Department of Public Education) established a touring company called Teatro del Periquillo, to take theater out into the provinces. Other such initiatives followed.

The most interesting development in the early efforts to take theater to the people was probably the regional Maya-based theater that flourished in the Yucatán Peninsula, although there is evidence that such theater had already been in existence there in the middle of the nineteenth century. The works performed appear to have been mostly short and costumbrista in style and to have often involved music and dance. That regional theater was at its peak in the second decade of the twentieth century, a time when the Yucatán became a sort of haven for theater people, so much so that in 1917 there were more theaters in Mérida than in Mexico City. One of the dramatists involved was Ermilo Abreu Gómez, who brought the Murciélago company to Yucatán.

While companies like Murciélago promoted indigenous material, the group that came to call itself the Grupo de los Siete (Group of Seven) sought to establish a tradition of quality modern and even cosmopolitan theater among Mexico's own playwrights; they were nicknamed "The Pirandellos." Together with the Italian, their artistic idols were playwrights such as Chekhov, Strindberg, and O'Neill. Though their manifesto was rather more impressive than their artistic achievements, they did increase the awareness of the need for change and they opened up the way for renovating Mexican theater. Vasconcelos invited Camila Quiroga's Argentine theater company to tour Mexico between 1921 and 1922, and the Grupo de los Siete authors, indeed the whole Mexican theatergoing public, were inspired by the way the company's actors used authentic Argentine speech, instead of the Spanish Castilian accent that was still being employed on stage by many actors in Mexico. In 1923 Group of Seven members helped establish a Mexican Playwrights' Union (Unión de Autores Dramáticos), and a short season of exclusively Mexican works was offered at the Teatro Virginia Fábregas. The group launched another season at the Fábregas between 1925 and 1926, at which point Monterde claimed they had staged more Mexican plays than had been offered in the preceding quarter century. The most distinguished of the writers amongst the Group of Seven were José Joaquín Gamboa and Víctor

Manuel Díez Barroso; Díez Barroso, the more prolific of the two, delved into psychology and dreams in his plays, and also used experimental techniques, such as viewing the same scene from different points of view. Two of his most highly regarded plays are *Véncete a ti mismo* (*Overcome Yourself*, 1925) and *El y su cuerpo* (*He and His Body*, 1934). Another important member of the Seven was Francisco Monterde, who was not only a dramatist but also a tireless promoter of theater, a critic, historian, teacher, and president of the Mexican Academy of Language (Academia Mexicana de la Lengua).Ulises was the name adopted by another group whose cosmopolitan theatrical experiments would more profoundly influence the subsequent evolution of Mexican theater. Ulises was founded by Salvador Novo and Xavier Villaurrutia; Novo explained that they had chosen the name because Ulysses had been driven by curiosity. Novo and Villaurrutia, as well as many of the other participants, like Gilberto Owen and Celestino Gorostiza, would soon be known as members of the avant-garde group Contemporáneos. Many other prominent artists of the day collaborated with them; it was a youthful, heady, and precocious group that liked to be provocative and heretical, and perhaps just a little bit snobbish. The plays that Ulises put on were primarily translations of the likes of Jean Cocteau and Eugene O'Neill, done by the group's own members, who also saw to all the staging, lighting, and other production details. Ulises was short-lived, but it fed directly into the government-sponsored Teatro de Orientación (1932–38), a group directed by Celestino Gorostiza and involving most of the same artists and intellectuals who were associated with the Contemporáneos. The Teatro de Orientación steadily expanded and solidified the achievements of Ulises, and slowly built up a significant following for its highbrow theater. There was a widening of the repertoire, increased use of experimental techniques, and a lessening of the cult of personality; there was a firm eye on the future, rather than on the Mexican tradition. The first seasons included translations of works by Sophocles and Gogol, Shaw and Shakespeare, Chekov and Cervantes. Gradually, the group began staging more and more of their own original works, such as Villaurrutia's *Parece mentira* and *¿En qué piensas?* By 1938, Gorostiza had left to direct the Departamento de Bellas Artes, but he left Teatro Orientación in the hands of three outstanding directors: Villaurrutia, Rodolfo Usigli, and Julio Bracho, each in charge of his own team. Bracho, also a filmmaker, had been busy independently working on similar innovations in Mexican theater, though with more of a Mexican emphasis; he founded Escolares del Teatro in 1931, Trabajadores del Teatro in 1933, and the Teatro de la Universidad in 1936. These people renovated theater and kept quality alive through times of crass commercialism, but they found that experimentalism did not provide a living, and so veered towards the sort of realism they had previously been at pains to break away from. However, it was to be a realism handled with skill and depth.

Both Villaurutia and Usigli received grants from the Rockefeller Foundation to study at the Yale Drama School. Among the most important experimental works of the twenties were Villaurrutia's *Parece mentira* (*Whoever Would Believe It?*) and *¿En qué piensas?* (*What Are You Thinking?*); these works brought the sort of existential concerns already apparent in his poetry to the stage, and that undermined their initial atmosphere of realism. For example, in the first of the two, characters called The Husband, A Clerk, and The Curious Person find themselves in a lawyer's waiting room. The husband is there because he has received an anonymous call about his wife's infidelity, and the action boils down to three women (whose separate identities are in some doubt) coming in to see the lawyer and reacting to each other's appearance. The perhaps happy but colorless life of the husband acquires new dimensions; he loses predictability and faces a future that is freer but uncertain. Though its setting is simple and realistic, the play has many enigmas; Villaurrutia seems to be saying that we live bound by conventions and symbols, but that these things are less stable, less clear in their meanings, than we realize. As a result, his play could be said to anticipate the sort of suspicions about language and symbols that came to occupy intellectuals in the last three or four decades of the twentieth century.

Another notable feature of *Parece mentira* is its humor. Many of these same characteristics, and a lifelong obsession with solitude and death, are found in other works by Villaurrutia. His first full-length play was *Invitación a la muerte,* written in 1940 but not premiered until 1947, a Mexicanized, personalized adaptation of *Hamlet. Invitación* makes effective use of light contrasts, something that would become characteristic of the playwright's subsequent works. It also further explores the idea of the double, and deals with incest, subjects that would reappear in Villaurrutia's plays *El pobre barba azul* (1947) and *La tragedia de la equivocaciones* (1950). The works written in the 1940s were intended for the commercial theater and were less aggressively experimental than others. Villaurrutia's language is generally stylized and ironic, and the emotions of his characters are contained to a degree that led Gorostiza to say that theirs were "mathematical lives."[4] Finally, it may be worth noting that Villaurrutia (1902–50) was openly homosexual at a time when few dared to be.

His friend Salvador Novo (1904–74) was another poet turned dramatist, but he was also much more: a translator, director, social commentator, and author of books about Mexico City, and even official chronicler of the capital under President Díaz Ordaz, in the 1960s. Novo was a winner of the Premio Nacional de Letras (National Prize for Literature). He was also head of theater at the Instituto Nacional de Bellas Artes (National Institute of Fine Arts). Villaurrutia and Novo had several things in common, including their use of realism as a stepping stone, but whereas Villaurrutia was given to delving into personal problems, Novo began by satirizing public life, and later turned to classical and pre-Hispanic matters. Even in Novo's early theater there are clear signs that realism is to be left behind. *Divorcio* (1924) touts itself as a drama in the style of Ibsen, but it is only Ibsenian in its theme; in style it is avant-garde, making fun of social and theatrical conventions. Somewhat more realistic, and certainly very different, is another early play, *El tercer Fausto* (*The Third Faust*); this dates from the same year as *Divorcio,* but it was first published in 1934, in French, because Novo felt that Mexico at that time would not take kindly to it. In *El tercer Fausto,* Alberto (coincidentally the name of the protagonist of Villaurrutia's *Invitación a la muerte*) seeks the Devil's help in order to change into a woman, because he is in love with his friend Armando; the Devil agrees, but it transpires that Armando cannot love the new woman, because he is in love with his male friend (the original Alberto). After 1924 Novo concentrated on directing and teaching, and ceased writing for the theater, but he returned to it 25 years later. In the 1950s he wrote a number of brief, sardonic, and anachronistic *Diálogos* involving famous people, ranging from Adam and Eve, to Sor Juana, to Malinche. *La culta dama* (1951) is a full-length work of powerful social criticism, more weighty than the earlier satires, and more realistic in style. From the mid-1950s on, Novo's plays move away from realism again, and they show the structuring influence of Greek tragedy, though in some respects they become Anglo-American in style. His view of the world becomes more skeptical, even cynical, and he reveals real concern at the powers of the media. At one point in *Yocasta, o casi* (*Yocasta, or Almost,* 1961) he writes "La gente no advierte hasta qué punto todos los mitos siguen vivos, latentes, reiterados como la corriente metálica y subterránea de nuestra cotidiana vulgaridad" ("People don't realize how far all those myths are still alive, latent, reiterated in the underground, metallic current of our daily commonness").[5] *Cuauhtémoc* (1962) marks a turn towards indigenous themes; here Novo plumbs a key personage of Mexican history, using the techniques of Greek tragedy tempered with anachronism. Perhaps the culmination of the exploitation of such anachronism is a comic opera first performed in 1972, not long before Novo's death. This is *In Ticitezcatl o El espejo encantado* (*The Enchanted Mirror*), a Gilbert-and-Sullivanesque parody of a Greek-style tragedy set in Teotihuacán, the site of one of the great pre-Columbian civilizations. A guide and a couple of tourists are joined by a motley group of indigenous deities associated with other places, and the play's language makes use of outrageous rhymes. In general, Novo's tragedies are farcical, playful, and ironic, but beneath the surface lie serious concerns.

Another important figure in Teatro de Orientación was its founder, Celestino Gorostiza (1904–67), whose works follow a similar evolution from avant-garde to realism. *El nuevo paraíso* (*The New Paradise*, 1930) portrays Adam and Eve as victims of convention and self-deceit; *La escuela del amor* (*The School of Love*, 1933) centers on a group of people who take refuge in dreams and illusions because they cannot deal with reality; *Ser o no ser* (*To Be or Not to Be*, 1934) is another development of the Faust theme. In all, Gorostiza's theater has many shared features with Villaurrutia's. Gorostiza, somewhat like Novo, gave up writing for the theater for a long time, coming back to it in 1952, with a box office hit in *El color de nuestra piel* (*The Color of Our Skin*), an exemplary tale of a mestizo family who try to hide their mixed ancestry and fall victims to their own prejudice. Though this play is quite old-fashioned in design it created a stir, highlighting latent feelings among the Mexican nouveaux riches. Like other dramatists of the group, Gorostiza also dealt with indigenous themes, particularly in his last play, *La Malinche* (1958), which covers the encounter of the two cultures. In this somewhat melodramatic play, Malinche's greater moral fiber helps Cortés rise above greed and the pursuit of power. In fact, Gorostiza's later works grow increasingly didactic, attacking the ways in which poor or mestizo people are used and abused by others. Gorostiza was perhaps more important as a director and promoter of theater than as a dramatist. He held important positions, including that of director of the Instituto Nacional de Bellas Artes, in which capacity he invited the U.S. dancer and choreographer Waldeen to create Mexico's first modern dance company, the Ballet de Bellas Artes.

Yet another group opted for a social realist theater that would engage issues of rural politics. This was the Teatro de Ahora group in the 1930s, led by Mauricio Magdaleno and Juan Bustillo Oro, who would both go on to participate in the Golden Age of Mexican cinema, the former as a screenwriter and the latter as a director. All the attention given to the work of Ulises and Orientación has tended to obscure the merits of an early play by Juan Bustillo Oro: *San Miguel de las Espinas: Trilogía dramática de un pedazo de tierra mexicana* (*San Miguel de las Espinas: a Trilogy about a Mexican Plot of Land*, 1933). The story is not unlike the one in Usigli's *El gesticulador* (see following discussion) insofar as it concerns political intrigue, double-dealing, and murder. What is distinctive about this Bustillo play, however, is its style, which has been described in the following terms: "To speak of the operatic... is not mere hyperbole, for this is a play grand in scope, tone and theatricality" (Nigro, 224). It is a didactic, social-realistic play, as were those of Teatro de Ahora generally; however, it is also self-consciously theatrical, highly visual, episodic in structure, and experimental in its staging in ways that reveal that its author was fully aware of techniques being used in Europe at the time.

No discussion of theater in modern Mexico is complete without Rodolfo Usigli. Usigli (1905–79) was only on the fringes of the Ulises and Teatro de Orientación activities. He was once a friend of Novo's, but the two fell out. Usigli, too, was a translator, a poet, and a propagandist for theater; his plays are richer, more varied, and much better known in Latin America than are those of his contemporaries. A theatrical novel of Usigli's, *Ensayo de un crimen* (*Rehearsal for a Crime*, 1944) was filmed by Buñuel. As to his theater itself, that has been described as "moral rather than moralizing" (Dauster, 152). Usigli deals with contradictions in (Mexican) human nature and owes a good deal to Ibsen, and particularly Shaw, whose works he admired. *La familia cena en casa* (*The Family Dines In*, 1942) has been compared to Shaw's *Pygmalion*, for example.

Usigli's refusal to paint a flattering portrait of his fellow Mexicans inevitably brought the wrath of many upon him. The first of his two most famous plays was influenced by Ibsen: *El gesticulador* (*The Impersonator*, 1937) is a satire on provincial politics and, because of its political sensitivity, it was not performed for 10 years. The perversion of Revolutionary ideals is under attack here, and the Partido Revolucionario Institucional (PRI) saw itself, no doubt rightly, as in the firing line. But *El gesticulador* has a broader target than just the PRI; as one critic says, it is "a play about politics and corruption, human relationships, the conflict between truth and lies, reality and appearance, and role-playing in all its multiple dimensions" adding that it is "clearly a self-reflexive play, an example of meta-theater."[6]

In fact, Usigli faced forms of censorship for much of his career. The other famous play, his most celebrated, was *Corona de sombra* (*Crown of Shadow*, 1943) and it lasted for only two performances when it was premiered in 1947. *Corona de sombra* is part of a trilogy (three "crowns") dealing with significant Mexican historical moments, in this case the short-lived reign of Emperor Maximilian. In a preface, Usigli calls his play an "anti-history" and says that his aim is not so much to present facts as to consider their implications for modern Mexicans, the ways in which historical moments have contributed to national consciousness, and to do so without political or ideological bias. The play is cleverly structured, framed by scenes that take place in Brussels in 1927, where the aged and crazed Empress is nearing death; the scenes in the middle are set in Mexico in imperial times. The stage is split in two; when the actors pass from one space to another, they also pass from one time to another. This, combined with extensive use of stage effects, such as lighting, facilitates the establishment of a set of opposites and doubles. At the end there is a tragic understanding of the suffering caused to the Mexican people and of the way in which the imperial experience has shaped the nation. (The other "crowns," *Corona de fuego* and *Corona de luz*, deal with the trauma of the conquest and with the appearance of the Virgen del Tepeyac, the patron saint of Mexico. Neither is as good as *Corona de sombra*.)

The plays of Usigli have many faces. *Noche de estío* (*Midsummer Night*, 1933) is one of what Usigli termed "three impolitic comedies" in which any resemblance to real persons or events, he said, was "absolutely coincidental and clearly to be avoided"; in fact, the play's relevance to the authoritarian rule of President Plutarco Elías Calles is quite clear. The title's reminder of Shakespeare is fairly apt; this is a piece of buffoonery that leaves virtually no one unscathed. There are several plays exploring social and individual pathologies, such as *Otra primavera* (*Spring Again*, 1938) and *El niño y la niebla* (*The Child and the Fog*, 1951). *La mujer no hace milagros* (*Women Don't Perform Miracles*, 1939) is about the love lives of the Rosas sisters, a play full of stock misunderstandings, complications, and heavy-handed jokes, that comes complete with a couple of rather dim-witted lovers and a pair of clowns. Social criticism becomes stronger in the years following World War II, a period during which Usigli was also a diplomat. The tile of *La exposición* (1955) might be rendered as "The Exhibition" since it deals with the art world, but it also implies "Exposé" in that this play pokes fun at the Mexican art world (together with the police and rich people). A curious late work is *Buenos días, señor Presidente* (1972), inspired by the events of 1968; Usigli paints a future in which young people take over the country and introduce true democracy, only to dissolve into internecine fighting.

The sort of difficulties faced by dramatists who dared cast a critical eye on authority or national icons are illustrated by the case of Vicente Leñero (1933–). An engineer by training, Leñero is also an important journalist and novelist, and a pioneer in Mexico both of the non-fiction novel and of documentary theater. However, the fact that he was a respected writer and known outside Mexico did not save him from trouble. Two of his finest plays are *Martirio de Morelos* (1983) and *Nadie sabe nada* (1988). The first of these deals with the last days of José María Morelos, one of the revered figures of the movement towards national independence; Leñero based his play on research that suggested that Morelos was not quite the superhero who weathered torture and died a martyr, as official history had it, but was rather a noble man of human proportions who in fact broke under torture. Within the play there is a character called The Reader who reads from a huge tome of Mexican history while Morelos listens in disbelief to what the official version says about him. Such indignation was provoked by this play, even before its official premier and extending to the then president, Miguel de la Madrid, that an attempt was made to suppress it. A public outcry ensued and there was a face-saving compromise. *Nadie sabe nada* is about contemporary corruption and collusion between government and the media. This play's opening was delayed while officials demanded that certain clear political and personal references be deleted and that the national anthem not be played ironically in acknowledgment of nefarious political behavior. Leñero has had several successes, including the theatrical adaptation of his novel *Los albañiles* (*The Bricklayers*), which won the Ruiz Alarcón prize for best play of the year in 1969. *Los albañiles* was also made into an award-winning film by director Jorge Fons in 1976.

Luisa Josefina Hernández (1928–) studied under Usigli and taught for more than 30 years at the Universidad Nacional Autónoma. Although also a novelist, she is better known for her plays, of which there are about 30, with themes ranging from human relationships, to social injustice, to mysticism. Along with Leñero and Emilio Carballido, she would help nurture a new generation of playwrights that emerged in the 1960s. Carballido was born in Córdoba, near Veracruz, in 1925 but he studied and worked in Mexico City for years, and became one of the most consistent dramatists to surface under the guidance of Salvador Novo, during the latter's tenure as director of theater at the Instituto Nacional de Bellas Artes (1946–52). A prolific playwright, Carballido has employed a wide variety of styles, from allegory to the comedy of manners. Some of his plays deal with provincial life, such as *Un pequeño día de ira* (*A Small Day of Wrath*, 1962) which won him Cuba's Casa de las Américas prize; but *El relojero de Córdoba* (*The Clockmaker of Cordoba*, 1960) is an example of a farce with a colonial theme, *Medusa* (1960) an example of a mythological play, and *El día que se soltaron los leones* (1960), of a fantastic one. Disapproval of human inauthenticity and respect for spontaneity and creativity are what tie together most of his work. There is social realism in *El censo* (*The Census*), written expressly for the working-class audience at the theaters of the Social Security Administration. There is rich experimentation in *Yo también hablo de la rosa* (*I, Too, Speak of the Rose*, 1966), which takes its title from a Villaurrutia poem and employs allegorical and meta-theatrical elements from Brecht's epic theater. Over the course of this last play the audience is witness to a bewildering array of social, political, and philosophical interpretations of a simple accident; but none of them adequately captures the intricate and fragile web of human emotion of the working-class children actually involved in the events.

Theater was to spend another of its apparently cyclic periods in the doldrums before new generations would emerge. Perhaps the accessibility first of film and then television was taking its toll. In any event, in spite of the success of playwrights like Carballido, Hernández, and Leñero, it was difficult to sustain an audience for critically sophisticated and original theater. Too often it seemed that for paying theatergoers, foreign works, flashy spectacles, melodrama, musicals, and money-making were all that counted. No doubt tensions and sensitivity to potential censorship of the kind suffered by Usigli and Leñero played a role too. But new signs of life did come, and although plays dealing directly with Tlateloco do not seem to have been numerous, that misfortune must have encouraged what amounted to a theater of generational protest and disaffection. The new dramatists seemed often to be expressing their hatred of their parents and teachers, saw their lives as controlled by others, and painted a bleak picture of human relationships.

Two dramatists stand out in the initial years of this revival; they are Oscar Villegas and Willebaldo López. The two share some thematic concerns— broadly put, the destructive effects that society has on people—but their approaches are different, Villegas relying much more on the verbal than López, whose plays are more readily accessible. Villegas portrays people who may be anywhere but who are generally victims of circumstance, and sometimes victimizers of others, and structurally his plays are highly fragmented, sometimes absurdist. An example is *La paz de la buena gente* (*The Peace of Good Folk,* 1987), which has almost as many scenes as pages, is set on a darkened and empty stage, and has faceless, numbered characters.

López, by contrast, stresses the Mexicanness of his characters and places, and his technique is basically realist, coupled with humor; his early plays have a meta-theatrical dimension—they are about playacting and writing plays— but he turned increasingly to historical and cultural issues. For example, in *Vine, vi y mejor me fui* (*I Came, I Saw and I Thought it Better to Leave,* 1974) he questioned the effectiveness of his own technique. The main character, called The Dramatist, interacts with others and with the audience in an apparently directionless manner until a violent act off stage draws the other characters away to investigate, while it leads the The Dramatist to sit and start writing. He imagines a scenario for a murder next door, and then learns that the murder has indeed occurred, so that reality has conformed to his imaginings, his fiction. But he decides that the event is too melodramatic for a play, and therefore he decides to adapt it. As an example of a historical theme we may take *Yo soy Juárez,* 1972, in which a group of students are rehearsing a play about Benito Juárez, one that portrays his human side; but their efforts are viewed as a slight on Juárez's heroic image and so they are forced to abandon their project. During the course of the rehearsals, however, the students have become the historical characters they are portraying. This play calls to mind the theme (and fate) of Leñero's *Martirio de Morelos,* mentioned earlier.

José Agustín, primarily a novelist, and leader of the Onda movement in the 1960s, published only three plays but drew some attention for his provocative experiments, such as *Abolición de la propiedad* (*Abolition of Property,* 1969). Several of the dramatists of the period wrote intermittently, and one or two even abandoned writing for the stage, because of economic necessity or the difficulties in getting plays staged. Villegas is a case in point. By the late 1970s Gerardo Velásquez was becoming significant for plays that foreshadowed the preoccupations of later dramatists. Thematically, like his immediate predecessors, Velásquez wrote about difficult human relationships, but he shifted the focus away from young people, away from Mexico City, and toward women. Structurally, his plays are inventive and demanding, inviting audience participation. *Toño Basura* (*Tony Garbage*) will serve as an example; it is subtitled "a Cubist portrait." The play consists of four acts, each of which has associated with it certain motifs or symbols, such as colors, seasons, and material objects. While these acts portray the title character's rise and fall, they do not follow the predictable life order, nor do they follow that of the seasons of the year with which they have been associated. Thus, the play has a typical puzzle-like quality, inviting the audience to make correspondences and discover patterns, but undermining any absolute certainty regarding events and their meaning. This is in contrast to the didactic nature of much previous writing, but it heralds the future.

In some ways the plays of newer writers like Sabina Berman, Tomás Espinosa, Oscar Liera, and Víctor Hugo Rascón Banda build on Willebaldo López's experiments with historical themes. Berman and Espinosa cast doubt on the believability of history and even question the nature of one's reality. Espinosa's characters emphasize their personal realities rather than any objective notion of reality, while Berman suggests that if history is open to question, then so is our present existence. Symptomatic is her *Rompecabezas* (*Brainteaser*), which makes doubt the focus of its plot at the same time as it questions its own trustworthiness. Based on the assassination of Trotsky, which took place in Mexico in 1940, the play is about the authorities' attempts to discover who was responsible, but it presents conflicting versions of the facts and sows a certain amount of confusion. There is a confession that is shown to be false, and the identity of the supposed killer is masked by the use of five different names for him. The proceedings are transcribed by a secretary who remains on stage throughout, as if recording another account of the facts. So it might be said that there is a basic truth in the fact of the assassination, and many versions or distortions of it, the most overarching of which is the play itself.

Berman, perhaps as much as any contemporary author, has breathed new life into the Mexican theater, demonstrating that commercial viability and sophisticated, critical treatment of Mexican themes are not necessarily mutually exclusive. Like Julio Bracho and Bustillo Oro in the 1930s, she has constructed a bridge between her theater and the cinema: before becoming a popular and critically acclaimed film, Berman's play *Entre Pancho Villa y una mujer desnuda* (1993) enjoyed a long and successful run on the Mexican stage (see pages 155, 160). This work, too, deftly combines historical reflections with utterly contemporary issues relating to social and gender relations. Her work is a theatrical counterpart of the critical and commercial success of women novelists like Sara Sefchovich, Laura Esquivel, and Angeles Mastretta. And, just as in fiction, contemporary women in the theater in Mexico have ranged over the whole gamut of styles. Jesusa Rodríguez, for example, a product of the Centro Universitario de Teatro, has developed her own radically experimental brand of theater; she has done innovative adaptations of theater classics—such as an adaptation of Mozart's opera *Don Giovanni* with an all-female cast—and she is the owner of a cabaret where she has created and staged some provocative one-woman shows.

Tomás Espinosa's most interesting play, according to Burgess, is *Santísima la nauyaca*. It concerns two older women who lead their lives vicariously, through mass media stars, especially through La María. Myth combines with religion here. A snake (*nauyaca*), erroneously reported by the media to be responsible for María's death, becomes sanctified (*santísima*) in the popular imagination. A María from the real world, María Cruz ("Mary Cross") assumes the identity (perhaps is trapped by the identity) of the media María; she is later is said to walk on water. At bottom it seems that people need myths, that the latter must be made to survive. Yet another real woman in this play becomes identified with a crocodile. It is she who will point out to María Cruz that she is no longer mistress of her own life or death, and it is she who will come to represent escape. At one point the characters receive news that a crocodile has escaped; symbolically pushing aside a painting of the *Last Supper* they encounter a glass partition behind which they can see the crocodile swimming to freedom. It is a window on the world outside, but it also looks rather like a television screen.

Liera and Rascón both comment on society and its institutions; they are committed to Mexican reality but are iconoclastic in technique. Liera suggests that life itself is theater, that people are always wearing masks, while Rascón sees reality in terms of a struggle between good and evil. We shall conclude our account of modern theater with some comments on a play by Liera, whose works are both varied and interesting. *Cúcara y Mácara* enjoys a certain notoriety. The first thing to note is the playfulness suggested by its title, which comes from a familiar children's rhyme. The play is based on the legend and history of the Virgin of Guadalupe, and it begins with an allusion to a failed attempt in 1921 to vandalize her image. But Liera's version of events is to provide a biting satire on the clergy and the lengths to which they will go in order to keep up appearances. So he invents a thinly masked clone he calls the Virgin of Siquitibum; he gives us to believe that she has appeared to two orphans named Cúcara and Mácara, and that her image has appeared on a shawl (an echo of the appearance of the image of the Virgin of Guadalupe on a shawl in early colonial times). "Siquitibum," we should note, is not altogether reverent, being a word one normally hears cried out in encouragement by supporters at sports events. Furthermore, Liera has the act of vandalism in his play destroy the shawl completely; the action then hinges on the need for a cover-up (no pun intended!). First, some priests use the day's collection money to buy police silence about the event, and then there ensues a somewhat cacophonous quest for ways to hide the loss and keep the faithful in happy ignorance. Clearly, the play is about the power of information and controls upon it, and it portrays the clergy as self-important and manipulative. *Cúcara y Mácara* provoked loud protests and it was accused of being unpatriotic and disrespectful. Early performances were interrupted by protesters shouting such things as "¡Viva la Virgen de Guadalupe!" (ironically, rather as one might hear cheers at a sports event). In later performances the voices of protest were joined by those of other theatergoers who simply thought that it was a matter of audience participation (something that by this time—the 1980s—was commonplace). Things culminated in June 1981 during a performance in Mexico City, when about 30 members of the audience invaded the stage. At first they were assumed to be a legitimate part of the theatrical experience, another example of audience participation, but then they attacked the actors and director and left them bleeding.

Despite Liera's experience—or perhaps in part because of it—the last decades of the century found the theater very much alive. The 1960s had cast aside many of the old taboos, ushering in a willingness to tackle almost any theme. An explosion of interest in the 1980s encouraged new writers and increased possibilities for publishing and staging plays, thanks in good measure to a New Dramatists series put on by the Universidad Autónoma Metropolitana. It was starting in 1979 that Sabina Berman had a streak of successes. At about that time Carballido, who had written so much for the stage himself and who had done so much to encourage younger dramatists, published two volumes of plays by young dramatists, *Teatro joven de México* and *Más teatro joven*. As it has most aspects of Mexican life, Mexico City has always ruled the world of theater, so much so that regional dramatists and players have had little choice but to migrate to the nation's capital or face marginalization. But we should note that there is a long and varied tradition of theatrical writing and performance in some other parts of the country, particularly Yucatán. The developing U.S. border culture has also generated some quite innovative theatrical activity, such as the provocative performance art of Guillermo Gómez Peña. In street installations and performances like *Two Undiscovered Amerindians Visit Madrid* (1992), offered on the occasion of the quincentenary of Columbus's voyage, Gómez Peña and his collaborator Coco Fusco underscore painful historical ironies and make fun of cultural stereotypes, in hilarious performances that have moved out of the Border Art Workshop in San Diego to the streets of Madrid, New York, and Los Angeles.

NOTES

1. Arguably, Mexico can claim the famed tenor Plácido Domingo as its own. He was born in Madrid but when he was nine moved to Mexico with his parents, who were singers in a peripatetic *zarzuela* company. Domingo himself has recorded examples from that genre. In the 1990s he starred on television in an "Anthology of the Zarzuela," widely shown in Latin America and coupled with a personal concert tour.

2. Aaron Copeland wrote a number of compositions inspired by Mexican popular melodies and motifs.

3. Both could be considered counterparts of the murals Rivera painted for Henry Ford, in Detroit.

4. Celestino Gorostiza, "El teatro de Xavier Villaurrutia," *Cuadernos Americanos* XI (1952), p. 2.

5. Salvador Novo, *Yocasta, o casi* (Mexico City: Los Textos de la Capilla, 1961), p. 118.

6. Catherine Larsen, "'No conoces el precio de las palabras': Language and Meaning in Usigli's *El gesticulador,*" *Latin American Theatre Review* 20/1 (fall 1986), p. 21.

7

Literature

They shall not wither, my flowers,
They shall not cease, my songs.
I, the singer, lift them up.
They are scattered, they spread about.
Even though on earth my flowers
May wither and yellow,
They will be carried there, to the innermost house
Of the bird with the golden feathers.

THIS POEM, BY NEZAHUALCÓYOTL, a Texcoco king of the fifteenth century, was translated into English from a translation into Spanish of a Nahuatl original. It is available to us thanks largely to the efforts of Miguel León-Portilla, a scholar to whom we owe much of our knowledge of literature from Aztec times. The fact that the poem is a version of a version of the original speaks of the difficulty in gaining access to the literature of pre-Hispanic times. For the most part, what we now know of that literature comes to us secondhand, and our understanding of it is inevitably mediated by that of others, by the process of translation. We know what little we do know mostly because some early Spanish missionaries worked with native informants to preserve or reconstruct literature. Another thing that this poem shows is that our modern ideas about what literature is, and how it can be categorized into genres, are not easily applicable. For this is not just a written poem; the poet writes songs, he is a singer, and clearly a performance is implied, not a private act of reading. Furthermore, understanding obviously depends on having a communal sense of occasion, and of the meaning of the imagery. All of this emphasizes both our cultural distance and how difficult it is to say when Mexican literature began. We know that there was a thriving pre-Hispanic literary culture (if by "literary" we understand something more all-embracing than that which is expressed and understood solely via the written word). From the start, the Spanish conquerors and early missionaries took an active, strategic interest in the fruits of pre-Hispanic culture, but as a free, autonomous undertaking, pre-Hispanic literature was effectively put to rest by the Spanish conquest; the "flowers" of the Aztec poet did indeed wither. Yet today indigenous literatures not only survive but are being actively revived. Especially since the 1970s, and with renewed focus following the 1994 Zapatista rebellion in Chiapas, voices have been raised in defense of indigenous rights to self-expression and self-determination, and international activists and prominent Mexican advocates such as Carlos Montemayor have supported indigenous populations in their grassroots revival of a literature of their own. Somewhat in line with the rhetoric of post-Revolutionary governments, much of this new literature has appeared under the imprint of federal agencies and the state governments in Chiapas, the Yucatán, and Oaxaca.

To whom, then, does this literature belong? To the modern Mexican nation state or to the semi-autonomous, indigenous-language communities? And how, in the light of such circumstances, is one to define Mexican literature? Is it rightly traced back to the products of the earliest, pre-Hispanic civilizations that inhabited the land? Should it be dated only from the time of the conquest, when the Spanish language took hold? Should we perhaps consider only what was written after independence, when Mexico shed its colonial inheritance and the modern nation was born? These are theoretical issues, and rather controversial ones at that. Our answer for present purposes will be a practical one that is in line with our approach in other parts of this book; our main focus will be on the period since independence, and especially on modern times.[1]

New Spain

The first works commonly held to be part of Mexico's literary heritage were in fact written by Spaniards and often published and circulated in Spain for Spanish readers. Furthermore, such works require a more permissive understanding of what constitutes literature than one based on aesthetics and imagination. Put simply, the first works in Spanish were *crónicas,* more like historical accounts or personal travelogues than works of the creative imagination. Nonetheless, the many histories of the New World penned in the sixteenth century and, above all, the personal chronicles of discovery and conquest, are essential parts of the history of Latin American literature; they are quite frequently exploited by modern writers.

After Christopher Columbus's logbook, his *Diario de navegación* (*Diary of Navigation*), most of the chronicles and histories have to do with Mexico and Peru, the main seats of colonial power. These documents, detailing the encounter between the European and American worlds, were written primarily for Europe. Cortés, the conqueror of Mexico, sent five long *cartas de relación (Report Letters)* back to the Spanish emperor, Charles V. One of Cortés's soldiers, Bernal Díaz del Castillo, wrote a full account of the conquest of Mexico: *Historia verdadera de la conquista de la Nueva España* (*True Account of the Conquest of New Spain*), a classic amongst the crónicas. And Fray Bartolomé de las Casas attracted the Emperor's sympathy with his account of maltreatment of the Indians: *Brevísima relación de la destrucción de las Indias* (*Most Brief Account of the Destruction of the Indies*). Another friar, Bernardino de Sahagún (1500–90), used quite sophisticated ethnographic techniques to gather information for his *Historia general de las cosas de Nueva España* (*General History of Things in New Spain*), a compendium of information about indigenous cultures, and an indispensable tool for modern scholars (though the good friar died believing that it would never be published, having incurred the suspicion of Spanish authority). Perhaps to compensate for the fact that he had previously destroyed many priceless indigenous documents, Fray Diego de Landa wrote the *Relación de las cosas de Yucatán* (*Account of Things in Yucatán*), another essential source of information, about Maya civilization.

In the early years of the colony, popular theater was important for purposes of evangelization and indoctrination, and useful in the management of the Indians, whose ritual practices were incorporated and assimilated through it. Many of the early works, most of them lost today, were composed by missionaries and staged in Indian languages. But in contrast to the early theater and the chronicles, which were largely functional, the ornamental genre that soon held sway among the criollos and peninsulares was poetry. There were frequent poetry contests, often associated with public events such as the arrival of new dignitaries. Poetry thus served official interests. For example, the students of the newly founded Royal and Pontifical University (1553) were trained to produce verse celebrating such things as religious effigies and the canonization of saints. The underlying purpose was propagandistic; the forms employed were those favored in the Spain of those times, and there was much recourse to classical mythology. Similarly, the prose writers mentioned above were inclined to compare events with the exploits of European heroes such as Caesar and Roland. On the popular front there were improvised ballads, based on the conventions of the Spanish romance; these were often satirical, and they were to provide the basis for the later corrido (see pages 174–75). The two styles—the one learned, the other popular—came increasingly together as time passed. These and other verse forms flourished in the hands of writers from Spain who had come to the New World, and increasingly in those of criollos. What is clear, however, is the extent to which the New World was slavishly immitating the Old World; significantly, even the criollo poets in the learned tradition had their poems published in Spain. The local presses were busy producing official documents and, in any case, the readers for poetry were mainly in Spain. Much of the poetry of the times is lost. In 1980 an important manuscript dating from 1577 was published, *Flores de varia poesía* (*Flowers of Assorted Poetry*); in addition to well-known peninsular poets, it includes work by the criollos Francisco de Terrazas, Carlos de Sámano, Miguel de Cuevas, and Martín Cortés, son of the conquistador.

The rise of the novel in sixteenth- and seventeenth-century Europe was not reflected in the American context, and the Spanish Inquisition, founded in 1478, was largely to blame. There were numerous official edicts designed to suppress cultural activities and forms that did not enjoy official approval, and the novel was effectively banned, for fear that it might detract from the monolithic purposes of officialdom and sow seeds of nonconformity among the populace. But some works did slip through the net. The imaginative prose work that has attracted most critical attention is Carlos Sigüenza y Góngora's *Infortunios de Alonso Ramírez* (*The Misfortunes of Alonso Ramírez*, 1690). Its author, from a prestigious family, joined the Jesuits at the age of fifteen but was expelled for misconduct. He later became professor of mathematics at the university and also royal cosmographer, while traveling widely and writing chronicles, learned treatises, and creative works. He was the source of some controversy both in his own time and since. *Infortunios* is only about 30 pages long and it is a work that mixes elements of chronicle, travelogue, and novel. In picaresque fashion, it tells how Alonso leaves Puerto Rico to seek his fortune in Mexico, then in the Philippines, where he falls prey to English pirates. After a shipwreck he comes back to Yucatán and makes his way to the capital, where he meets the viceroy, who puts him in contact with the author. So this work is not conventionally picaresque, with the hero narrating his own life story and the real author keeping well out of the picture; in a small way it is metafictional (which explains its fascination for modern scholars). Nor is the hero as amoral as conventional heroes. In fact, Sigüenza endows Alonso with knowledge and puts words in his mouth that show that he, Sigüenza, is there in disguise. In passing, Sigüenza has Alonso extol the virtues of the viceroy, which was no doubt in the author's interest, and perhaps a device to make his work acceptable.

Sigüenza was a friend of the real star of early colonial literature, Sor Juana Inés de la Cruz (1651–95). Although of illegitimate birth, she became a member of the viceregal court and was lady-in-waiting to the viceroy's wife before she retired from it to a nunnery, some say in retreat from amorous problems, but undoubtedly because she wanted the sort of conditions that would allow her to satisfy her love of learning and her wish to write. She was a prodigy of intelligence and wit in a world that looked askance on such qualities in a woman. Once in the convent she was hardly a recluse; her cell became a place for intellectuals to visit and share in literary discussions. Her erudition and her curiosity about things secular and mundane led to her being publicly reprimanded by a bishop in a document which, to hide his identity, he signed as Sor Filotea de la Cruz. Her response was to be one of her most famous works, her *Respuesta a Sor Filotea* (*Reply to Sor Filotea*). In it, perhaps tongue in cheek, she declares herself unworthy of dealing with theological issues and argues that her passion for secular knowledge is God given; she also takes advantage of the bishop's assumed female identity to wax satirical.

Sor Juana's works—essays, plays, and, above all, poetry—were almost all published in Spain.[2] Her many sonnets deal with moral and philosophical issues, with history, with mythology, with things sacred and things profane. About a quarter of her poetry is religious. She was sometimes respectful, sometimes satirical. "Este que ves, engaño colorido" ("This colored lie you see before you") is the first line of a clever philosophical poem that deals with the vanity of portraiture and challenges the value of art. She wrote many quite erotic love poems, discreetly couched and believed to be based on purely fictitious relationships. Among these love poems, which speak of the conflict between reason and passion, "Detente, sombra de mi bien esquivo" ("Stay, Shadow of My Elusive Joy") is a well-known example. She also wrote poems at the expense of men, which has endeared her to modern feminists: "Had Aristotle known how to cook," she wrote, "he would have written more" and, famously, "Hombres necios, que acusáis / a la mujer sin razón / sin ver que sois la ocasión / de lo mismo que culpáis" ("You stupid men who blame women without reason, unaware that you yourselves are the cause of that which you criticize"). Her long poem "Primero sueño" is considered her masterpiece, a "First Dream" that has no vision in it, being at bottom a literary exercise. She delighted in clever plays on words and erudite allusions in the baroque, *culterano* style associated with the Spanish poet Góngora; her writing is eminently intellectual, clever, and astute. She even seems arrogant at times, feigning humility in order to be seen to toe the line of acceptability. Sor Juana stands out among all Latin American colonial writers. She was a legend in her time, but her work fell into neglect until it was resurrected by the group known as the Contemporáneos in the early twentieth century.

Poetry in the late colonial period became less interesting, more conformist, and even reactionary. In eighteenth-century Mexico, literature was very much the province of the aristocrat and the cleric, and a good deal of what was written was in Latin, in a classical vein. An exception is to be found in the work of the most intriguing and eccentric figure of Enlightenment literature, Fray Servando Teresa de Mier (1763–1827), a Dominican priest who claimed to be related to Moctezuma, the Aztec emperor. The ideas in support of an independent Mexico that he expressed in 1794 in "Notes for the Sermon on the Appearance of the Virgin of Guadalupe," and his questioning of the apparitions of the Virgin, met with the displeasure of the Inquisition. In the presence of the viceroy and other high-ranking officials, he suggested that Mexico had actually been evangelized in the sixth century and that miraculous appearances there had paralleled others in Spain, thus implying Mexico's equality. Mier was forced into exile, to spend ten years in a Spanish monastery. He escaped and was recaptured several times, and traveled widely, meeting other exiles (especially Jesuits) and ending up penniless in London, where he wrote one of his most important works, which he published under a pseudonym, *Historia de la revolución de Nueva España* (1813). In all, he wrote volumes and in every imaginable genre. His most interesting work from a modern standpoint is, like Sigüenza's *Infortunios,* in the picaresque style: *Apología y relaciones de su vida* (*Apology and Accounts of His Life*).[3] This he wrote after his return to Mexico, in prison. But with independence came recognition for his patriotism. The end of his florid life was orchestrated in style by Mier himself; he is said to have toured the streets of Mexico City in a carriage inviting people to witness his last rites, then to have delivered an eloquent address to the assembled crowd, after which he confessed and was administered his rites, to die 16 days later.

José Joaquín Fernández de Lizardi died in the same year as Mier. Fernández de Lizardi is nicknamed "The Mexican Thinker" after the title of the most successful of several newspapers that he published.[4] He was a true revolutionary, more by virtue of his journalism than his creative works, but is widely remembered for his first novel, *El Periquillo Sarniento* (*The Itching Parrot,* 1816), which for a long time was held to be the first fully fledged novel in Latin America. It is frequently suggested that Lizardi turned to the novel as a means of obviating censorship, but any political message in this book is quite muted. Significantly, in its prologue, the author laments the shortage and the high cost of books under colonial rule (a reference to repressive policies) and he dedicates his book to his readers, instead of aiming to please the colonial elite. The novel is a first-person account of a life told from the protagonist's deathbed, and it is full of ridiculous didactic passages that undermine the apparently serious aim of having his children learn from his errors. This novel adapts the rather outmoded picaresque form and is very much a product of its age with its classical references and endless moralizing; but Lizardi was enlightened in his awareness of the power of the printing press to transcend colonial patronage and address the broader reading public directly.

INDEPENDENCE

Literature in nineteenth-century Mexico was a fledgling enterprise with an air of improvisation and amateurism about it. Such an assertion may come as a shock, given that we are talking of a nation whose literary inheritance reached back across 300 years of Spanish colonial rule and into the pre-Hispanic period. But by 1821 the slate was all but wiped clean, the country suddenly set adrift down the path toward modern nationhood, with hardly any preparation or precedent.

Mexico produced few, if any, literary giants in the nineteenth century. Sandwiched between the importance of art and architecture during the colonial period, and that of the new media of the twentieth century, literature in the nineteenth went largely unchallenged as the main means of ideological and cultural expression. Because of its size and relatively advanced level of social development, Mexico was something of an exception to the general Spanish American nineteenth-century rule that most of the major authors came from the upper crust of society and did double duty as statesmen. While many Mexican authors were also important statesmen, many came from less privileged social strata, and a surprising number of intellectuals and statesmen were of predominantly Indian heritage, including Benito Juárez, and his literary counterpart and contemporary, Ignacio M. Altamirano.

Perhaps because there was so little in the colonial literary past to escape from, and because the novel was in any case a relatively new genre, prose fiction began to play a much more interesting role than did poetry. While Fernández de Lizardi had adapted the Spanish picaresque tradition, other writers, such as Francisco Zarco (1829–69), Guillermo Prieto (1818–97) and José de Tomás Cuéllar (1830–94) wrote in the style of Spain's costumbrista sketch of local manners, sometimes to considerable satirical effect. Such sketches were published in the suddenly ubiquitous literary magazines produced by the newly liberated printing presses, where fledgling novels, too, began to appear in installments. Many of these early nineteenth-century novels were loosely organized constructs, and they held together, if at all, not because of any significant aesthetic design, but thanks to the constant and reassuring presence of the author's narrative voice and his melodramatic or paternalistic tone. An early fiction writer of interest is Juan Díaz Covarrubias (1837–59), who in his short life managed to write five works of fiction that at least evinced his awareness of the possibilities of the genre. His best-known work is an historical novel, *Gil Gómez el insurgente o la hija del médico* (*Gil Gómez the Insurgent, or the Doctor's Daughter,* 1859), in which he declares that he is abandoning the frivolity of poetry (at the time, poetry was often thought frivolous) in favor of the novel, despite which he launches into descriptions that have the air of Romantic poetry. The action, narrated by the author rather than distanced through a fictionalized narrator, develops in two largely independent plotlines, one historical or sociopolitical and the other amorous and personal, and these are made to converge only at the rather unlikely ending.

Another significant example of a costumbrista work is Luis G. Inclán's *Astucia* (*The Shrewd One,* 1865), unusual in that its style seems so natural and unpretentious. It provides a picture of life in rural Michoacán and concerns the trade in contraband tobacco, managing to be didactic but not heavy-handed. Beyond the basic conflict of good versus evil, Inclán raises other oppositions such as the individual versus society, common sense versus formal education, and freedom versus order. Although it is clear that the author is in sympathy with the former in each of these cases, his message is neither overstated nor unambiguous. Most interestingly, at the time he was one of few to suggest that civilization might be the cause of corruption, and he did so long before there came general disillusionment with progress and the sway of reason.

As to poetry, the nineteenth century began with Manuel Carpio (1791–1860) and José Joaquín Pesado (1801–61) both of whom are representative of neoclassical tendencies, of poetry that still served to uphold the status quo, to educate and instruct. Poets such as Guillermo Prieto and Ignacio Ramírez (1818–79) devoted as much of their energy to public polemic as to literature. Prieto, the founder of a society called the Academia de Letrán, is still known today by his pseudonym Fidel and as the National Poet par excellence; in his *Romancero* (1885) he chronicles in verse the major events of the independence movement; in the famous collection *Musa callejera* (1883) he paints tender portraits of many popular types. Ramírez, though generally conservative as a writer, proved to be an ardent reformer and liberal educator, active not only in the Academia de Letrán but also in the ground-breaking Instituto Literario de Toluca, which was committed to the education of students of Indian extraction. It was there that he taught Ignacio Altamirano. The first wave of Romantic poetry, with its excesses of melodramatic angst and melancholy, is represented by poets Manuel Flores (1840–85) and Manuel Acuña (1849–73). The most popular of all the nineteenth-century poets, however, somewhat to the chagrin of certain *littérateurs,* was Juan de Dios Peza (1852–1910), perhaps because his poetry avoided some of Romanticism's excesses and used natural, everyday language, advocating traditional values like patriotism, religion, and the family.

ALTAMIRANO'S NATIONALIST RENAISSANCE AND THE PROGRESS OF FICTION

In chapter 4, "The Media," we discussed the rise of literary magazines and the role of Ignacio Manuel Altamirano (1834–93) in that process, particularly his involvement with *El Renacimiento*. He was one of the most fervent promoters of the idea of a unified national literature, and one of the first to appreciate the role that serious literature could play in laying the foundations of a modern nation. Altamirano was a jack-of-all-trades, trying his hand at many genres, but his most important contributions were in prose fiction. The novel by Altamirano that signaled formal progress in the genre, for it is a well-structured and controlled piece of writing employing a cleverly self-conscious framing device, was *Clemencia* (1869); but his most popular and enduring works of fiction were the costumbrista sketches, *La navidad en las montañas* (*Christmas in the Mountains*, 1870) and *El Zarco* (*Zarco the Bandit*, 1901). Though Altamirano wanted to lift writing above the level of political partisanship, in his fiction his didactic temperament is very apparent, and he tends to fall rather simplistically into portraying good versus evil; this is true of *Clemencia,* in which two suitors represent the glamour of superficial appearance (Flores) and the soulful depths of moral integrity (Valle).

Even late in the century, *costumbrismo* was still evident in the works of Manuel Payno, who compiled perhaps the most complete inventory of social customs and types in nineteenth-century Mexico. The fact that Payno's voluminous *Los bandidos de Río Frío* (*The Bandits of Río Frío,* 1889–91), which appeared serially in Spain, so resembles his novel *El fistol del diablo,* of some 50 years earlier, suggests how slow literary and social progress were. Generally speaking, it was difficult for Mexican writers to accept the tenets of realism, with its pretension to objectivity and its erasure of the presence of the author from the surface of the text. In this regard, Emilio Rabasa (1856–1930) was a key figure. A distinguished lawyer for whom literature still seemed to have the taint of frivolity, under a pseudonym he produced a series of four Mexican novels, linked by a shared protagonist who also serves as narrator. In these novels the unthinking nationalism of earlier years is left behind, together with most of the Romantic sensibility associated primarily with poetry, to make way for a more discerning, constructively critical view. The narrator-protagonist retains a certain faith in the goodness and simplicity of things provincial, even while he acknowledges the corruption and brutalities of the burgeoning metropolis of Mexico City that is around him. The criticism that is implicit in these novels is leveled primarily at individuals of the more affluent classes, while the masses remain outside the sweep of Rabasa's picture. His style contrasts with those of the other two important realist novelists, José López Portillo y Rojas (1850–1923) and Rafael Delgado (1853–1914), who were artistically more accomplished than many others but who wrote with a certain detachment that communicates itself to the reader. Both were traditionalists in terms of attitude and social values; López wrote sympathetically but condescendingly about the popular classes, as in *La parcela* (*The Piece of Land*, 1898) and *Fuertes y débiles* (*The Strong and the Weak*, 1919), while Delgado painted the upper crust as pretentious and immoral and the middle class generally as God-fearing and humble, in novels such as *La calandria* (*The Love-Bird*, 1891) and *Los parientes ricos* (*Rich Relatives*, 1903).

Few Mexican novels since Lizardi's *El Periquillo Sarniento* have been as widely read and celebrated in their time as was *Santa* (1903) by Federico Gamboa, the leading practitioner of naturalism after the fashion of Émile Zola. This novel's popularity would later be exploited in several film versions, among them Mexico's first sound film. The emergence of naturalism in prose, like that of Spanish American *modernismo* in poetry, coincided at the turn of the century with the growth of the upper- and middle-class reading public. No doubt Gamboa's popularity had to do with his focus on marketable issues like sex and morality; his writing generally married psychological insights with what at the time were rather lubricious accounts of licentious behavior. Indeed, another significant Gamboa novel, *Suprema ley* (*The Supreme Law*, 1896), suggests rather directly that passion and sexual desire are more powerful forces than morals.

A writer who was important because he was an embarrassment to the government of Porfirio Díaz was Heriberto Frías (1870–1925). Frías had been a member of Díaz's army, and his military service inspired his most notable novel *Tomóchic*, which was first published anonymously in an opposition newspaper in 1893. This novel, which takes its name from a village where the army crushed an Indian rebellion, employs an unpolished mixture of the realist, Romantic, and naturalist styles. It is sharply critical of excesses on both sides in the conflict portrayed, and so remarkably evenhanded. The work's impact derives from its economy and its evident need to document contemporary political reality; in this respect, it anticipates the novels of the Mexican revolution.

MODERNISMO: PROFESSIONALIZATION AND ALIENATION IN THE LITERARY ARENA

We come now to what has often been said to be the first truly Spanish American literary movement, Modernism (not to be confused with avant-garde European and North American modernism). Modernismo was distinctly Spanish American but drew on French artistic forms, notably Parnassianism and Symbolism. Its prose dates back to the early 1880s, the most characteristic prose genre being the journalistic chronicle, whose principle exponent in Mexico was Manuel Gutiérrez Nájera (1859–95). Another form favored by the modernists was the *cuento azul* ("blue tale"), a whimsical tale modeled on the work of writers like Alphonse Daudet. Modernismo is associated above all with the figure of Rubén Darío, a Nicaraguan (1867–1916), but it spread through Central America and Mexico and down to the Southern Cone of South America. In its early phase, modernismo was anything but nationalistic; it exploited cultural references and images drawn from Greek and Teutonic mythology, from pre-revolutionary Versailles, even from the Orient. This stage of modernismo was programmatically aesthetic, emphasizing the cult of beauty for its own sake and the visual and musical properties of language. The refinement and luxury of the poetic objects and ambiances evoked probably reflect the pretensions and the materialism of the Spanish American bourgeoisie; the poems of this phase are replete with ornate gardens, statues, and fountains, desirable women, and other attractions that money could buy, although the crass bourgeoisie might find it hard to appreciate the refined aesthetics. The principles of *modernista* poetry and the very forms and language of the poems reflect the new, modern situation of the poets; literature was becoming not a hobby, a sideline, but a vocation and a life-style. Before coming to an end, modernismo went through a final phase represented by the work of poets who turned modernista style against itself through parody and exaggeration.

Modernismo was not quite the phenomenon in Mexico that it was in many other Spanish American capitals and cultural centers, where the national literary culture had weaker traditions on which to build. Manuel Gutiérrez Nájera is the most anthologized and prototypical representative of modernismo from Mexico. For many years waves of modernista influence colored the output of a whole gamut of poets in Mexico—from late Romantics such as Manuel José Othon (1858–1906) and Luis G. Urbina (1869–1934), through such central figures as Salvador Díaz Mirón (1853–1928), José Juan Tablada (1871–1945), and Amado Nervo (1870–1919), to the outstanding work of Enrique González Martínez (1871–1952) and especially Ramón López Velarde (1888–1921). With the exception of Gutiérrez Nájera, few of the Mexican poets at the turn of the twentieth century produced quintessentially modernista poems of exquisite sensibility and exotic refinement; rather, most responded to local circumstances and developed personal styles and sensibilities. As a group, they constituted a second, more refined and often decadent generation of modern Romantics; largely excluded from the political realm during the Porfiriato, and unable to assume the nation-building and heroic roles played by the early Romantics, they became specialized and professional authors, and took refuge in audacious sentiment and imagery. The modernista period culminated in two original figures, Juan José Tablada and López Velarde, whom many consider the first authentically modern poets in Mexico.

Salvador Díaz Mirón, celebrated in his home state of Veracruz, was a significant transitional figure in the passage from Romanticism to Modernismo, and he is said to have had some influence on Rubén Darío, the leader of the modernista movement. A staunch individualist who worked outside of established literary circles, he saw his role as that of an aristocratic, heroic, and tragic figure. He was once jailed for having killed a braggart in a fight, and his poetry is often remarkable for its passion and even violence; in the second half of his career, his work evolved towards greater purity and objectivity. Díaz Mirón's poetry seems to express the frustration and tragedy of the vocation in Porfirian times, and poems such as "El desertor" and "Ejemplo" are a long way from the civic poems of patriotic praise and national virtue that had been common earlier in the nineteenth century. Often Díaz Mirón is almost Nietzschean in his inversions of conventional wisdom, and his unusual vision and imagery lend considerable complexity to social and amorous themes.

Gutiérrez Nájera was the first of Mexico's full-time creative writers, and it was he who truly defined and promoted modernismo in Mexico; he helped found the famous *Revista Azul,* which was known throughout the Spanish-speaking world and was the most important literary magazine in Mexico since Altamirano's *El Renacimiento.* More than any other poet, he embodied the pretense to European, particularly French, refinement that swept through the elite of the time. His poetry enshrined the modernista cult of musicality ("La serenata de Schubert"), of form and color and sensorial effect ("De blanco"). Generally, Gutiérrez Nájera viewed poetry as a means of escape from the everyday world; in "Non Omnis Moriar" ("I Shall Not Die Completely"), for example, poetry is a means of achieving immortality, both for the poetic voice and the beloved. Gutiérrez Nájera began publishing at the tender age of thirteen, and all of his work bears the mark of his complete dedication to a life of writing; his vast critical output, sketches of local color and travel, and short stories (or fantasies) appeared almost exclusively in newspapers and magazines. He excelled particularly at the genre known in Mexico as the journalistic chronicle, in which he skillfully detailed things such as the ins and outs of high society at the theaters, salons, cafés, and the Jockey Club. He has been described as a "professional modernist *roué*" who celebrated "blindingly perfect beauty" and lived out the life of a "dandified aesthete."[5] This helps explain his slightly ambiguous attitude to his reading public, on which he depended, but which he also rather despised. He himself once described his approach toward his audience as "biting with the lips."

Still at the heart of Mexican modernismo are two other rather flamboyant and eccentric figures. One was Amado Nervo, who as a youth studied for the priesthood, becoming immersed in the writings of the mystics. Although he left to pursue a career as a journalist, the influence of the mystics became evident in his later works. In 1898, along with Jesús E. Valenzuela, Nervo founded the modernist journal *Revista moderna* (1898–1911). His first works show the influence of the French Parnassians, emphasizing formal perfection and exotic imagery, with mystical overtones. *Místicas* (*Mystics,* 1897), *Poemas* (*Poems,* 1901), *Perlas negras* (*Black Pearls,* 1898), *El éxodo y las flores del camino, Lira heroica* (*The Exodus and the Flowers Along the Path, Heroic Lyre,* 1902), and *Los jardines interiores* (*The Interior Gardens,* 1900) fit into this first category. The second stage was one of turning inward and exploring religious themes influenced by oriental philosophies, especially Buddhism. *En voz baja* (*In a Low Voice,* 1909), *Serenidad* (*Serenity,* 1914), *Elevación* (*Elevation,* 1917), and *Plenitud* (*Plenitude,* 1918) belong to this period, the last two being especially influenced by a pantheistic view of nature and by love for mankind. The third stage is one of simplicity and profound questioning of the meaning of life and death. One of Nervo's most famous works, *La amada inmóvil* (*The Motionless Beloved,* 1920), appeared during this period, later becoming a film; it is dominated by the theme of love. Nervo's poetry is subjective and sincere, soothingly pure, expressing metaphysical anguish but also resignation in the face of the unknown. Like so many writers of the time, for whom literature became a full-time vocation, Nervo wrote prolifically and in many genres. He tried a variety of narrative styles, from the morally provocative naturalism of *El bachiller* (1895) to the more ethereal *El donador de almas* (1922). Nervo was internationally recognized and extremely popular during his lifetime. Today his work meets with varied reactions, though some people think him among the best of Latin American poets.

José Juan Tablada is the other major and truly eccentric figure of Mexican modernismo, one whose work passed through extraordinarily diverse phases, spanning the whole gamut from late Romanticism, through modernismo, to the avant-garde. Though his work was celebrated by his contemporaries, both nationally and internationally, many of the ground-breaking values of his work have only recently been fully recognized. Even in his earliest poems, Tablada delighted in provocative frivolity, sacrilege, decadence, and eroticism. Some critics believe that he is the one truly original Mexican modernista, especially by virtue of the poems collected under the title *El florilegio* (1899), such as "Onix." Tablada was one of Mexico's first true cosmopolitans and orientalists; he visited and cultivated poetic innovations from France, Japan, and the United States. His global vision is beautifully captured in his "Nocturno alterno," which Octavio Paz considered his best poem; it evokes the immense distance between worlds but also the unity that binds them together. Tablada's zest for vanguard experimentalism is amply demonstrated in later works: he was the first to bring to Spanish the suggestive powers of the haiku, in *Un día* (1919) and *Un jarro de flores* (1921), while in *Li-Po y otros poemas* (1928) he experiments graphically with ideogram-like compositions deriving from the Orient, and intoxication, somewhat after the fashion of Apollinaire's *Calligrames.*

Among the stock symbols of modernist writers was the swan, which stood for absolute beauty. As the appeal of the rarified aesthetic pretensions of the modernists began to wear thin, another Mexican poet, Enrique González Martínez, famously called for the swan's neck to be wrung (in the poem "Tuércele el cuello al cisne," 1911) for, while he appreciated the refinement of poetic form, he felt that it was frivolous and symptomatic of moral decay. With Ramón López Velarde, González Martínez thus embodies the post-modernista spirit, which turned away from the exotic and the exquisite to revive more traditional topics: simple objects, provincial life, religion, home, and family. González Mártinez and López Velarde are often viewed as the poetic counterparts of the novelists of the Revolution: their return to simpler values was not only a reaction against modernista decadence emanating from the capital, but also a nostalgic refuge and a rejection of the chaos, violence, and vulgar banditry into which the Revolution had degenerated. But this is a very limited understanding of the achievements of López Velarde, based on selected compositions such as the return of the prodigal son in "Retorno maléfico" ("Malefic Return," 1919) or the patriotic "Suave Patria" ("Tender Homeland," 1932). In fact, López Velarde had a thoroughly modern, ironic style and was a transitional figure on the road to contemporary poetry. López Velarde was born in the province of Zacatecas, studied law at the University of San Luis de Potosí and then, like most aspiring artists, moved to Mexico City, where he worked during his brief life as a journalist, professor, and public servant. Like Tablada, but in a different way, López Velarde bridges Modernismo and the avant-garde, and together they laid the foundations for subsequent poetry. His works manage unselfconsciously to marry a thoroughly Mexican reality with literary sophistication and originality. The sentimental provincial themes of his early poetry (*La sangre devota* [*Devout Blood*], 1916), rich with sensual Catholic imagery, change in later years, becoming more urbane in *Zozobra* (*Anxiety,* 1919) and *El son del corazón* (1932). López Velarde was essentially a poet of feelings, manipulating language with daring metaphors and erotic imagery that appealed to sight, smell, and touch and cast universal emotions in an entirely original, subtle, and complex light.

INTELLECTUAL PRECURSORS OF THE REVOLUTION: THE ATENEO DE LA JUVENTUD

The story of modern Mexican literature demands recognition of the contributions made by a society known as the Ateneo de la Juventud. Founded in 1909, it was short-lived as a collective enterprise, but many of its members went on to illustrious careers, making fundamental contributions to Mexican culture. It is often suggested that the *ateneístas,* as they are known, were the first to professionalize literary and intellectual activity in Mexico, but they were not alone in this respect: the same could be said of several of the modernista authors. Like the modernistas, the ateneístas felt excluded from the public sphere under the Díaz regime, but in contrast to the isolation and alienation of the modernistas, the ateneístas pursued direct involvement. They gave new life to higher education, with many new programs of study and pedagogical initiatives, and they became revered teachers and mentors of future generations of intellectuals. Plain old Revolutionaries the lofty-minded ateneístas most definitely were not, even though their activities as a group coincided exactly with the outbreak of the Revolution. Revolutionary artists and intellectuals they most certainly were, and their vocal and very public opposition to the positivistic scientism that dominated cultural and educational policy under Porfirio Díaz paralleled the political opposition to the Díaz regime embodied in the Revolution itself.

Broadly speaking, the ateneístas stood for the revival of the universal and humanistic values of culture, and the reassertion of mankind's philosophical and spiritual dimension. Rather than novelists and poets, the ateneístas were humanists and philosophers, and since there was little by way of an established tradition in these areas, they broke considerable new ground. Figures such as Alfonso Reyes (1899–1959), a formidable intellectual from Monterrey, and the Dominican expatriate Pedro Henríquez Ureña, for example, gave new weight to literary criticism, and their torch would be taken up by the writers of the avant-garde group known as the Contemporáneos. Other ateneístas, most notably Antonio Caso (1883–1946), did much to establish philosophy as an academic discipline in Mexico, thus paving the way for the work of Samuel Ramos, Luis Villoro, and many others. The more literarily inclined of the ateneístas excelled especially in the essay and similar forms; often they combined characteristics of different genres into highly effective personal styles. Others fused fictional and non-fictional forms, as is the case with the four-volume, novel-like autobiography penned by José Vasconcelos (1882–1959), and Martín Luis Guzmán's chronicles of the Revolution and his fictionalized autobiography, *Memorias de Pancho Villa*. All the Ateneo participants sided politically with the Revolution, at least at the outset; as the stark realities of the political and military battle became clear, however, the group dissolved.

LITERATURE AND THE (NOVELS OF) REVOLUTION

The final triumph of the Mexican Revolution of 1910, and particularly the consolidation of a range of social and political institutions in its wake, helped to put a distinctive mark on future Mexican culture. So sweeping were the changes, in theory and rhetoric if not in actual practice, that there was bound to be some literary spin-off. The novel of the Revolution, in particular, was as a uniquely Mexican variant on the Spanish American regionalist novel of the 1920s and 1930s. Yet it would be wrong to assume that the dramatic and chaotic events of the 1910 Revolution immediately transformed literature. The turmoil, of course, influenced and often inconvenienced cultural activity, but daily life went on: newspapers, magazines, and books continued to be published, cultural and literary events took place as best they could. Aspiring writers from the provinces continued to make their way toward Mexico City in the hope of getting their voices heard and establishing a reputation.

By the 1930s the novel of the Mexican Revolution was so widespread as to appear to be obligatory. Together with the artwork of the muralists, the novel of the Revolution fed into the classic films of the Golden Age of Mexican cinema that, in turn, have helped define the face that Mexico has presented to the world. In fact, one would have to acknowledge that novels of the Revolution are still being written: witness the surprise bestseller of 1985, Angeles Mastretta's *Arráncame la vida* (translated as *Mexican Bolero*) and her more recent *Mal de amores* (*Lovesickness*, 1995), which are nostalgic revivals, or romancings, of the genre. Any novel that aims seriously to explore Mexico's twentieth century must perforce come to terms with the effects of the Revolution. Nowhere is this more apparent than in the three mid-twentieth-century masterpieces: Agustín Yáñez's *Al filo del agua* (*The Edge of the Storm*, 1946), Juan Rulfo's *Pedro Páramo* (1954), and Carlos Fuentes's *La muerte de Artemio Cruz* (*The Death of Artemio Cruz*, 1962). All of them are revaluations of the Revolutionary inheritance.

The novel of the Revolution had quite inauspicious beginnings. Significantly, like the circumstances surrounding Fernandez de Lizardi's first Mexican novel of some 100 years earlier, the first examples of the novel of the Revolution appeared as alternatives to news reports. Rather as in the case of the chronicles of discovery and conquest, the attraction of the very first novels of the Revolution lay outside Mexico, not inside, perhaps because events felt too painfully near for reading about them in novels to have much appeal. Mariano Azuela's *Los de abajo* (*The Underdogs*) and Martín Luis Guzmán's *El águila y la serpiente* (*The Eagle and the Serpent*) are early novels in the genre, and many critics would say that they are the outstanding examples. In form and style the two are quite dissimilar, but in the visceral reactions to the Revolution that can be read between their lines, and in the circumstances surrounding their genesis, the two have things in common. Both authors were educated men and intellectuals of sorts: Guzmán a respected member of the Ateneo circle in Mexico City, Azuela a rural physician from the state of Jalisco. Both authors favored the goals and premises of the Revolution in theory, and apparently found its mysteries, particularly the charisma and power of leaders like Pancho Villa, alluring. Both took up with bands of Revolutionaries in the north. Both, in the process, came in some degree to be disillusioned by the chaos, the violence, and the lack of respect for moral and political ideals. Their novels are more or less fictionalized accounts of what they witnessed and experienced. Azuela's *Los de abajo* first appeared in periodic installments in an El Paso (Texas) Spanish-language newspaper in 1915, but it received scant attention until it was reissued in book form in 1924. Guzmán's *El águila y la serpiente* made its first appearance not in Mexico but in Spain, in 1928. After the possibilities of the genre were revealed by the publication of these two books, other narrative accounts of the Revolution began to appear.

Los de abajo is episodic in structure, and its rapid-fire, fervent style seems to mimic the flavor of the Revolution itself. Each chapter is short and expressionistic, and the whole novel barely runs to 100 pages. The main action follows the circular participation in the Revolution of the small, essentially anonymous, rebel group from the north-central plateau. No dates are given, but reference points scattered throughout the novel show that the main action follows precisely, though selectively, the advances of 1914 and 1915. The rebels are small landowners of the lower middle classes. The hero is their leader and he is counterbalanced by a character who is a hypocritical intellectual ideologue. More than the coherence of the story line, Azuela emphasizes the attitudes of the characters, in a series of powerful, loosely connected episodes. The ultimate effect is one of disillusionment; the Rvolutionaries, who have lived by the sword, die one by one, presumably as a consequence of their greed and moral bankruptcy. The intellectual readily abandons the cause when the opportunity for material gain presents itself. In the end, the hero returns alone to his point of origin; his integrity leads him to a death that is portrayed in deliberately ambiguous terms and has symbolic overtones.

Guzmán was more sophisticated than Azuela, though his values, prejudices, and gut reaction to the Revolution were similar. In many ways *Los de abajo* and *El águila y la serpiente* provided complementary accounts of the same phase of the Revolution; each covers the rise and fall of Pancho Villa between 1913 and 1915, but they focus on very different parts of the Revolution's pecking order. Instead of the anonymous commoner, Guzmán pays ample attention to the larger-than-life caudillos. Pancho Villa is in effect Guzmán's equivalent to Azuela's hero Demetrio Macías; *El águila y la serpiente* reveals Guzmán's mixed feelings as he attempts to vindicate Villa's moral character. The triumphant general, Venustiano Carranza, is the foil in Guzmán's novel; he is indicted for his greed and personal ambition. This novel lacks the immediacy and passion of Azuela's but it makes up for them with its elegance and coldly penetrating analysis. While also episodic—many of its chapters are anthologized as short stories—*El águila y la serpiente* runs some three or four times as long as Azuela's novel. Where Azuela gets close enough to the Revolution to feel it as a pathetic, yet heroic tragedy, Guzmán presents it from a more critical distance, as a farce full of the strangest of incongruities.

The figure of Pancho Villa had clearly become an obsession with Guzmán. Through the 1930s and into the 1940s, he published a multi-volume fictionalized autobiography of Pancho Villa, titled *Memorias de Pancho Villa*. He also produced an outstanding political novel, *La sombra del caudillo* (*The Shadow of the Political Boss*, 1929). This novel deals with machinations around the time of the infamous assassination of General Obregón, the work of a political ally turned enemy. To many people the assassination of Obregón has come to epitomize the corruption of the institutionalized Revolution. It inspired the well-known play by Rodolfo Usigli, *El gesticulador* (censored by government officials for a number of years). Indeed, when a film version of Guzmán's novel was finally made in 1960, it too suffered from government censorship for the next 30 years.

Narratives of the Revolution now proliferated. For most authors, the substance of what they had to tell took precedence over any concern for style or artistic form. Often they adopted an episodic structure, as had Azuela and Guzmán, yielding a series of quick sketches, short stories, or vignettes, as if the unwieldy events of the Revolution could still not be brought together into a larger, meaningful whole. Two authors who produced valuable works of this type, Rafael Muñoz and Nellie Campobello, also focused their narratives on the activities of Pancho Villa's troops in the north. But these two authors were both much younger than Azuela and Guzmán and, perhaps as a result, they take a more emotionally distanced view of the horrors of the Revolution. Muñoz's *Vámonos con Pancho Villa* (*Let's Ride with Pancho Villa*), originally published in Madrid in 1931, first shows the excitement that the Revolution generated and the powerful attraction that Villa's charisma exerted over many young men. The novel goes on, however, to depict the tragic consequences of undying loyalty to Villa; each of the six young country boys the novel presents is sacrificed. (Muñoz's novel provided the basis for an important 1935 film directed by Fernando de Fuentes.) Nellie Campobello's memoirs, published in *Cartucho* (*Cartridge*, 1931) and *Las manos de mamá* (*Mother's Hands*, 1937), are powerful works that provide a unique perspective. Long the object of neglect, Campobello's works have recently received attention because she was one of very few women writing at the time in Mexico. *Cartucho* organizes a series of snapshot anecdotes and vignettes into three general thematic categories: "Men of the North," "Victims of Execution," and "Under Fire." Though colored by her own experience of the Revolution and its protagonists as a very young girl and presented in the first person, most of the selections recount what family members, especially her mother, had told her or witnessed. From a child's perspective, there is no basis for putting the figures who serve as protagonists in her anecdotes on pedestals; moreover, their calculated cruelty contrasts vividly with her innocence and openness.

While the Revolution had begun in the north as a principled demand for true and effective democracy, only to evolve into factionalism and banditry, in the south it took the form of an agrarian revolt on behalf of peasants and Indians led by the legendary figure Emiliano Zapata. The literary champion of this side of the Revolution was Gregorio López y Fuentes, who produced a rash of propagandistic novels of dubious effectiveness and literary value in the 1930s, including *Campamento* (*Bivouac*, 1931), *Tierra* (*Land*, 1932), and *El indio* (*Indians*, 1935). López y Fuentes's novels are also constructed as a series of episodes, scenes, or sketches loosely connected around some organizing principle. *Campamento*, for example, focuses one by one on the diverse types and interests brought together in a single night in the bivouac of a typical Revolutionary band. *Tierra* paints the progress, or lack thereof, on a typical hacienda. *El indio* portrays the plight of the Indians. López y Fuentes strongly sympathizes with the social reforms championed by the Revolution, and he deplores its many shortcomings. His novels capture the way larger events of the Revolution affected, or failed to affect, inhabitants of the social fringes. His somewhat condescending focus is primarily on anonymous, representative types, as opposed to the more individualized and larger-than-life figures populating the novels from the north.

The novel of the Mexican Revolution—if we take that label in a restrictive sense to apply to works that deal with the events of the Revolution's armed phase—sprang up and ran dry in the early to mid-1930s. While almost all

Mexican novels for some time to come were bound to deal in some way with the causes and effects of the Revolution, they generally took a wider and more critical view of things. In some ways López y Fuentes's *El indio* signaled the path followed by many writers in the 1930s and 1940s who were concerned with the marginalization and exploitation of the Indian. *Indigenismo* is the term generally used to refer to artistic products that treat such matters. Mauricio Magdaleno's *El resplandor* (*Sunburst*, 1937), though less well known than López y Fuentes's novel (*El indio* was translated into both English and German, and it won Mexico's National Prize for Literature), makes a more sophisticated contribution to indigenista writing. This novel, too, tends to mystify and distance Indians, portraying them as a timeless presence closely tied to the land. But because of its greater psychosocial and artistic complexity, Magdaleno's novel heralds the more broadly interpretative treatments of the Revolution that we find in much later fiction. Magdaleno went on to have a very successful career as a writer for the film industry, working on some of the classic Golden Age films by the Emilio Fernández/Gabriel Figueroa team (see page 133–37).

THE AVANT-GARDE

Mexico had a vigorous avant-garde culture in the 1920s and 30s. The fact that the international (mostly European) avant-garde movements coincided with the early post-Revolutionary years made this period a particularly dynamic and polemic one, full of anomalies and contradictions. For a time, a shaky alliance of different artistic approaches and political agendas was held together by the plans of José Vasconcelos, then minister of education. Vasconcelos proposed to implement a radical new cultural program of universal literacy, and he wanted to make art a thing of the people, following the Russian model. Mexico was seen by many people, both inside and outside the country, as a testing ground for the new art and ideas that flourished in the post–World War I period. These included a rejection (but sometimes also a celebration) of technological progress and capitalist development, of science and of reason, coupled with a return to the natural simplicity of primitive community, to the magic of myth, intuition, and the unconscious. Such developments greatly enriched the intellectual and artistic culture of Mexico, and they brought with them a parade of renowned, radical, European and North American avant-garde figures: from such precursors as the English novelist D.H. Lawrence and the American journalist John Reed, to Eisenstein the filmmaker and later Leon Trotsky the Bolshevik, to the photographer Edward Weston and the artist Tina Modotti, to Copeland, to Breton and

Artaud, and perhaps in a final, fully decadent stage, the Canadian novelist Malcolm Lowry.

As one might expect, the avant-garde in Mexico expressed itself above all though the more intuitive arts of music and painting, such as Carlos Chávez's music and Diego Rivera's murals. The Mexican avant-garde epitomized the perennial dilemma of post-colonial nations, driven simultaneously to modernize, to catch up and gain respect, but also to affirm their difference. Virtually none of the works of the authors of the avant-garde in Mexico have filtered down to us today as part of the literary canon. What they wrote was generally difficult and experimental, polemic and programmatic. But they do have a cult following, and there is little doubt that their innovations and defenses of unpopular ideas make them one of the most significant groups in the history of Mexican letters. Most of what subsequent literature in Mexico has accomplished seems unthinkable without their influence.

Two literary groups, both Mexican originals, represent the avant-garde spirit of the 1920s and 1930s; they had very different programs and strategies, outcomes and successes. One, the *Estridentista* movement, in typical vanguard fashion set out to meld together socialism and futurism, politics and literature, in a program involving the new machine age and emerging cadres of organized labor. Their efforts were a kind of literary counterpart to the murals Rivera produced for the Ford family at the Detroit Art Institute, exalting the power and possibilities of new industrial technology. Estridentista authors printed broadsides, published literary manifestos in sporadic reviews in the early 1920s, and produced some poetry and novellas, whose primary effect was to shock. Manuel Maples Arce (1900–81) was the founding father and leading figure of *Estridentismo*. The movement proved short-lived; the works of its authors were too extravagant and esoteric for the social realists and too naively proletarian for those who were more cosmopolitan. But the flames did not burn out before one of Maples Arce's poems, "Urbe" (1924), found its way into English as "Metropolis," in a translation by the renowned U.S. novelist John Dos Passos.

A group of writers who came to be known as the Contemporáneos took a very different approach from the Estridentistas and in the end they left a more enduring legacy. Much less partisan and programmatic, if no less polemic and controversial, the Contemporáneos did not favor any particular ideology; in the partisan and polemic post-Revolutionary period in which they did battle, their work seems almost apolitical, and they often considered themselves to be "the group that wasn't a group." The Contemporáneos defended the kind of cosmopolitan literary culture that was the heritage left by the modernistas two generations before them. And like the members of the Ateneo de la Juventud, they added to the modernista legacy a reverence for the broad social and political benefits of humanist culture. Several of the Contemporáneos worked under Vasconcelos's guidance in the cause of the new Mexican cultural renaissance; one of them, Jaime Torres Bodet, worked at the Secretariate of Public Education for many years. The Contemporáneos saw through the reigning exuberance of their time, and they came to define themselves in direct opposition to what they saw as the false, touristy nationalism epitomized by the work of people such as Rivera. Rather than project a proletarian, Indianist image, which they thought patronizing and folklorish, the Contemporáneos practiced their own particular combination of dandyism and bohemianism. They opposed the macho brutalism of the Revolutionary hero with a more refined sensibility, one which, as many saw it, was dangerously effeminate, if not unabashedly homosexual. If their work appeared to be un-Mexican, then at least, they said, it involved fewer blatant hypocrisies. Above all, the Contemporáneos possessed highly independent and dissident, often haughty spirits; they championed free thinking and open critical exchange. Some suggest that while such elder members of the group as Bernardo Ortiz de Montellano, José Gorostiza, and Jaime Torres Bodet tended to share the kind of optimism that inspired Vasconcelos's vision, among the younger members of the group, such as Gilberto Owen, Salvador Novo, Jorge Cuesta, and Xavier Villaurrutia, skepticism, disillusionment, and melancholy were more prevalent.

One reason why the group's contributions were so substantial yet generally under-appreciated was that its members concentrated on day-to-day involvement in public issues and intellectual debate rather than on the production of major works. As with avant-garde groups elsewhere, much of their energy went into magazines, the most famous of which was the one that gave them their name, a magazine that appeared monthly between 1928 and 1931. In its pages, the group members' writings appeared alongside the work of cutting-edge international authors and many other Mexican artists and intellectuals of the time, whatever their ideological inclinations.

In the area of aesthetic theory and practical criticism of the arts, Xavier Villaurrutia and Jorge Cuesta were the most distinguished of the group. Cuesta addressed all of the pressing cultural and ideological issues of the time, channeling most of his energy into voluminous essays on literature, art, philosophy, and science, as can be seen in the posthumous, five-volume collection entitled *Poemas y ensayos* (*Poems and Essays*, 1964, 1981). The revitalization of the theater was another of the Contemporáneos group's invaluable contributions to Mexican culture (see chapter 6), with Villaurrutia, Novo, and Celestino Gorostiza (1904–) at the forefront of this initiative. Several of the Contemporáneos also wrote short novels, and Torres Bodet produced full-length ones. Their impact on the novel was to interiorize, to psychologize, to urbanize, and to aestheticize the genre. Anglo-European innovations were introduced in such works as Gilberto Owen's *Novela como nube* (*Novel Like a Cloud*, 1928) and Torres Bodet's *Primero de enero* (*First of January*, 1934). Still, of all the main genres, poetry was the one to which they were best attuned, and it was religiously written by all of them.

In poetry, "Canto a un dios mineral" ("Song to a Mineral God," 1942), by Cuesta, and "Muerte sin fin" ("Death without End," 1939), by José Gorostiza (1901–73), are the poetic masterworks of the group; the Contemporáneos' creative fusion of the material and the spiritual is apparent in the very titles of these compositions, which were also, as detractors often pointed out, arcane and difficult. While Gorostiza's poem tackles philosophy and mysticism with eloquence and musicality, Cuesta's confronts the possibilities of science and logic. "Muerte sin fin" comes across as lucid, transparent, and susceptible to multiple readings, while "Canto a un dios mineral" seems so opaque is to be virtually unintelligible. Both poems venture to the outer limits of language. From this, many readers have concluded that the best poetry produced by the Contemporáneos group is not found in these works but rather in the minor poems that Villaurrutia collected under the title *Nostalgia de la muerte* (*Deathly Nostalgia*, 1938). Generally, compositions such as "Poesía," "Nocturno de la alcoba," and "Nocturno en que nada se oye" capture the surrealistic character of much Contemporáneos poetry, and they compensate for some of its excesses.

AFTER 1940

In literature, as in most realms of Mexican life and culture, 1940 serves as a convenient and instructive watershed. It marked the end of the populist and nationalist reforms of the Lázaro Cárdenas presidency, and the transition to the first civilian post-Revolutionary governments, with their more liberal programs favoring modernization and capitalist development. Authors who produced their first mature works after 1940 were not participants in the Revolution but rather the intellectual progeny of its populist and often paternalistic style. Before 1940, the Revolution had seemed to demand a visceral or partisan reaction, seemed inevitably to involve publicity or polemics. Now that the cultural arena no longer had such a circus air, theorists and practitioners no longer found themselves pushed by their ideological adversaries into exaggerated and untenable positions. And social consciousness and aesthetic value no longer seemed so mutually exclusive: artists and writers were freer, because Mexico was no longer being seen as a testing ground for socialist revolution, or as a primitive paradise.

One could say that in many respects the two halves of the twentieth century mirror those of the nineteenth. Following independence in the one case and Revolution in the other, the century opened full of passion and idealism, life seemed to take priority over art, actions over words. In the second half of the twentieth century, as idealism gave way to disillusionment, as institutional stability (and corruption) took over (as the dollar gained sway), there was also greater critical distance and a more reflective, aesthetic attitude in art and literature.

Several members of the Ateneo de la Juventud in the early years of the twentieth century, especially Antonio Caso, led a resurgence of interest in philosophy that would carry over into the substantial and provocative work of Samuel Ramos and beyond. (Mexico's best known contemporary philosophers would include Adolfo Sánchez Vásquez, Luis Villoro, and Leopoldo Zea.) One clear indication of the shifting currents in Mexican literature at mid-century is found in a rising tide of deeply self-searching works exploring what has come to be known as *la filosofía de lo mexicano* ("the philosophy of Mexican identity"). This vein of thought was first explored by Ramos in his treatise entitled *El perfil del hombre y la cultura en México* (*Profile of Man and Culture in Mexico*, 1934). Ramos's criticism of provincialism and cultural dependence (on European civilization), and his controversial characterization of the inferiority complex of the Mexican, were almost enough by themselves to justify the collective neurosis. Octavio Paz produced the most famous volume in the genre, *El laberinto de la soledad* (*The Labyrinth of Solitude*, 1950 and 1959), in which he endeavored to mollify Ramos's negative view by suggesting that a more universal solitude was at the heart of Mexico's identity, and that this was a means of distinguishing Mexican culture from that of its economically and politically more powerful neighbor to the north. These famous works were only two of many that dealt with the philosophy of Mexican identity. Much less well known, but more intriguing as a kind of minor cult classic of the filosofía de lo mexicano works, was Jorge Portilla's *Fenomenología del relajo* (1966).

The kind of political stability and economic development that Mexico enjoyed between 1940 and 1968 met few intellectuals' ideals. The accompanying urbanization and Americanization of the 1940s and 1950s, and the consequent erosion of values and traditions, were explored in a wonderful 1981 novella by José Emilio Pacheco, entitled *Las batallas en el desierto*. But arguably, these same factors made the times propitious for the undisturbed cultivation of literature. Octavio Paz heads a list of quality poets who made their reputations during these years; at that time Paz produced some of his best poetry, with such collections as *Libertad bajo palabra* and *La estación violenta*, not to mention the extended piece, inspired by the Aztec Sunstone, entitled *Piedra de sol*. In the 1940s and 1950s Mexico also made its own contributions to the new Latin American novel; complex and stylistically sophisticated novels by Agustín Yáñez and Juan Rulfo confirmed the arrival in Mexico of the techniques of European modernism and paved the way for Boom novelist Carlos Fuentes.

The government's violent repression of the 1968 student movement had a chilling effect on artistic and intellectual activity for a while, and it marked the beginning of a crisis of legitimacy that still affects Mexico's social and political institutions. Two prominent members of the generation of 1940, Octavio Paz and José Revueltas, took significant and courageous stands in opposition to the government repression. Revueltas, a longtime political activist and Communist Party member, became the most visible martyr of the cause of 1968. Having been an active organizer of the demonstrations, he was jailed in the aftermath of the Tlatelolco massacre and his imprisonment became the cause of vigorous protests by international writers groups and radicalized Mexican students alike. Paz's opposition, though primarily symbolic, received greater attention because of his reputation, and perhaps because it came more from within official circles, in the form of his resignation from his diplomatic post as Mexican ambassador to India. In fact, the contrasting styles and ideologies of Paz and Revueltas have done much to shape subsequent literary developments. While Paz, a figure of international stature, a cosmopolitan and universal man, inspired much of the work produced by the Boom generation of the 1960s, Revueltas, who was always a marginal figure and who is still virtually unknown outside Mexico, became a counter-cultural hero and mentor to many authors of the post-Boom generation. Some of the latter, such as Salvador Castañeda, went on to produce testimonial fiction documenting their participation in guerrilla bands in the early 1970s; all of them reacted in some way against what they saw as the cosmopolitan pretentiousness of their immediate predecessors.

THE "NEW NOVEL"

Al filo del agua (*The Edge of the Storm*, 1947), by Agustín Yáñez, is widely recognized as the major milestone of twentieth-century Mexican fiction, too often as if it appeared out of nowhere and transformed the literary scene overnight. Yáñez's novel is the outstanding Mexican contribution to a handful of works that paved the way for the new Spanish American novel of the 1950s, and the Boom novel of the 1960s. Like other outstanding works of the time, this one brings the technical innovation and literary sophistication of European modernism to the Spanish American novel, and it applies them in the service of a penetrating sociocultural analysis. It combines the social, political, cultural, and historical preoccupations of social realism with avant-garde interests in formal innovation, experimentation, and symbolic or allegorical resonance. For its setting *Al filo del agua* returns to the time immediately preceding the Revolution of 1910. Yáñez's focus here falls not on things military or political, but on the moral and emotional dynamics of a small, closed, and ostensibly self-sustaining provincial town. Here the Revolution does not come noisily, but rather with subtle winds of change; itinerant musicians and mysterious liberated women, students and migrant workers return home with a larger vision of the world, to challenge the self-assurance and sanctimoniousness of the town's suffocating worldview. Breaking with the episodic structure of many novels of the Revolution, Yáñez's work dissolves linear chronology through fragmentation and interior monologue, through stream of consciousness and other techniques. He moves easily in and out of the minds of the town's inhabitants, and so portrays both the town and the way in which it affects them.

Agustín Yáñez was a careful stylist who produced a slow but steady stream of novels over the course of his career, including such sequels to *Al filo del agua* as *La creación* (*Creation*, 1959) and *Las vueltas del tiempo* (*The Twists of Time*, 1973). He was not, however, the only 1940s writer of fiction to transform the novel; the presence of José Revueltas on the scene at the same time shows that alternative strategies had become available. Ideologically, intellectually, and even stylistically, Yáñez was almost the antithesis of Revueltas; the former became a respected cultural bureaucrat, while the latter throughout his life was persecuted as a radical activist, a social misfit. Yet Yáñez and Revueltas had comparable effects on the evolution of Mexican literature; both enriched social and political themes with psychological depth, philosophical reflection, and broad historical perspective; both recognized Mexico's singularity without falling prey to any stereotypes or facile simplifications.

Revueltas came from an artistically gifted and inspired family that included his sister Rosaura, an actress, and brothers Fermín and Silvestre, the former a muralist painter, the latter an internationally known composer of classical music. Though scarcely known outside of Mexico, José was easily the most fascinating figure of all of them. He still has a certain legendary aura in Mexico, and his life and work have generally provoked strong opinions, both pro and con. His works all reflect his very personal amalgamation of primitive Christianity, from the heart of the Hispanic tradition, and modern proletarian utopianism, for which he drew on Marxist socialism. Yet neither his mysticism nor his utopianism were ever sufficient to cure his rather Nietzschean fascination with the human will, or his personal despair at humanity's shortcomings and civilization's imperfections. These, the strengths of Revueltas's vision, also factor into the frequently cited weaknesses of his works—extensive moral and philosophical digressions, internal contradictions, and forced or unconvincing symbolism. It seems that overstepping the boundaries of accepted form was *de rigueur* for Revueltas. He frequently seems to be trying to show the way towards human communion, but in laying bare our defensive mechanisms, our essential solitude, our capacity for degradation, he often undercuts the message. His first novel, *Los muros de agua* (*Walls of Water*, 1941), drew on personal experience; it concerns the fate of a group of political prisoners on a desolate island prison, despised by fellow inmates and brutal guards alike. His second novel, *El luto humano* (*Human Mourning*, 1943) brought him some critical acclaim, and is considered by some to rival Yáñez's *Al filo del agua*, in spite of its unevenness. Through flashbacks and interior monologues *El luto humano* brings into focus Mexico's recent and distant pasts, as if in search of the national soul. It is a vigorous denunciation of social injustice and a desperate search for redemption.

In response to criticism from fellow Communist Party members, Revueltas once went from bookstore to bookstore removing from the shelves what today is believed to be his best novel, *Los días terrenales* (*Life on This Earth*, 1949). This novel remained out of circulation until it was reprinted in 1962. Revueltas's last published work of fiction, *El apando* (*Solitary*, 1969), was a stylistically forceful novella that was made into a movie in 1975. *El apando* avoids some of the excesses of his longer works, but with its extensive use of prison slang it makes very difficult reading. Revueltas uses the prison setting to explore the depths of human brutality and degradation, as he had in his first novel. This time the setting is the infamous Mexico City dungeon of Lecumberri, now closed and converted into a museum, where Revueltas spent most of his final years as a result of his participation in the events of 1968.

Outstanding works of fiction continued to appear through the decade of the 1950s, mostly with little fanfare and outside the spotlight of notoriety. Carlos Fuentes closed the decade with a book of short stories and his first novel. There was also another of Mexican literature's fascinating juxtapositions of contrasting characters, the coincidence of Juan Rulfo and Juan José Arreola. Like so many modern Mexican literary figures, both were from the state of Jalisco. Neither of them apparently wrote with any real agenda, other than the wish to exercise the creative imagination, a fact that has given their work considerable weight and moral authority. It seems that both were perfectionists; neither was prolific. But here the similarities fade away. Arreola had a quick wit, a cosmopolitan, philosophical outlook, and an upbeat sense of humor. He was also an actor. A thoroughly social being, he conducted workshops for young authors, and in later years hosted television programs focused on the Mexican cultural scene. Though the author of the short novel *La feria* (*The Fair*, 1963), Arreola is best known for his short stories and vignettes, most of which were first collected under the title of *Confabulario total* (*Collected Confabulations,* 1962). The short story "El guardagujas" ("The Switchman") is the most widely anthologized of his texts; this entertaining satire may be read, on one level, as an indictment of Mexican systems and their inefficiencies but on another level as a celebratory allegory of life's mysteries and the twists and turns of fate.

By contrast Rulfo cuts an eerily brooding and laconic figure, and he caused both awe and consternation. For years a humble bureaucrat in the Instituto Nacional de Antropología e Historia (National Institute for Anthropology and History), Rulfo so carefully guarded his privacy that an aura of mystery came to surround him. His published writings and public appearances were so few that some have marveled at how such a figure could have produced works of such profound literary significance. Yet, as the Chilean novelist José Donoso once said, Rulfo's fame grew with every book he failed to write. His complete works barely total 300 pages; they comprise one filmscript, *El gallo de oro,* one short novel, *Pedro Páramo,* and one brief collection of short stories, *El llano en llamas,* all three cut from very similar cloth. Yet on the basis of these few works the most dissimilar Mexican authors and critics pay him homage as a crucial figure, one whose work most decisively demonstrates the potential for universal resonance of profoundly Mexican, regionalist subject matter. What is more, the idiosyncratic characters and the starkly surreal, hermetic fictional universe that Rulfo creates, with its archetypal and biblical undertones, are perhaps the real precursors of the magical realist style that García Márquez's *One Hundred Years of Solitude* later made famous internationally.

Whereas Arreola was cosmopolitan and humorous, Rulfo was dark and provincial. Part of the fascination his works exercise derives from the (misleading) impression that his experimental techniques do not derive from any knowledge of up-to-date literary ideas but rather from a natural and instinctive accommodation of style to substance. Arguments still rage today as to whether Rulfo's fiction authentically re-creates the speech of rural communities in the north-central provinces, or whether it is simply a brilliant stylistic creation. His novel, *Pedro Páramo,* is set against the background of the Cristero War, a somewhat violent religious rebellion against government policy at the end of the Revolution. Rulfo paints a depressed rural community dominated by a ruthless cacique, a community that lives in fear and has been let down by religion, but he moves freely between the world of the living and that of the dead, between different time frames and from character to character, challenging the reader to compose his fragmented tale into a coherent pattern.

OCTAVIO PAZ

Octavio Paz won Mexico's first and so far only Nobel Prize for Literature in 1988 and, as such a distinction might suggest, no other figure in modern Mexican letters can rival his stature. For many throughout the world possessed of a minimal acquaintance with Mexican art and culture, the name of Paz is synonymous not only with Mexican literature but with modern Mexican critical thought as well. Paz, who died in 1996, was a prolific and multi-talented author: poet and art critic, essayist, and cultural historian. Spanning seven decades, his prolific literary output often defies classification, becoming a kind of island unto itself. One of the ironies has been that as his international status grew, his relative isolation in the Mexican cultural milieu increased.

Rather than the Mexican Revolution, it was the Spanish Civil War (1936–39), and later the aftermath of World War II and the Stalin purges in Russia, that most indelibly marked the formative years for Paz and many others of his generation. The Spanish Civil War signified the advent of a new internationalist consciousness, and it led to political radicalization and activism. In 1937, Paz, together with other left-leaning writers from across the globe, attended a famous international conference of anti-fascist intellec-

Octavio Paz (middle) meets with J.L. Borges (left) and Salvador Elizondo under a painting of the Virgin of Guadalupe. Photo by Paulina Lavista.

tuals that took place in Valencia, Spain. Paz would later help welcome the many intellectual exiles from the Spanish Civil War who came to Mexico and had a decisive impact on contemporary cultural developments.

Paz is first and foremost a master poet, and he has steadfastly subordinated his other activities to this calling, even though his essays on politics and cultural history have been more widely discussed and read. Right up to the end of his long and illustrious career, he stubbornly retained his faith in poetry as an experience with transcendental potential, and an essential, heroic undertaking, particularly at a time when its readership was fading. Over the course of his career, Paz's poetry underwent a remarkable evolution, assimilating a broad array of influences: from dialectic materialism to surrealism, from the classics of the Western poetic canon to the major authors in the Mexican tradition, from the thought and vision of the pre-Hispanic civilizations in Mexico to the pantheistic premises of far Eastern philosophy and religion. His poetry over the course of his evolution was remarkably consistent, in the sense that each new poetic composition was like a recasting of previous ones, in unwavering pursuit of the total and immaculate poetic artifact. While continuing periodically to produce a fresh volume of poems, he found time to revise his previous volumes, repeatedly retooling his collected works.

As a young poet, Paz originally established his artistic identity in opposition to the supposed apoliticism of many of the Contemporáneos, and in the 1930s he produced a number of poems committed to international socialist and revolutionary causes. Soon, however, there began a series of changes that would shape the course of his poetics and his politics. Virtually all of Paz's early political poems were erased from later editions of his complete poetic works (the poem "Elegía a un compañero muerto en el frente" ["Elegy for a Comrade Killed at the Front"] is one of the few to have survived, albeit in revised form.)

Paz was always interested in the power and potential of language, the written and spoken word. Though with his rhetorical skill, his eroticism, and his constant recourse to the elements of earth, wind, water, and fire, he can take on the appearance of a materialist, he remains at heart an idealist, a man with a visionary approach to poetry. Paz sees mankind as above all a user of language, and it is through words, for all their inadequacies, that the mystery of life can be revealed and a way found toward understanding and harmony with material creation. This way of transcending the horrors of history is invoked in the very title to Paz's first volume of collected poetry, *Libertad bajo palabra* (*Freedom in Words*, 1949, 1960, 1968), a collection that has undergone constant revision and been published in several versions. Paz delights in poetic abstraction and reduction, in binary opposition and conceptual paradox; at the same time he affirms the vital and dynamic interdependence of the spiritual and the material, the you and the I, the yin and the yang. The essential premises of Paz's theory of poetry are eloquently expressed in *El arco y la lira* (*The Bow and the Lyre*, 1956).

In the late 1930s and early 1940s his poems are synthetic, elemental, blindingly clear; a good example is "Bajo tu clara sombra" ("In Your Lucid Shadow," 1937). Paz then becomes more allusive and elusive, and more ambitious—for instance, in "Piedra de sol" ("Sun Stone," 1957) and "Himno entre ruinas" ("Hymn among the Ruins, 1949), which both appeared in what is perhaps his crowning poetic achievement, *La estación violenta* (*The Violent Season*, 1958). The latter poem alternates descriptions of a mystical instant when the sun is at its zenith and when material creation is perceived in all its spiritual transcendence, with an inventory of the ravages of history. The former is a longer, meticulous poem based on numerical principles from pre-Hispanic cosmology; it circles back upon itself and bites its own tail, as it were, with the last verse repeating the first and setting the cycle in motion again. Still later in his career Paz becomes more earthy and carnal, more aloof and hermetic, more graphically and audaciously experimental, even writing some concrete poetry. Other books of note are *Salamandra* (*Salamander*, 1962) and *Ladera este* (*The Eastern Slope*, 1969)—which most thoroughly embody the influences of the Orient and his stint as Mexican ambassador to India—*Pasado en claro* (*Clarified and Revisited*, 1975), a poetic biography, and *Vuelta* (*Return*, 1976) and *Arbol adentro* (*The Tree Within*, 1987), which document a kind of return to the poet's cultural, historical, and poetical roots.

ROSARIO CASTELLANOS AND WOMEN'S WRITING IN THE 1950s AND 1960s

Women were rare but by no means invisible on the Mexican literary scene in the 1950s and 1960s. Rosario Castellanos, for one, wrote with great poignancy and often with acerbic irony of the challenges and social impediments faced by the female intellectual. This is particularly true of her very personal poetry and of certain essays. Castellanos brings an active feminist consciousness to Mexican letters, and it would be hard to imagine the success of contemporary women writers had she not provided a precedent. Castellanos was not a programmatic feminist, but in those times her self-defense, her search for fulfillment and meaning were bound to stand for women in general (even though she sometimes lashed out at the temerity of her sisters). Her attitudes and concerns in essence are a continuation of those of the famous seventeenth-century nun, Sor Juana Inés de la Cruz. This connection is especially evident in the allegorical overtones of Castellanos's play *El eterno femenino* (*The Eternal Feminine*, 1975), and in such poetic compositions as

"Lamentación de Dido," in which she employs erudite allusions while enumerating women who are prominent in myth and world history.

Castellanos's work dramatizes the situation of the female caught painfully between traditional roles of domesticity and motherhood, on the one hand, and her intellectual passion and commitment to the rights of women to public life on the other. Much of her poetry, which treats amorous, domestic, and carnal themes as well as self-consciously literary and intellectual ones, reflects the bitterness of her struggle for intellectual respectability in a hostile sociocultural ambience. The essay "La liberación del amor" ("The Liberation of/from Love," 1972), however, involves a scathing attack on the superficiality of feminism. Her poetry was collected in 1972 under the defiant title *Poesía no eres tú* (*You Are Not Poetry*, 1972), which rejects the romantic enshrinement of the object of the poet's love on a pedestal.

Castellanos had another issue at heart; in her two novels, *Balún Canán* (*Nine Guardians*, 1957) and *Oficio de tinieblas* (*Dark Craft*, 1962), and in the short stories collected in *Ciudad real* (*City of Kings*, 1960), she describes the plight of the indigenous population in her native state of Chiapas. No doubt she saw the oppression and marginalization of Indians as analogous to the position of women. These works are classifiable as indigenista fiction. They are basically social realist in technique, but the stylistic expertise and the nuanced sensitivity she brought to her indigenista writing advanced the genre in ways comparable to those achieved in Peruvian indigenista fiction by José María Arguedas. On the one hand, the objective detachment with which she explores Indian ritual and superstition approaches ethnography. On the other, Castellanos gives considerable psychological complexity and individuality to her Indian characters. Some of her short stories show the inadequacy of social programs set up for remote regions by people working in the national capital, but also reveal the degree to which transculturation in the backwoods has always been a two-way phenomenon, affecting members of the Hispanic-based culture as well as the Indians.

Other women produced outstanding though largely unheralded novels in the 1950s and 1960s. One, Josefina Vicens, cut a solitary, laconic, Rulfian-type figure and produced two little-known but critically acclaimed novels, *El libro vacío* (*The Empty Book*, 1958) and the brooding *Los años falsos* (*False Years*, 1982), both dark, existential, and meta-fictional exercises filled with resignation and determination. Another, Elena Garro, has unfortunately drawn more attention for her criticisms, whether well-founded or not, of her former husband Octavio Paz's abuse of his political and cultural capital, than she has for her own literary accomplishments. But in *Los recuerdos del porvenir* (*Recollection of Things to Come*, 1963) she produced a highly regarded novel somewhat in the vein of Rulfo's *Pedro Páramo*. Set in a small town during the Cristero revolt of the late 1920s, Garro's novel follows the divergent fates of two female protagonists in a context of suffocating conservatism. The town itself functions as a kind of collective narrator, and the novel's complex manipulations of time and point of view give the events and situations depicted a mythic, larger-than-life resonance that heralds the work of Gabriel García Márquez, who acknowledged his debt to Garro.

CARLOS FUENTES

Two figures in contemporary Mexican letters stand head and shoulders above all the rest in terms of international prominence and reputation. One is Paz and the other is Carlos Fuentes. Fuentes became one of the "big four" novelists of what came to be known as the Boom in Spanish American fiction, in the 1960s (the others being Julio Cortázar of Argentina, Mario Vargas Llosa of Peru, and Gabriel García Márquez of Colombia). Rivalry and tension between Paz and Fuentes came to a head when one of Paz's protégés, a historian called Enrique Krause, published an indictment of Fuentes's work in *The New Republic,* claiming it was showy and superficial. The rivalry is tinged with irony for, like many writers of his generation, Fuentes had matured under the tutelage of Paz, and the career-defining, major novels that Fuentes produced early in his career thoroughly embody the view of Mexico's identity that Paz had proposed in *El laberinto de la soledad.* In many ways their rivalry epitomizes the sort of betrayal, pettiness, and virulence that sometimes clouds Mexican literary and cultural politics. But Paz and Fuentes have been just as much victims of these things as causes of them. Both, because of their international prominence and visibility, have been targets for criticism, no doubt born of a mixture of envy and resentment.

Carlos Fuentes was born in 1928 into a diplomatic family and spent his childhood and adolescence in a variety of countries, beginning his primary school education in Washington, D.C., where he became fluent in English. He has held important university posts in Mexico and the United States, and has himself served as a diplomat in Switzerland and France. His first book of short stories, *Los días enmascarados* (*The Masked Days,* 1954), draws somewhat on Aztec mythology and blends historical and mythical time, juxtaposing the ancient and modern cultures. Such a use of myth to interpret history became Fuentes's trademark in later works. For example, in his first novel, *La región más transparente* (*Where the Air is Clear,* 1958), Fuentes draws upon elements of Mexico's mythical past to reinterpret the present realities of Mexico City's inhabitants. He shows skill with a variety of novelistic techniques, using allegories, symbolism, interior monologues, fragmented time, rich metaphors, and vivid, cinematic imagery. In fact, it is this sort of narrative skill that has made him vulnerable to the charge that his work has more technique than substance. The novel most associated with the early years of the Boom is *La muerte de Artemio Cruz* (*The Death of Artemio Cruz,* 1962), which traces the history of Mexico from the latter part of the nineteenth to the mid-twentieth century, concentrating especially on the period of the Mexican Revolution; but the techniques and structure employed here differentiate this novel from others of the Mexican Revolution, and to a large extent from Fuentes's own previous work. During the twelve hours before the protagonist's death, the twelve most important moments of his life are reviewed. These represent the triumphs and failures of the Revolution, the gradual disillusionment of the idealists who had thought that it would transform their society into a more equitable one. But the originality of the novel really lies in its narrative strategies, which have attracted a good deal of critical attention; in passages related in the first, second, or third person, the inner musings of the narrator in the present, future, and past are, respectively, explored. A similar experiment with grammatical person is deployed in *Aura,* published in the same year (1962). Here the second person is used as an elusive narrative voice to tell the story of Felipe, a young Mexican historian who enters into a magical world representing Mexico's past; as he transcribes the memoirs of a general from the time of the Emperor Maximilian, he is transformed into the general's double. There are also two female archetypes: Consuelo, the general's wife, is an enchantress who relives her youth through Aura, the embodiment of youth and beauty. As these personalities blend into each other, it seems that the "you" employed by the narrator may be referring to himself, to his double, to Consuelo or her double, Aura, or even to the reader. Another important novel, *Cambio de piel* (*A Change of Skin*), was published in 1967. In this extremely complex, meta-fictional work, Fuentes again looks for the roots of contemporary Mexico in its mythical past, paralleling a current reality lived by the main characters with scenes from other times and places. Time and point of view shift freely, and the language runs the gamut from the vulgar to the lyrical. The structure of the novel itself reflects what is an existentialist struggle to find oneself in the face of an absurd and tragic human condition.

Many people regard *Terra Nostra* (1975) as the culmination of Fuentes's fiction; it links European and Mexican history and myth, with little respect for rigorous historical chronology, and compressing significant events that occured after 1492. In the protagonist, Señor Don Felipe, who is supervising the construction of the palace-cum-mausoleum of El Escorial near Madrid, Fuentes fuses the characteristics of various Spanish rulers (notably the Catholic monarchs, the Emperor Charles V, and Philip II). Don Felipe epitomizes the rigid, intolerant absolutism of the Spanish monarchy, and his mausoleum marks its mummification. Fuentes's aim is to understand Hispanic culture on both sides of the ocean. He has also published several plays which deal with the same sort of concerns; the best known is *Todos los gatos son pardos* (*All Cats Are Grey*, 1970), about the encounter between the Spanish conquistador, Hernán Cortés, and the Aztec monarch, Moctezuma, mediated by Malinche.

Some other novels by Fuentes, such as *La cabeza de la hidra* (*The Hydra Head*, 1978), are less complex. In recent years Fuentes has turned his attention to the relationship between his country and its neighbor to the north, in *Gringo viejo* and in *Cristóbal Nonato* (*Christopher Unborn*, 1987). Raymond Williams calls this last novel Fuentes's "most irreverent fictional critique of postmodern Mexico...with images of a nation lost in garbage and defecation that are products of its own development" (37). The *suave patria* ("gentle fatherland") of which Ramón López Velarde had written has been mutilated, its debt is not so much foreign as forever, its jungles have been lost under concrete and filth, acid rain falls constantly, people speak "Anglatl," and the government spends its time devising new national symbols and holidays. *Cristóbal Nonato* is Fuentes's most postmodern novel, a very self-conscious work, like many before it. Prolific though he has been as an author of fiction, there are also significant works of criticism, which include his book on *La nueva novela hispanoamericana* (*The New Spanish American Novel*, 1969).

POPULAR POETRY AND COMMERCIAL FICTION

Luis Spota (1925–84) was of the same generation as Fuentes but was a very different writer and a polemic figure for other reasons. In the mid-twentieth century he was one of few writers who were able to live off their writing, for he wrote popular bestsellers, proving that a large-scale readership for novels was there, provided that one knew how to write accessibly and how to tap into its interests. Spota did so by concentrating on the popular classes and pandering to the taste for gossip and scandal involving prominent people; *Casi el paraíso* (*Almost Paradise*, 1956) is one of his successful novels. It is interesting to note that Spota, often dismissed as a writer who was not serious, has attracted renewed interest in recent years, a time when the incorporation of elements of popular culture into fiction has become widespread. Spota also wrote an apologetic novel based on the Tlatelolco massacre: *La plaza* (*The Square*, 1972).

In the realm of poetry, author Jaime Sabines (1925) has fulfilled similar functions, producing a body of work, collected as *Recuento de poemas*, that has proved to be accessible to large number of readers from the vast middle and lower-middle strata of society. His public readings, which have attracted audiences numbering in the thousands, prove that literary icons can still meet social needs in Mexico. Sabines is a spontaneous writer who wears his emotions on his sleeve, in a way comparable to a popular balladeer, or perhaps to a Pablo Neruda without the philosophical depth. Sabines unleashes frustrations, disappointments, feelings of impotence and deception or, alternatively, confessions of tender feelings and of the softer side of his masculinity, things with which readers easily identify.

ONDA AND ESCRITURA

The boom of Latin American fiction in the 1960s, in which Carlos Fuentes was Mexico's major representative, generated considerable interest and excitement and gave literature across Spanish America new confidence and vigor. Nonetheless, and perhaps particularly in Mexico, the Boom was far from the only game in town; in the 1960s, Mexican fiction had its own complex and highly charged dynamics, involving several competing trends or factions. Two of the most prominent of these came to be defined, thanks primarily to a volume entitled *Onda y escritura en México,* as the *Onda* ("new wave") and *Escritura* ("writerly") groups. The Escritura group was the older of the two, involving people born roughly between 1925 and 1935; several of them, informally at least, became protégés of Octavio Paz. They came together as staff writers and shaped the editorial line for several of the most important literary reviews of the 1960s, such as the *Revista de la Universidad de México* and the *Revista Mexicana de Literatura* (sometimes they are called the Revista Mexicana de Literatura group). On the whole, these authors were very highbrow, cosmopolitan, even elitist and un-Mexican, and their fiction was deeply philosophical and experimental, metaphysical and meta-literary. The Onda group was made up of precocious, younger writers, born roughly between 1935 and 1945; they began to write and publish in the 1960s and early 1970s, and their youth is often reflected in narratives that focus on the language and life-style of adolescents, chiefly in urban areas. (Thematically, something similar would happen in the theater; see chapter 6.) In their own minds, and partly with good reason, the Onda writers associated Paz and Fuentes with the Escritura group. They tagged them as the "mafia," and accused them of blocking access to new and alternative voices in the major literary publishing venues—in fact, in the late 1960s Luis Guillermo Piazza published a kind of *roman à clef* entitled precisely *La mafia,* about the politics and personalities of the 1960s literary scene. The work of the Onda made new use of techniques from earlier generations, such as shifting points of view, fragmented, non-chronological time, multiple narrative voices, and the incorporation of other genres into the narrative. And, like the Escritura group, they rejected the nationalistic concerns of previous generations. But what set the Onda apart was their openness to new forms of popular culture, their brashness and irreverence, their recourse to new electronic communications media, both as subject and technique, and their adoption of issues drawn from the international youth culture and protest movements of the 1960s, from drugs and homosexuality to the sexual revolution and the antiwar movement, to jazz and rock.

For a long time, Salvador Elizondo (1932–) and Juan García Ponce (1932–) were the leading and most productive writers of the Escritura group. They are still well known and respected in Mexico as major figures of their generation, but their works, which reveal the essential characteristics of the group in very different ways, have always had more of a cult following than a broad readership, and for that reason they have not become well known outside of Mexico. Elizondo made a huge splash with his first and most acclaimed novel, *Farabeuf* (1965), which, exceptionally, was translated into several languages. It is a disturbing, experimental tour de force, a Mexican *nouveau roman;* it involves violent erotic rituals, ancient Asian systems of divination, and primitive, nineteenth-century surgical techniques, while fusing and confusing grammatical persons, time, and physical space. Most of Elizondo's subsequent works spiraled deeper into a kind of hall of mirrors, in which he experimented with pure forms of literary self-consciousness, to such a point that he himself was ready to admit in the mid-1970s that he found himself at a dead end, though the journey had been exhilarating. García Ponce also seems to live primarily through and for literature, though in a very different stylistic key. He has written with impressive dedication—some might say monotony—over the course of a career that now spans more than 40 years. Rather like the poetry of Octavio Paz, García Ponce's novels seem to embark on a frankly carnal and profanely mystic quest to transcend conventional social identity and morality. Most of his characters seem free of the mundane concerns of the workaday world, which no doubt accounts for some of the seductiveness of his novels; the two-volume *Crónica de la intervención* (*Chronicle of Intervention*, 1982) is representative. García Ponce has also been a lucid and prolific essayist, and his greatest contribution to Mexican culture has perhaps been as a friend and critic of most of the outstanding painters of his generation. The shock effect of works by García Ponce and Elizondo has now faded; their brilliance has been eclipsed by a late-bloomer, Sergio Pitol (1932–), one of Mexico's most accomplished narrators. Pitol spent much of his early career in the diplomatic corps, in Eastern Europe, but after his return to Mexico his work blossomed, and he tempered the self-conscious excesses of works such as *El tañido de una flauta* (*The Sound of the Flute,* 1972). Though still faithful to high-brow literature, in more recent Pitol novels such as *El desfile del amor* (*The Parade of Love,* 1984) and *Domar a la divina garza* (*Taming the Divine Heron,* 1987), he has brought in popular and historical elements—for example, from mystery and detective fiction. These works first became popular in Spain, which indicates how the market for writers in Spanish has opened up.

In the mid-1960s, the first works of the Onda writers—most notably José Agustín (1944–) and Gustavo Saínz (1940–)—had even more shock value than those by members of Escritura, and they were far and away better sellers, thanks to word-of-mouth publicity. Though Agustín's *La tumba* (*The Tomb,* 1964) was the first to appear (he was scarcely 20 years old at the time), it was Gustavo Saínz's first novel, *Gazapo* (*Tall Tale,* 1965) that made the biggest impression; almost immediately it was reprinted and it was soon translated into several languages. *Gazapo* concentrates on the inconstant, conflicting world of adolescence, depicted through tape-recorded conversations, letters, diaries, and telephone dialogues. The adolescent protagonist reviews and reinvents the past through the use of the tape recorder, which to him and his friends represents an escape from the restrictions of the adult world, and allows them to explore sexual fantasies and adventures. The fragmented structure of the novel represents the unsettled lives of the adolescents, and the experimentation with various kinds of language, from the colloquial to the flamboyant, reflects the quest for artistic as well as social freedom. As for Agustín, he mixes colloquial speech with descriptive prose in his novels *La tumba* (*The Tomb,* 1964) and *De perfil* (*In Profile,* 1966) to reflect the frustrations of youth, while criticizing middle-class values. *La tumba* is the story of an adolescent whose wealthy family pays no attention to him, so that he turns to a bohemian life-style. Perhaps the single most representative and entertaining work from the Onda group is Agustín's story "¿Cuál es la onda" ("What's up?"), from the collection *Inventando que sueño* (1968); it is full of delicious, contagious word play and free associations, mixes several languages, and alludes to all kinds of pop cultural icons. The literature of the Onda has been attacked as purely adolescent, and that it certainly was, more of an attitude than a literary style. This became apparent when Saínz's second novel finally appeared; *Obsesivos días circulares* (*Obsessive, Circular Days,* 1969) is pretentious and hermetic. Similarly, Agustín's broody *Se está haciendo tarde* (*final en laguna*) (*It's Getting Late* [*Blank Ending*], 1973) is a kind of epitaph to the Onda experimentation with drugs and sex. Though Agustín and Saínz have both continued to evolve and produce new work, neither has matched his initial impact; still, Mexican literature could not have become what it is today had they not opened up the way for a more frank, democratic, and variegated literary culture.[6]

One should not conclude that the two groups we have been discussing account for all significant fiction writing in the 1960s and 1970s. The works of Vicente Leñero, Jorge Ibarguengoitia, and Fernando del Paso are cases in point. Ibarguengoitia (1928–83) belonged to the Escritura generation by birthright, but there is little obvious connection between his work and theirs. Perhaps there is a shared disillusionment with contemporary Mexican politics and society. But where writers like Elizondo and García Ponce's response was to refuse to include such things in their fictions, Ibarguengoitia made them the very substance of his, often deploying his irrepressible sense of humor and sarcasm. Ibarguengoitia wrote quickly, in a variety of styles and on popular Mexican subject matter. One of his early works was a much celebrated send-up of both the novel of the Revolution and the Revolution itself, entitled *Los relámpagos de agosto* (1964). Later works herald certain characteristics of post-Boom fiction—for example, recourse to popular subgenres such as detective fiction, and the use of a flat, pseudo-documentary style, of direct speech and interior monologues unmediated by any authorial presence. Examples of this are *Las muertas* (*Dead Girls,* 1977) and *Dos crímenes* (*Two Crimes,* 1979), which take their storylines from the tabloids. Del Paso (1935–), too, followed a solitary path, at a distance from the literary circles of Mexico City; for a number of years, he lived in England, and worked for the BBC. He had some affinities with the younger Onda writers, notably his levity and irreverence, but his work took the form of voluminous and intricate compendia, and in this respect it was more in tune with the ambitions of writers of the Boom. Over some 40 years, he has produced just four imposing novels. *José Trigo* (1966) draws parallels between the conquest of the Aztec empire and government suppression of a strike by railroad workers in 1960 in Tlatelolco, an event that foreshadowed those of 1968. In the ambitious and comic *Palinuro de México* (*Palinuro of Mexico,* 1975), del Paso uses the events of 1968 as the climax of his narrative; it is an episodic compendium of the comic and erotic, with fleeting apearances by a host of literary characters drawn from other writers' works.

AFTER TLATELOLCO: MONSIVÁIS, PACHECO, AND PONIATOWSKA

Apart from Paz and Fuentes, three people have played crucial roles in leading younger writers in Mexico's transition from the Boom to the Post-Boom. Elena Poniatowska (1933–), Carlos Monsiváis (1938–), and José Emilio Pacheco (1939–). They were active while still young in the 1960s, in journals such as *Nuevo Cine, Revista Mexicana de Literatura,* the *Revista de la Univer-*

sidad, and the "La cultura en México" supplement of the weekly *Siempre.* Each of them went on to find a distinctive personal style and purpose as a writer. Though they have worked independently, their efforts have led Mexican literature in a common direction; above all, they have renounced the high aesthetic pretensions of their predecessors. In other words, the social and humanitarian consciousness and the irreverence that marks much of their work have done much to bring literature back to the people. All three have been active as journalists, in such new wave periodicals as the monthly *Nexos* and the investigative news weekly *Proceso.* Monsiváis and Poniatowska, in particular, have focused not on the classic literary genres, but on the instinctive and non-systematic development of new, hybrid, largely nonfiction writing that displays their commitment to chronicling the everyday life and experience of voiceless and anonymous people. They have managed to stay above dogma, party lines, and narrow polemics, and to respect alternative positions, including those of their elders and mentors, even while giving passionate reign to their own ideas. Their focus has been on the national scene, and they have apparently been unconcerned about the kind of cosmopolitanism that might foster international fame.

Poniatowska, the oldest of the three, is in fact one of the Boom generation; perhaps the fact that she is a woman drove her down a different path from her contemporaries. Like some other intellectually gifted women elsewhere, Poniatowska has provided a behind-the-scenes glimpse of leading figures from her generation, and she is well known for her penetrating sensitivity as a journalist and her incisive wit as an interviewer. She is the author of several outstanding works of fiction, from the stories collected in *Lilus Klikus* (1954) to the recent *Paseo de la Reforma* (1996). Poniatowska has also assiduously chronicled Mexico's worst contemporary tragedies and shortcomings, yet her works manage deftly to remain beyond the pale of partisanship and political interests. Her irrepressible wit and playful innocence allow her to unearth what is redeeming and uplifting in the human spirit. Though some would see her magnanimity in interviews as a fault, her ability to gain her subjects' confidence and make herself seem a mouthpiece for them, from the famous and powerful to the forgotten and anonymous, has allowed her to tread where few dare. Selected Poniatowska interviews with both the odd and the famous have been collected in such volumes as *Palabras cruzadas* (1961) and *Todo empezó el domingo* (1963). Most recently, in addition to a major biography of the avant-garde personality Tina Modotti (*Tinísima,* 1992), she has edited a selection of her interviews with Octavio Paz, woven together with an intimate look at his life and revealing anecdotes of their encounters over the years; this is entitled *Octavio Paz: Las palabras del árbol* (*Octavio Paz: Fruits from the Tree,* 1998). Among Poniatowska's most critically celebrated works have been her fact-based fictions. One, *Hasta no verte, Jesús mío* (*Until We Meet Again,* 1969), a first-person narrative based on extensive personal interviews, captures the courage of a representative soldadera (female camp-follower) who is faced with the trials and tribulations of life after the Revolution. Another, *Querido Diego, te abraza Quiela* (*Dear Diego,* 1978), creates imaginary correspondence between the famous muralist painter Diego Rivera and a lover, and it brings the legendary Rivera down to earth, exposing his vulnerability.

Poniatowska's talents as a journalist and interviewer, as well as her ability to insinuate herself into politically treacherous terrain, are revealed in a different way in a work that brought her instant notoriety and wide acclaim: *La noche de Tlatelolco* (*Massacre in Mexico,* 1971), a contemporary classic which, together with *Hasta no verte, Jesús mío,* is a forerunner of the popular testimonial genre that became quite widespead in Latin America. *La noche* takes the form of a powerful, largely anonymous documentary collage of the 1968 student movement, the massacre at Tlatelolco, and its aftermath. There is little explicit authorial intervention. The book brings together extracts from press accounts and published interviews, dramatic and previously unpublished photographs, protest slogans and graffiti, transcriptions of extensive interviews with public figures, and testimony from participants and witnesses. Thus, it captures a range of perspectives on the events. *La noche de Tlatelolco* is on a par with Octavio Paz's *Posdata* as a representation of the events of 1968 in Mexico. The diametrical contrast between their two approaches, however, could not be more striking or revealing. Paz, exclusively in his own authoritative voice, offers a powerful but abstract, synthetic interpretation in the context of Mexican history at large; many critics feel that in doing so he mystifies rather than clarifies the causes and effects of the events in question. His work may even be a symptom of the kind of absolute authority that it diagnoses. Poniatowska's volume, on the other hand, manages, as if intuitively, to convey a more postmodern approach—perhaps a more democratic and egalitarian one. She stops short of interpretation and synthesis, allowing the various individuals involved to speak for themselves, as it were, and leaving her readers to ponder possible conclusions. A subsequent Poniatowska volume, *Nada, nadie: las voces del temblor* (*Nothing, Nobody: Voices in Tremor,* 1988), did for the major earthquake of 1985 in Mexico City what *La noche de Tlatelolco* had done for the events of 1968: it presents a varied and moving collage of photographs, testimony, and reports about the disaster. While indicting injustice, corruption, and ineptitude in the management of the disaster, it seeks above all to pay tribute to the many spontaneous displays of heroism, humanitarianism, and community solidarity that the tragedy inspired, and to the potential for new forms of broad-based social organization and activism.

In his own inimitable way, and with a similar postmodern spirit *avant la lettre*, Carlos Monsiváis has covered much of the same terrain as Poniatowska, and more. Monsiváis is a prolific author and a brilliant stylist with an incisive wit and an almost facile intelligence; since the 1960s he has established a considerable following and a fearsome reputation not as a fiction writer or poet, but as a cultural historian, art critic, and social commentator. To Monsiváis must be attributed much of the popularity that the new journalistic chronicle of contemporary life enjoys today. The new chronicle is as much a creative exercise as an academic one, an exercise in which the style, personality, and attitudes of the author count as much as what is chronicled. It could be regarded as a modern version of the local color (*costumbrista*) sketches that were so common and popular throughout the nineteenth century. Indeed, in Mexico the form has had a virtually continuous history, with exemplary practitioners in almost every intellectual generation, including the modernista poet Gutiérrez Nájera at the turn of the century, and the flamboyant Contemporáneos group author Salvador Novo, a prolific chronicler of Mexican life in the 1930s, 1940s, and 1950s. The notoriety that Monsiváis has achieved with this genre amply demonstrates the star appeal that the all-purpose intellectual in Mexico can still command. Beginning with *Días de guardar* (*Days of Penance*, 1970), his account and evaluation of the events of 1968, Monsiváis has produced a steady stream of volumes collecting his chronicles of contemporary life, each anxiously awaited by his readers. *Entrada libre: crónicas de la sociedad que se organiza* (*Free Admission: Chronicles of a Society in Movement*, 1988) covers the neighborhood organizations and citizen activism that arose in response to the 1985 earthquake, as well as the increasing power of opposition parties in Mexican politics.

Monsiváis's work as a cultural historian and critic of art and literature has been just as fundamental, but he has rarely proceeded systematically with it. Rather, his key articles and essays are dispersed in magazines, conference proceedings, and special topics volumes, and as prologues written for anthologies edited by himself and others. From the start, Monsiváis's major contribution in this area has been his insistence on giving popular culture and the mass media the same respect and attention as highbrow art and literature. In this vein, he sustained a famous, public debate with Octavio Paz in 1977, in an exchange of magazine articles that would shape the discussion of cultural politics in Mexico for years to come. More recently, Monsiváis's stance on popular culture has made him a leading figure from Mexico, alongside Argentine immigrant Néstor García Canclini, in the international cultural studies movement. Monsiváis is a star on the cultural circuit. With his explorations of the theatricality of Mexican politics and culture, he has made himself into a popular, even legendary, figure, an analyst who evaluates and interprets with the seduction of melodrama.

Whereas Monsiváis has become a visible guru, José Emilio Pacheco has worked more quietly, behind the scenes, but to similar effect, in a much more measured and traditional way, acting as a kind of spiritual figurehead for younger generations. First and foremost a poet, though he has also produced some outstanding fiction and cultural journalism, Pacheco has responded better than anyone else to the decline of highbrow poetry that has come with the rise of science and technology and the spread of mass media. While such early volumes of poetry as *Los elementos de la noche* (*Elements of the Night*, 1963) showed Pacheco's command of poetic diction and the inevitable influence of Octavio Paz, later works like *Irás y no volverás* (*You Will Leave and Not Return*, 1973) and *Islas a la deriva* (*Islands Adrift*, 1976) became playful, witty, epigrammatic, aphoristic, and original. Poems like "Disertación sobre la consonancia" ("Dissertation on Consonant Rhyme") turn literature against itself to create new literature. Poems like "Tres poetas novohispanos" ("Three Poets from New Spain") demystify and humanize the historical tradition. Delightful epigrams like "Autoanálisis" poke postmodern holes in the certainties of the human sciences. Poems like "H & C" playfully combine philosophical meditations on language with reflections on cultural imperialism. Other poems, like "Shopping Center" and "Malpaís" provide critiques of rampant commercialism and environmental devastation. With Pacheco, we see that while much of twentieth-century prose fiction has become poeticized, poetry has found new life in the so-called prosaic. The death of high culture, Pacheco seems to say, should not simply be lamented or passively acquiesced to but, rather, actively embraced and explored to discover what new doors it might open. Though primarily a poet, Pacheco also wrote a significant short novel in *Morirás lejos* (*You Will Die Far Away*, 1967).

THE WOMEN'S BOOM AND OTHER RECENT DEVELOPMENTS

Without question, the most celebrated and widely discussed literary phenomenon in recent Mexican letters has been the quality and quantity of literature by women. Awareness of the phenomenon, and controversy surrounding the coining of a new term, "light literature," to describe some women's writing, rose to new heights with the resounding popularity, at home and abroad, of Laura Esquivel's *Como agua para chocolate* (*Like Water for Chocolate*, 1991), in both its novel and film versions. But in Mexico, the breakthrough work was actually Angeles Mastretta's first novel, *Arráncame la vida* (*Mexican Bolero*, 1985), which circulated for some time as a national bestseller before it was picked up for foreign translation. In the Mexican national context, her work has fulfilled many of the same trailblazing functions as that of Isabel Allende in the wider Spanish American context, and also sparked similar critical polemics: like Allende, both Mastretta and Esquivel have drawn successfully on their own adaptation of the larger-than-life, tender, and discreet style of fabulation characteristic of Gabriel García Márquez's magical realism.

Arráncame la vida exploits the Mexican public's interest in looking behind the scenes at the lives of the rich and famous, and it is somewhat in the pattern of the commercially successful novels of Luis Spota. The historical background and the eminent figures alluded to in *Arráncame la vida* are not difficult to identify. It is the tale of a young girl who is swept off her feet by an older man, a general who becomes a provincial governor, who is well-connected, unscrupulous (even to the point of arranging for the murder of adversaries), and philandering to boot. A certain solidarity develops between the heroine (the novel is narrated through her voice) and the governor's children. She also discovers love in the arms of a famous orchestral conductor, but is fated to lose him. Apart from exposing the machinations of the powerful, this novel illustrates women's lot in a patriarchal society. It is the multifaceted character of the heroine that saves the novel from being simplistic; she is spirited and intelligent, aware of her husband's wrongdoing, but her feelings towards him are somewhat ambivalent and she not quite principled or strong enough to break away and renounce the material privileges to which she has become accustomed. It would be hard to argue that she acquires any real moral perspective on life. Other books by Mastretta are *Mujeres de ojos grandes* (1991), a series of sketches of people, events, and situations affecting women, and *Mal de amores* (1996), a lengthy novel which harks back to the armed phase of the Revolution for its primary setting; the protagonist, the charming and gritty daughter of a very progressive, liberal family, grapples with love and life, and meets with considerable success, even becoming a kind of unsung hero of the Revolution, in a society which does not allow women equal opportunity. The novel has many elements of the romance genre: the heroine serves the national cause as a rather unlikely, elite version of the soldadera, healing the sick and wounded with the medical knowledge learned in her father's pharmacy; and she is so fortunate in love as to manage to maintain two loves of her life simultaneously, men who cover the whole range of her needs: one is a dashing young adventurer, the other a discreet and elderly doctor of medicine.

Almost all the women authors who have burst onto the literary scene in recent years share feminist concerns to some degree, but it would be misleading and simplistic to speak of a uniform women's writing today. The new women authors have brought their perspective to bear on the whole range of literary styles, and their work has just as much variety and diversity as that of the men. At one pole, for example, we have the work of Carmen Boullosa (1946–). Her first novel, *Mejor desaparece* (*Better to Disappear*, 1987), is a challenging, experimental book that alternates narrative with reproductions of her own paintings and recreates, in fragments, the childhood of the narrator and her relationships with her siblings and father. The father is authoritarian, hypocritical, half-crazed, and the girls learn to hate him and his second wife. One of the girls escapes into a life of music, another becomes an actress. A third, as if symbolically, turns to wax. The sanctity of family is under attack here; perhaps the disintegration of the narrative stands for that of the family. *Antes* (*Before*, 1989) is also a reconstruction, a reconstruction of the life of the child narrator before her death at the age of eleven, but it is less hermetic; it appears that the author has recognized the need to be more comprehensible. Speaking of *Antes* in an interview, Boullosa stated that she had tried to write a gothic novel in the English manner, but set in Mexico, and to evoke the anguish of a conciousness that cannot find a way of reaching others.[7] *Son vacas, somos puercos* (1991) is yet more conventional in form; it is marked, like *Llanto* (1992), by nostalgia for an ordered world. In the latter case, that world is the one of the Aztecs. 1989 is 9 times 52 years since the fall of Tenochtitlán. (52 was the pre-Columbian equivalent of our notion of century.) Moctezuma comes alive again in Mexico City and is taken by a group of women on a tour of twentieth-century life, which he cannot comprehend. In the course of the novel, we are told that Moctezuma is a symbol of the way we have conquered our own certainties about the world;[8] this is a very postmodern attitude. Interestingly, this novel, once again a complex one, contains a number of meta-fictional passages dealing with the difficulties in writing a (historical) novel in the postmodern era. Other novels by Boullosa are *La milagrosa* (1993) and *Cielos en la tierra* (1997).

Somewhere in between the poles of Boullosa's postmodern explorations, on the one hand, and tender, popular, and nostalgic romances by Mastretta and Esquivel, is to be found the steady output of novelist María Luisa Puga (1944–), who uses a variety of modern but accessible techniques to explore social issues, both local and global. Puga's first book, *Las posibilidades del odio* (*The Possibilities of Hatred*, 1978) was unusual due to its focus on the effects of colonialism on Kenyan society, on ethnocentric and racist attitudes, and cultural and economic domination by others; the considerable parallels with Mexico's situation are obvious. In another Puga novel, *Pánico y peligro* (1983), a secretary working in Mexico City reflects on her relationships with men and women; she is, in a sense, the writer—of notebooks that are the chapters of the novel—but she is not one bound by literary norms. The book is structured around a central metaphor, the main Mexico City thoroughfare known as Insurgentes, and it gives a picture of Mexico's recent past. Esquivel and Mastretta, Boullosa and Puga represent just a sampling of the large number of women producing significant work today in Mexico, including Sara Sefchovich and Beatriz Novaro, Bárbara Jacobs and Silvia Molina.

Women's have by no means been the only voices in recent Mexican literature. Rather like those of the young Onda writers, the works of Héctor Manjarrez (1945–) and Jorge Aguilar Mora (1946–) have stood for modern involvement in global culture. In the former's *Lapsus* (1971), the characters, who are less naive than the innocents of the first new wave novels, delight in the rather schizophrenic possibilities of youth counterculture; here literature derives from "sending up" literature, somewhat in the manner of *Tristram Shandy*. More maturely, in Manjarrez's *No todos los hombres son románticos* (1984), the emptiness of counterculture is abandoned in favor of committed political action, in the form of support for the Sandinista revolution in Nicaragua. Aguilar Mora is more daringly experimental (pretentious and obscure) in *Cadáver lleno de mundo* (1971) and *Si muero lejos de ti* (1979). Both of these writers have the whole world, the whole of Western culture, as their frame of reference, but for another two writers Mexico City *is* the world, or at least stands for it, and the cultural frame of reference is the popular one of radio, television, and film. Luis Zapata (1951) and Armando Ramírez (1950) have made serious art of popular culture, rather as Manuel Puig did in Argentina, and they have signaled the emergence of new cadres of gay and blue-collar writers in Mexico. *El vampiro de la colonia Roma* (1979) and *De pétalos perennes* (1981), both by Zapata, and *Chin-Chin el teporocho* (1972) and *Volación en Polanco* (1980), by Ramírez, document daily life among different segments of contemporary society in a way that might be considered neo-costumbrista, and they show emotions ranging from violent to tender. Along the way, Zapata and Ramírez have demonstrated the market potential of fiction covering a wide range of styles and special interests; authors such as José Rafael Calva, Luis Arturo Ojeda, and Sara Levy have furthered gay and lesbian writing; detective fiction in the old style has new proponents in Paco Ignacio Taibo II and Rafael Ramírez Heredia. Other popular new authors have crossed over and enlivened national cinema; Eusebio Ruvalcaba's *Un hilito de sangre* became a hit movie, and Guillermo Arriaga produced the screenplay for the prize-winning film, *Amores perros* (see chapter 5).

There was a point when popular and commercial literature had grown to such an extent that it did appear that highbrow fiction might fade from the Mexican literary scene. Recently, however, there has emerged a new young generation of art novelists, the Crack Generation (not in reference to crack cocaine, but in parodic allusion to the earlier Boom). Jorge Volpi has become the leading figure among the authors of this (some would say) precocious and pretentious group. The group manifesto published in 1996 provoked rather harsh reactions, perhaps as it had meant to. Their work, though by no means lacking in Mexican reference points, might be described as universalist with a vengeance; it features erudite speculation and allusions, somewhat after the fashion of the Italian author Umberto Eco's *The Name of the Rose*. Other Crack Generation group members include Pedro Angel Palou, Ignacio Padilla, and Eloy Urroz, but the group's breakthrough work was Volpi's novel *En busca de Klingsor* (*In Search of Klingsor*, 1999), which won Spain's prestigious Seix Barral prize. Though it has been challenged as another all-male club, this group is in the tradition of cosmopolitan groups before it, like the Contemporáneos and Escritura. One significant and revealing difference between this group and its predecessors is that almost all of the members of the Crack group are university educated, and many hold advanced degrees from institutions both at home and abroad; members of the earlier groups were often self-educated.[9]

In the 1980s, many of the small, traditional publishing outlets for serious literature, such as Joaquín Mortiz, were taken over by larger, international Spanish-language houses, like Planeta. This understandably fueled fears that serious Mexican literature would be phased out of the market and be replaced by translations of foreign authors, by commercial fiction, self-help titles, and other bestsellers. But, in fact, these fears have been unfounded; some of the smaller, less commercial imprints have been kept going as subsidiaries and even enhanced, and publications have multiplied and diversified through segmentation and specialization of the market into various niches. In virtually all of the Spanish American countries literature benefited from a big boost thanks to the Boom of the 1960s; the Boom brought the kind of external validation that seems essential to the confidence of writers and the success of cultural products, and it opened the eyes of authors and especially publishers to the commercial possibilities of serious literature. As regards Mexico specifically, we might add the fact that in the mid- to late twentieth century there was an unprecedented expansion of the middle classes, of education and literacy. What has occurred in this respect in Mexico is roughly analogous to what took place in much of the Anglo-European world in the nineteenth century; then and there, as now in Mexico, it produced a ripe potential market for literature. This couples with another factor, which is the continued prestige of literature and the literary artist in Mexico, in part out of respect for tradition, but equally because Argentina (and to some degree Cuba) are the only serious rival traditions in Spanish America. That said, we must remember that large numbers of Mexicans remain illiterate and lack access to education, and that the cost of books, magazines, and newspapers is still prohibitive for many people. Few writers (Fuentes, perhaps Esquivel) can make a decent living solely by the sale of their books.[10]

Still, literature of all kinds has unquestionably flourished in Mexico in the post-Boom era, and publishing has undergone tremendous growth and diversification. If one considers that all the new urban and urbane literature exists alongside a concerted revival of indigenous-language literature in the southern provinces of Chiapas, Yucatán, and Oaxaca, and alongside the work of quality young writers from the state capitals—such as David Toscana (1961–) from Monterrey and Luis Humberto Crosthwaite (1962–) from Tijuana—one surely must conclude that the health of literature in Mexico, in terms of quality and diversity, has never been better. Whereas not so very long ago there was only highbrow literature at one extreme, and a couple of successful pulp-fiction authors, plus fotonovelas, at the other, today there is a huge proliferation of writing to appeal to all sorts of readers.[11] Inevitably, our account here only samples an immensely rich field.

NOTES

1. Theater is dealt with in chapter 6, "Performing Arts."

2. Her theater is discussed on pages 172–73.

3. The modern Cuban novelist Reynaldo Arenas fictionalizes Servando's life in *El mundo alucinante* (*The Ill-Fated Peregrinations of Fray Servando,* 1969).

4. Lizardi as journalist is discussed on page 84.

5. Bart L. Lewis, "Modernism," in ed. David William Foster, *Mexican Literature: A History* (Austin: University of Texas Press, 1994), p. 162.

6. At about the same time as the Onda writers were becoming known in the 1960s and 1970s, Chicano literature began to win recognition. This is literature by Mexicans or Mexican Americans living in the United States, and it is naturally associated above all with the Southwest. Such literature emphasizes Chicano history and culture, and it frequently deals with forms of social oppression. Among events that encouraged a heightening of Chicano consciousness were the civil rights movement, anti-war protests, and particularly the unionization of farmworkers led by César Chávez and Dolores Huerta, the creation of the Teatro Campesino (Popular Theater) by Luis Valdéz, and the women's movement. In the process of delving into cultural roots, Chicano literature sometimes evokes the mythical Aztec land of Aztlán, which becomes a metaphor for the Southwest; other cultural milestones are the Mexican-American War of 1848 and the Mexican Revolution. Chicano writers react to being outsiders broadly in two ways. One is by trying to create their own history and culture and denying that of the dominant society, and the other is a more conciliatory approach which involves recognizing that their history is part of the history of the United States. The latter approach led Chicanos to make connections with other marginalized ethnic groups in the United States. For the most part, Chicanos write in English, but there is quite frequent switching between English and Spanish, and at times there is a sprinkling of Nahuatl and Tex-Mex. Among the works that have received most attention are *Heart of Aztlán* (1976) by Rudolfo Anaya (1937–), *El sueño de Santa María de las Piedras* (*The Dream of Santa María de las Piedras,* 1986) by Miguel Mén-

dez-M. (1930–), *Generaciones y semblanzas* (*Generations and Sketches,* 1976) by Rolando Hino-josa-Smith (1924–), and *Pocho* (1959) by José Antonio Villareal (1924–); Gloria Anzaldúa with *Borderlands/La Frontera: The New Mestiza* (1987), Ana Castillo with *My Father Was a Toltec* (1984), Lorna D. Cervantes with *Emplumada* (*The Plumed One,* 1981), Helena María Viramontes with *The Moths and Other Stories* (1985), and Sandra Cisneros with *The House on Mango Street* (1985).

7. Interview published in *La Jornada* (Mexico City) on December 24, 1989.

8. *Llanto* (Mexico City: Era, 1992), p. 96.

9. In literary criticism, the Octavio Paz protegé Christopher Domínguez Michael has ful-filled the same function for high-art authors as has José Joaquín Blanco for popular and work-ing-class ones.

10. Millions of books by the authoress known as Corín Tellado are sold in Mexico (and all over the Hispanic world), but she is in fact Spanish (her real name is María del Socorro Tellado López).

11. Fotonovelas are discussed in chapter 4.

8

Visual Arts

Most of the attention received by Mexican art has been focused on two bodies of work that are generally held to be the country's most distinctive: on the one hand, the pre-Hispanic monuments and artifacts, and on the other, the equally imposing products of twentieth-century muralism, a movement led by Diego Rivera, José Clemente Orozco, and David Alfaro Siqueiros. However impressive they may be, pre-Hispanic artifacts do not convey the syncretic spirit of modern Mexican culture. Moreover, the idea that the pre-Hispanic ruins and the grandiose, post-Revolutionary murals are the essentials of Mexican art is largely a European and U.S one. Some people point out that there is also a vibrant tradition of frequently anonymous art that has served more mundane social purposes.

In the architecture of La Plaza de las Tres Culturas (The Square of the Three Cultures) at Tlatelolco in Mexico City, a site upon which cultural and political battles have been waged for centuries, we have an explicit emblem of Mexico's combination of the indigenous American, the Spanish colonial, and the modern: a carefully preserved pre-Hispanic temple stands alongside a colonial church in the shadow of a modern skyscraper. Walking the streets of the historic centers of many of the ancient cities of Mexico's central plateau, where skyscrapers and discotheques are squeezed into the interstices between crumbling colonial cathedrals, built in the shadows, or upon the cinders, of pre-Hispanic structures, one feels that the past is still alive. One is also aware of the fact that these buildings have seen continual use, aware of their relatively unkempt state (and of the surrounding poverty). The feeling would not be the same were these buildings artificially maintained, as happens, for example, in Japan, where completely modern reproductions of ancient temples destroyed by earthquakes have been built. Nor is it quite the same in modern Europe, where imposing Gothic cathedrals are still in use, but in the context of a society that has progressed and in which more or less everyone enjoys the fruits of modern development. True, Europe's cathedrals were lavish constructions built at a time when the majority of the population was living in poverty. The difference in Mexico is that that sort of contrast still exists, and so the historical buildings seem even more astonishing.

What also becomes acutely apparent is the degree to which the pomp of art in Mexico has been linked to the exercise of power. Mexico's great monuments are related to the subordination of man to the larger powers of the gods, and to the imposition of one culture on another. Mexican art also embodies what one has left behind, and perhaps longs to recapture. Curiously, the world thinks of Mexico as a key contributor to human cultural history, but virtually no part of its art has ever been valued in the canon or considered to be original, superior, or truly significant. It is therefore ironic that in order to hold on to the respect of dominant nations and cultures in the modern world, Mexico seems to feel the need to celebrate and preserve its ancient heritage and to play on its aura of primitiveness.

THE PRE-HISPANIC

What comes down to us from pre-colonial times can only be a fraction of what once was. Not only was much destroyed by the Spaniards, but much, too, was lost or it simply decayed. Even so, a visit to the Museum of Anthropology in today's Mexico City provides a fascinating glimpse at past glories. There is pottery and sculpture in abundance, representing people engaged in mundane activities, also entertainers, warriors, and gods; some of the pieces are utilitarian, such as drinking vessels; some are ceremonial; some, purely decorative. In fact pottery is a major research resource for modern anthropologists. While the conquerors systematically burned documents, thinking them heretical, some survived and their illustrations in bright colors and somewhat geometric images record the events of ordinary life, acts of war, and tales of the gods. Some of their images recall the encounter with the Spaniards, the fall of Tenochtitlán, and times of disease and oppression. There is a telling image of Malinche standing between Spaniards and Indians, acting as interpreter. From her mouth there emerges a series of squiggles representing the message she is conveying; the portrayal is curiously reminiscent of medieval European religious paintings that didactically represent the word of God being conveyed from the heavens by an angel.

As to the monuments that survive, these range from the massive stone carvings of heads by the Olmecs, the first significant civilization of Meso-

Teotihuacán viewed from Pyramid of the Moon. Photo by Steven Bell.

America, to the temples, play areas, and pyramids of later civilizations. For example, the two imposing pyramids at San Juan Teotihuacán, close to the capital city, are dedicated to the sun and the moon. Many Mayan ruins have survived in Yucatán, and these include pyramids that may not be as massive, but are more delicately designed. Their precipitous sides have steps so narrow that one almost inevitably has to climb them in a zig-zag manner, thus showing due respect for the gods. The best-known examples are in Chichén Itzá and Uxmal, where impressive friezes carved in stone can also be seen, together with a ball court. The buildings of the Aztecs, the dominant civilization at the time of conquest, fared less well; as we have noted previously, the Spaniards razed Tenochtitlán to the ground and built Mexico City on top of it. But late in the twentieth century, workers on a construction site there discovered a huge buried Aztec representation of a god, and thus began the lengthy process of excavating what was found to be the site of the main Aztec temple.

THE COLONIAL

Much Latin American colonial art is considered inferior in quality to the European, and highly derivative of it. However, if there is one Latin American country that can rival Europe in this respect, it is Mexico. Even though it was basically imitative, from the start colonial art took on distinctive characteristics, determined by the distance between New Spain and the European metropolis, and by the influence of native Mexican artisans. Mexican colonial art evolved as a by-product of evangelization and colonization, both cultural and economic. The Church was the principal patron. It is interesting to note that many, perhaps most, of the impressive and distinctive works of colonial art and architecture are found not in Mexico City but in the countryside and in regional or provincial capitals. In Mexico City, the force of the colonial past has been diluted by successive reconstruction, and the insertion of nineteenth- and twentieth-century buildings. In such regional capitals as Puebla, Morelia, and Guanajuato, however, it is another story.

Somewhat paradoxically, in the visual arts, perhaps more than in any other realm of cultural activity, the most significant shift in style came not with independence, but well before, at the start of the eighteenth century. The prime style of colonial church architecture became baroque; instead of the harmonious moderation of the Renaissance style, elaborate façades and indigestibly overdecorated interiors became the norm. What is fascinating about these churches and about religious artifacts, however, is the way in which indigenous craftsmen fed in their own ideas and images, fusing Catholic religious icons with native deities, dressing nobles and saints and the Virgin Mary in feathers and giving them Indian facial features. Among the churches

Eighteenth-century Indian Baroque-style Iglesia de San Francisco de Acatepec, Puebla. Photo by Steven Bell.

that exemplify this phenomenon is Santa María Tonantzintla, in Puebla; another, San Francisco de Acatepec.

THE NINETEENTH CENTURY

Consider the fact that the first ruler of the independent Mexico called himself an emperor, as if aping Napoleon. Throughout most of the nineteenth century, criollo statesmen and liberal intellectuals emulated what was happening in Europe (especially in France) as much as ever and in some ways even more desperately; there, it seemed, were to be found the means of bringing enlightenment to Mexico. French cultural dominance remained the norm right through to the end of the nineteenth century and into the start of the twentieth. Strangely, the Porfirio Díaz regime that ruled Mexico from 1876 until the outbreak of the Revolution in 1910 was even more Francophile than the government that had preceded it; by contrast, Maximilian of Hapsburg, who had been installed in Mexico by Napoleon in 1864, had often promoted native and nationalistic expressions of culture, if only in an effort to overcome his unpopularity as a foreign interventionist.

For the most part, early nineteenth-century painting followed classical and Romantic figurative styles, depicting religious and historical subjects, and continuing the line of late colonial painting. Some effort was made to turn to Mexican, and especially to legendary, pre-Hispanic subjects, but most often, the choice of subject matter was in harmony with European preferences and interests. It was an effort made almost against the better instincts of the Mexican painters, to judge by the unrealistic, classical trappings with which the Mexican figures were depicted. An example is José Obregón's *The Discovery of Pulque* (1869), in which the pre-conquest Indians are portrayed rather in the manner of Greek gods. Another is the careful depiction of the Mexican features of two young artists in the classically trained Juan Cordero's *Portrait of the Sculptors Pérez and Valero* (1847). A third is the outstanding sculpture of the legendary Aztec leader Cuauhtémoc, done by the Spanish-born and Italian-trained artist Manuel Vilar, and placed on the Paseo de la Reforma (the major thoroughfare in the center of Mexico City) in 1887; this sculpture has bas-relief work on its huge pedestal, representing the torture of Cuauhtémoc by Cortés.

Against this background, the landscape artist José María Velasco stands out. The flora and fauna of the country, its people, and particularly its awe-inspiring physical geography, are the main, almost the only, focus of the many canvases he produced during a career that spanned some 40 years. He developed a distinctive, personal style, neither concerned with nor influenced by the latest styles in Europe, and instead allowed himself to be led

by the requirements of his subject matter and by his own interests. As it
happens, the most direct and significant precedents for Velasco's painting
are to be found not in the previous work of Mexican artists but rather in the
work of foreign artists and prominent visitors of the late eighteenth and
early nineteenth centuries, people who took a new, scholarly and scientific
interest in Mexico, in its physical and human geography. Besides the writings of Fanny Calderón de la Barca (the wife of Spain's first ambassador to
the independent Mexico) and the German naturalist Alexander von Hum-
bolt, these included painters and lithographers such as the Italian Claudio
Linati and the Englishman Daniel Thomas Egerton. Today, only Gerardo
Murillo (otherwise known as Dr. Atl), who in any case was of a later generation, remotely rivals Velasco as the foundational figure of modern Mexican
painting. Though they came of age at very different historical junctures,
and had radically different temperaments and ideologies, Atl and Velasco
shared key features that help account for their pervasive influence. Rather
than being narrowly specialized, both were intellectual leaders with wide-
ranging interests and broad visions, very much after the fashion of the
many intellectual statesmen who led Mexican public life during the nineteenth and early twentieth centuries. Both used art as a tool (Velasco apply-
ing it to natural history and Atl to science) in the service of a nationalistic
exploration of Mexican reality.

Prior to Velasco, large-scale landscape painting had never existed in Mexico, at least in any realistic or naturalistic form. When Velasco entered the
Academia de San Carlos in 1858, he soon gravitated toward the Italian master Eugenio Landesio, who had been brought in to teach perspective, natural
form, and landscape composition, and who put his students to work drawing
colonial interiors, rock formations, trees, and shrubbery. Several of Velasco's
early works derive directly from these studies, such as *Patio del Ex-convento de
San Agustín* (1871), *Peñascos del Cerro de Atzacoalco* (1873), *Ahuehuetes
de Chapultepec* (1872), and *La Alameda de México/Un paseo en los alrededores
de México* (1866), in which Mexico City's Alameda Central gives the appearance of a rural or provincial scene, with small human figures representing all
strata of Mexican society. Velasco is renowned today primarily for his vast
landscapes of the central valley, with the imposing shapes of the Popocatépetl
and Iztaccihuatl, and the vast expanses of the remaining Texcoco lake beds.
The first of these were composed between 1873 and 1875. Over the next 30
years, Velasco would produce numerous variations on this theme, far and
away his favorite. Each painting is crafted with precise and accurate detail
from a specific and always changing vantage point. The detailed but diminu-
tive human figures in the foreground and the seemingly miniature Mexico

City in the distance emphasize the grandeur of the natural geography, which is portrayed in soft outlines and understated colors that make it warm and inviting rather than intimidating.

Velasco's many contributions to the causes of Mexican natural history and scientific investigation have been less readily acknowledged. He produced a series of lithographs on the flora of the central valley that earned him recognition by the Mexican Society of Natural History, for whose official journal he often provided detailed illustrations. To decorate the recently constructed Museum of Geology, he painted a number of canvases. To document archeological explorations that were underway at Teotihuacán in 1877, he produced two lithographs of the famous Pyramid of the Sun and Pyramid of the Moon. From 1880 to 1910, he held the position of illustrator for the National Museum, and frequently traveled across the country documenting discoveries. His trip to Oaxaca in 1887 yielded one of his most impressive canvases, a painting of Oaxaca Cathedral that dramatically captures its majesty by means of a brilliant control of perspective; this painting was given to Pope Leon XIII. Only late in his career did Velasco travel outside of Mexico: in 1889 he went to Paris as a government delegate to an international exhibition; in 1893 he traveled to Chicago to show 14 of his canvases at another international exhibition. His work was well received internationally, and it has been considered equal to that of the best European landscape painters of this time.

A highly significant popular engraver of the nineteenth century was José Guadalupe Posada (1852–1913), a man who created some the most important and influential examples of graphic art in the Americas. He began drawing and making pottery at an early age and later studied at the Academia de Arte y Artesanía (Academy of Art and Handicrafts). During the 1860s, Posada became an apprentice in lithography and intaglio and started to publish illustrations in popular magazines. His early illustrations and cartoons are characterized by their delicate drawing and halftones, a little like French political cartoons of the 1860s. By 1888 Posada had his own engraving workshop where passersby could observe him work, including art students from the nearby Academia de San Carlos, such as Orozco, whose cartoons of the 1920s would reflect his admiration for Posada's work. Posada produced political cartoons for popular magazines and also worked for a publishing house illustrating thousands of penny sheets called the *Gaceta Callejera* (*Street Gazette*). These wood and metal cuts were made in a simplified expressionistic style and later hand colored in garish tones by other people. Posada intended his prints to be readily accessible to everyone. Their messages were explicit, conveyed in dramatic images addressed primarily to the urban poor and to Indian peasants. Posada's themes were as varied as was the news itself, ranging from horrific to comic, from edifying to outrageous, and his illustrations reached every part of Mexico.

Posada's best-known technique involves transforming public figures into skeletons. For instance, *Calaveras de periodistas* (*Skulls of Journalists*, 1889–94) shows a bony press group on bicycles trampling a fallen skeleton, and the famous *Calavera Catrina* (1913), portrays a ladylike skeleton wearing a large hat, a feathered boa, and a fancy gown. Like the anonymous photographers whose work is included in the Archivo Casasola, Posada created some of the most memorable images of the Revolution. In later life he adopted a freer technique, illustrating ballads, battle scenes, and the life of the soldiers—for instance, as in *Despedida de un maderista y su triste amada* (*The Farewell [The Kiss]*, 1910s), which was probably inspired by a photograph now in the Casasola Archive. Posada's works not only influenced the development of graphic art, but also inspired interest in Mexican popular culture amongst other artists. (His printmaking tradition has also been continued by Chicano artists.)

Hermenegildo Bustos was among the many prolific, nonacademic artists who earned a living painting portraits in the nineteenth century. It is often noted that Bustos's portrait subjects appear to be staring directly out as if into the lens of a camera. During the nineteenth century photography was all the rage, and there is no doubt that it was a major influence on both portrait and landscape painting. Perhaps photography was perceived as a threat to the livelihood of artists, even though it is clear that some of them based their compositions on it. The daguerreotype arrived in Mexico around 1840. Many of the professional photographers in Latin America in the 1840s and 1850s were temporary visitors from Europe and the United States. Some set up commercial studios to fill the upper-middle-class demand for portraits, while others employed in scientific cataloguing and exploration produced photographs as an aid for the engravers who made book and journal illustrations.

The world's first accurate war photos were the work of an anonymous Mexican photographer who documented the horror and hardships of the war with the United States in 1847. Technical innovations made in Europe in the 1850s, which permitted smaller formats and reduced costs, made photographic portraits accessible across class lines in Latin America after 1860. Many studios were set up by local photographers in the 1860s and 1870s, but the photographic journals, clubs, and exhibitions that proliferated in late nineteenth-century Europe and the United States came later in Latin America, in part due to the lack of readily available photographic supplies. However, even in Cuba and Mexico, where supplies were available, such organizations were not widely formed until the 1950s. In some ways this had a positive effect on photographers, some of whom became socially integrated into major artistic and intellectual circles and less isolated in photographic niches than their European or United States contemporaries.

INTO THE TWENTIETH CENTURY

At the beginning of the twentieth century, Mexico and Central America turned away from the pictorialist trends of European photography. During the Mexican Revolution a strong documentary tradition of black-and-white photography was developed. The photojournalist Agustín Víctor Casasola, who worked in Mexico City, created numerous official portraits of figures such as Porfirio Díaz, Pancho Villa, and Emiliano Zapata. Such images acquired enormous historical value and influenced the work of several generations of artists and photographers. While many famous photographs of the Mexican Revolution were directly attributed to Casasola, they were in fact shot by others, by journalists and soldiers who were in the field. Casasola collected them and created an impressive archive, which later published several photographic albums, such as the ten-volume set titled *La historia gráfica de la revolución* (*Graphic History of the Revolution*). Foreign photographers working in Mexico in the late 1920s, such as Edward Weston and Tina Modotti, emphasized their interest both in modern forms and Revolutionary themes.

A significant tradition of popular or amateur art was revitalized in the post-Revolutionary period, when Mexican nationalistic sentiment was strong. The naive style of anonymous, religious ex-voto painting was an important influence on many twentieth-century century artists, particularly on those who sought in one way or another to revalue Mexican popular art; examples are Roberto Montenegro, Diego Rivera's friend Antonio Ruiz, and, most notably, Frida Kahlo, Rivera's wife. (The couple amassed a collection of ex-votos that are now on display at the Frida Kahlo Museum outside Mexico City.)

In Mexico, perhaps more than elsewhere, intellectuals and artists working in various media have been extraordinarily collaborative. This may be a result of colonialism and underdevelopment; generally, low levels of literacy, education, and social, cultural, and economic development have limited the number of artists and intellectuals, discouraging narrow specialization. In fact, many artists and intellectuals have also been prominent as statesmen, wearing more than one hat, as has happened elsewhere in Latin America. The marked centralization that has always characterized public life in Mexico, whereby everyone who wants to be anyone is required to come to the capital to make his or her mark and stay abreast, no doubt further facilitates close collaboration. The effect overall on art has generally been salutory; the fact that artists maintain broad interests and stubbornly pursue a holistic, humanistic vision surely is one of the underlying reasons why much of the highly developed world has looked to Mexico for artistic, intellectual, and spiritual renewal, for something other than a culture beset by technification and over-specialization. It could even be said that collaboration between Mexican artists and intellectuals led them to practice multi-media arts *avant la lettre.*

Among the artists at the turn of the twentieth century who led up to the famous muralism of the Escuela Mexicana de Pintura, Julio Ruelas clearly exemplifies this phenomenon. Ruelas served as the principal illustrator for the *Revista Moderna,* one of Mexico's first outstanding literary reviews, and the principal mouthpiece of the modernista poets. The *Revista Moderna* was by no means a magazine of mass appeal, but artists and intellectuals who were in the know throughout the Spanish-speaking world regarded it highly. Besides the work of leading Mexican and Spanish American modernista poets, including the movement's leader, the Nicaraguan Rubén Darío, the *Revista Moderna* published translations of works by Novalis, Baudelaire, and Edgar Allan Poe, along with essays on new trends in art and architecture, and topics such as the occult. Ruelas worked with figurative forms, but he used them symbolically and allegorically to represent dark forces, or spiritual and arche-typal aspects of existence. His two best-known works in this vein are a self-portrait entitled *Criticism,* in which a little monster with a top hat and a rolled-up newspaper appears to be drawing blood from the artist's forehead,

Museum of Popular Arts, Mexico City. The hotel next door was damaged by the 1985 earth-quake. Photo by April Brown.

Painting by Raul Anguiano at the Museo de Arte Moderno; from the "La Espina" (Thorn) Series. Photo by Steven Bell.

and another widely known as *La Revista Moderna* (1904), which playfully depicts the principal collaborators of the magazine as a gathering of satyrs and centaurs, with their Maecenas don Jesús Luján approaching the group on a white unicorn.

One of the first people to adopt indigenista themes was Saturnino Herrán (1887–1931). He undertook the difficult task of visually portraying the native heritage of his country during the dictatorship of Porfirio Díaz, and was influenced by Díaz's attempt to Europeanize the culture of Mexico. Better known as a printer, draftsman, and illustrator during his lifetime, Herrán produced cover illustrations intermittently throughout his career, for publications like *El Universal Ilustrado*. He was first employed as a draftsman in 1907 by the government's Archaeological Monuments Inspection Service, and in that same year he was commissioned by the Museo Nacional to copy Teotihuacán frescoes, a commission that enhanced his interest in pre-Columbian cultures. To indigenous subjects and popular genre scenes Herrán brought the stylized realism, lyricism, and classically structured compositions typical of symbolist art. Herrán's earliest paintings focused on the common Mexican and his plight. *Labor* (1908) is a particularly poignant composition: in the foreground it shows a humble couple feeding their child in the shadow of a building, and in the background there are laborers struggling to move a huge construction stone under the blazing sun. While always focused on typical, popular human figures, Herrán's work encompassed all facets of Mexican life and cultural history. He produced a memorable trio of canvases depicting the legend of Iztaccihuatl. *Nuestros dioses* (*Our Gods*, 1918), conceived as part of a decorative frieze for the new Teatro Nacional building, depicts an Aztec ritual of reverence and sacrifice. *Nuestros Dioses* clearly anticipates the thematics of muralism; in it Indian and Spaniard stand side by side, together with their respective gods, Coatlicue and Christ. Herrán's work is not documentary, but rather a Europeanized representation of Aztec times as the golden age of Mexico. The languidness of the Indians made them palatable to the French-oriented public of Porfirio Díaz's day, and their effeminate quality rendered them unthreatening to the dominant culture. Herrán's work often paralleled that of his close friend the poet Ramón López Velarde. *Nuestros dioses* and *La viejecita* (*The Little Old Lady*, 1917), for example, have thematic counterparts in Lopez Velarde's poetry. Herrán was also very much in tune with the conservative nationalism of another of his friends, the composer and musicologist Manuel Ponce. All three men reacted against what they saw as the foreign pretensions of Porfirian high society, as well as against the exotic refinement, the noisy cosmopolitanism, and frivolous decadence of the symbolists and modernistas. Each in his own way undertook a defense of the simple values of traditional Mexican mestizo culture—God, home, and country.

In marked contrast to his contemporary Rivera, who as a young student gladly accepted the opportunity to travel and study in Europe, Herrán preferred to stay at home at the Academia de San Carlos, where he gradually developed his own synthesis of new styles in painting, emphasizing poetic and subjective expression rather than trying to represent nature in traditional academic ways. Herrán was attempting to reveal the inner and outer beauty of the Mexican people, and human forms were consistently the central focus of his painting. A surprising number of the key features of Diego Rivera's muralist art are heralded in Herrán's paintings, particularly the reverence for the strength, dignity, and stoicism of the Mexican people. Herrán was perhaps not the most accomplished stylist, but his paintings were arguably the first clearly to express a social consciousness.

Francisco Goitia (1882–1960) is another painter of this generation, one with a powerful, subjective vision. Some of his stark and dramatic landscape studies approach the kind of surrealism that makes the animal, vegetable, and mineral seem to come alive. Other compositions focus darkly on human figures and suggest the omnipresence of fear and suffering, of powerful and oppresive spirits, of pain and death in indigenous life; examples are *Campo mortuorio revolucionario del Charquito Colorado* (1922) and the highly regarded *Tata Jesuscristo* (1927). Goitia is best known for his bleak images of the Mexican Revolution and for his indigenista paintings. After studies at the

Academia de San, in 1904 he left for Spain, where he became familiar with the work of Velázquez, El Greco, and Goya, whose paintings influenced his own. Goitia exhibited his work with such success that the Mexican government gave him a scholarship to travel in Spain, France, and Italy. However, at the beginning of the Mexican Revolution, his grant was suspended and he had to return. He joined the forces of Francisco (Pancho) Villa and recorded the desolation of the war, creating some of the most somber images of the Revolution, comparable to those produced by José Guadalupe Posada and the anonymous photographers included in the Archivo Casasola. After the Revolution Goitia traveled throughout Mexico, taking part in archaeological and ethnological research projects. In his works he recorded not only indigenous peoples and their traditions, but also different psychological states—for example, in *Viejo en el muladar* (*Old Man on the Dung Hill*, 1926).

MURALISM AND THE ESCUELA NACIONAL DE PINTURA

Of all the popular artists of the nineteenth century it was the engraver José Guadalupe Posada who most captured the imagination of the muralists. Their regard for his prolific work lifted it from the obscurity in which it had languished since his death in 1913, and they made him a legend. His stylistic and thematic influence can be seen in Diego Rivera's murals: the skeleton and skull motifs, the cartoon-like quality in some compositions, and particularly the festive, almost orgiastic scenes of urban life. But above all it was the general approach that Posada took toward art, the critical gaze that was cast on all classes and social types, that inspired Rivera.

Mexican muralism, a programmatic, ideological project, has had few equals in the history of modern art. Its critics have identified the more glaring of its many tensions and contradictions. Particularly in the work of Rivera, its leading practitioner, muralism glorified the ancient Meso-American civilizations, and postulated that the Indian was the essence of Mexican cultural identity. It did so under the auspices of a Revolutionary government that in the final analysis only paid lip service to the cause of social justice and equality for the Indian. In its most notorious manifestations, muralism expressed a vehemently anti-capitalist, Marxist, and utopian ideology, one that nonetheless was underwritten by unabashedly capitalist patrons. Inevitably, many of the movement's more far-flung ideals went unrealized. For example, it is doubtful whether the murals ever worked as a mirror in which the masses saw themselves reflected, learned their history, or recognized their destiny. But in spite of many gaps between its intentions and its effects, the accomplishments of muralism were not insignificant; the murals became a source of national pride and inspiration.

Diego Rivera murals in the corridors of the National Palace, Mexico City. Photo by Steven Bell.

Especially through the work of the "big three" (Diego Rivera, José Clemente Orozco, and David Alfaro Siqueiros), muralism placed Mexico at the forefront of the international art world. It was an artistic counterpart of the social, political, and military Revolution that had captured the attention of people throughout the world. It was a novel, provocative undertaking, one that provided precisely the kind of ideological vision that the Revolution itself had lacked. It was in tune with the many radical and avant-garde intellectuals who had proclaimed the decadence of the West and who therefore flocked to Mexico in the early post-Revolutionary years, in search of a cause or of spiritual renewal. Above all, the murals lent dignity to ordinary Mexican people, plastering them larger than life on the walls of the most important public buildings at home and abroad. Despite the extent to which the murals have been exploited by post-Revolutionary governments of questionable moral authority, muralism established a commitment to two Revolutionary principles: art for the people and government sponsorship for the arts (something that, whatever it shortcomings, continues to enrich cultural life in Mexico to this day).

Like Carlos Chávez's Indianist music, muralism dominated the art scene in Mexico for some 30 years, beginning in the early 1920s. So profound was the impact of the work of the big three that most previous and much subsequent art in Mexico is defined by its degree of affinity with or opposition to their principles and practices. Muralism was to affect the work of Andean Indianist painters such as Eduardo Kingman and Oswaldo Guayasamín. It was also important as an influence on art in the United States; apart from its influence on individual artists, the uses to which muralism had been put in Mexico did not go unnoticed by the leaders of the Chicago movement of the 1960s, and muralism remains popular in Mexican American artistic circles as a means of raising historical consciousness.

Let us look briefly at the beginnings of modern Mexican muralism. One of its first champions was Gerardo Murillo (Dr. Atl), an eccentric promoter of avant-garde nationalism. Amid his comings and goings between Mexico and Europe, he was at the forefront of a number of rebellions against the reigning conservatism of the Mexican Academy. Around 1910 there was a series of Escuelas de Pintura al Aire Libre (Open Air Art Workshops), and there was a mural project at the Escuela Nacional Preparatoria (National Preparatory School) that was cut short by the outbreak of the Revolution. Later, when muralism came into its own, it was as a cornerstone of the new Education Minister José Vasconcelos's visionary program for national cultural regeneration and social change. Inspired in part by the Soviet socialist model, Vasconcelos's plans involved an ambitious program to combat illiteracy, the promotion of the fine arts for pedagogical purposes, the integration of Indian minorities into the mainstream by means of a rural school system, and the revitalization of popular arts and crafts. In his book *La raza cósmica* (*The Cosmic Race*, 1925), Vasconcelos envisaged a Latin America peopled by mestizos. All three of the major muralists, in varying fashions and degrees, would subscribe to this vision, and according to it the artist had to don his overalls and work boots every morning just like any other worker. All three were swept up in the Revolutionary enthusiasm and signed a 1923 manifesto issued by the union of technical workers, painters, and sculptors. Rivera would even be led disingenuously to suggest that his techniques derived from pre-Columbian sources.

In the main, muralism was concocted at a far and comfortable remove from the Revolution itself, in enthusiastic discussions between Siqueiros and Rivera that took place in Paris. The movement cohered to an extraordinary degree through to the end of the Lázaro Cardenas presidency and even through the transition to modernizing, capitalist civilian governments that began in 1940. This was so despite the fact that Vasconcelos's tenure as secretary of education ended abruptly in 1924, and in spite of the many political differences between the artists, who were somewhat influenced by fame and fortune. In fact, the three major muralists had strikingly different temperaments and visions, and their individuality is apparent even to the casual observer. These differences are reflected from the start in their several reactions to the Revolution's armed phase. Orozco, ideologically the most independent and the most skeptical, stayed at home and witnessed the full course of the Revolution's drama. Rivera, in sharp contrast, remained in Europe, where he had gone in 1907; he was there throughout the armed phase, and while there he assimilated many international avant-garde premises and techniques, most notably cubism. Siqueiros, the youngest of the three, was far and away the most staunchly Marxist ideologue and the most dogmatic defender of committed, proletarian art; he was jailed for political activism for the first time at a very early age, took up with Revolutionary groups for a while (in between visits to Europe), and later joined the republican cause in the Spanish Civil War.

The muralist movement's very first work was painted by Rivera over the stage of the tiny Anfiteatro Bolívar, in the Escuela Nacional Preparatoria, located off the corner of the Mexico City square known as the Zócalo, where today the excavation of the main Aztec temple can be viewed. The Anfiteatro is sometimes used by Mexico's presidents for political functions, while the school was one through which most of Mexico's political and intellectual leaders of that time passed. This first mural, titled *La creación* and completed between 1922 and 1923, is very different from all subsequent ones. Though most of its human figures—particular the Adam-and-Eve types at the bottom of composition's hierarchy, on each side of the amphitheatre's stage—have clearly Indian and mestizo features, the symmetry of the overall design and its allegorical message are European Renaissance in inspiration. Here we have the product of Rivera's then very recent travels to Italy and the embodiment of Vasconcelos's vision of the cosmic race and its perfection through enlightenment. Hovering over the two naked progenitors are their teachers, and ascending to the heavens on each side are allegorical and increasingly ethereal figures representing various arts and sciences and heavenly virtues.

Rivera's next major commission was the walls of the interior courtyards of the newly constructed Secretariat of Education building. The murals were begun in 1923 and finished in 1929. Here, Rivera truly began to develop his dramatic and distinctive treatment of Mexican themes. Each section of the mural is a complex and powerful composition. On the lower floors, Rivera depicted a variety of scenes from Mexican daily life: scenes of rural education and of labor in mines and mills and in the countryside. Lighter scenes of busy activity and popular celebration are in the *Courtyard of Fiestas,* including a famous depiction of the Day of the Dead, which employs the tradition of *calaveras* ("skulls") that Posada had made his trademark. Rivera himself is portrayed with his then wife, the actress Lupe Marín, caught up in the festive, pulque-drinking crowd and coyly staring back at the viewer. On the walls of the upper corridors Rivera painted a series of 42 panels embodying his strident vision of the Revolution. It encompassed both his idealization of the peasant and the Revolutionary combatant, and his acerbic criticism of their enemies: the rich and powerful, the priests and politicians. This series is symbolically linked by a continuous banner that runs across the top, and bears the lyrics of Revolutionary ballads (the famous corridos). Included is a panel entitled *The Sages,* which depicts a group of peasants, workers, and Revolutionaries jeering at a group of self-absorbed and mystified intellectuals, who appear to be addressing a stooped-over pupil generally believed to represent Vasconcelos. (It was now 1929, and Vasconcelos was a candidate for the presidency.) However one is to interpret the images, clearly they are a long way from espousing the same view of the value of education that was present in Rivera's first mural.

In 1926 and 1927, for the Salón de Actos (Assembly Hall) of the National Agricultural School at Chapingo, Rivera produced a totally different kind of mural art in which he gave free rein to his creative spirit. Some consider this work his masterpiece, because of the voluptuousness and sensuality of his human forms, and the way in which the various figures, as well as the overall design, are so well integrated into the baroque twists and turns of the build-

Diego Rivera mural in the Palacio Nacional depicting Hernán Cortés and the Spanish conquest. Photo by Steven Bell.

ing, which was formerly the chapel of a large hacienda. On one side of it, Rivera presents his vision of the biological evolution of human life ("La evolución natural"), while the opposite side depicts man's social development ("La transformación social"). The two sides are brought together at the back wall of the chapel, in an allegory dominated by a huge female nude representing Mother Earth, surrounded by images of man's technical mastery of nature and his harmonic and fructiferous existence in it.

In 1929 Rivera began his famous work at the Palacio Nacional in Mexico City. The murals on the staircase are a powerful vision of Mexican history, and they include numerous portraits of notable figures and forces in that history. On the staircase, the right wall depicts *Pre-Hispanic Mexico,* an idyllic vision of social and cultural practices, set against a volcanic backdrop. The long center wall, titled *From the Conquest to the Present,* emphasizes the violence and turbulence of Mexican history, with the lower sections dedicated to the conquest, and the upper arches depicting the protagonists of such major events as independence, the war with the United States, the era of reform, the struggle against French intervention and, finally, the Revolution. The left wall, which Rivera completed in 1935, is titled *The Mexico of Today and of the Future;* this section portrays Rivera's vision of the Revolutionary future, and his criticism of reactionary, capitalist forces in the contemporary world. In the late 1940s Rivera would return to the palace to work on a series of panels intended to ring the upper corridor of the courtyard and depict in chronological fashion a series of scenes and moments from Mexican history, but he was unable to complete this work before his death in 1954. Among these panels is his widely reproduced representation of the Aztec capital of Tenochtitlán, viewed from a nearby hillside, perhaps as it might have appeared when first glimpsed by the Spanish conquerors.

By 1930 Rivera's work had attracted world attention and earned him the first of a number of commissions in the United States (though Orozco had been the first Mexican to complete a mural in the that country, at Pomona College in California). Among Rivera's first works in the United States is a mural for the San Francisco Arts Institute titled *The Making of a Fresco,* a lighter, self-reflexive composition in which the painter himself is shown at work. In New York, he produced a painting entitled *Frozen Assets,* which contains a bitter critique of stockmarket speculation and the capitalist system. Rivera then went on to Detroit and produced a mural for Henry Ford at the Detroit Institute of Arts, titled *Detroit Industry,* an arguably naive celebration of the power and beauty of technical progress. Among the many fascinating instances of political intrigue in Rivera's life is the story of the murals he was commissioned by Nelson Rockefeller to produce for Rockefeller Center in New York; once Rivera's patrons realized that the composition included a portrait of Lenin, he was paid off, the project was canceled, and the unfinished mural destroyed. Two years later, Rivera got his own back, producing a version of this same mural for the Palace of Fine Arts in Mexico City, under the title of *Man, Controller of the Universe,* and including Rockefeller in it. Finally, one of his last murals was to become one of his most celebrated; in *Dream of a Sunday Afternoon in the Alameda Park* (1947–48), originally produced for the Hotel del Prado, Rivera combined his fascination with Mexican history and his love of Mexican popular culture and festivities. He placed together many of his favorite Mexican props and contemporary and historical figures, with the legendary graphic artist José Guadalupe Posada and one of his skeleton figures at the center of the composition, and with Rivera and his second wife, the painter Frida Kahlo, beside him.

History has bound the three great muralists, Rivera, Orozco, and Siqueiros, irrevocably together. Moreover, the sheer scope of the muralist project, the number of images plastered across the walls of so many of the major public buildings in Mexico, can have the effect of blurring their work together. José Clemente Orozco has undeniably suffered under the immense shadow cast by Rivera. In contrast to Orozco, Rivera relished the attention he received as a larger-than-life public figure. His mural compositions generally entailed much more flamboyant and provocative designs, often highlighting easily recognizable portraits and caricatures of famous figures. Thanks in part to his extensive European training and reputation, Rivera secured many of the best mural commissions in the most famous and important public spaces. But many art historians, among them Justino Fernández, believe that Orozco had the greater and more original talent. Orozco has also been the most influential of the three among more recent generations of Mexican painters; his anarchic and apocalyptic vein, his rejection of all idealism and dogma, are appreciated more than ever today, and they make him in some ways a precursor of postmodernism.

By no means was Orozco immune to the kind of modern trends in painting that had been so central to Rivera's formation, but in Orozco's case it is not clear how much this was a matter of direct influence, and how much grew out of his own stylistic development. The sharp, geometric lines that define Orozco's *The Trench* (at the Escuela Nacional Preparatoria), one of his most frequently reproduced works, suggest an affinity with cubism. Teresa del Conde says that Orozco has many points of contact with the German expressionist Max Beckmann, though there is no evidence that Orozco had any acquaintance with the man or his work. In most respects Orozco was both a more authentically Mexican artist and a more universal muralist than Rivera. While Rivera studied in Europe, Orozco was at home witnessing first hand the ravages of the Revolution. Arguably, Orozco's theory and practice were

often at odds, and paintings such as *The Trench*, with their violent and powerfully expressive abstraction of anonymous human forms, lend themselves to
diverse interpretations. Orozco's compositions appear to run the gamut from
impassioned grieving over tragic human flaws and denunciation of the violence, destruction, and exploitations of history, to deep admiration for the
strength and endurance of the human spirit, and a certain faith in human
potential for renewal. This last is perhaps best seen in his giant *Prometheus* at
Pomona College (1930). Orozco often expressed these ideas through the
motif of the cleansing power of fire, as for example in *Man of Fire*, which is a
segment of his masterpiece at the Hospicio Cabañas, in Guadalajara. Much of
his mature work is dominated by violent, dramatic, even chaotic compositions that emphasize the grotesque and the sinister. This aspect of Orozco's
vision also comes through in his repeated references to the crucifixion, specifically in his several paintings on the theme of *Christ Destroying His Cross*.
These convey Orozco's anti-clerical attitude, but they also capture his rejection of all false hope, hypocrisy, and idealism. Orozco's realistic depiction of
some of the horrors of the Revolution compares with the verbal picture of it
given in some of the novels of the Revolution. All in all, he was a realist, a
skeptic, and a pragmatist, never an ideologue, and these are the things that set
him apart from Rivera and Siqueiros. It is somewhat ironic that in the early
days of the muralist movement, it was not the party-line defending Rivera,
but the staunchly independent Orozco who suffered the brunt of the public
outrage that muralism initially provoked. Orozco's first major commission
was for the patio corridors at the Escuela Nacional Preparatoria; it gave rise to
protests by radical students and members of high society alike, and was subject to repeated instances of vandalism while in progress.

If Orozco was stylistically, temperamentally, and ideologically to the right
of Rivera, then David Alfaro Siqueiros was unequivocally to the left. While
Orozco roundly rejected party lines and dogmas, while Rivera rather oppor-
tunistically seemed to embrace every cause, style, or trend that came along,
and maintained a rather tumultuous, sporadic relationship with the Communist Party, Siqueiros remained a dogmatic Marxist, an orthodox communist, and a staunch defender of the proletarian Revolution. In his youth he
was a political activist, he lived through periods of political exile, and in his
final days he spent time in jail. Under the influence of Vasconcelos's ideals,
Siqueiros worked on a series of allegorical murals, *Los elementos*, in the early
1920s but soon moved on to more propagandistic work. *Entierro de un már-
tir obrero* (*Burial of Martyred Worker*, 1923–24), inspired by the execution of
a liberal politician, incorporates the hammer and sickle along with Aztec-style
faces. In Los Angeles he produced the ambitious but controversial *Tropical
America* (1932); in an obvious attack on U.S. imperialism, it featured an

Indian being crucified beneath the U.S. eagle, led to his deportation, and was subsequently whitewashed over. But he later returned to work in New York. One of his last and most complex murals was *Marcha de la humanidad en Latinoamérica* (*The March of Humanity in Latin America*), which was installed at the Poliforum Cultural during the 1960s.

Juan O'Gorman (1905–82) was an architect associated with the muralist movement. During the 1930s he designed houses in the functional style for a number of Mexico City's elite figures, including Rivera. But O'Gorman designed a host of other buildings besides, including mass housing projects and 28 schools. In the 1950s, however, he left functionalism behind on the grounds that it failed to accommodate either nature or Mexico's indigenous traditions; instead he moved toward an organic approach like that of Frank Lloyd Wright. O'Gorman's name is most often associated with the main library building at Mexico City's Autonomous University, whose façade he covered with mosaics depicting scenes from the nation's main historical periods, together with allegorical portrayals of the arts and sciences. This work was done between 1949 and 1951. O'Gorman was also a painter of canvases and murals, examples of which can be seen at the Chapultepec Castle and at the Palacio de Bellas Artes (Palace of Fine Arts).

Muralism presented the most visible and newsworthy face of Mexican art in the period 1920 to 1945. It was practiced not only by the big three, but also by others such as Fernando Leal, Roberto Montenegro, Fermín Revueltas (brother of the composer Silvestre and of the writer José), and even by foreigners like the French-born Jean Charlot and the American born Pablo O'Higgins, who came to support the movement and made themselves into artists who seemed more Mexican than the Mexicans. Many of these figures took part in the open air painting classes led by Dr. Atl, whose aim, as we noted earlier, had been to distance art from the conservative academy and give it back to the people.

One should in no way leave the impression that muralism was the be all and end all of Mexican art at the time. Estridentismo was an artistic movement that began in Mexico City in 1921, under the leadership of the poet Manuel Maples Arce, with Charlot and Revueltas among its members. They used to meet at the Café de Nadie (Nobody's Café), which would itself become one of their subjects, and there they fostered avant-garde activities such as exhibitions and poetry readings. Their artistic rationale, promulgated in a series of scandalous manifestos, involved a utopian vision of a society improved by technology. But the avant-garde activities of this movement were overshadowed by muralism. In the meantime, conventional easel painting not only continued to be cultivated but flourished, being the preferred form for some artists and being seen by many as a source of a steady income.

In fact, some of the best works by Siqueiros and Rivera were painted not on walls but on canvas, such as Siqueiros's striking compositions *Ethnography* (1939) and *Our Present Image* (1947).

Though muralism was far and away its most visible manifestation, the Escuela Mexicana de Pintura (Mexican School of Painting) brought under its umbrella a broad mix of avant-garde and nationalist initiatives that paved the way for a renaissance in art. Perhaps the two most significant developments were the explosion of interest in popular and folk art, and the cultivation by several significant artists of a variety of pseudo-naïve or primitive styles of portraiture focusing on humble or folkloric subjects. As in so many other aspects of the Mexican artistic renaissance, Dr. Atl played a key role. He encouraged scholarly interest in folk art and popular traditions, and in the context of post-Revolutionary fervor, coinciding with the heady atmosphere of the international avant-garde in the 1920s and 1930s, these things became unprecedentedly fashionable. Together with fellow painters Roberto Montenegro and Jorge Enciso, Atl received government support in 1921, on the occasion of the centennial of independence, to organize an exhibition of Mexican popular art. In conjunction with this project, Atl produced his ground-breaking multi-volume treatise titled *Las artes populares en México* (1922). By that time, many of Mexico's leading artists and intellectuals had begun to develop personal collections of Mexican folk arts and crafts, Kahlo and Rivera among them. Others soon followed suit. Many international avant-garde and leftist artists and intellectuals, anthropologists, and folklorists, who were drawn by the excitement and the untapped political, cultural, and artistic possibilities of early post-Revolutionary Mexico (from Artaud and Bretón to Weston and Strand, from Eisenstein and Modotti to Brenner and Toors), supported the trend and collaborated in artistic projects that were part of it. Ironically enough, the popular arts and crafts and culture that Mexican intellectuals were suddenly keen to preserve and celebrate (and exploit) were at the time on a fast track to extinction, due to the modernizing pressures to which avant-garde art itself was contributing. While perhaps encouraging the demise of living popular art forms, the activities described did give them a new lease of life as commercialized commodities.

ALTERNATIVES TO MURALISM

Only in the 1950s did muralism loosen its hold on Mexican art; yet all along there had been other artists who had taken different paths. Rufino Tamayo (1899–1991), from a mestizo family that owned a wholesale fruit company in the predominantly Indian state of Oaxaca, best exemplifies this (not that Tamayo's work was anti-nationalistic or anti-Mexican). His works are indirectly reminiscent of pre-Hispanic art; their coloration and figuration are distinctive; and they make frequent use of the elements, of animal and vegetable motifs. Tamayo favors dark-skinned, native human forms, cast in his own geometrically abstracted and rather two-dimensional style. Tamayo had no time for the strident didacticism of the muralists, and he questioned whether they were truly close to the Mexican people. Those works that Tamayo did produce in a historic-nationalistic vein—his two early homages to *Juárez* (1932) and to *Zapata* (1935), for example—express a simple, lyrical nationalism appealing to people's admiration for the achievements of two men of humble origins. The Juárez painting has the face of an Indian woman in the foreground contemplating a bust of the former president; the Zapata one situates the Revolutionary hero's bust in folkloric celestial surroundings that call to mind classic representations of the Virgin of Guadalupe. There is no political agenda here; in fact, the figures are statuesque. In general, instead of the superficial and picturesque views of the muralists, what Tamayo tried to capture was a poetic view of Mexico, and to do that he made use of form and color. Whether Tamayo achieved his aim is open to question, and it should be noted that his works, too, have been criticized for giving in to primitivism and oversimplification. But what he undeniably did do, in his own special way, was assimilate different artistic styles and techniques. During the 1940s he produced a series of expressionistic works, such as *Muchacha atacada por un extraño pájaro* (*Girl Attacked by a Strange Bird*, 1941) and thereafter his work became increasingly abstract, as in *Sandías* (*Watermelons*, 1968). Tamayo left Mexico a legacy in the form of a museum devoted to pre-Columbian art in his native Oaxaca. In 1981 a museum in his own honor was opened in Mexico City. He had few obvious disciples, but in some ways his fellow Oaxacan Francisco Toledo follows in his footsteps.

By the early 1950s such was Tamayo's stature that he had been invited to add his own contribution to the walls of the Palacio de Bellas Artes in Mexico City, alongside the works of the Rivera, Orozco, and Siqueiros. The titles of the two huge canvases he produced, *The Birth of our Nationality* and *Mexico Today*, might suggest that he was acquiescing to muralism's grandiose nationalism, but Tamayo's works could not be more strikingly different from the others'. Though Tamayo's paintings contain a number of highly abstracted symbols of the nation, these serve primarily as an excuse for a powerful display of geometric forms and color.

Tamayo's presence in the hallowed halls of the Palace of Fine Arts was enough to provide encouragement to a group of younger artists who have come to be known as the Generación de la Ruptura (Breakaway Generation). Beginning in the 1950s, this group gave art a completely new direction; suddenly the dominant style in Mexican painting became abstract, experimental,

Palacio de Bellas Artes, Mexico City. Photo by Steven Bell.

and decidedly cosmopolitan. The leading lights were Manuel Felguérez and Vicente Rojo, Roger von Gunten and Francisco García Ponce, and Lilia Carrillo and Alberto Gironella. The change was deliberate and strategic, in opposition to the straightjacket that had been imposed by the muralists—what the ruptura leader, José Luis Cuevas, called not the "iron curtain" but the "nopal curtain"—against the stereotypical expectations of what Mexican painting could and should be. In point of fact, the work of the rupturistas would have been unthinkable without the muralists; it came about because of their achievements, and built upon them. The muralists had assimilated many of the latest, European avant-garde techniques, adapting them for their own purposes. They had brought Mexico up to date, had placed it at the art world's cutting edge, and won it international recognition. From this experience, the rupturistas undoubtedly derived the kind of self-confidence they needed in order to strike out on their own and establish their own artistic identities.

Moreover, besides Tamayo there were a number of other precursors, many of them foreign artists who had emigrated to Mexico, whose work never received the public attention enjoyed by the muralists, but who produced an important body of work in the Mexico of the 1940s and 1950s. Leonora Carrington, originally from England, and Remedios Varo, from Spain, were both influenced by surrealism; independently of one another they produced oddly delicate, fantastic, and personal pictorial universes that have won a certain cult following. Both Carrington and Varo had had direct contact with European surrealists, but other painters who had not had such contact also revealed surrealist tendencies, including Frida Kahlo, Rivera's wife.

André Breton, the leader of the surrealist movement, once said that Mexico was the land of surrealism par excellence. Certainly it attracted a lot of surrealist artists. In fact, an international surrealist exhibition was held in Mexico City in 1940. It was Breton who called attention to the surreal quality of Frida Kahlo's work, though she herself did not see it in that way. There is undoubtedly a dreamlike side to her work, but just as evident are its naïve qualities, and the influence of Mexico's ex-voto folk art tradition. She was particularly interested in the idea of Mexicanness. Even her self-portaits are full of obviously Mexican trappings. Kahlo (1907–54) won fame and financial success late in her life and had her first one-woman exhibition only in 1953; but since then she has become a popular icon. Her subject was often her own suffering: she was a victim first of polio then of a serious traffic accident, and was unable to have children and in an unhappy marriage. (Her relationship with Rivera is explored in the feature film by Paul Leduc titled *Frida, naturaleza viva;* see pp. 149–50.)

María Izquierdo (1902–55) drew on similar sources and was similarly interested in the notion of Mexicanness. Just as Breton claimed Kahlo for surrealism, so Artaud claimed Izquierdo, and in doing so he enhanced the international appeal of her work. Izquierdo cohabited with Tamayo in the 1930s, and later with Lola Alvarez Bravo, a famous photographer; their house became a popular meeting place for intellectuals. Bravo was by then estranged from her husband Manuel, also a significant photographer; at one time or another both husband and wife had taught at the National Institute of Fine Arts. During the 1920s both became interested in documenting ordinary indigenous life, but Lola's approach to the subject was more documentary, Manuel's more lyrical. An important pioneer of photojournalism, she was a staff photographer for a number of magazines. She also photographed artists and their works, and is well known for her photos of Frida Kahlo. Lola died in 1993. Her husband Manuel (1902–) had in fact introduced her to photography. Closely associated with the muralists, though less blatantly propagandistic in his art that they were, he preferred subjects drawn from the working class. His photographs were inventive, with dreamlike elements, and some of his work was included in the surrealist exhibition previously mentioned. His most famous photo, whose title, *Obrero en huelga, asesinado* (*Assassinated Striker,* 1934) is a closeup of the upper half of a bloody, dead worker, taken in such a way as to make the viewer feel he is crouching beside the body.

Juan Soriano (1920–) was a brilliant, precocious and highly idiosyncratic enfant terrible who consistently followed his own artistic course. His paintings invariably employ striking color combinations, sometimes expressionistically, with sharp boundaries, sometimes impressionistically, with the lines blurred and confused. They can be simple and elemental, or chaotically complex. They run the gamut from the light and playful to the macabre, from the cosmopolitan to the primitive, from traditional to contemporary, from stylized figuration to geometric abstraction. Initially his work was figurative, with allegorical, symbolic, and surreal elements, and later, after a stay in Italy, there were avant-garde tendencies. But Soriano was always a free spirit. He is another example of an artist who has worked in several media—painting, sculpture, and ceramics—and who has collaborated with artists in other fields, for example as a theater scenographer.

The group of artists who came to be called the Generación de la Ruptura is clearly related to the avant-garde literary group known as the Contemporáneos; both were loosely constituted groups. What united the ruptura artists was their resistance to the programmatic, dogmatic, doctrinaire aspects of the Mexican School of Painting. The ruptura group, whose name became current in the 1950s, freely pursued their individual inclinations down such paths as post-Romanticism, neo-expressionism, geometrical and lyrical abstraction, and various combinations thereof. They preferred the cosmopolitan and universal to the nationalistic, and they had a much more multi-media approach than the muralists (who were almost exclusively painters), emphasizing texture as often as color and using a variety of materials. Among the more abstract artists of La Ruptura were Manuel Felguérez, a sculptor, Vicente Rojo, and Gunther Gerzso.

To complicate matters, there was another group that was an offshoot of La Ruptura, called *Nueva Presencia* (New Presence), which was active from 1961 to 1963 and which also went under the name of *Los Interioristas* (The Insiders). This group's members had denounced the emphasis on social realism and the didacticism of the dominant schools of muralism and indigenism, but unlike others they rejected the use of abstract modes in favor of neo-figuration; they were to become one of the most important neo-figurative groups in the Americas. Neo-figuration was a generalized trend away from abstraction and towards the representation of the human figure, a trend that emerged in Europe, the United States, and Latin America during the 1950s. Many of the European artists who worked in neo-figurative styles expressed existentialist concerns relating to the individual in the anxious context of post-war Europe. In Latin America, the industrialization and urban growth of the 1940s and 1950s resulted in an increasingly alienating urban life-style which also made artists receptive to existentialist ideas. The members of Nueva Presencia became aware of existentialism through the writings of Octavio Paz, the U.S. Beat poets Allen Ginsberg and Lawrence Ferlinghetti,

European writers like Albert Camus and Franz Kafka, and especially the U.S. author Selden Rodman, whose book *The Insiders: Rejection and Rediscovery of Man in the Arts of Our Time* (1960) explains the label Los Interioristas.

One of the most important members of this last group was Alberto Gironella (1929–99). Influenced by his Catalán father, Gironella became interested in the culture of Spain, especially the writings of Ramón Gómez de la Serna and Ramón del Valle-Inclán. He studied Spanish at the Universidad Nacional Autónoma de México (National Autonomous University of Mexico), and later his studio became a meeting place for Spanish and Mexican writers and artists. In the early 1950s Gironella turned to painting and together with fellow artist Vlady (Vladimir Kibalchich Rusakov) founded the Galería Prisse, which supported artists who wanted to break away from the dominance of the muralists. In the late 1950s, Gironella reached artistic maturity, although this involved appropriating the work of the Spanish painters El Greco, Velázquez, and Goya. Gironella was fascinated by the most sinister aspects of Spanish culture, sometimes using it to comment on Mexico. In his painting *Entierro de Zapata* (*Burial of Zapata*, 1957), he took as his source of inspiration El Greco's *Entierro del Conde de Orgaz* (*Burial of the Count of Orgaz*); Zapata had come to represent the traditional values of the campesino, was the sanctified political figure. Gironella was by no means alone in painting variations on the works of old masters; to quote two other examples, the same painting by El Greco was used by Alejandro Colunga as the basis for his *La pasión de los locos 1* (*Passion of the Lunatics 1*, 1981), while another of the Spaniard's most famous canvases, the *Vista y mapa de Toledo* (*View and Plan of Toledo*, c.1609), lies behind Juan O'Gorman's *Ciudad de México* (*Mexico City*, 1942).[1] It has been suggested that "there is a nice irony in the idea of producing an Old Master in the New World, where the one is not old and the other not new" (Fraser and Baddeley, 8).

Gironella's key works are those in the *Serie de las reinas* (*Series of the Queens*, 1960s–1970s), in which he deconstructs images of Queen Mariana of Austria painted by Velázquez. Gironella's sinister vision of Mariana was influenced by Valle-Inclán's writings about the decadence of the Spanish monarchy. At the beginning of the series, Gironella reinterpreted Velázquez's portraits in an expressionistic style, giving the figure of the queen an almost abstract quality. Soon he began to introduce found objects into his compositions, which eventually became complex collages. The metamorphosis of Mariana reached an important stage in collages such as *Gran obrador* (*Great Maker*, 1964), in which he represented her as a dog. *La reina de los yugos* (*The Queen of the Yokes*, 1975–78) becomes a statement about subjection under Spanish colonial power. This paradoxical identification of Mexico with Spain also appears in Gironella's painting *El sueño de Doña Marina 2* (*The Dream of Doña*

Marina 2, 1977), where Mariana becomes Malinche, both a traitor to and a symbol of Mexico.

Another major figure in La Ruptura and Nueva Presencia was José Luis Cuevas (1934–). By 1953 the self-taught Cuevas had already had an important exhibition at Gironella's avant-garde Galería Prisse in Mexico City. He rapidly rose to national prominence not only due to his considerable talent, but also because of his public attacks on well-established artists like Rivera and Siqueiros, and his demands for greater artistic freedom. The young Cuevas achieved international fame in the late 1950s thanks in part to the support of José Gómez Sicre, then director of the Division of Visual Arts at the Pan-American Union in Washington, D.C. The expressionistic, subjective representation of the human figure in Cuevas's work, which consists mainly of drawings and prints, is comparable to the work of neo-figurative artists active in many parts of the world during the 1950s and 1960s, including Gironella. *Loco* (*Madman*, 1954), *Estudios de Kafka y su padre* (*Studies of Kafka and His Father*, 1957), and *Autorretrato en la noche* (*Self-Portrait at Night*, 1978) are drawings in which Cuevas identified with the dark vision of human nature found in the works of Goya and Orozco; Cuevas portrays a nightmarish universe populated by alienated, marginal, and grotesque figures.

With the possible exception of Cuevas's drawings, the works of the artists of this generation never approached the level of international recognition enjoyed by the big three muralists and Tamayo. But, paradoxically, it was within Mexico that these decidedly universally minded artists were significant; they renovated Mexican art at a time when it sorely needed it, opening it up to new horizons. Their success in this is reflected in the creation of the Museo de Arte Contemporáneo, an official and very public sign of recognition of their achievements. Their role parallels that of the composers of classical music who sought to break away from Carlos Chávez's nationalism, and that of the Boom or "mafia" generation writers (see p. 240) who rallied around the figure of Octavio Paz. As Paz put it, "We [Mexicans] are now the contemporaries of all men." (Paz, *El laberinto de la soledad*, 174). Moreover, all of these changes in the creative arts could be seen as fruit of the shift that began in Mexican society and politics in 1940, towards modernization and the free-market economy. Unlike the muralists, the ruptura artists never claimed to be escaping the realm of high art; they did demonstrate that muralism had itself never truly done so.

We come now to a small selection of artists who came to prominence towards the end of the twentieth century. Rocío Maldonado (1951–) is one of the most important exponents of neo-Mexicanism, a loosely connected group of contemporary Mexican artists that emerged in the 1980s and also included Nahum Zenil and Julio Galán. Neo-Mexicanism has signaled a return to ideological issues in Mexican art. Maldonado's style is related to neo-expressionism, which emerged in Europe and the Americas during the early 1980s and is favored by a number of other Latin American painters. Her interest in the history of art and in Mexican popular culture is characteristic of neo-Mexicanism. She exposes cultural stereotypes that present women as weak and subordinate to men. Recurrent motifs in her early works, such as *La virgen* (*The Virgin,* 1985), are Mexican folk craft dolls made of painted leather or papier-mâché, often accompanied by representations of male and female reproductive systems and genitalia; these are intended to symbolize the passive role that has traditionally been expected of women. In more recent paintings, Maldonado expresses feminist concerns through a postmodern combination of images taken from the history of art and religion. For instance, in *Extasis de Santa Teresa II* (*Ecstasy of Saint Teresa II,* 1989), she makes use of a well-known sculpture by Bernini, the Italian baroque artist, and she explores the relationship between past and present, between sacred and profane, between passive and active female sexuality.

Somewhat similar is Nahum Bernabé Zenil (1947–), one of the most important artists to have emerged in Mexico in the late twentieth century. Like Frida Kahlo and José Luis Cuevas before him, Zenil's principal subject is himself, but by means of exploring the self Zenil also questions broad cultural and sexual attitudes. In his startling works, most of them small, intimate mixed-media paintings, Zenil includes images of himself in religious and traditional contexts. In *Retrato de boda* (*Wedding Portrait,* 1988), the self-representation approaches narcissism: he gives all members of the wedding

Museo de Arte Moderno, designed by Pedro Ramírez Vásquez. Photo by Steven Bell.

party his own face. In *Bendiciones* (*Blessings*, 1987), Zenil adopts the format of the ex-voto and paints himself together with Gerardo, his look-alike, long-time companion and lover, standing below that well-known Mexican icon, the Virgin of Guadalupe. Her blessings are showered upon them in the form of roses, which are flowers traditionally associated with her. Zenil reinterprets and subverts established symbols in order to challenge sexual stereotypes and expose the homophobic prejudices of a conservative Catholic society. Sexual intolerance is the obvious subject of *Esperar la hora que cambiará nuestra costumbre no es fácil* (*Waiting for the Time When Our Customs Will Change Is Not Easy*, 1984).

Late twentieth-century photographers include Flor Garduño (1957–), whose work suggests both the present and the eternal by portraying indigenous people in daily activities that perpetuate tradition. Garduño studied in Mexico City and also worked as a studio assistant for Manuel Alvarez Bravo in the late 1970s. She continued Alvarez Bravo's tradition of lyricism in black-and-white photography as well as his synthesis of formal concerns with a strong interest in the culture of Mexico. However, her first internationally acclaimed photographic series, *Bestiario* (*Bestiarium*, 1987), presents a renewed Indianist outlook, one that makes no political assumptions. In this series, which features indigenous peoples dressed in the zoomorphic costumes from pre-Columbian rituals, indigenous traditions are often integrated with the Catholic faith and modern trends. In perhaps an idealized way, Garduño illustrates the close relationship between mankind, animals, and nature in traditional Mexican culture. She also worked and traveled in Central America and the Andes, continuing the photographic survey of native lives and traditions that she had begun in Mexico. Her photographs capture moments of spirituality and death. *Huilancha-Sacrificio* (*Huilancha-Sacrifice*, 1990) offers the viewer a ceremonially sacrificed llama. From its slit throat, blood has poured over the bouquet of flowers beneath its head and soaked into the fissures of the earth. In *Camino al cementerio* (*Road to the Cemetery*, 1988), we see a burial procession in which a child's coffin is tied to the back of the person in the middle, while a figure on the right is carrying a shovel. They have their backs to the camera, and it is as if the viewer were following them. Throughout her work, Garduño uses anonymity to draw the viewer into indigenous lives and rituals.

Graciela Itúrbide (1942–), another important photographer, became professionally active in the 1970s. Itúrbide, the daughter of a photographer, has used a camera since she was a teenager. She studied at the Centro Universitario de Estudios Cinematográficos (University Center for Cinematic Studies) and she too was once an assistant to Manuel Alvarez Bravo. In 1974 she became a full-time professional, but instead of focusing on advertisements or photojournalism, she has supported her documentary black-and-white photography mostly through grants and commissions from the United States and Europe. The main theme of Itúrbide's oeuvre is the dignity of human life and the efforts of different groups and individuals to maintain a sense of identity. She tends to work in series of images reflecting the lives of marginal groups and often concentrating on women. While in Spain and Portugal she produced a series about gypsies, and in Newcastle, England, she photographed a group of unemployed women. In Cuba, she took photographs of *santería* celebrations which were later included in her book *Sueños de papel* (*Paper Dreams*, 1985), and in Mexico she explored the theme of death, in photographs relating people to animals that are dead or about to be killed or sacrificed; examples are *Los pollos* (*The Chickens*, 1980) and *Gansos* (*Geese*, 1980). Itúrbide's Mexican work often explores the traditional ways of life of indigenous groups. Perhaps the most important of these suggestive but ultimately ambiguous images are her photographs of Juchitán women, published in her book *Juchitán de las Mujeres* (*Women's Juchitán*, 1989). In the late 1980s Itúrbide traveled to east Los Angeles, where she produced powerful images based on her exploration of the private and collective activities of members of Mexican American street gangs.

In addition to the aforementioned photographers, we should mention Mariana Yampolsky, who often works in the countryside documenting the difficult life of impoverished but tenacious and dignified indigenous people. Since the 1960s Mexican photographers such as Lázaro Blanco, Ignacio "Nacho" López, and Pedro Meyer have documented a wide variety of themes, ranging from urban life and psychological conditions to the shocking effects of poverty and violence. Their work often goes beyond simple documentation to create images that can be poignantly dramatic or subtly poetic. Yolanda Andrade, a younger photographer, also depicts urban life, but her images have a more stark and gritty quality.

ARCHITECTURE

Finally, a word about the evolution of architecture since independence. Early twentieth-century architecture in Mexico was based almost entirely on European precedents. Mexican independence in the early nineteenth century had provided little impetus for architectural innovation, but during the periods of French occupation and the Porfirio Díaz dictatorship, Mexico City fully embraced French neoclassical architecture at the expense of both Iberian and indigenous Mexican designs. Although the phenomenon spread somewhat to Central American capital cities, it met with limited acceptance in Mexico's state capitals and even less in agrarian communities, where elaborate

View of the Villa de Guadalupe, looking up toward the early colonial buildings. Photo by Steven Bell.

folk styles imported from Spain continued into the early twentieth century. Some Mexican cities, like Puebla and Zacatecas, which had forged artistic and architectural traditions that were different from those of Mexico City, continued to utilize local tile and stone-carving traditions.

After the Revolution, the styles of European modernism were introduced. Several architects from Mexico studied in Europe, and many of those who studied at home also adopted the principles of Le Corbusier's functionalism. The functional structures that first appeared in Latin America in the late 1920s were not merely a bastion of the elite intelligentsia, they were also recognized by practically minded governments throughout the region as an efficient means of housing a rapidly growing population and providing the expanding the concomitant social services. We noted earlier that Juan O'Gorman designed some of the earliest functional buildings in Mexico.

One cost-effective technique was the concrete shell construction, which was to be widely used in Latin American. One of the early innovators in this technique was the architect Félix Candela, a Spaniard who emigrated to Mexico. Candela (1910–97) believed that the form of a structure rather than its mass offered resistance and stability, a belief that at first found few supporters in Mexico City, where most architects doubted that Candela's structures could last in an area known for its poor subsoil and frequent earthquakes. Candela

Zócalo and cathedral, Puebla. Photo by Steven Bell.

defended his designs in *A New Philosophy of Structures* (1951), which attacked standard architectural theories and stated that the elasticity of reinforced concrete surpassed previous assumptions. Most of Candela's commissions in the early 1950s came from the business and industrial sectors, which had become aware of the relatively low cost of concrete shell construction. The simplicity of reinforced concrete groin vaults led to Candela designs being used even in rural communities; an example is the school at Ciudad Victoria, Tamaulipas (1951). However, such clients did not allow Candela much latitude of expression. The formal freedom to pursue hyperbolic forms that was offered by concrete consumed Candela throughout his career. Sometimes he used it to mimic traditional forms, as can be seen in the Gothic-inspired Iglesia de la Virgen Milagrosa (Church of the Miraculous Virgin, 1954–55) in Mexico City. Among Candela's most elegant works is a restaurant in Xochimilco called Los Manantiales (1957); the groin-vaulted octagonal structure allowed him to manipulate the concrete shell into soaring free-form edges, with seemingly unsupported exterior roof lines. This demonstrated Candela's philosophy of concrete shell construction, asserting that form, not mass, was the essential element in support systems.

The International Style that was dominant during the twentieth century arrived in Latin America shortly after its European inception, but it was not readily expressed in large-scale vertical structures prior to World War II, due to Mexico's strong continuing tradition of stonemasonry and, more signifi-

Gardens and chapel, Palacio Nacional, Mexico City. Photo by Steven Bell.

cantly, due to the scarcity of steel. The mid-century International Style build-ings in Mexico City, largely the work of architect Mario Pani, greatly influ-enced construction in other Latin American capitals. Pani (1911–) embraced the International Style more fully than most other Mexican architects of his time. Born in Mexico City into a diplomatic family, Pani was raised in Europe and studied architecture in Paris. After returning to Mexico in 1934, he received a commission to design the Hotel La Reforma, which became the leading tourist hotel in Mexico City and a flagship of modern architecture. Over the following three decades, Pani designed numerous buildings along major Mexico City thoroughfares. Most are more significant in scale than in design. Because of the use of constructional steel, which, as noted, had not been readily available in Mexico prior to World War II, Pani was instrumen-tal in binging the modern skyscraper into the Mexico City skyline.

Like most of his contemporaries, Pani thought that architecture and urban planning were inseparable. Already concerned with Mexico City's growth rate in the 1930s, Pani's answer to the strain of rapid urbanization was to promote massive residential building programs. Tlatelolco, his largest project, was begun in 1964. The 101-building complex provided space for 70,000 resi-dents and included 11,916 apartments, 13 schools, 3 medical clinics, a movie theater, shops, and social gathering areas. Tlatelolco was successful in its mis-sion to provide affordable housing, thanks to the sensitivity of preliminary

Museo Rufino Tamayo, Chapultepec Park, Mexico City. Photo by Steven Bell.

social surveys and the experience gained by Pani in previous Mexico City complexes. During the 1950s, Pani joined Carlos and Enrique del Moral as chief architects of the campus of the Universidad Nacional Autónoma de México (UNAM), at the time one of the most important architectural projects in Latin America. Although not as successful as the campus designs for the University of Caracas, the designs for UNAM integrated visual arts with functionalist architecture. Several of the buildings were covered with large-scale mural mosaics, the most famous being the central rectangular block of the library, designed by O'Gorman and others. Another important building in the Ciudad Universitaria is its Olympic Stadium, one of the largest in the world, which features a mosaic by Rivera on its façade. The entire campus project covered an area of 1,500 acres and included the work of more than 100 architects.

While functionalism played a vital role in the architecture of Mexico during the 1950s and 1960s, several architects such as O'Gorman and Luis Barragán reacted against its influence and adopted the principles of organic architecture proposed by Frank Lloyd Wright. Barragán (1902–88) was known primarily for his upscale single-family residential structures. In the late 1920s he and three other Guadalajara architects were known as the Guadalajara Four, and they were associated with the conservative Partido de Acción Nacional (National Action Party), which denounced the changes brought about by the Revolution and rejected indigenism, then being institutionalized in Mexican art. However, Barragán was not antagonistic to other cultural influences. His first period of study in Europe in 1925 had led to an interest in Islamic architecture, African art, and Art Deco, all of which influ-

enced his neo-colonial designs of the late 1920s and early 1930s. During the
1930s, after he moved to Mexico City, Barragán adopted the style of functionalism, influenced as much by the Cárdenas administration's promotion of
rational and economic architecture as by European aesthetics. At this time,
Barragán produced designs he believed were neither unique nor noteworthy
and felt displeased with the constraints placed upon his work. He came into
his own in his work on domestic architecture and residential urban planning,
which together allowed him a greater freedom of design. His first widely
acclaimed residential development was Los Jardines del Pedregal (The Pedregal Gardens, begun 1945). In this, Barragán followed Frank Lloyd Wright's
idea of harmonizing architecture with the landscape, rejecting both functionalism and International Style. Barragán was a deeply religious man who
believed that residential architecture was only successful if it accomplished
the spiritual mission of providing an atmosphere of serenity and intimacy.
While International Style architecture prescribed walls of glass which opened
the interior living space to the exterior landscape, Barragán preferred a central
garden onto which interior spaces converged. Central gardens and largely
windowless exterior walls were traditional design features that dated back to
ancient Mediterranean and Meso-American origins. Such gardens allowed an
interior space to be sculpted by changing patterns of light and shadow
throughout the day, and these were intended to foster thought and spirituality. One of Barragán's masterpieces in Mexico City, the Casa Gilardi (Gilardi
House, 1976), is a particularly good example of his accommodation of monumental forms to a human scale, as well as the transformation of colonial
antecedents for modern contexts.

Barragán's designs have influenced a number of followers. Younger archi-
tects fused the International Style with Barragán's organic, eclectic approach,
thereby bringing a previously unknown warmth to large structures, as in
Ricardo Legorreta's Hotel Camino Real (1968). Mathias Goeritz also challenged the principles of functionalism by designing, in collaboration with
Barragán, what Goeritz called "emotional architecture." His structure called
Las Torres de Satélite (Satellite City Towers, 1957–58), at the entrance of the
Ciudad Satélite neighborhood of Mexico City, consists of five triangular con-
crete towers with an average height of 156 feet, painted in different colors.
These towers are not inhabitable, but neither are they merely sculptures; they
identify an inhabitable area.

NOTE

1. One could add the highly successful modern Colombian artist Fernando Botero to the
list.

Conclusion

It is tempting to imagine that one can still identify areas in Mexico where something like a pure form of indigenous culture survives, and other areas where Spanish colonial culture still endures, and yet other areas, particularly urban locales, where all traces of the historical and cultural strata have been erased by modernization. Yet the reality is that no such clear distinctions can be made. Moreover, new trans-cultural contacts are influencing the old order. We can see this at the international level in the consequences of the North America Free Trade Agreement (NAFTA) and nationally in the Zapatista rebellion in Chiapas. NAFTA has led to arrangements that run the gamut from partnerships between huge conglomerates to import/export agreements between, for example, a local company in Houston and a family enterprise in Chihuahua. In the case of Chiapas, complex national alliances have come about among people in remote Indian villages, underground revolutionaries, Mexico City students, artists, and intellectuals; international activists and organizations have become involved, too, bringing together such strange bedfellows as scholarly anthropologists, evangelical and ecumenical church people, and students and business people.

Mainstream historians of Mexico, such as Octavio Paz and Edmundo O'Gorman, emphasize the Spanish foundations of modern Mexico: the language; the Catholic religion; the economic, social, and legal structures; and political institution that were erected upon the ruins of the conquered Indian civilizations. Yet because of the many Indian cultures, communities, and languages that survive today, and because of the extent to which so many pre-Hispanic cultural elements underlie the cultural practices of the majority of Mexicans, other historians such as Guillermo Bonfil Batalla argue that what keeps Mexico from realizing its true potential is its continuing failure, for all the rhetoric, to respect its indigenous origins and its present-day indigenous populations. Still others, such as Roger Bartra, have decried the overemphasis on both the indigenous and the colonial heritages, pointing out that while these do much to explain Mexico's past, they have little direct bearing on the lives and consciousness of Mexicans today. Is the true origin of the Mexico we know today to be found in the ancient Indian civilizations, in the Spanish conquest, in the war for independence from Spain at the beginning of the nineteenth century, or in the fabled Revolution of 1910? The answer is yes to all of them, but not to any one of them alone.

Mexico is a young nation, younger than the United States; like the majority of Spanish American nations, Mexico achieved its independence from Spain during the first quarter of the nineteenth century, and part of the inspiration came from the very liberal ideals that had guided the French and (North) American Revolutions. It is also a young nation in terms of its population. Whereas the population of industrialized countries is in decline and the average age is rising, in today's Mexico some 40–50 percent of the population is thought to be 15 years old and younger. And there are no signs of a loss of vigor in the debate about the essence of its identity. Mexico is still actively reinventing and recombining its traditions, still trying to find its place in the world, still striving for the modern development that its leaders ostensibly have sought since independence, and still full of problems and potential.

Glossary

Amiguismo   Use of personal acquaintances to make social contacts and advance in society.

Bolero   A song genre (romantic ballad).

Bracero   Mexican guest worker in the United States.

Cabaretera   Film genre based on cabaret life and in a melodramatic vein.

Cacique   Regional strong man. The word is of pre-Hispanic derivation.

Campesino   A person from the country, peasant.

Canción ranchera   Song genre popular in films of the Golden Age of Mexican cinema.

Cantinflas   Screen name for the actor Mario Moreno.

Caudillo   Regional strong man.

Charro   Stereotypical, traditional Mexican cowboy.

China poblana   Stereotypical, traditional young Mexican female figure.

Cine de arrabal   Urban melodrama (film genre).

Cofradías   Guilds or brotherhoods devoted to the veneration of particular saints.

Comal   A form of hot plate, usually clay, for preparing tortillas.

Compadre   Godfather figure; also connotes very close, family-like friendship.

Corrido   Narrative song ballad telling of life in the northern region and/or exploits of the famous.

Costumbrismo   Artistic tendency involving the highlighting of local manners and human types, often with a satirical purpose.

Criollo/a   Person of European descent but born in the Americas.

Cuate   Close friend, "buddy." A slang term of pre-Hispanic origin.

Curandero   Healer, medicine man.

Ex-voto   An object or artifact that is offered to a saint, Christ, or the Virgin Mary, as public testimony and thanks for their intercession. Usually displayed at a church or shrine.

Fotonovelas   Picture books telling soap opera–style stories.

Gacetilla   News sheet (sometimes indirectly) under government control.

Gringo   Person from the United States (though the term is frequently applied to non-Hispanic foreigners in general).

Hacienda   Ranch.

INBA   Instituto Nacional de Bellas Artes (National Institute of Fine Arts).

Indigenismo   Artistic portrayal or advocacy of the Indian.

Jarabe tapatío   A dance form associated with Guadalajara: the "Mexican Hat Dance."

Ladino   Person from outside the Indian community.

Malinchismo   Betrayal of the nation to foreign interests; or more loosely now, a preference for things foreign (European or North American) over things Mexican. (Malinche was an Indian woman who served as translator for Cortés in his conquest of Mexico and was his mistress.)

Maquila(dora)   Assembly (and sometimes manufacturing) plant located close to the U.S. border.

Mesa/meseta   Plateau.

Meso-America   Term used to refer to areas (parts of present-day Mexico and Central America) that were inhabited by ancient Indian civilizations.

Mestizo/a   Person of mixed European and Indian descent.

Metate   A stone vessel with concave upper surface, used for grinding corn and other grains.

Mordida   Bribe, most often associated with the police.

Norteño   Music associated with the northern part of the country, particularly the U.S. border region.

Partido Revolucionario Institucional   The Institutionalized Revolutionary Party that held power for some 70 consecutive years during the twentieth century.

Pelado   A complex term with variable connotations, but essentially a negative stereotype of the working-class Mexican. Literally denotes stripped clean, penniless, raped, or peeled. According to Pilcher, during Porfirian times *pelados* referred to the poor migrants from rural areas who attempted to fit into city life and became the urban underclass. The term is also used to refer to the stock comic figure made famous by the actor Cantinflas. In the view of Samuel Ramos, he represents the Mexican macho who covers his feelings of inferiority with an aggressively self-confident exterior: a streetwise character who lives by his wits and survives through verbal dexterity (or obfuscation).

Peninsulares   Native-born Spaniards.

Petate   A straw mat or bedroll.

Plaza mayor   Main square, usually housing the town hall and also serving as the focus of a town's social activity.

Porfiriato   The period of despotic rule, political stability, and economic and industrial modernization dominated by President Porfirio Díaz (1877–1911).

Pulquerías   Bars specializing in *pulque,* a drink fermented from cactus.

Quinceañera   (Party for) girl celebrating her fifteenth birthday.

Remesas   Sums of money sent back home by Mexicans working abroad.

Retablo   Originally a series of decorative or didactic religious paintings, usually of saints or biblical scenes, displayed behind the altar of medieval Catholic churches. Today it also applies to small devotional paintings, such as ex-votos.

Soldadera   Female camp-follower.

TLC   The Tratado Libre de Comercio, Mexico's name for the North American Free Trade Agreement (NAFTA).

Telenovelas   TV soap operas.

Tianguis   Open-air markets; a term of Náhuatl origin.

UNAM   Universidad Nacional Autónoma de México (National Autonomous University of Mexico, the country's largest).

Zambo   A person of mixed Indian and black parentage.

Zarzuela   Light Spanish operatic genre in which costumbrismo is frequent.

Selected Bibliography

Ades, Dawn. *Art in Latin America: The Modern Era (1820–1980)*. New Haven: Yale University Press, 1989.

Aguayo Quezada, Sergio, ed. *El almanaque mexicano*. México: Grijalbo/Proceso/Hechos Confiables, 2000.

Aguilar Camín, Héctor, and Lorenzo Meyer. *In the Shadow of the Mexican Revolution: Contemporary Mexican History 1910–1989*. Translated by Luis Alberto Fierro. Austin: University of Texas Press, 1993.

Agustín, José. *Camas de campo (campos de batalla)*. México: Universidad Autónoma de Puebla, 1993.

Alducín Abitia, Enrique, et al. *Los valores de los mexicanos: presentación del tercer tomo*. México: Banamex, 1994.

Alvarez, José Rogelio. *Enciclopedia de México*. México D.F.: Secretaría de Educación Pública, 1988.

Barabas, Alicia, and Miguel Bartolomé, eds. *Etnicidad y pluralismo cultural: la dinámica étnica en Oaxaca*. México: Conaculta, 1990.

Barry, Tom, ed. *Mexico: A Country Guide*. Albuquerque: Inter-Hemispheric Education Resource Center, 1992.

Bartra, Roger. *Oficio mexicano*. México: Grijalbo, 1993.

Becerra Acosta, Manuel, et al. *Prensa y radio en México (Comunicación y dependencia en América Latina)*. México: UNAM, 1978.

Beezley, William H., and David E. Lorey, eds. *Viva Mexico. Viva la Independencia: Celebrations of September 16*. Wilmington, DE: SR Books, 2001.

Beezley, William H., et al., eds. *Rituals of Rule, Rituals of Resistance: Public Celebrations and Popular Culture in Mexico*. Wilmington, DE: SR Books, 1994.

Béhague, Gerard H. *Music in Latin America: An Introduction*. Englewood Cliffs: Prentice Hall, 1979.

———. "Latin American Music, 1920–1980." In *The Cambridge History of Latin America,* Vol. 10. Edited by Leslie Bethell. Cambridge: Cambridge University Press, 1995.

Bell, Steven M. "Mexico." In *Handbook of Latin American Literature,* edited by D.W. Foster. New York: Garland, 1992.

Bethell, Leslie, ed. *The Cambridge History of Latin America.* Volume 10: *Latin America since 1930: Ideas, Culture and Society.* Cambridge: Cambridge University Press, 1995.

Billeter, Erika, ed. *Images of Mexico: The Contribution of Mexico to 20th Century Art.* Dallas: Dallas Museum of Art, 1987.

Blanco, José Joaquín. *Crónica de la poesía mexicana.* México D.F.: Katún, 1977.

———. *Crónica literaria.* México: Cal y Arena, 1996.

———. *Esplendores y miserias de los criollos: la literatura de la Nueva España.* Mexico D.F.: Cal y Arena, 1989.

Bonfil Batalla, Guillermo. *México profundo: Reclaiming a Civilization.* Translated by Phillip A. Dennis. Austin: University of Texas Press, 1996.

Brushwood, John S. *La novela mexicana (1972–1982).* México D.F.: Grijalbo, 1985.

———. *Mexico in Its Novel.* Austin: University of Texas Press, 1966.

Burgess, Ronald D. *The New Dramatists of Mexico: 1967–1985.* Lexington: University of Kentucky Press, 1991.

Burton, Julianne. *Cinema and Social Change in Latin America.* Austin: University of Texas Press, 1986.

Butler Flora, Cornelia. "Photonovels." In *Handbook of Latin American Popular Culture,* edited by Harold E. Hinds, Jr., and Charles M. Tatum, pp. 151–71. Westport: Greenwood Press, 1985.

Cadwallader, Sharon. *Savoring Mexico.* Tucson: Ironwood Press, 1999.

Calderón de la Barca, Fanny. *Life in Mexico.* Edited by Howard T. Fisher and Marion Hall Fisher. New York: Doubleday, 1966.

Carrasco Puente, Rafael. *Bibliografía de Catarina de San Juan y de la china poblana.* México: Secretaría de Relaciones Exteriores, 1949.

———. *La caricatura en México.* México D.F.: Imprenta Universitaria, 1953.

Castellanos, Pablo. *Horizontes de la música precortesana.* México: FCE, 1970.

Chase, Gilbert. *Contemporary Art in Latin America.* New York: Free Press, 1970.

Cooper Alarcón, Daniel. *The Aztec Palimpsest: Mexico in the Modern Imagination.* Tempe: University of Arizona Press, 1997.

Cosío Villegas, Daniel, et al. *Historia mínima de México.* México: El Colegio de México, 1983.

Cueva, Alvaro. *Lágrimas de cocodrilo: Historia mínima de las telenovelas en México.* México: Tres Lunas, 1998.

Dájer, Jorge. *Los artefactos sonoros precolombinos desde su descubrimiento en Michoacán.* México: Empresa Libre de Autoeditores/Fondo Nacional para la Cultura y las Artes, 1995.

Dallal, Alberto. *El "dancing" mexicano.* México: Oasis, 1982.

———. *La danza en México en el siglo XX.* México: CONACULTA, 1994.

Dauster, Frank N. *Perfil generacional del teatro hispanoamericano.* Ottawa: Girol Books, 1993.

Debroise, Olivier. *Fuga mexicana: un recorrido por la fotografía en México.* México: CONACULTA, 1998.

Del Conde, Teresa. *Historia mínima del arte mexicano en el siglo XX.* México: Átame Ediciones, 1994.

De la Cruz, Sor Juana Inés. *Obras completas.* Mexico City: Porrúa, 1981.

Domínguez Michael, Christopher. *Servidumbre y grandeza de la vida literaria.* México: Joaquín Mortiz, 1998.

Duncan, J. Ann. *Voices, Visions, and a New Reality.* Pittsburgh: University of Pittsburgh Press, 1986.

Fernández Christlieb, Fátima. *Los medios de difusión masiva en México.* México: Juan Pablos, 1985.

Fernández, Justino. *A Guide to Mexican Art.* Chicago: University of Chicago Press, 1969.

Ferrer, Elizabeth. *A Shadow Born of Earth: New Photography in Mexico.* New York: American Federation of Arts/Universe Publishing, 1993.

Five Decades of Mexican Photography. Catalogue text by Mónica Amor. Throckmorton Fine Art, Inc./Mexican Cultural Institutes of New York and Washington, 1996.

Florescano, Enrique, ed. *El patrimonio nacional de México.* 2 vols. México: CONACULTA/FCE, 1997.

————, ed. *Mitos mexicanos.* México: Aguilar/Nuevo Siglo, 1995.

Folgarait, Leonard. *Mural Painting and Social Revolution in Mexico, 1920–1940: Art of the New Order.* Cambridge, Cambridge University Press, 1998.

Foster, David William, ed. *Mexican Literature: A History.* Austin: University of Texas Press, 1994.

Fox, Elizabeth. "Latin American Broadcasting." In *The Cambridge History of Latin America,* Vol. 10, pp. 519–68. Cambridge: Cambridge University Press, 1995.

Franco, Jean. *Plotting Women: Gender and Representation in Mexico.* New York: Columbia University Press, 1989.

Fraser, Valerie, and Oriana Baddeley. *Drawing the Line.* London: Verso, 1989.

García Canclini, Néstor. *Hybrid Cultures: Strategies for Entering and Leaving Modernity.* Translated by C.L. Chiappari and S.L. López. Minneapolis: University of Minnesota Press, 1995.

García Riera, Emilio. *Breve historia del cine mexicano: primer siglo (1897–1997).* México: Ediciones Mapa/CONACULTA/IMCINE, 1998.

————. *Historia documental del cine mexicano.* 9 vols. México: Era, 1969–78.

García Rivas, Heriberto. *Historia de la literatura mexicana.* México D.F.: Textos Universitarios, 1971.

García Silberman, Sarah, and Luciana Ramos Lira. *Medios de comunicación y violencia.* México: FCE and Instituto Mexicano de Psiquiatría, 1998.

García, Gustavo, and José Felipe Coria. *Nuevo Cine mexicano.* México: Editorial Clío, 1997.

García, Gustavo, and Rafael Aviña. *Epoca de oro del cine mexicano.* México: Editorial Clío, 1997.

Gillespie, Jean L. "Gender, Ethnicity and Piety: The Case of the *china poblana."* In *Imagination Beyond Nation,* edited by Eva P. Bueno and Terry Caesar. Pittsburgh: University of Pittsburgh, 1998.

Glantz, Margo. *Repeticiones: Ensayos sobre literatura mexicana.* México D.F.: Universidad Veracruzana, 1979.

Goldman, Shifra. *Contemporary Mexican Painting in a Time of Change.* Austin: University of Texas Press, 1981.

González Gortázar, Fernando, ed. *La arquitectura mexicana del siglo XX.* México: CONACULTA, 1996.

González Peña, Carlos. *Historia de la literatura mexicana: desde los orígenes hasta nuestros días.* México D.F.: Porrúa, 1984.

Granados Chapa, Miguel Angel. *Examen de la comunicación en México.* México: Ediciones El Caballito, 1981.

Harmony, Olga. *Ires y venires del teatro en México.* México: CONACULTA, 1996.

Hayes, Joy Elizabeth. *Radio Nation: Communication, Popular Culture, and Nationalism in Mexico, 1920–1950.* Tucson: University of Arizona Press, 2000.

Hellman, Judith Adler. *Mexican Lives.* New York: New Press, 1994.

Hernández Castillo, Rosalva Aída. *La otra frontera: Identidades múltiples en el Chiapas poscolonial.* México: CIESAS/Miguel Angel Porrúa, 2001.

Hinds, Harold E., and Charles M. Tatum. *Handbook of Latin American Popular Culture.* Westport: Greenwood Press, 1985.

Historia general de México. 2 vols. México: Colegio de México, 1981.

Iturriaga, José E. *La estructura social y cultural de México.* México: FCE, 1951.

King, John. *Magical Reels: A History of Cinema in Latin America.* London: Verso, 1990.

Lafaye, Jacques. *Quetzalcoatl and Guadalupe: The Formation of Mexican National Consciousness.* Translated by Benjamin Keen. Chicago: University of Chicago Press, 1976.

Langford, Walter M. *The Mexican Novel Comes of Age.* Notre Dame: University of Notre Dame Press, 1981.

León Portilla, Miguel. *Literaturas de Mesoamérica.* Mexico City: SEP, 1984.

Leonard, Irving. *Baroque Times in Old Mexico.* Ann Arbor: University of Michigan Press, 1959.

Lombardo, Irma. *De la opinión a la noticia: el surgimiento de los géneros informativos en México.* México: Medios Utiles, 1992.

Lomnitz, Claudio. *Deep Mexico, Silent Mexico: An Anthropology of Nationalism.* Minneapolis: University of Minnesota Press, 2001.

Lozano, José Carlos. *Prensa, radiodifusión e identidad cultural en la frontera norte.* Tijuana: El Colegio de la Frontera Norte, 1991.

Magaña Esquivel, Antonio. *Imagen y realidad del teatro en México, 1533–1960.* México: CONACULTA/INBA, 2000.

————. *La novela de la Revolución Mexicana*. México D.F.: Instituto Nacional de Estudios Históricos, 1964.

Martínez Rentería, Carlos. *Cultura-Contracultura*. México: Plaza y Janés, 2000.

Mayer-Serra, Otto. *Panorama de la música mexicana: desde la Independencia hasta la actualidad*. 1941. México: El Colegio de México, 1996.

McAnany, Emile G., and Kenton T. Wilkinson, eds. *Mass Media and Free Trade: NAFTA and the Cultural Industries*. Austin: University of Texas Press, 1996. (Especially see articles by C. Monsiváis, N. García Canclini, and J.C. Lozano.)

Mejía Barquera, Fernando. *La industria de la radio y la televisión y la política del estado mexicano*. Volumen I (1920–1960). Mexico: Fundación Manuel Buendía, 1989.

Memoria del tiempo: 150 años de fotografía en México. México: CONACULTA/ INBA/MAM, 1989.

Mendoza, Vicente T. *El romance español y el corrido mexicano: estudio comparativo*. México: Ediciones de la Universidad nacional autónoma, 1939.

Mexico: Splendors of Thirty Centuries. New York: Metropolitan Museum of Art, 1990.

Meyer, Michael C., and William L. Sherman. *The Course of Mexican History*. Oxford: Oxford University Press, 1995.

Meyer, Michael C., and William H. Beezley, eds. *The Oxford History of Mexico*. Oxford: Oxford University Press, 2000.

Miller, Robert Ryal. *Mexico: A History*. Norman: University of Oklahoma Press, 1985.

Monsiváis, Carlos. *Del rancho al internet*. México: Biblioteca del ISSTE, 1999.

————. "Notas sobre la cultura mexicana en el siglo XX." In *Historia general de México Tomo. II*. 3rd ed. México: El Colegio de México, 1981.

————, and Carlos Bonfil. *A través del espejo: el cine mexicano y su público*. México: Ediciones el Milagro/Instituto Mexicano de Cinematografía, 1994.

Montemayor, Carlos. *La literatura actual en las lenguas indígenas de México*. México: Universidad Iberoamericana, 2001.

————. *Los pueblos indios de México hoy*. México: Planeta, 2000.

————, ed. *Situación actual y perspectivas de la literatura en lenguas indígenas*. México: CONACULTA, 1993.

Mora, Carl J. *Mexican Cinema: Reflections of a Society*. Berkeley: University of California Press, 1989.

Moreno Rivas, Yolanda. *Historia de la música popular mexicana*. México: CONACULTA/AlianzaEditorial Mexicana/Editorial Patria, 1989.

————. *La composición en México en el siglo XX*. CONACULTA, 1996.

Musacchio, Humberto, ed. *Milenios de México*. 3 vols. México: Hoja Casa Editorial, 1999.

Nigro, Kirsten. "Twentieth Century Theater." In *Mexican Literature: A History*, edited by D.W. Foster. Austin: University of Texas Press, 1994.

Noriega, Chon A., and Steven Ricci, eds. *The Mexican Cinema Project*. Los Angeles: UCLA Film and Television Archive, 1994.

Noriega, Luis Antonio de, and Frances Leach. *Broadcasting in Mexico*. London: Routledge & Kegan Paul, 1979.

Ochoa Campos, Moises. *Reseña histórica del periodismo mexicano*. México: Porrúa, 1968.

Ochoa Serrano, Alvaro. *Mitote, fandango y mariacheros*. Zamora: El Colegio de Michoacán, 1994.

Orme, Jr., William A., ed. *A Culture of Collusion: An Inside Look at the Mexican Press*. Miami: North-South Center Press, 1997.

Ortiz de Zarate, Juan Manuel. *Breve historia de la música en México*. México: Manuel Porrúa, 1970.

Oster, Patrick. *The Mexicans*. New York: Harper & Row, 1990.

Padúa, Alfredo Naime. *El cine: 204 respuestas*. México: Editorial Alhambra Mexicana, 1994.

Paranaguá, Paulo Antonio, ed. *Mexican Cinema*. Translated by Ana M. López. London: British Film Institute, 1995.

Paz, Octavio. *El laberinto de la soledad*. México: Fondo de Cultura Económica, 1972.

———. *The Labyrinth of Solitude and the Other Mexico*. New York: Grove Press, 1985.

Pick, Zuzana M. *The New Latin American Cinema*. Austin: University of Texas Press, 1993.

Pilcher, Jeffrey M. *Cantinflas and the Chaos of Mexican Modernity*. Wilmington, DE: SR Books, 2001.

Poniatowska, Elena. *Hasta no verte, Jesús mío*. Mexico City: Era, 1969.

Quiroz Malca, Haydée. *Fiestas, peregrinaciones y santuarios en México*. Mexico City: CONACULTA, 2000.

Raat, W. Dirk, and William H. Beezley, eds. *Twentieth-Century Mexico*. Lincoln: University of Nebraska Press, 1986.

Ramírez Berg, Charles. *Cinema of Solitude: A Critical Study of Mexican Film, 1967–1983*. Austin: University of Texas Press, 1992.

Ramos Smith, Maya. *El ballet en México en el siglo XIX*. México: CONACULTA/AlianzaEditorial Mexicana/Editorial Patria (Los Noventa), 1991.

———. *La danza en México durante la época colonial*. México: CONACULTA/AlianzaEditorial Mexicana/Editorial Patria (Los Noventa), 1990.

Reed Torres, Luis, and Maria del Carmen Ruiz Castaneda. *El periodismo en Mexico: 500 anos de historia*. México: Edamex, 1998.

Retablos y Exvotos. México: Museo Franz Mayer/Artes de México, 2000.

Revisión del cine mexicano. Special issue of *Artes de México*. No. 10, Nueva Época. Septiembre-Octubre 1994.

Riding, Alan. *Distant Neighbors*. New York: Knopf, 1985.

Rodríguez Prampolini, Ida. *El surrealismo y el arte fantástico de México*. México: UNAM, Instituto de Investigaciones Estéticas, 1983.

Romo, Cristina. *Ondas, canales y mensajes: Un perfil de la radio en México*. Guadalajara: ITESO, 1991.

Ross, John. *Mexico: A Guide to the People, Politics and Culture.* London: Latin American Bureau, 1996.

Rowe, William, and Vivian Schelling. *Memory and Modernity.* London: Verso, 1991.

Rubenstein, Anne. *Bad Language, Naked Ladies, and Other Threats to the Nation: A Political History of Comic Books in Mexico.* Durham: Duke University Press, 1998.

Rudolph, James D., ed. *Mexico: A Country Study.* Washington D.C.: The American University, 1985.

Sanchez de Armas, Miguel Angel, coordinator. *Apuntes para una historia de la television mexicana.* México: Revista Mexicana de Comunicacion, 1998.

Schmidt, Henry C. *The Roots of Lo Mexicano: Self and Society in Mexican Thought, 1900–1934.* College Station: Texas A&M University Press, 1978.

Schneider, Luis Mario. *Ruptura y continuidad.* México D.F.: Fondo de Cultura Económica, 1975.

Sefchovich, Sara. *México: país de ideas, país de novelas.* México D.F.: Grijalbo, 1987.

Shaw, Donald L. *Nueva narrativa hispanoamericana.* Madrid: Cátedra, 1999.

Siqueiros, David Alfaro. *Art and Revolution.* London: Lawrence and Wishart, 1975.

Skidmore, Thomas E., and Peter H. Smith. *Modern Latin America.* Oxford: Oxford University Press, 1992.

Smith, Clive B. *Builders in the Sun: Five Mexican Architects.* New York: Architectural Book Publishing Company, 1967.

Sommers, Joseph. *After the Storm: Landmarks of the Modern Mexican Novel.* Albuquerque : University of New Mexico Press, 1968.

Stabb, Martin S. *In Quest of Identity: Patterns in the Spanish American Essay of Ideas, 1890–1960.* Chapel Hill: University of North Carolina Press, 1967.

Stevenson, Robert. *Music in México: a Historical Survey.* New York: Thomas Crowell, 1952.

Suárez Radillo, Carlos Miguel. *El teatro neoclásico y costumbrista hispanoamericano.* Madrid: Ediciones Cultura Hispánica, 1984.

———. *El teatro romántico hispanoamericano.* Madrid: Ediciones Cultura Hispánica, 1993.

Toor, Frances. *A Treasury of Mexican Folkways.* New York: Crown, 1947.

Trejo Delarbe, Raúl. *La sociedad ausente.* México: Cal y arena, 1992.

———. *Ver, pero también leer. Televisión y prensa: del consumo a la democracia.* México: Instituto Nacional del Consumidor, n.d.

———, coordinator. *Televisa: el quinto poder.* México: Claves Latinoamericanas, 1985.

Ureña, Pedro Henríquez. "Observaciones sobre el español de América." *Revista de Filologia Española* 8 (1921–2): 357–90.

Usigli, Rodolfo. *Mexico in the Theatre.* Translated by W.P. Scott. Oxford, Mississippi: University of Mississippi Romance Monographs, 1976.

Van Young, Eric, ed. *Mexico's Regions: Comparative History and Development.* San Diego: UCSD Center for U.S.-Mexican Studies, 1992.

Williams, Raymond L. *The Postmodern Novel in Latin America.* New York: St. Martin's Press, 1996.

Winn, Peter. *Americas: The Changing Face of Latin America and the Caribbean.* Berkeley: University of California Press, 1992.

Yúdice, George. "La industria de la música en la integración América Latina-Estados Unidos." In Néstor García Canclini, et al., *Las industrias culturales en la integración latinoamericana.* México: Grijalbo, 1999: 181–243.

Zarauz López, Héctor L. *La fiesta de la muerte.* México: CONACULTA, 2000.

———. *México: Fiestas cívicas, familiares, laborales y nuevos festejos.* México: CONACULTA, 2000.

Zea, Leopoldo, ed. *Características de la cultura nacional.* México: UNAM, 1969.

WEB SITES

General Information

LANIC is the richest source of information on the web for information on Latin America in general:
http://www.lanic.utexas.edu/la/mexico/

General info plus photos:
http://www.mexconnect.com/mex_/
http://www.mexico.com/index.html

Links to a wide variety of sources:
http://www.mexico.web.com.mx

Ancient civilizations:
http://www.angelfire.com/ca/humanorigins/index.html

Cinema

Official site of the film institute:
http://www.imcine.gob.mx/
http://www.cinemexicano.mty.itesm.mx/front.html
http://www.wam.umd.edu/_dwilt/mfb.html

News and Media

http://www.newslink.org/nonus.mex.html

Border Culture

http://www.lib.nmsu.edu/subject/bord/laguia
http://www.utep.edu/border

Index

About the Authors

PETER STANDISH is Professor of Spanish at East Carolina University.

STEVEN M. BELL is Associate Professor of Spanish and Latin American Studies at the University of Arkansas.